Smart Green Cities

T0371689

Smart Green Cities: is a comprehensive overview of what global cities are doing to become sustainable. Woodrow W. Clark II and Grant Cooke have produced a book that is both practical and visionary. They have examined the infrastructure needs – sustainable development, communications, energy, water, waste, and transportation to develop guidelines, processes and best practices. City leaders are key to mitigating climate change who must plan, design and implement solutions.

Smart Green Cities (SGC) offers a global perspective that includes implementing the Green Industrial Revolution the title of their last book. SGC discusses innovative emerging technologies, and the new economics paradigm that move beyond the out-dated neo-classical economics. The authors present examples from around the world including Europe, the U.S, China and the Middle East, which discuss the best green technologies from renewable energy power generation to smart on-site grid development. The extraordinary shift from a rural to an urban world is described; national plans are analyzed; so that future cities will be designed, built and implemented now – not 50 years from now.

The struggle for the planet's survival is being waged by the world's cities. Clark and Cooke argue that cities are the key to mitigating climate change and reducing toxic greenhouse gas emissions. SGC introduces sustainable technologies; discusses the economics for implementing the solutions; and offers numerous examples to serve as pathways for cities to become smart, green, and thus carbon neutral.

Dr Clark is an expert in economics, renewable energy, and sustainable communities who was a contributing scientist to the United Nations Intergovernmental Panel on Climate Change which as an organization won the Nobel Peace Prize in December 2007. In the 1990s, he was the first Manager of Energy Technology Transfer at Lawrence Livermore National Laboratory. At the turn of the 21st Century he was California Governor Davis' Renewable Energy Advisor and then in 2004 formed Clark Strategic Partners, an international renewable energy, economics, and environmental consulting firm.

Grant Cooke is a journalist and Silicon Valley businessman with experience in emerging technologies and sustainability. In 2006, he was one of the first businessmen involved with California's $3.5 billion world-leading energy efficiency program. He is also an established writer with numerous publishing credits including "The Green Industrial Revolution: Energy, Engineering and Economics", with Clark.

This book is dedicated to Woody's wife Andrea Kune-Clark, and Grant's wife Susan Cooke, and their children and grandchildren as well as all those who envision a better life through smarter, greener cities.

Smart Green Cities

Toward a Carbon Neutral World

WOODROW CLARK II
and
GRANT COOKE

Routledge
Taylor & Francis Group

LONDON AND NEW YORK

List of Tables

Acknowledgments

With 7 billion people now on this fragile planet, the sands of time are marking our existence if we continue to use the atmosphere and the environment as garbage cans. The mitigation of global warming and climate change is crucial to our future and the health of our children and grandchildren.

Cities have become the focus for the effort to address the solutions to climate change. The mass migration of the world's rural population to the urban centers has put increasing pressure on city leaders to develop strategies for the sustainability of their natural resources and sustainable development. Adding to the cities' burdens are the ineffectiveness of national governments—except China and other BRIC (Brazil, Russia, India and China) nations who are resolving these issues directly in both planning and economic support—to address this issue because of the historic dependency and political power of the oil and other carbon industries.

Fortunately, cities and local leaders across the globe are responding to this challenge. Efforts to reduce greenhouse gas emissions are taking hold in cities throughout Europe and Asia, and some in the US. Obviously, more needs to be done, but there is a growing trend in the smart, green direction. Renewable energy, reasonably priced energy storage, and smart grids that flexibly share power are gaining acceptance and market share for systems that are on-site and distributed via smart grids. This shift is growing and significant.

Smart green cities need not be just large new cities or restructuring of historical and older cities. "Smart green" can apply to on-site and distributed power to subsets of large cities. It can also be the basis for the growth of these new cities in different areas. Denmark did this over 40 years ago to counter the population moving to Copenhagen. The national government started universities with specialized expertise in other areas of the country, hence attracting scholars and new businesses. The program proved to be a big success and is now being considered by China, a country facing similar problems.

In examining and explaining these developments, the authors wanted to bring together this emerging phenomenon so that city leaders across the globe would be encouraged to continue with their efforts and share useful ideas. By learning that the residents of Copenhagen, after decades of pollution in their busy harbor, now are able to swim in clean, healthy water, other leaders of cities with busy ports may be encouraged to take similar actions.

Books and scholarship of this type build on the work of others now and from the past when communities were protected for their tradition and historical values. We are fortunate that this topic struck the interest of acclaimed scholars who offered comments, case studies, and suggestions. Several teams of global experts graciously contributed researched appendixes that we have gratefully included. We are indebted to Quay Hays, CEO of GROW Holdings, Los Angeles for sharing the Preliminary Design Plan for Quay Valley; to Professor Steffen Lehmann, Curtin University, Perth, Australia for Lessons from Asia-Pacific Region; to Professor Natalija Lepkova and Dalia Bardauskienne from Technological Vilnius University; to Cornina Alternburg, Fritz Reusswig, and Wiebke Lass from Germany for Berlin Insights; to Corinna Altenburg and Fritz Reusswig for The Case of Potsdam; to Professors V. Oree, A. Khoodaruth, and M.K. Elahee for the case study of Mauritius; and finally Naved Jafry and Garson Silvers for their discussion of the Smart Green MicroCity that has been started in India.

There are other scholars, academics, and scientists whose work influenced our writings. We have done our best to note their opinions and give credit where credit is due. Some of our mentors included Herbert Blumer and Norman Cousins who have passed away. Then there are Professor Noam Chomsky who is Dr Clark's life long role model and mentor along with Herbert Blumer and Jeremy Rifkin, who inspired us to write books about the solutions to climate change along with others including the creators and members of the US Green Building Council and other organizations.

We are particularly beholden to the hundreds of scientists from around the world who have contributed their time, expertise, and scientific inquiry to the United Nations' work on climate change. They have provided a warning to and a call to action for the international community to address this serious global crisis. Without their credible work, our planet would not have a chance for long-term survival.

We want to acknowledge the City of Beverly Hills in southern California where Dr Clark lives. Beverly Hills celebrated its 100-year anniversary in 2014. Clark chaired The Next 100 Year Committee for Beverly Hills. Our current work helped to push the City of Beverly Hills to move faster in a smart and green process and to plan and implement those activities. Clark spent over a year with his team and the City Technology Committee investigating how the city could be smart as well as green. The Next 100 Year Committee issued a Report at the Centennial with the Mayor and City Council taking notice.

While intelligence, experience, and insight can help in the recognition of what makes a city smart, green, and livable, hard work and economic support are what captures the transformative ideas and hones them into a coherent strategic plan that must be implemented. This hard work is impossible without the support of loved ones, and the authors would like to thank their respective families for their forbearance and patience as time and the research went on and the manuscript came together.

Woodrow W. Clark II and Grant Cooke

Reviews of
Smart Green Cities

Smart Green Cities *highlights and documents the transformation that has and is taking place to place cities at the center of the space of 'solutions science' to meeting our energy, food, and even water demands. As urban populations grow and the target of 2 degree C warming presents even greater challenges on our urban footprint, this book provides an outstanding guide to the innovations needed to make our cities part of the solution instead of the problem.*

Daniel Kammen, Goldman School of Public Policy,
University of California, Berkeley

While reviewing the Smart Green Cities *book, I found this book's content to be not only profound and eloquently written, but also extremely timely, since most of the issues addressed in 2015 by the UNECE symposia in the summer and then the UN FCCC Conference in Paris, are very much in line with subject matters discussed and reviewed in the book.*

As author of numerous books in solar and alternative energy technologies, and as an engineering design consultant specializing in large scale solar and alternative energy systems, I consider Dr. Clark to be one of the most informed, and visionary applied academics who has devoted several decades on green energy economics.

The book covers some of the most significant issues that are extremely essential in resolving some of the most challenging issues that we presently face in our urban areas ranging from climate change to the solutions just as infrastructures, systems, health, food and others. Anyone who has had an opportunity to visit some of the largest cities across the globe will appreciate the importance of the book's message.

In my professional opinion, this book is a must read by everyone who is in position of affecting change to the present challenges facing our only habitat. I wish to congratulate Dr. Clark and Grant Cooke for their outstanding work.

Dr. Peter Gevorkian Ph.D.,
P.E.CEO/ President, Vector Delta Design Group, Inc.

Introduction

Anthropocene is the term geologists use to describe the current age. It roughly began in the eighteenth century with the First Industrial Revolution, and it refers to the period during which human activity has been the dominant influence on climate and the environment. A key characteristic of this era is the mass migration from an agrarian society to an urban one. The Anthropocene period is being populated by city dwellers, in contrast to the rural demography of the past millennia, and has profound implications for human society.

This vast migration to an urban environment is being fueled by a variety of factors including the jobs, social services, and safety against violent marauders, but it can be summed up by the human sense that a better way of life is available in a community. This sense, or need, that humans have to belong to a group is one of the most powerful driving forces in human history.

The United Nations estimates that there are 7 billion people living on the planet now, and by the mid twenty-first century that will be 10 billion. Furthermore, the global workforce that amounts to about 3 billion people will almost double by the middle of the century. Every year, hundreds of thousands of young, energetic people are crowding the job market, looking for work. This burgeoning workforce and growing population is focused on the cities. Half of today's 7 billion people, or about 3.4 billion, live in cities and by mid-century 75 percent, or about 7 of the world's 10 billion people, will live in a city.

This is most apparent in China, home today to more than 1.4 billion people. Urbanization is one of the critical factors in China's extraordinary economic growth and rapid industrialization over the past three decades, providing essential labor and new consumers. More than half the population now lives in cities, which at 690 million is more than double the entire US population. In 1980, less than 20 percent of the Chinese population lived in cities. By 2030, this number is predicted to rise to 75 percent.

For China this rapid rise in urbanization brings serious societal challenges, including housing, infrastructures, water, food, and jobs, as well as rising pollution and social and wealth inequality issues. Most of the world's cities and, particularly, its megacities with populations of over 20 million, face similar problems. The most severe of these problems are congestion, air pollution, and the related effects of global warming and climate change.

While city populations continue to accelerate, they are producing more and more of the world's wealth. Fewer residents are generating this great wealth while at the same time global poverty is on the rise and becoming an increasingly urban-based phenomenon, causing new problems. The middle class is shrinking as cities grow and economies become more knowledge-based and technology dependent. Urban inequality is verging on the crisis level, with measures of inequality growing rapidly.

As the migration continues, the urban population is also becoming less dense, sprawling out and taking over vast land mass. The sheer number of people moving to the cities has been pushing the cities further and further away from the center. To city planners and political leaders this is agglomeration, and it results in urban development that extends in hundreds of square miles in every direction. Shanghai, China is a prime example; the city is steadily spreading out to include almost the whole region. It is becoming harder for the cities to provide and support basic infrastructure needs of energy, transportation, water, waste, and telecommunications.

Fortunately, circumstances and technologies are coming together to accelerate the change away from carbon-based energy generation. The era of sustainability and renewable energy has begun—northern Europe and Asian nations started it. In spring 2015, the State of California declared that it will have 50 percent renewable energy by 2050. The push for renewable energy and a carbonless lifestyle will become history's largest social and economic megatrend, with the potential of extraordinary benefits in the form of economic revival, innovation, emerging technologies, and significant job growth for those cities capable of fast entry.

The authors call this new era, the Green Industrial Revolution (Clark and Cooke, 2014), and it is emerging in several parts of the world. Cities can now address their problems by becoming greener and smarter, particularly as to the way energy is generated, supplied, and used. The Green Industrial Revolution is a revolutionary global change from fossil fuels to renewable energy sources that has extraordinary potential and opportunities. It includes remarkable innovations in science, technologies, and energy. These advances are leading to sustainable, smart, and carbonless communities whose economies are powered by non-polluting technologies like solar, wind, and geothermal.

Creating smart green cities requires solutions to old and new problems. Changing from the twentieth century dependency upon fossil fuels and their carbon-intensive, polluted urban environment to one that is sustainable, healthier, and with low toxic emissions is doable—and there are many cities around the world that are succeeding.

Human needs remain constant in urban environments, particularly in large, global cities. People need the basic infrastructure components such as energy, water, waste, telecommunications, and transportation, to work well. In a smart green city, the components are linked and integrated. That way, components overlap, reducing costs for construction, operations, and maintenance.

The quality of urban space must improve. The architecture should be inventive with sensitive urban design and a dynamic atmosphere. Sustainable living and sustainable business development must be promoted. Cities must become more walkable, bike friendly, and livable. They need to focus on the environment as well as economic sustainability. They need to become smart and maximize the use of smart technologies to optimize the resources available for infrastructure upgrading. Smart cities need to capitalize on IT solutions to develop a smart economy, smart governance structures and procedures, smart people, a smart environment, smart mobility, and smart living. Smart cities make use of IT and human capital solutions to become greener.

In short, the world needs to develop and implement smart green cities, which are capable of stopping climate change and addressing the other looming challenges of the twenty-first century. At the same time, cities need to be smart as they are urban centers that must encourage sustainable economic development, which promotes a high quality of life. Smart, emerging technologies can smooth the way for a more sustainable existence.

In the following chapters, we will explore the problems facing today's cities; what solutions are available; and how many of the world's cities have radically reversed course and are now moving to become smart and green.

Reference

Clark, Woodrow W. II and Grant Cooke, 2014. *The Green Industrial Revolution*. Elsevier Press, New York.

Chapter 1

Modern Civilization is The City

Great cities are extraordinary monuments to civilization. These dynamic metropolises with their glittery aura of prosperity and human fulfillment are like enormous magnets, pulling people to them. The massive tide of immigrants swarming to the urban life grows daily. The rural poor, clutching hopes, dreams, and all their worldly goods give up subsistence farming and stream to the cities to find work, social services, and schools for their children to escape the poverty cycle.

The phenomenon of the city has been developing since the end of the Holocene era, about 12,000 years ago. Human pre-history was dominated by small, nomadic groups of hunter–gatherers who roamed the world's vast regions in search of food. These ancients lived in family or extended family groupings, clinging together and dwelling in caves for shelter and protection.

As the Holocene era ended, a broad transition took place. Close to the same time, in vastly divergent parts of the world, hunter–gatherers and fisher–gatherers learned to grow grains and vegetables, and to domesticate large mammals. This transition was the Neolithic, or Agricultural Revolution, and as the ancients learned to cultivate food, they slowly changed from nomadic to small sedentary societies. Extended families cooperated for food production and protection against marauders, and slowly, larger settlements took shape. With agriculture and animal protein came higher survival rates and increased populations.

Settlements became villages where humans radically changed the environment. Hills were deforested, marshlands drained, pastures reshaped, and rivers and streams were redirected for irrigation. Survival was no longer in constant peril and specialization of labor developed. Trading became an economy as goods, tools, and people passed between villages. A stable food supply with excesses allowed some people to turn to other pursuits such as arts and music. Human curiosity emerged and scientific questions, explorations, and discoveries began. Over time came centralized administrations, governmental structures, and property ownership that impacted business growth and political influence. Religions and hierarchical ideologies helped bind the community, and succored the afflicted. Spoken language became written, and knowledge and experience were expanded and shared.

Ancient Sumeria in southern Mesopotamia, which is now Iraq, is cited as the best example of these Neolithic settlements. By 4000 BCE, Sumeria had divided into settlements big enough to be classified as city–states. Each city had their own particular patron god or goddess and was separated by canals and boundary stones.

Eridu in Sumeria was probably the first of the world's great cities. On the Euphrates River, near the Persian Gulf, Eridu was formed around 5400 BCE by groups of ancient people seeking access to fresh water in the desert. They lived in reed and mud-bricked huts, hunted and fished along the river, and worshipped the god Enki, who was considered to have found the city. On the rough hills, near Enki's temple, they grazed goats, and built a complex system of canals and waterways for irrigation. By 2900 BCE, Eridu was in its splendor with 4,000 residents, and covering more than 25 acres (Leick, 2002).

As the saline water table rose, and sand dunes pushed against the city's structures, Eridu declined and was eventually abandoned by the sixth century. However, for hundreds of years this thriving, robust complex contained the requisite infrastructure as well as the artistic, social, political, and legal dictums and behaviors that define a city.

A later example of an ancient city is Matera, established by the Romans in 3 BCE, in southern Italy. Matera was awarded in 2015 for being the European Union's (EU) Green City of the year as well as the European Union Cultural City for 2019 due to its preserving, restoring, and then making its homes within its rock mountains green, smart, and sustainable. Matera continues to respect its cultural heritage through the preservation of its buildings.

That tradition continues with modern infrastructures like water, energy, and wireless telecommunications that do not destroy its past history. Additionally, Matera has also been leading the larger region of southern Italy, Basilicata, in its efforts to curb the use of fossil fuels from northern Africa. The region plans on having both large renewable energy resources like wind and solar farms as well as on-site systems for local business, homes, and the government.

The Greeks, and Hippodamus, their fifth-century BCE philosopher, are regarded as the first town planners in the civilized world. The Greeks developed an orthogonal urban layout with more or less square street blocks. As the Greeks started to develop colonies along the coasts of the Mediterranean, these city–states used the classic orthogonal plans. Gradually, the new layouts became more regular. In the fourth century BCE, Alexander used an orthogonal layout for his new city of Alexandria.

The Ancient Romans were the early engineering geniuses. Inspired by the Greeks, they employed regular orthogonal structures to mold their colonies. The Romans used a consolidated scheme for city planning, developed for military defense and civil convenience. The basic plan consisted of a central forum with city services and a marketplace, surrounded by a compact and a rectilinear grid of streets. Surrounding the city was a wall for defense. To reduce travel times, two diagonal streets crossed the square grid, passing through the central square. A river usually flowed through the city, providing water, transport, and sewage disposal (Vitrivius, 1914).

Throughout Europe, Roman engineers originally laid out hundreds of towns and cities including London and Paris. Many still show the logical way that the Romans designed cities, laying out the streets at right angles in the form of a square grid. All roads were equal in width and length, except for two, which were slightly wider than the others. One of these ran east–west, the other, north–south, and intersected in the middle to form the center of the grid. Roads were made of carefully fitted flagstones and filled in with smaller, hard-packed rocks and pebbles.

Creating infrastructures were embedded in the Roman way of life. Their brilliance stretched from aqueducts and bridges, to roads, mining, and water-powered technology. According to Frontinus, who wrote "De aquaeductu" in the first century, 14 different aqueducts delivered 260,000 gallons of water to Rome each day. Per capita water usage in ancient Rome matched modern-day cities like New York.

The aqueducts stretched as long as 100 km or 60 miles, and descended from an elevation of 300 m above sea level at the source, to 100 m when they reached the city's reservoirs. Roman engineers even invented inverted siphons to move water across a valley if it was impractical to build a raised aqueduct.

Urban development in the Middle Ages focused on a fortress, or fortified nucleus, with growth extending outward in rings. In Europe, a large migration to towns and cities occurred from the ninth to fourteenth centuries, and hundreds of new towns were built.

Eventually, the design of cities changed to include aesthetics like the star-shaped layout of Florence. Paris was rebuilt in the nineteenth century when Napoleon III had Baron Haussmann rebuild the city with the mission of making it healthier, less congested, and grander. For two decades, Paris was under construction as Haussmann created vast boulevards, parks, and neighborhood squares. To bring fresh water to the city, a new aqueduct and reservoir were built, and to connect the city with the rest of France, Napoleon III built two new railroad stations. He completed Les Halles, the great iron and glass produce market in the center of the city, and built a new municipal hospital, the Hotel Dieu, in the place of crumbling medieval buildings on the Ile de la Cite. The signature architectural landmark was the Paris Opera, the largest theater in the world, designed by Charles Garnier, crowning the center of Napoleon III's new Paris.

The Industrial Revolution of the eighteenth and nineteenth centuries brought a huge growth of industrialized cities, with a pace and style dictated by business interests. Eventually, the quality of urban life became a matter of concern and urban planners explored ways of providing residents, especially factory workers, with healthier environments.

Modernism began to creep into city planning in the 1920s, bringing skyscrapers and steel-framed office buildings encased in huge walls of glass curtains. New York City's Manhattan with its great canyons formed by cloud-touching office towers is the iconic example. Others soon copied Manhattan and vied for the distinction of having the world's tallest building. It was not long before cities like Chicago and Shanghai constructed buildings taller than NYC's Empire State building.

While Europe-centric, this brief overview of how settlements slowly evolved into cities is similar to how most of the world's regions developed. While the experiences in Asia, South America, and the rest of the world were unique to their respective regions, the process of moving from hunter–gatherers to agrarian settlements and then into ever-larger and more populous cities was essentially the same. As agrarian societies flourished and provided a food source beyond subsistence, knowledge-based and complex-skilled tasks were taken on and developed that improved the overall welfare of the community.

From the very beginning, cities offered protection and safety. Historically, settlements were built near fresh water and on higher ground or some other location that was easy to defend. For example, London is built on a promontory overlooking a plain bordered by the Thames River. Paris, on the other hand, originated on an island in the middle of a river, which allowed defense in either direction. The people of Venice were so tired of the raiding barbarians from the north that they escaped from the mainland to the nearby marshes. Here they drove wooden stakes into sandy islands and constructed wooden platforms on top of these stakes. Finally, buildings were constructed on the platforms and Venice's streets are waterways and getting around is far easier and more popular by boat.

Besides protection and safety, cities have always offered commerce, trade, and the potential to prosper. Trade is as old as humankind, with archeological evidence that goes back to the very origins of species. Great financial centers like London were originally a point of land where clans met to exchange animal hides for sharp pieces of rock to be used as tools or weapons.

Besides development and commerce, cities have essential infrastructure elements of energy, transportation, water, waste, and telecommunications. This is as true for today's modern cities as it was true for Eridu in Sumeria. How a city addresses and provides for these elements determines much about the prosperity and health of its citizens.

Cities are Getting Bigger

Humanity has been trending toward ever-larger social organizations since humans adopted the agrarian lifestyle. The more humans evolve, the less willing they are to tolerate a rural existence. Currently, we are witnessing billions of people striving with all their might for a share in the spoils of modern civilization. They want homes with running water and electricity, a plentiful supply of food, household appliances, medical care, education, computers, televisions, cell phones, and personal transportation. They are not worried about how much is enough as they work hard to escape poverty and invest for their children's futures. These billions are moving to the cities, or like in Africa, struggling to create new cities.

About a million years has passed since the emergence of Homo Sapiens. From then, except for the medieval plagues, worldwide human population has grown continually. It is estimated that around 8000 BCE, there were about 20 million people on Earth. At the beginning of the Common Era, (AD) there were about 200 million. Industrial development accelerated population and by 1930 there were already 2 billion on Earth. Thirty years later another billion was added, then 15, then 13, then 12, then about 11 years to reach the current count of over 7 billion. At the moment, global population is growing by the equivalent of the population of Germany today, or about 80 million per year.

The fastest growth is in Africa which, by the middle of the twenty-first century, will have about twice as many people as today, assuming that the spread of the Ebola disease can be stopped and population growth continues. China will lead the world in population with India not far behind. For Asia and the rest of the world, such large population growth means also the increase and spread of greenhouse gases, pollution, and dangerous toxic emissions for housing, food, jobs, and transportation. Infrastructures worldwide will be challenged to meet the local demands while curbing and reversing climate changes.

The UN estimates that there are 7 billion people living on the planet now, and by the middle of the twenty-first century that will be 10 billion. Furthermore, the global workforce that amounts to about 3 billion people will almost double by the middle of the century. Every year, hundreds of thousands of young, energetic people are crowding the job market, looking for work. This burgeoning workforce and growing population is focused on the cities. Half of today's 7 billion people, or about 3.4 billion, live in cities and by the middle of the century 75 percent, or about 7 of the world's 10 billion people, will live in a city.

The world's largest cities are increasingly concentrated in Asia, where 56 percent of the world's population lives. China and India each have over 1 billion people. North America ranks second to Asia, with only 14 percent of the largest cities. Only three high-income world cities are ranked in the top ten (Tokyo, Seoul, and New York) and, with present growth rates, Tokyo will be the lone high-income representative by the middle 2020s.

China's workforce is estimated to grow by 250 million by the middle of the twenty-first century, and jobs and incomes must be found for these people. This will pressure China to continue its pro-growth policies for the future. China already has several cities with more than 10 million residents. In 1975 there were five megacities with populations of more than 10 million around the world. By 1995 there were 14 megacities according to the UN, and in 2015 there are 29 (UN DESA, 2011).

According to the *2014 Demographia World Urban Areas* (Demographia, 2014), the world's most populous megacities are (note the population numbers include the urban areas, not just city limits):

Table 1.1   World's most populous megacities

City	Population
Tokyo-Yokahama	37 million
Jakarta	30 million
Delhi	24 million
Seoul-Incheon	23 million
Manila	22 million
Shanghai	22 million
Karachi	21 million
New York	21 million
Mexico City	20 million
Sao Paulo	20 million

Source: Cox, 2014.

Land Area

Despite its image as a dense environment, the urban area of New York continues to cover, by far, the most land area of any city in the world. Its land area of nearly 4,500 square miles (11,600 square km) is one-third higher than Tokyo's 3,300 (8,500 square km). For example in the US, Los Angeles, which is often thought of as defining low density, ranks only fifth, behind Chicago and Atlanta, with their substantially smaller populations. Perhaps more surprising is the fact that Boston has the sixth-largest land area of any city in the world.

Table 1.2   City urban areas per square kilometer

City	Urban Areas per Square Kilometer
New York	11,000
Tokyo–Yokahama	8,500
Chicago	6,500
Atlanta	6,500
Los Angeles	6,200
Boston	4,700
Dallas–Fort Worth	4,500
Philadelphia	4,500
Moscow	4,300
Houston	4,300

Source: Cox, 2014.

Boston's strong downtown (central business district) and relatively dense core can result in a misleading perception of high urban density. In fact, Boston's post-Second World War suburbanization is at urban densities little different than that of Atlanta, which is the world's least dense built-up urban area with more than 3 million population. Now, 29 cities cover land areas of more than 1,000 square miles or 2,500 square km (Demographia, 2014).

Urban Density

On the other hand, the world's densest cities are on the India subcontinent and Asia. Dhaka in Bangladesh is the densest, with 114,000 residents per square mile (44,000 per square km). Hyderabad (Pakistan, not India) ranks a close second. Mumbai and nearby Kalyan (Maharashtra) are the third and fourth densest cities. Hong Kong and Macau are the only cities ranking in the densest 10 outside the subcontinent. Despite its reputation for high urban densities, the highest-ranking city in China (Henyang, Hunan) is only 39th (Demographia, 2014).

Humans have been trending toward ever-larger social organizations since they gave up the nomadic lifestyle. The lures of bright lights, easy money, and the benefits of modernity are too much to ignore and so the steady march to the cities continues.

Table 1.3   Urban population per square kilometer

City	Urban Population per Square Kilometer
Dhaka	45,000
Hyderabad (PAK)	40,000
Mumbai	32,000
Kalyan (IN)	30,000
Chittagong (BD)	29,000
Vijayawada (IN)	28,000
Hong Kong	26,000
Malegaon (IN)	25,000
Macau	23,000
Aligarh (IN)	23,000

Source: Cox, 2014.

While planners, architects, and politicians have watched and profited from this phenomenon, they have allowed most cities, particularly those in America, to grow without regard to available resources, ecological, or environmental impacts. Why else would a city like Las Vegas be allowed to sprawl unchecked across a fragile desert without concern? There are about 2 million people living in this water-constricted environment. It's just a question of time until the water runs out.

Climate Change Impacts Cities

Climate change is happening, with noticeable consequences, but what is it exactly? The simplest answer is that climate change is the permanent change in the world's weather patterns over time. It may be a change in weather conditions, or in average weather conditions, like more or fewer extreme weather events.

Several factors cause climate change. For example, oceanic circulation, variations in radiation from the sun, movement in the Earth's tectonic plates, and eruptions of volcanoes can all cause significant changes in regional and global weather patterns. However, the most crucial factor in climate change is the warming of the Earth's environment, which scientists are now convinced comes from human or anthropogenic impacts.

In 2014, the World Meteorological Organization (WMO) said the global average temperature from January to October was 0.57 Celsius (1.03 Fahrenheit) above average, tying it with 2010 for the hottest year on record. Ocean temperature set a record while land temperatures were the fourth or fifth highest since record keeping began in the nineteenth century.

In addition, Arctic sea ice shrunk to the sixth lowest level, while Antarctic sea ice grew, indicating the extraordinary shifts occurring as the ocean's temperatures absorb the excess energy trapped in the atmosphere by greenhouse gases from fossil fuel and other human activity. The concentration in the atmosphere of carbon dioxide (CO_2), a key greenhouse gas, rose to a new high of 396 parts per million last year, the WMO said. This is 42 percent above the level before the Industrial Revolution, when people started burning fossil fuel for energy (Richter, 2014).

Since the world is round, not flat, weather in one part of the world impacts the rest. When different weather patterns occur, as they are doing more frequently because of changes in climate, the results can be tornados, hurricanes, and extreme weather patterns never before experienced in history.

Hurricane Sandy is a case in point. Sandy, the largest Atlantic hurricane on record, slammed into the northeastern section of the United States October 29, 2012. Propelled by twisting cyclonic winds and torrential rain, Hurricane Sandy crushed coastal New Jersey and New York, killing 253 people, destroying homes and businesses and wrecking havoc and destruction for over 72 hours. Airports were abandoned, and millions of people were threatened as New York City's subway tunnels sparked, then shorted, and became eerily quiet as they filled with water.

Hurricane Sandy was not an isolated case. Global warming is real, it is here now, and it is having a serious impact on the planet's weather. For example, Climate Central reported that 2012 was the third straight hurricane season with 19 named storms on the US east coast. Hurricane records go back to 1851, and 2010, 2011, and 2012 were the busiest on record except for 2005 and 1933. Scientists think one reason for this increase in storm activity comes from the warming of the Atlantic sea surface temperatures (Sandy Hurricane, October 2012).

Hurricanes are exceptional because of their size, but they are not the only results of climate change. On land, hurricanes are called tornados. They are caused by the same weather impacts from wind from different directions and temperatures hitting one another causing vast circles of energy that are out of control. The number of tornados in the US has doubled each of the last 10 years. The damage cannot be calculated due to the loss of lives.

Massive though Hurricane Sandy was, it paled in comparison to super-typhoon Haiyan that ripped through the Philippines in November 2013. The sheer magnitude of the typhoon was unprecedented as the archipelago was shattered with 250 miles per hour (mph)-sustained winds, and water surged over 16-foot barriers. The scale of the destruction and damage was shocking. President Benigno Aquino declared the devastation a national calamity (*The Economist*, 2016).

Some parts hit by Typhoon Haiyan were remote; however, the government said that more than 2,300 people were killed, and 11 million were affected.

Roads and villages were destroyed, trees felled, crops flattened, power lines and houses blown away and about 600,000 were made homeless. Cost estimates were well over $15 billion.

Typhoon Haiyan may be the strongest storm in recorded history, and scientist and politicians are blaming climate change. Naderev Sano, the Philippines representative at the 2013 Warsaw climate summit, was convinced that the severity of the storm was the result of climate change. "The trend we now see is that more destructive storms will be the new norm," he told reporters (*The Economist*, 2016).

From 2010–2012, Pakistan struggled with unprecedented flooding, and Mongolia in China and Texas in the US suffered from torturous droughts. Texas cattle ranchers were rushing steers to slaughter before they died from dehydration. Also in 2010, western Russia had its hottest summer on record, with 500 wildfires around Moscow. In 2011, East Africa was ravaged by famine, the result of a drought that was linked to the Indian Ocean warming. The western Amazon region had its worst drought, with record low water levels in Rio Negro. The spring of 2011 was the hottest and driest ever in France. A year later, the summer of 2012 was the wettest April-to-June period ever recorded in the United Kingdom. The rain blighted much of the Queen's diamond jubilee river pageant on London's Thames.

A road melted in Oodnadatta, an outback town in south Australia in summer 2013, and fires swept across the Tasman peninsula. Australia, one of the countries most vulnerable to global warming, is getting ever hotter. The 2013 heat wave set new records (40.3C) for the highest national temperature ever recorded. To measure these new recordings, Australia's Bureau of Meteorology added new colors, purple and pink, to its weather map. The new colors denote temperatures once considered off the scale (*The Economist*, 2016).

"Freaky," which are extreme weather patterns, are becoming the new normal as global warming changes everyone's climate. The year 2014 has now become the world's hottest in recorded history.

Fossil fuels and carbon emissions are not the only source of greenhouse gases, though they are the major contributors to CO_2. Methane and nitrous oxide are two major greenhouse gases that are 300 times more potent than CO_2. While both gases are a small part of the fossil fuel emissions, the bulk of these gases come from cattle and hogs.

In fact, livestock production is a primary cause of climate change and may be responsible for almost a fifth of the emissions produced by human behavior (*The Economist*, 2014). The faster the planet's population grows, the more livestock is grown for feed. The more poor nations push toward development, the more people want animal protein for themselves and their children.

The problem is particularly acute in China, where pig farming has taken on epic proportions. China has a long tradition that features pigs—according to the Chinese zodiac, those born in the Year of the Pig are diligent, sympathetic, and generous. Pigs are celebrated in poems and songs and they signify prosperity, fertility, and virility. For centuries, eating pork and sacrificial pigs figured prominently in Chinese festivals and commemorations.

As China has emerged into a world-leading economy, prosperity has replaced decades of deprivation. Not surprisingly, meat eating and especially pork has become a symbol of the Chinese miracle. The average Chinese person now eats 39 kilos, or about a third of a pig, a year—five times more per person than they ate in 1977.

Traditionally, each farmer or family had a pig, which was prized for its manure as much as its meat. Now hog farming has reached epic production levels with millions of pigs being raised at facilities housing hundreds of thousands at a time. Pigs and pork eating are so vital to the stability of Chinese society and population that the government subsidizes hog farming to the tune of about $50 per animal.

While the government prizes self-sufficiency in food, each kilogram of homegrown hog requires 6 kg of feed, usually corn or soybeans. China does not have enough water or land to feeds its pigs. Chinese pigs that previously ate household scraps are now relying on imported feed. With so many hogs to feed, soon half the world's feed crops will be eaten by Chinese pigs. Already, in 2010, China's soy imports accounted for more than 50 percent of the total global soy market.

This huge distortion is leading to drastic changes in land use in other parts of the world. Brazil is cutting down forests and parts of the Amazon jungle to plant soy. Argentina has chopped down thousands of hectares of forest and shifted its traditional cattle breeding to plant soybeans. Since 1980, the Argentine acreage for soybeans has quadrupled, and entire species of plants and trees are being sacrificed to fatten China's pigs.

Pig manure, which was once desirable as a fertilizer, has become a critical problem for China. The billions of tons of waste are a major source of water and soil pollution, contributing huge quantities of methane and nitrous oxide gases to the Earth's atmosphere. Greenhouse gas emissions from Chinese agriculture increased by 35 percent between 1994 and 2005. Not only is the Earth losing the "cooling effect" from the forest and trees being cut down for feed, but also China's insatiable appetite for pork is creating millions of tons of toxic GHGs that are being poured into the atmosphere (*The Economist*, 2014).

Cities Are the Battle Ground for Climate Change

The world's cities only occupy about 3 percent of the planet's land. Yet, they contain half the world's population, and are responsible for up to 70 percent of the harmful greenhouse gases. This major discrepancy caused the UN to say that urban centers have become the battle ground against climate change and cities will "neglect their role in responding to this crisis at their peril. Not just their own peril but that of the world" (Cities and Climate Change, 2011).In a 2011 report called "Cities and Climate Change: Global Report on Human Settlements," the UN notes that the key issues are what goes in cities and how they manage their impact on the environment. It is the fast pace of urbanization and the demand for development that poses the major threats.

Cities in developing nations are growing the fastest. Every year sees the addition of 67 million new urban dwellers, and 91 percent of these are added to the populations of cities in developing countries.

According to the UN, a variety of factors influence the total and per capita CO_2 emission:

- a city's geographic situation—influencing the amount of energy required for heating, cooling and lighting;

- demographics—the size of the population influences the demand for space and services;

- urban form and density—sprawling cities tend to have higher per capita emissions than more compact ones;

- the urban economy—types of economic activities and whether these emit large quantities of greenhouse gases;

- the wealth and consumption patterns of urban residents.

CO_2 emissions by cities vary substantially, with those in Europe tending to be relatively low compared to other regions. European urban areas tend to be more compact, with better public transportation, higher levels of densification, and lower levels of sprawl, particularly compared to North American cities.

The UN estimates greenhouse gas emissions by sector, and accordingly, on a global level, 14 percent of GHGs are related to agricultural activities and 17 percent to forestry. For the rest, the main sources of greenhouse gas emissions tend to be urban-based and include the combustion of fossil fuels for electricity, cooking, transportation, and industrial production.

Globally, transportation is responsible for about 23 percent of total energy-related greenhouse gas emissions, and 13 percent of global greenhouse gas emissions, 19 percent of greenhouse gas emissions are associated with industrial activities. Global emissions from residential and commercial buildings are estimated at 10.6 billion tons of CO_2 equivalent per year, or 8 percent of global greenhouse gas emissions. Emissions from waste represent about 3 percent of total emissions.

Global climate change is happening, with significant consequences. Hurricanes, typhoons, draughts, coastal flooding, diminished air quality, and famines are just some of the catastrophic events battering our fragile planet.

According to "A Guide to the Cold Calculus of a Hot Planet," published in the fall of 2012 by Climate Vulnerable Forum (Monitor Climate, 2012) more than 100 million people will die and the international economy will lose out on over 3 percent of gross domestic product (GDP) by 2030, if the world fails to tackle climate change. The report's authors calculate that 5 million deaths occur each year from air pollution, hunger, and disease as a result of climate change caused by carbon-intensive economies, and that toll would likely rise to 6 million a year by 2030 if current patterns of fossil fuel use continue (Monitor Climate, 2012).

Tragically, more than 90 percent of those deaths will occur in developing countries, since the world's poorest nations are the most vulnerable to increased risk of drought, water shortages, crop failure, poverty, and disease.

Economically, the world's poorest nations could see an average 11 percent loss in GDP by 2030 due to climate change. Agriculture and fisheries, two areas that most poor nations are dependent on, face losses of more than $500 billion per year by 2030 (Monitor Climate, 2012).

If the world is going to address climate change and its devastating effects, cities must be at the forefront of the effort. Greenhouse gas emissions have to be reduced significantly, and cities play a major role. With 70 percent of all greenhouse gas coming from cities, some big cities emit more than some states: the total annual CO_2 emissions of New York City roughly corresponds to those of Bangladesh, London's are almost equal to those of Ireland, and Berlin's equal those of Jordan.

What is the Answer?

The answer for New York City or Beijing and for all the world's megacities, regions, and communities is to become green, smart and sustainable. Cities, particularly large cities, must focus on environmental sustainability as well as economic sustainability. The quality of urban space must improve, and they must become more walkable, bike friendly, and livable. The architecture should be inventive with sensitive urban design and a dynamic atmosphere. Sustainable living and sustainable business development must be promoted, along with infrastructure needs of water, recycling, transportation, waste, and materials. Above all else, a green sustainable city needs to generate renewable energy and use energy storage with a smart integrated grid system to balance and share energy.

Cities can follow Berlin's example as it works to be "climate-neutral." Germany's capital, Berlin, is the nation's largest city with 3.75 million inhabitants. Becoming more attractive and growing steadily, Berlin has made a city-wide effort to become climate-neutral by 2050. A city can be regarded as "climate-neutral" if its greenhouse gas emissions can keep global warming below the dangerous threshold of 2°C. Given these conditions, Berlin could become climate-neutral if total urban CO_2 emissions can be limited to 4.4 million tons by 2050—a reduction of about 85 percent compared to 1990 levels.

Becoming climate-neutral is only a part of the drive for sustainability. A city needs a heart and soul, or a center, where people have congregated for work and leisure based on its culture, history, and traditions. Today, smart cities are well connected locally and internationally, along with a sustainable lifestyle and places where people come first. A "smart green city" has these elements, plus a core value of conservation, a respect for natural resources, and an appreciation for the environment.

References

Cities and Climate Change, 2011. Global Report on Human Settlements, http://mirror.unhabitat.org/downloads/docs/E_Hot_Cities.pdf.

Cox, Wendell, 2014. Largest World Cities: 2014. November 16, http://www.newgeography.com/content/004280-largest-world-cities-2014.

Demographia, 2014. World Urban Areas, http://www.demographia.com/db-worldua.pdf.

Leick, Gwendolyn, 2002. *Mesopotamia: The Invention of the City*. Penguin Books, London.

Monitor Climate, 2012. http://daraint.org/climate-vulnerability-monitor/climate-vulnerability-monitor-2012/.

Richter, Karl, 2014. UN Weather Agency Says No Pause in Global Warming, Associated Press. December 4.

Sandy Hurricane, 2012. October 29, http://news.blogs.cnn.com/2012/10/29/hurricane-sandy-strengthens-to-85-mph/.

South Florida's Desperate Secession Movement, 2014. Future Tense. October 23, http://www.slate.com/blogs/future_tense/2014/10/23/south_florida_as_51st_state_the_city_of_south_miami_votes_to_break_away.html.

The Economist, 2014. Empire of the Pig, December 20.

The Economist, 2016. November 16.

Vitrivius, 1914. *The Ten Books on Architecture, Bk I*. Morris H. Morgan (translator). Harvard University Press, Cambridge, MA.

UN Department of Economic and Social Affairs (UN DESA), 2011. World Population Prospects: The 2010 Revision, http://esa.un.org/unpd/wpp/index.htm.

Chapter 2

Key Problems Facing Modern Cities

Los Angeles is an iconic city; its sunshine, beaches, and freeways are forever encased and displayed on film and television screens. Its mythic legends of wealth, excess, and indulgence are known to viewers worldwide who have grown up with the Los Angeles of myths like Beverly Hills and razzle-dazzle of Hollywood, along with the bountiful beauty of Pamela Anderson in Baywatch, the nitty-gritty gangster playground of Pulp Fiction, and the wondrous innocence, beauty and charm of Marilyn Monroe and Mickey Mouse.

It is a City unlike any other, with a media and screen influence that reaches from Buckingham Palace to the mud huts of the Serengeti, from the Burj Al Arab Jumeirah in Dubai to a Mongolian yurt, and from the Amazon's Manaus to Shanghai's International Finance Center. It is the best, and the worst of cities, with huge houses in beautiful sun-drenched and green-lawn suburbs that are hours away from the office. People live in their cars.

It is not uncommon for Angelinos to spend two-to-four hours a day in a car, getting back and forth to work. To accommodate that insular and auto-centric lifestyle, the city is wrapped like a mummy in thousands of miles of concrete freeways. With all those cars stuck in traffic, greenhouse emissions and bad air quality have plagued the city for decades. The overbuild pattern has since occurred in other cities around the world.

Los Angeles is the US's second-largest city behind New York City. Powered by cheap fossil fuel and a massive defense industry, Los Angeles burgeoned after the Second World War, quickly growing into expansive suburbs with big houses and swimming pools for the wealthy; with slums and poor neighborhoods for the average workers. During the 1950s, it became the American ideal of security, prosperity, and success. As the City built out from its downtown core, more and more freeways were needed to link homes to offices and businesses.

Expansion of land and real estate development took over and any sort of logical regional planning caved into urban sprawl. Pressure and influence keep getting in the way of coherent and efficient infrastructure. Public transportation shriveled in the flood of cars and cheap gas, as the freeways systematically replaced train tracks that were used since the 1920s. As the population surged, towns as large as the original city were created so that today, the Los Angeles County has dozens of separate and independent cities in it, including Los Angeles.

As the first of the mega auto-centric cities, LA was dependent on cheap fossil fueled-powered cars for transportation. This behavior was encouraged by the large and profitable US auto industry without much regard for ecology or the environment. Other global cities have followed the LA model, with land development linked to city centers by highways.

Today, the greater Los Angeles region has a population of about 15 million people, which is almost half of the population of California. The region is locked into a fossil fuel addiction that pushed the auto-centric culture that controls the region. The Los Angeles Commission on 2020 describes in its early 2014 report release, "A Time for Truth" that "Los Angeles is barely treading water while the rest of the world is moving forward. We risk falling further behind in adapting to the realities of the 21st century and becoming a city in decline" (Los Angeles Commission on 2020, 2013).

Not only does Los Angeles have the largest high-speed roadway network in the world, but it also has the highest per capita car population. While the US may be the country with the most registered vehicles (around 232 million), California, and in particular Los Angeles, are the places most committed to and dependent upon the automobile. The Greater Los Angeles region holds the highest concentration of cars in the world, with more than 26 million, or about 1.8 cars per person. Los Angeles is the most car-populated area of urban sprawl in the world.

With more than 12 million fossil-fueled cars daily on its freeways, congestion and pollution are major problems. Los Angeles holds the number one spot on the list of North America's most congested and polluted roadways, according to the 2014 Congestion Index (Los Angeles Commission on 2020, 2014: 1).

More automobiles and more driving, therefore, equals more air pollution. The Los Angeles Basin, surrounded by mountains on three sides and the Pacific

Ocean on the west, is susceptible to atmospheric inversion. This meteorological anomaly traps pollution and keeps it close to the ground, capturing exhaust from road vehicles, airplanes, locomotives, shipping, and manufacturing (Los Angeles Commission on 2020, 2014).

Millions of tons of toxins are released daily into the atmosphere, so pollution accumulates as a dense cover of smog, threatening the health and well-being of the residents (Los Angeles Commission on 2020, 2014). This heavy layer of carbon-intensive pollution finally triggered enough concern that lawmakers passed environmental legislation, including the Clean Air Act in the late 1990s. Today while the number of days registered as being extensive in pollution has lowered, the problem has not gone away. Nor will it in the near future, if the same factors that are creating greenhouse gases and pollution continue.

Despite improvement, the 2014 Annual Report of the American Lung Association (ALAC) ranked Los Angeles as the most polluted city in the country (ALAC, 2014). In addition, Los Angeles' groundwater is increasingly threatened by Methyl Tertiary Butyl Ether (MTBE) from gas stations and perchlorate from rocket fuel (SCAQMD, 2010). Making matters worse is the fact that California is now in a serious drought with the Governor pushing for a 36 percent reduction in water usage in 2015 and more thereafter.

Congestion and Air Quality is a Global Problem

Like Los Angeles, most cities around the world struggle with the impacts of a fossil-fueled auto-centric culture. In fact, as intense as the auto problems are for Los Angeles, the US city did not make the world's top 10 worst cities for traffic congestion as compiled by TomTom, the GPS manufacturer. One factor may have been the large number of German VW cars in southern California, whose use of diesel power engine were "documented" to be lower in greenhouse gas emissions. Then in September 2015, the investigations by California Energy Agency revealed that the software used to measure and validate the low environmental impact of the VW cars was false and misleading. By October 2015, over 11 million VW cars were recalled from around the world. And significant legal and corporate actions have been taken against VW, once the largest car manufacturer in the world.

TomTom's index measures the sharpest increases in travel times between non-congested periods and peak periods. Russia's Moscow was rated the world's most congested city. TomTom's most congested cities are:

Moscow, Russia	Worst congested city overall.
Istanbul, Turkey	Large bodies of water in the heart of a city create traffic jams, with drivers unable to avoid using popular, busy bridges. The Bosphorus strait through commercial center creates problems.
Rio de Janeiro, Brazil	Most congested city in the Americas. Brazil is working to add metros and improve road infrastructure.
Warsaw, Poland	Car ownership has doubled, but road-building programs are failing to keep up.
Palermo, Italy	Low population, but world-class traffic jams.
Marseille, France	Harbor and coastline create problems and few ways in and out of city center.
Sao Paulo, Brazil	Transportation authorities tried to raise bus and metro fees sparking massive public protests.
Rome, Italy	Very old street network that wasn't built for cars.
Paris, France	Some alternative routes for drivers, but very congested.
Stockholm, Sweden	Network of waterways and bridges add to city's congestion.

Source: CNN, 2013.

Along with congestion comes declining air quality as harmful particulates envelop the city. Los Angles, Mexico, and Beijing are legendary for their thick, gray smoke. However, those three cities did not make the World Health Organization's (WHO) most polluted city list for 2014.

WHO measures air quality with a rating of PM2.5, which refers to the diameter in microns of particulates such as ammonia, carbon, nitrates, and sulfates. These micro particulates can lodge deep in the lungs as they are breathed in, and are especially harmful to asthmatics, those with emphysema or heart disease, or the elderly. They also contribute to illnesses like cancer as they pass through the bloodstream. WHO considers 25 microns a safe level, and says that, unfortunately, most cities that monitor their pollution exceed that level.

Delhi in India is the city with the worst air quality, WHO reports. Delhi's air quality as measured by PM2.5 averaged 575 micrograms per cubic meter. By contrast, London's average PM2.5 is below the safe zone at 20 (CNN, 2014).

Not far behind Delhi is Patna, another large Indian city with terrible air quality. It is rated at 149 micrograms per cubic meter. Half of the worst polluted cities in the world with the highest levels of PM2.5 are in India, according to WHO. Other megacities with high levels of toxins are in Pakistan and Bangladesh. Smaller cities with health-threatening smog problems include Anwaz in Iran and Gaborone in Botswana.

India's Center for Science and Environment reports that during the 2013 winter, Delhi's level jumped to 60 times higher than safe levels. The center said that India's cities were becoming victims of killer pollution, congestion, and a crippling car-dependent infrastructure. Delhi adds about 1,400 cars a day, and Indian car manufacturers fit only basic emission-cutting apparatus to their vehicles. Smoke from the burning of rubbish, industrial emissions, and pollutants from the country's predominantly coal-fired power stations add to the dangerous atmosphere. Medical studies point to the toxic risk of smog in the wide prevalence of acute lung diseases, eye disorders, and Vitamin D deficiency leading to rickets among Delhi inhabitants.

Of particular concern to tourists, pollution levels inside vehicles traveling in the Indian capital could be eight times worse than outside.

In contrast, the report noted that the Chinese government has made "consistent and aggressive efforts" to improve air quality in smoggy cities like Beijing. The efforts include limiting annual car sales, banning odd or even number-plated vehicles during "red alert" pollution periods and fining local governments for failing to curb smog as more and more cities are doing successfully (CNN, 2014).

Milan, Italy restricts traffic in the city by odd and even license plate numbers along with encouraging more walking and bike borrowing in the city. Central London has a congestion charge and campaigners have suggested a ban (*The Telegraph*, 2014). People need to walk, bike or take mass transportation.

Climate Change and Global Warming

Congestion and air pollution are part of a global dependency on carbon and fossil fuel-controlled economies. Too many autos and too much pollution are contributing to climate change and global warming, which are probably the most severe problems facing global cities, particularly those along the world's coasts. Climate scientists say that the Earth's northern polar region is entering a new warmer era, and the ice cap is melting at an unprecedented rate. They warn that the new era has warmer air and water temperatures, less summer sea ice and snow cover, and changed ocean chemistry. In 2011, the average annual air temperatures over the Arctic Ocean were 2.5 degrees greater than the 1981–2010 baseline and that ocean acidification from the increased absorption of CO_2 was rising.

As Arctic Sea ice declines in thickness it alters the flow of heat between the Arctic Ocean and the air. As the sea ice declines, the corresponding dark ocean surface absorbs more incoming solar radiation. This has a dramatic influence on Arctic air temperatures, and can alter atmospheric circulation. Warmer air weakens the high-altitude winds that circle the North Pole, causing a decline in the "polar vortex." This provides more chances for Arctic air to flow south into the US and Europe, causing major changes in weather (Arctic Map, 2014).

As the ice cap melts, sea levels rise, which gives a boost to high tides. Coastal cities are experiencing high tides that are overtopping streets, floorboards, and low-lying areas. The trend is projected to worsen sharply in the coming years.

The Union of Concerned Scientists released a report in October 2014 that forecasts that at least 180 floods will strike Annapolis, Maryland, US by 2020. By 2045, Washington, DC, Atlantic City, New Jersey, and 14 other east Coast and Gulf Coast locations will experience similar floods. The researchers have issued warnings about future coastal flooding rates, based on their projections of a rise in sea level of 5 inches between 2012 and 2030, and a rise of a foot between 2012 and 2045 (Climate Central, 2012).

Independent of the Union of Concerned Scientists' report, the City of Miami in Florida passed a resolution to become the US 51st state. The resolution expresses concerns that Miamians and others living in the south Florida area have with global warming and the subsequent rise in sea level. The combination of the sea level rising and the threat of evermore powerful storms means that Miami will likely become the first major American city to slide out of existence because of climate change (South Florida, 2014).

Worldwide, coastal cities are just as vulnerable as the US eastern seaboard is to flooding as sea levels rise. In an August 2013 report (World Bank, 2014), the World Bank estimated that costs of flood damage to the large coastal cities could reach $1 trillion a year as sea levels rise.

The report says that climate change, rapid urbanization, and subsiding land are putting the world's coastal cities at increasing risk of dangerous flooding. The World Bank economists forecast that average global flood losses will multiply from $6 billion per year in 2005 to $52 billion a year by 2050 with just social–economic factors, such as increasing population and property value, taken into account. Add in the risks from sea-level rise and sinking land, and global flood damage for large coastal cities could cost $1 trillion a year if cities don't take steps to adapt (World Bank, 2014).

Coastal cities' defenses against storm surges and flooding are designed for current conditions. They aren't prepared for the rising sea levels accompanying climate change that will make future floods more devastating. Protecting these cities in the future will take substantial investment in structural defenses, as well as better planning.

The World Bank says that in terms of the overall cost of damage, the cities at the greatest risk are: 1) Guangzhou, China; 2) Miami, US; 3) New York, US; 4) New Orleans, US; 5) Mumbai, India; 6) Nagoya, Japan; 7) Tampa, US; 8) Boston, US; 9) Shenzhen, China; and 10) Osaka, Japan. The top four cities alone account for 43 percent of the forecasted total global losses (World Bank, 2014).

However, cities in developing countries are at greater risk, when flood costs are measured as a percentage of gross domestic product (GDP). Many cities in developing nations are growing rapidly, with large populations that are poor, and exposure to tropical storms and sinking land.

The study lists the 10 most vulnerable cities when measured as percentage of GDP as: 1) Guangzhou, China; 2) New Orleans, US; 3) Guayaquil, Ecuador; 4) Ho Chi Minh City, Vietnam; 5) Abidjan, Ivory Coast; 6) Zhanjiang, China; 7) Mumbai, India; 8) Khulna, Bangladesh; 9) Palembang, Indonesia; and 10) Shenzhen, China (World Bank, 2014).

The poor are most at risk in these cities, because rapid urbanization has pushed them into the most vulnerable neighborhoods, into low-lying areas and along waterways prone to flooding. Often they must travel great distances to and from their daily work, and without mass transit they are dependent on individual vehicles that are usually older cars with antiquated combustion fuel systems.

The report also notes that several port cities face increasing risk, including Alexandria, Egypt; Barranquilla, Colombia; Naples, Italy; Sapporo, Japan; and Santo Domingo, Dominican Republic.

The World Bank calls for cities to act soon, by building better structural defenses. In addition, they need better crisis management and contingency plans, including early warning systems and evacuation plans. For small countries, protection and preparation are especially important. A devastating flood in a key city can stall the entire economy of a small country, making recovery and reconstruction even more difficult. For all of the cities, the preparation will save lives and money in the future (World Bank, 2014).

Wealth and Inequality

While cities' populations continue to accelerate, growth from migration is becoming less a function as natural populations increase. Mega cities like Delhi, Dhaka, Jakarta, and Mexico City are exploding with 30 million residents each, threatening to overtake the entire population of Canada—35.6 million in 2013. Soon over 500 cities globally will have more than a million residents. China alone has expanded its cities at a rate of one new Chicago (about 3 million people) every month for the past dozen years. Effectively, in little more than a century, human beings have gone from being rural animals to urban ones.

Not only are the cities growing, but also they are producing more and more of the world's wealth. According to the 2012 report from the Wilson Center, urban economic activity accounts for up to 55 percent of gross national product in low-income countries, 73 percent in middle-income ones, and 85 percent in high-income nations (Ruble, 2012).

Tragically, while great wealth is being generated by the cities, at the same time global poverty is on the rise and becoming an increasingly urban phenomenon. The middle class is shrinking as cities grow and economies become more knowledge-based and technology dependent. Urban inequality is verging on the crisis level, with measures of inequality growing rapidly.

The UN estimates that 1 billion people, or roughly one-third of the world's urban population live in slums (UN-HABITAT, 2006). Hundreds of millions of people in the world's cities exist in desperate poverty, without access to adequate shelter, clean water, and basic sanitation. Global poverty has become an urban phenomenon.

In the year 2002, 746 million people in urban areas were living on less than $2.00 a day. Over the last 20 years, the absolute number of urban poor has increased at a rate faster than in rural areas. Rapid urban growth has made Asia home to the largest share of the world's slum dwellers. However, the threat of urbanizing poverty is the gravest in Africa, which has the fastest rate of urban growth and the highest incidence of slums in the world. In the last 15 years the number of slum dwellers has almost doubled in sub-Saharan Africa, where 72 percent of the urban population lives in slums (Woodrow Wilson International Center for Scholars, 2007).

Overcrowding and environmental degradation make the urban poor particularly vulnerable to the spread of disease, for example the Ebola epidemic in West Africa. Slum dwellers' lives are permeated with insecurity, and what work there is comes with low pay and poor conditions.

Economic inequality gives rise to a wide range of chronic social problems like homelessness, criminal behavior, and gang violence that drain resources and distract politicians from large global issues like climate change. Gang violence is particularly pernicious. Gangs bring crime, injuries, and death that threaten the social fabric of local neighborhoods, and trigger social, economic, and physical decay.

European cities like Vienna, Paris, and London that have large immigrant populations with significantly different religions and cultures (mostly Muslim) now face serious social issues. Though not as criminally oriented as the gang cultures of some US cities, these large immigrant populations have increasing numbers of disaffected and underemployed youths. In many of these minority neighborhoods, men cannot marry without a job, and unskilled immigrants find little or no work.

Large numbers of restless, disenfranchised young men shut out from the normal patterns of modern life, leads to trouble. Terrorism is a critical concern for these cities, and many of the jihadist/terrorists fighters now in the Middle East have come from these neighborhoods.

In fall 2014, police and security crackdowns in London, Vienna, and cities in Bulgaria and Bosnia were aimed at arresting violent jihadists that were connected to the large Muslim populations. It seems that the radical Islamic group, ISIS, was actively recruiting fighters via online websites and through local mosques and radical imams.

In November 2014, Britain enacted tough laws that prevented citizens who traveled to Syria or Iraq to fight for terrorists groups from returning. Other European countries like Germany are pursuing radical jihadist and terrorist elements within their cities. Estimates are that 3,000 Europeans have travelled to Syria and Iraq to fight as jihadists, according to the EU anti-terrorism unit. The fear, particularly in cities like London, Paris, and Berlin, is that returning jihadists will generate terrorism, violence, and criminal activities (BBC, 2014).

Severe economic inequality like climate change is a major problem for the world's cities. It is more than just a question of whom, or which group, has more money. It is a question of being shut out of the body politic, of social disenfranchisement, and being marginalized from the benefits of modernity.

Economic inequality particularly impacts youths who are restless, unconnected, and vulnerable to outside groups who want to exploit them for their own purposes. Global cities are feeling the social stresses and restlessness created by these marginalized residents and the problem continues to grow.

Homelessness

Wealth inequality impacts the cities in other ways, particularly in terms of expensive or unavailable housing and corresponding homelessness. At the most basic economic level, homelessness is caused by poverty and unemployment. The poor simply cannot afford adequate housing or shelter. Scott Leckie, Director of the Centre on Housing Rights and Evictions in Geneva, adds that homelessness persists on a vast scale in both rich and poor countries because of economic and political disregard for the human rights of the poor (Share International, 2014).

The 2005 United Nations Commission on Human Rights estimated 100 million homeless worldwide. These are people with no shelter; they sleep on pavements, in doorways, in parks or under bridges. Or they sleep in public buildings like railway or bus stations, or in night shelters set up to provide homeless people with a bed.

Throughout the world, the problem is acute. It is estimated that in Europe, over 3 million are homeless. Even the wealthiest nations like the UK have homeless problems. According to Homeless World Cup, a global organization working to improve the lives of homeless people, the UK has one of the highest levels of homelessness in Europe with more than four people per 1,000 estimated to be homeless. The average life expectancy of a homeless person in the UK is 42 years, compared to the national average of 74 for men and 79 for women. This is lower than the life expectancy of Ethiopia or the Democratic Republic of the Congo. In the UK there are 10,459 rough sleepers and 98,750 households in temporary accommodations, and it is estimated that homelessness costs London £38.9 million a year in lost economic development and costs to its justice and health-care communities, and a much higher toll in human lives. Finally, the estimated cost for one homeless person in the UK to be provided accommodation and other support services is £15,000 per year (Homeless World Cup, nd).

In Brazil, there is a deficit of 6.6 million housing units, which equals an estimated 20 million homeless people, who live in favelas, shared clandestine rooms, hovels or under bridges and viaducts, or are squatters, in some of the country's largest cities. India is 63 percent slums, and in Mexico City an estimated 40 percent of people live in informal housing.

In Nigeria, 40 percent of the population lives in slums. There are an estimated 5 million people homeless in Russia, with 1 million of them children. Some 600,000 to 2.5 million are homeless in the US, and homelessness is particularly hard in expensive cities like San Francisco. Hawaii has one the worst rates of homelessness in the US because of the high cost of housing and low-paying tourist economy (Homeless World Cup, nd).

City Sprawl = Agglomerations

As cities grow in population, they consume more land. The urban population is also becoming less dense, sprawling out and taking over vast land mass. According to satellite photos by the Cities Alliance, the urban population density is two-thirds of what it was just a half-century ago. The sheer number of people moving to the cities has been pushing the cities further and further away from the center. To city planners this is "agglomeration," and it results in urban development that obliterates the landscape, extending in hundreds of square miles in every direction. Shanghai in China is a prime example; the city is steadily spreading out to include almost the whole region.

This sprawl is a global trend and probably means that the "urban age" is beginning and not ending. Global cities are becoming larger, more diverse, more fluid, and less manageable. Declining density and the sheer landmass, means the "city" as was once understood has grown into a sprawling, urbanized region.

Infrastructure Issues

Urban sprawl and declining density makes it harder and harder for cities to provide and support basic infrastructure needs of energy, transportation, water, waste, and telecommunications.

In December 2013, the US National League of Cities released a report that identified "The 10 Critical Imperatives Facing America's Cities." While US centric, most of the issues facing US cities are common to all the world's large cities. The report listed:

- Fragile fiscal health: Cities report their fiscal health is improving, but they continue to confront the prolonged effects of the recession and remain vulnerable to spending cuts.

- A deteriorating transportation infrastructure: Traffic congestion continues to worsen, choking the air with pollution and costing commuters millions of dollars in wasted gas and thousands of hours of lost time every year.

- A shrinking middle class: Over the past decade, middle-class families saw their median incomes decline by nearly 30 percent.

- Inadequate access to higher education: Higher education brings better-paying jobs, growing tax revenues, enhanced public safety and a better quality of life. Yet only 40 percent of American adults currently hold postsecondary degrees, and this rate is significantly lower for underserved minorities.

- The need for affordable housing: Foreclosures and vacant houses have destabilized neighborhoods resulting in increased crime, blight, shrinking local tax bases and more demand for social services.

- A less-than-welcoming return for veterans: Service members coming home from combat zones face a higher risk for unemployment, homelessness, and family problems. Among the solutions: local governments should work with non-profit and veterans groups to determine what service members need, create affordable housing for them, and partner with businesses to provide jobs.

- Gang violence: Gangs bring crime, injuries, and death that threaten the social fabric of city neighborhoods and trigger social, economic, and physical decay in affected neighborhoods.

- A broken immigration system: Millions of immigrants continue to arrive each year, generating substantial economic growth, revitalizing communities, and stabilizing neighborhoods.

- Climate change and extreme weather: Catastrophic storms, droughts, heat waves, and rising sea levels will increasingly impact cities, harming citizens, destroying property, disrupting local economies, and wiping out infrastructure.

- A lack of public trust in government: City leaders need citizens' input and cooperation more than ever before, yet recent surveys show public trust in government is falling (The National League of Cities, 2014).

Cities outside the US have infrastructure problems that are compounded by explosive growth. For example Mexico City is undergoing explosive growth as the nation continues to prosper. Mexico is projected to become the world's fifth-largest economy by 2050, and Mexico City contributes more than 30 percent of the nation's GDP. Like many global cities, it has grown piecemeal without a coordinated plan for urban infrastructure.

"The sheer size of the city makes planning difficult, and there will never be enough roads," says Adriana Lobo from Mexico's Center for Sustainable Transport. "Car growth is above five percent a year, and there are quite big mobility problems. You have got people travelling three hours each way to get to work. There is no way that we can match the growth of cars with growth of the roads" (Planetizen, 2008).

One partial solution is the Metrobus. One lane of the main carriageways in and out of the city is allocated solely to single-decker buses that ferry 250,000 people each day at high speed in and out of the city center. There are plans to expand the Metrobus system rapidly, as well as a twelfth line for the city's underground network, but gridlock in the city center is a major concern.

Not Enough Water

While coastal cities have been, or will be, ravaged by rising ocean levels and flooding, some inland cities are struggling to provide residents with a simple glass of water. California is suffering from a severe draught that has impacted San Francisco as well as Los Angeles. In fact, scientists are saying that the US's lakes, rivers, and aquifers are going to have a hard time quenching the thirst of the nation's growing population in a warming world.

A 2013 study from the US Columbia University Water Center (Huffington Post, 2013) on water scarcity detailed how a surging population plus climate change was impacting the availability of water, particularly in the southwest. Eleven US cities were listed that could be deeply affected by water shortages in the not too distant future.

The cities ranged from Salt Lake City in Utah's high desert to Lincoln, Nebraska in the farm belt, to Washington DC and Atlanta, Georgia on the east coast (Huffington Post, 2013).

Food and Water Watch, a US non-profit group focused on the world's food and water supplies, put together some overall facts about the world's water situation. For 2014, they reported that globally:

1.   780 million people live without clean drinking water;

2.   2.5 billion people—including almost 1 billion children—live without basic sanitation;

3.   more than one-third of Africa's population lacks access to safe drinking water;

4.   more than 130 million people in Latin America and the Caribbean lack access to safe drinking water;

5.   between 15 and 20 percent of the water used worldwide is not for domestic consumption, but rather for export.

Water and disease

•   Every 20 seconds a child under five years of age dies from waterborne illnesses;

- half of the world's hospital beds are occupied by people with an easily preventable waterborne disease;

- 80 percent of all sickness and disease worldwide is related to contaminated water, according to the WHO;

- diarrhea killed more children in the last decade than all armed conflicts since the Second World War;

- dirty water kills more children than war, malaria, HIV/AIDS, and traffic accidents combined;

- 75 percent of the people in Latin America and the Caribbean suffer from chronic dehydration because of poor water quality.

Water quality

- 90 percent of wastewater produced in underdeveloped countries is discharged untreated into local waters;

- 80 percent of China's major rivers are so degraded that they no longer support aquatic life;

- 90 percent of all groundwater systems under major cities in China are contaminated;

- 75 percent of India's rivers and lakes are so polluted that they should not be used for drinking or bathing;

- 60 percent of rural Russians drink water from contaminated wells;

- 20 percent of all surface water in Europe is seriously threatened.

Water scarcity

- More than 400 million Africans now live in water-scarce countries;

- unless we change our ways, two-thirds of the world's population will face water scarcity by 2025;

- compared to today, five times as much land is likely to be under "extreme drought" by 2050;

- by 2030, nearly half of the world's population—the majority living in underdeveloped countries—will be living in areas of high water stress;

- the percentage of the Earth's land area stricken by serious drought more than doubled between the 1970s and 2005;

- rapid melting will reduce the Tibetan glaciers by 50 percent every decade, according to the Chinese Academy of Sciences;

- more than two-thirds of Chinese cities face water shortages;

- 90 percent of the European alpine glaciers are in retreat (Food and Water Watch, nd).

These water issues hit the hardest in the large cities. Currently, they are acute in Brazil's Sao Paulo, South America's biggest metropolis with over 20 million people. Sao Paulo is quickly running out of water, with taps running dry, schools being suspended, and restaurants closing. The Candareira reservoir system, on which 6.5 million depend, is down to 7.1 percent of capacity, according to *The Economist*. At this time in 2013, it was half full, and Brazil's disaster-monitoring center is predicting that it will dry up by mid-2015.

There are numerous reasons for this impending crisis, including deforestation and the city's "heat island" effect, but it seems that the city authorities ignored the looming problem as it built up. Even now, conservation is not taken seriously and the average Sao Paulo resident consumes about 200 liters of water a day, well above the 150 in much of Europe (*The Economist*, 2014).

Of great concern to areas suffering from drought is that water shortages not only impact consumers, but they impact agricultural as well as energy. In Sao Paulo's case 80 percent of the city's power is generated by hydropower. Less water means less power and the city's economy will decline, adding to Brazil's economic woes.

Unprecedented Challenges

The challenges of twenty-first century urbanization seem unprecedented. They run the gauntlet from macro problems like climate change and global warming and wealth inequality to basic infrastructure issues like public transportation and water conservation.

Responding to these challenges begins by recognizing the new urban realities. First, as important as rural communities are, a majority of the planet's human population—and before too long the world's poor—now lives in cities. Second, an increasing percentage of the world's wealth is being produced in cities. Third, cities are spreading out and becoming less dense, thereby consuming tremendous amounts of land. Fourth, the present is one of the most active periods for human migration in history. Fifth, the impermanence of the present-day world necessarily means that the task of urban management becomes one of refining the process through constant learning, rather than one of simply identifying fixed solutions.

Many environmental crises that are linked to climate change will fall on our cities, particularly those along the world's coasts. Cities like Tokyo, Paris, Seoul, Shanghai, and many others, have undertaken large regeneration and infrastructure development. Now, they must face the challenges posed by climate change, which will hit hard.

Greening our cities is essential to mitigating climate change, since buildings, cars, and other city elements are the major sources of GHGs. We need to make our cities healthier and pollution free before we reach a "tipping" point where human action cannot save our fragile planet. New approaches to development and construction must be incorporated into how we work, live, and play. Instead of being centers for wealth inequality that bred alienation, resentment, and strife, our cities most be turned into centers that promote human interaction, healthy exchanges of ideas, and participation in a shared culture.

Most importantly, we need to replace our legacy dependence on carbon-based energy with renewable energy that is sustainable and distributed by efficient, non-polluting grid systems that are agile and responsive.

In short, we need to develop cities capable of slowing climate change and facing the other looming challenges of the twenty-first century. In the past, city governments have had to act long before international laws and treaties were passed. For example, Tokyo and Los Angeles had to act on air quality issues long before national or state governments got involved.

Climate change and the crisis of inequality are far too important for the cities to leave to national governments. For the survival and economic well-being of much of the world's population, global cities must become smart, green, and sustainable.

References

American Lung Association, 2014. http://www.lung.org/associations/states/california/advocacy/fight-for-air-quality/sota-2014/state-of-the-air-2014.html.

BBC, 2014. Islamic State Crisis: 3,000 European Jihadists Join Fight. September 26, http://www.bbc.com/news/world-middle-east-29372494.

Climate Central, 2012. Sandy Remembered. November 30, http://www.climatecentral.org/news/atlantic-hurricane-season-ends-sandy-will-be-long-remembered-15310.

CNN, 2013. http://money.cnn.com/gallery/news/2013/11/06/global-traffic-congestion/index.html.

CNN, 2014. http://www.cnn.com/2014/05/08/world/asia/india-pollution-who/.

Food and Water Watch, nd. http://www.foodandwaterwatch.org/water/interesting-water-facts/.

Homeless World Cup, nd. http://www.homelessworldcup.org/content/homelessness-statistics.

Huffington Post, 2014. http://www.huffingtonpost.com/2013/12/04/water-shortage_n_4378418.html.

Los Angeles Commission on 2020, 2014. A Time for Truth, December.

Los Angeles Highway Congestion, 2013. http://www.stateoftheair.org/2013/city-rankings/most-polluted-cities.html.

Planetizen, 2008. Mexico City Struggling with Infrastructure Problems, http://www.planetizen.com/node/29531.

Ruble, Blair A., 2012. The Challenges of the 21st Century City. The Wilson Center, December.

Share International, 2014. http://www.share-international.org/archives/homelessness/hl-mlaroof.htm.

South Coast Air Quality Management District (SCAQMD), 2010.

South Florida's Desperate Secession Movement, 2014. Future Tense. October 23, http://www.slate.com/blogs/future_tense/2014/10/23/south_florida_as_51st_state_the_city_of_south_miami_votes_to_break_away.html.

The Economist, 2014. Reservoir Hogs. Sao Paulo's Water Crisis. December 20.

The National League of Cities, 2013. The 10 Critical Imperatives Facing America's Cities. December, http://www.nlc.org/find-city-solutions/city-solutions-and-applied-research/governance-and-civic-engagement/10-critical-imperatives-in-2014.

The Telegraph, 2014. http://www.telegraph.co.uk/news/earth/environment/11280067/London-will-follow-Paris-and-ban-diesel-cars-campaigners-warn.html.

UN-HABITAT, 2006.

Woodrow Wilson International Center for Scholars, 2007. Global Urban Poverty: Setting the Agenda, www.wilsoncenter.org/sites/default/files/GlobalPoverty.pdf.

World Bank, 2014. Climate Change, http://climatechange.worldbank.org/sites/default/files/Turn_Down_the_heat_Why_a_4_degree_centrigrade_warmer_world_must_be_avoided.pdf.

Chapter 3

The Green Industrial Revolution

Human history is marked by extraordinary leaps in technology. When a technological window opens it triggers remarkable social, political, and scientific advances. The ancients advanced when they discovered fire and then entered the Stone Age.

So it went through history. Stunning developments in technology, science, and engineering allowed the great civilizations of the Egyptians, Mayans, and Chinese to flourish. Superior battle technology aided Hannibal as he conquered Italy; later, it made the Venetians the rulers of the Mediterranean Sea.

The First Industrial Revolution

In the middle of the 15th century, a German named Johannes Gutenberg, and two friends Andreas Deritzehn and Andreas Heilmann, became interested in a crude invention that pressed images on paper from a flat woodcut. Gutenberg began to work with a new form of type and an oil-based ink that was durable and lasting, and he used paper as well as vellum, a high-quality parchment.

When he had mastered the process, Gutenberg printed a beautifully executed Bible in 1455. Copies sold for 30 florins, or about three years' worth of wages. Through various iterations of his Bible, Gutenberg refined his technique for mechanical movable type printing. His inventions were astounding, revolutionary in their impact on society.

Printing spread to hundreds of cities throughout Europe, helping to stimulate the Renaissance and later Europe's scientific revolution of the sixteenth and seventeenth centuries. Historians estimate that by the end of the sixteenth century, European printing presses had produced 150 million books (Febvre and Martin, 1976).

These early printers unlocked the human mind on an unprecedented scale. Ideas crossed borders, and literacy broke the monopoly of the elite and bolstered a middle class. Mass communication had arrived, and ideas were emerging and suddenly accessible. Another advance in technology had pushed civilization forward.

Since the printing press was a European phenomenon, the rest of the world fell behind in science and social development. The rapid exchange of new ideas lead to the Age of Enlightenment, that extraordinary era of cultural, social, and scientific advancement led by Isaac Newton and Charles Darwin.

In the early 1700s, as the Age of Enlightenment emerged in Great Britain, a young Scottish inventor and mechanical engineer named James Watt started to tinker with the design of a crude steam engine that was used for pumping water from mines. In a flash of insight, he changed the steam so that it condensed in a chamber separate from the piston. Watt's change radically improved the power, efficiency, and cost-effectiveness of steam engines. Then he added rotary shafts and gears and a new world rose.

In 1775, Watt entered a partnership with Matthew Boulton, a businessman who quickly recognized the commercial potential of this new energy-generating source. Boulton and Watt were enormously successful with their steam engine, providing the power for a change in the way people lived, worked, and played.

By the end of the Napoleonic Wars in 1815, wood was scarce in Britain. However, Britain had an abundance of coal, which contained twice as much energy as wood. Coal quickly displaced wood as the fuel for the steam engine. Soon it was used to produce heat for industrial processes, to drive engines, and to create propulsion, as well as to warm buildings.

The combination of Gutenberg's printing press, which made the quick dissemination of innovation and ideas possible, and Watt's coal-driven steam engine, which created a whole new energy source, triggered an explosion in industrial activity. Chemical energy from coal was transferred to thermal energy and then to mechanical energy. The steam engine powered industrial machinery and steam locomotives.

The First Industrial Revolution surged. It was a turning point in human history and soon, all of western civilization was entrenched in this new industrial age, driven by steam, and surrounded by innovative ideas, which were distributed with the help of the printing press.

The machine age was born. At first, machines started to replace manual labor, horsepower, and wind and waterpower. This transition soon reached North America, hastened by the westward expansion and the 1849 discovery of gold in California. American communities, which were based on trade and agriculture and dependent on tools and animals, began to rely more and more on machines and engines.

The Second Industrial Revolution

America had its own version of the Enlightenment driven by the brilliant Ben Franklin. A Founding Father of the United States, Franklin was a prolific scientist and inventor. In 1752, this pudgy, pear-shaped physicist ventured out to a muddy field near Philadelphia. As rain clouds gathered and lightening sparked the dark sky, Franklin calmly fitted his kite with a key and then sailed the kite into the lightening. Luckily, he was spared electrocution as the lightening travelled down the kite lines to his Leyden jar. He had captured electricity in a jar, and his famous kite experiment ushered in the era of electricity.

Franklin's experiment led to a series of ideas, inventions, and breakthroughs from him and hundreds of people inspired by his concepts. People began to understand, harness, and commercialize electricity, which had been studied since 1600. Along with the discovery and nascent efforts to harness electricity, power and energy generation led to oil and the internal combustion engine.

In 1851, Samuel Kiers, an American from Pennsylvania, began selling kerosene to local coal miners, calling it Carbon Oil. Eventually, Kiers's efforts led to commercial oil drilling and production. With oil, the internal combustion engine became the force for modern industrialization.

In its simplest form an internal combustion engine harnesses a small intense explosion to drive a shaft or gears, like wheels on a car, or a turbine or propeller. A tiny amount of high-energy fuel like gasoline is placed in a small, enclosed space. Then air is mixed in and the mixture is ignited releasing energy in the form of expanding gas. The result is a mini-explosion that applies force to a part of the engine, usually to pistons, turbine blades, or a nozzle. This force pushes the engine part, converting chemical energy into useful mechanical energy.

The irony in the Second Industrial Revolution being totally dependent upon oil and gas was that one of the creative leads at the time was Henry

Ford who created the mass manufacturing of automobiles. Thus the costs of cars became very viable for all consumers, while the depend for oil, gas and then highways rose dramatically. However, the real irony was that Ford was a farmer and actually created fuel for cars from plants that would be made into a juice for powering cars. Until 1923, he had succeeded in making the "alternative fuel" to oil and gas. Then that industry forced him out of business and into their dependency on fossil fuels for automobiles.

By the end of the nineteenth century, the first of the world's major auto manufacturers was founded in Germany. Wilhelm Maybach designed an engine built at Daimler Motoren Gesellschaft (DMG), following the specifications of Emil Jellinek. As part of the deal, Jellinek required that the engine be named Daimler-Mercedes after his daughter. In 1902 automobiles with that engine were put into production by DMG (Georgano, 1990).

As the Second Industrial Revolution took hold, the internal combustion engine, fuelled by various types of carbon and oil-based gases, became the driving force behind this new age of extraordinary machines—cars, trains, boats, space ships, and so on—that soon defined modern life.

Manufacturing and jobs grew as the assembly lines made it possible to mass-produce goods and products at lower consumer costs. Except for some brutal wars in Europe, and the relentless genocide of the world's aboriginal natives, the planet's overall population expanded. With this expansion came evermore dependence on fossil fuels.

Along with machines, electricity, and transportation came the telephone—a technology that revolutionized the daily lives of ordinary people. This revolutionary technology provided the same explosion in communications as had Gutenberg's printing press. It was a new world of analog communications. Ideas, concepts, and images, now driven by electricity, could travel faster than ever before. Once more, science and knowledge exploded exponentially.

The Second Industrial Revolution's commercialization of fossil fuels opened the world to the wonders of the personal transportation vehicle. At first, fossil fuels allowed for the transition from an agrarian society to an urban one and provided a way to make electricity. But when used to power a car, fossil fuels allowed urban workers to leave their city apartments and settle in the suburbs. This led to the need to construct highways and build housing developments, and America's car culture took root.

Unfortunately, the western world's improving lifestyle—and the human passion for autos—have been dependent on fossil fuels. At one time, the coal, oil, and natural gas that powered this new economic model and the prosperity it entailed seemed relatively cheap, inexhaustible, and presumably harmless. More and bigger homes and buildings were built, more concrete poured, more fossil fuels extracted and burned. Frankly, there wasn't much to stop this social and economic juggernaut.

As industrialization led to urbanization, and urbanization to suburbanization, America built highways and thousands of miles of freeways that circled and interlaced our cities. Railroad and subway tracks were destroyed and covered over with paved highways and roads. The more concrete that was poured, the faster the suburbs grew and the American lifestyle was forever changed to be thoroughly dependent on fossil fuels.

By the middle of the 1990s, the world's undeveloped countries followed and soon were building highways and suburbs that sprawled along concrete ribbons, creating congestion, generating pollutants, and producing an atmospheric overhang of smog. Cities around the world evolved to require greater and greater amounts of energy for light, heat, locomotion, mechanical work, and communications; and then for smartphones, computers, televisions, microwaves, washing machines, coffee makers, and all the other technology and gadgets of modern living.

In fact, world energy consumption is predicted to grow by 53 percent from 2008 to 2035, according to the US Energy Information Administration. Much of the growth in energy consumption comes from developing nations like Brazil, Russia, India and China—known as the BRIC nations. Energy use has exploded in these nations and predicted to increase 85 percent by 2030.

To keep its energy-intensive lifestyle going, the US uses about 19 million barrels of oil a day, or about 7 billion barrels of oil a year. In 2011 this worked out to about 22 percent of the world's total consumption of oil, which was about 32 billion barrels in 2011, according to the US Energy Information Administration (USEIA, 2011). This high level of consumption is not sustainable.

Not Enough Supply, Too Much Demand

For over 100 years, oil and gas discoveries have made fortunes for those optimistic and smart enough to understand the Earth's geology to exploit it.

Or, as in the case of the Middle East, the nations there were lucky enough to live on top of enormous hydrocarbon deposits that made them rich and powerful.

Now, scientists believe that the world's traditional oil and natural gas supplies have peaked and are rapidly declining. As M. King Hubbert (1956), the Shell Oil geophysicist, observed in his startling prediction first made in 1949, the fossil fuel era will be of very short duration. In 1956, he predicted that US oil production would peak about 1970 and then decline. At the time he was scoffed at, now Hubbert looks extraordinarily prescient (Hubbert, 1956).

While traditional oil supply decreases, demand increases. Now with natural gas supplies and the use of questionable technologies like "horizontal drilling" or "fracting" which is now very questionable due to its documented negative environmental impact. In early 2011, China released customs data that showed that oil imports rose 18 percent in 2010. Platts, an oil industry research company, reported in October 2012 that China's oil consumption averaged 9.8 million barrels per day. Platts calculated that China's apparent oil demand is up 9.1 times year-to-year (China Oil Demand, 2013). The unfortunate result is that China has now become very dependent upon fossil fuel sources from other nations.

Driving this consumption is China's adoption of the automobile by its emerging middle class. Once a nation where everyone commuted by bicycle, China now has 60 million cars on the road, with 12 to 18 million more new cars predicted annually. To solve it's demand problem, China's state-controlled oil and gas companies have been buying massive amounts of oil and gas from around the world (BP, 2011).

However, as China prepares for its 13th Five-Year Plan (from 2016–2020), there is speculation that the nation will allow only electric and hydrogen fuel vehicles to be sold. That would be monumental for China's own auto manufacturing, and it would force other nations to convert rapidly to non-fossil fuel transportation (Hong, 2013). Furthermore, China plans on manufacturing these cars and then exporting them to other countries.

India is not far behind China in oil consumption. India consumes nearly 3 million barrels per day as car sales have jumped (Asian Age, 2010). India is expected to be the fourth largest car market in the next three years (Jafry and Silvers, 2014).

The rest of the world's undeveloped societies are modernizing and using more oil for cars, trucks, airplanes, and boats. For example, Saudi Arabia is the world's largest oil producer. However, it is also the sixth-largest oil consumer and internal consumption is growing rapidly. Increasing population and fuel subsidies are pushing internal demand growth to 7–9 percent per year (Luft and Korin, 2012: 33).

Meanwhile as more and more oil and other fossil fuels are burned, pollution increases and emissions grow, spreading around the world and causing climate change. The build up of greenhouse gases (GHGs) has marched in lock step with the expansion of fossil fuel use since the 1700s. While primarily composed of CO_2, greenhouse gases also include methane (CH_4), and nitrous oxide (N_2O). The gases float upward into the atmosphere and wrap themselves like a blanket around the Earth. As more and more are added, the blanket gets thicker and warmer.

Unlike empty beer cans, plastic bags, or the other garbage that pile up along our roads and rivers, GHGs pile up out of sight, in the Earth's atmosphere above our heads. Visualize all the CO_2 that is released from cars, from coal and gas burning power generation, and from the burning and clearing of forests and the deforestation of regions like Brazil or Indonesia.

As a consequence the planet is getting hotter. Each day, the Earth is gaining huge amounts of extra energy from greenhouse gas emissions. NASA climate scientist James Hansen says the current increase in global warming is equivalent to exploding 400,000 Hiroshima atomic bombs per day, 365 days per year (*The Economist*, 2012: 3). That is 278 atomic bombs' worth of energy every minute or more than four explosions per second. To be clear, this is the extra energy being gained each day. The results are devastating to the land areas and the atmosphere that is breathed daily around the world. Further, severe changes to weather patterns are created by the differences in temperatures and the impacts from evaporation as hot air streams hit cold water.

The Green Industrial Revolution

In the midst of this fossil-fuelled, internal combustion, greenhouse gas suffocating age, the Green Industrial Revolution, has emerged.

Social scientists argue that industrial revolutions are triggered by the confluences of a new energy-generating technology and a new form of communication technology that provides rapid dissemination of ideas to accelerate the adoption of inventions. In the First Industrial Revolution, it was the steam engine and the printing press, and in the second, it was the internal combustion engine and analog communications. For the Green Industrial Revolution, renewable energy has combined with digital communications.

While Jeremy Rifkin coined the term, the Third Industrial Revolution, in his 2004 work, *The European Dream* (Rifkin, 2004), the Green Industrial Revolution is more descriptive of what is already emerging. While Europe was and is environmentally conscious and aware of being "green," the Green Industrial Revolution actually began in Japan and South Korea many years before it emerged in Europe.

As a small and densely populated island nation of 130 million people, Japan has a tradition of "no waste" that dates back to the Middle Ages. For centuries, Japan relied on its own natural resources for energy and development. Natural resources were exploited, but because 70–80 percent of Japan is mountainous or forested, development of land for commercial, farm, and residential use was limited. Even today, human waste is recycled for fertilizer. It is no wonder that, for three decades, Japan led in the creation of PV and other renewable energy systems. Its concerns for water conservation led to the success of Toto, one of the greatest and most efficient water use companies in the world.

By the 1980s, Japan and South Korea were concerned with the need to become energy secure, and, as a result, they developed national policies and programs to reduce their growing dependency on foreign fuels. These countries realized after the Second World War and the Cold War that their futures were not rooted in the same carbon-intensive economies that had built the US and western Europe.

Decades later, Japan is once again struggling with an energy crisis, created by a devastating earthquake and tsunami in the northeast coastal region that destroyed one of the key Fukushima nuclear power plants. From this tragedy, Japan may leap even further ahead in developing a carbonless economy as it expands renewable energy generation to compensate for the loss of nuclear power. Other Asian nations are rapidly developing large-scale renewable energy generation as well.

The Green Industrial Revolution features fast-as-light communication of the digital age with its Internet access to almost all-scientific knowledge, and the Facebook and Twitter-led social networking that has truly created Marshall McLuhan's "global village." This digital age will intersect with renewable and sustainable sources for power. Smart grids, intelligent machines, and additive manufacturing will augment it.

The Green Industrial Revolution may be more significant and life changing than either the First or Second Industrial Revolutions. It may also turn out to be the planet's only real chance for survival. With an estimated 10 billion inhabitants by mid-century, there is so much more at stake.

Despite the claims by the oil and natural gas industries that there is an abundant supply, the reality is that the world is running out of fossil fuel, particularly oil. This alone threatens to shake the very foundation of human existence. Adding a heightened sense of urgency is the environmental degradation and the collapse of various parts of our planet's ecosystem, like the Brazilian watershed and the Arctic.

Fortunately, in some parts of the world, the Green Industrial Revolution has begun. Parts of Asia and Europe have been moving into it for over three decades, developing sustainable, energy-independent communities. South Korea has urban regions that are already energy independent and carbon neutral (Clark, 2000).

Japan was heading in this direction as well, but got redirected toward nuclear power stations and plants in the 1970s. However, after the March 2011 nuclear disaster at Fukashima, the Japanese government is replacing nuclear power with renewable energy systems for building complexes and individual homes (Adams and Funaki, 2009).

Meanwhile a large-scale effort is underway in China where the nation has overtaken other countries. In 2008 the Climate Group, an international think tank, reported China's rapid gains in the race to become the leader in developing renewable energy technologies via its 12th Five-Year Plan. This plan that started in March 2011 committed the nation to spending the equivalent of over three trillion dollars in funding for renewable energy (Climate Group, 2008).

Germany through its feed-in-tariff (FiT) program was the number one producer and installer of solar panels for homes, offices, and large open areas from 2006–2009. In 2015, Germany embarked on the most ambitious energy revolution anywhere in the industrialized world. In 2014, 26 percent of Germany's power supply came from renewable sources. By 2050, the figure is targeted to rise to 80 percent. The shift, Foreign Minister Frank-Walter Steinmeier said, is Germany's "man on the moon" project (Slater, 2015).

In 2010, Italy then copied the FiT and held that distinction of world leader in solar panel installation. China took the lead in 2011 and continues as the number one solar panel and PV manufacturer and installer. Japan is now leading in auto manufacturing, jumping ahead of the competition with its hybrid autos (Gipe, 2014).

Other European nations like Spain, Scotland, and the Nordic countries are pursuing policies to achieve energy independence through renewable energy. They are succeeding. Denmark has made extraordinary advances already. The Danes have a program that includes local plans and financing to develop on-site energy-renewable power systems. By 2015, several Danish cities will be energy independent with renewable energy power and smart green grids with the whole nation 100 percent using renewable energy by 2025 (Lund and Østergaard, 2010).

Sustainability is the Key

The decline in natural resources and fossil fuels and increasing climate change plus an accelerating population is pushing us closer to environmental catastrophe. If global energy policies do not change, political and social tensions will mount over the supplies and locations of fossil fuels as they become scarcer. The rise in climate change, particularly as it impacts food production, will exacerbate the difficulties that global cities face.

The way out is by embracing the Green Industrial Revolution and its promise of smart green cities powered by renewable energy. Asian and European nations have set the pace for sustainable and secure communities with their own renewable energy sources, storage devices, and emerging technologies.

Smart green cities represent an improved new design for how we can live. They can integrate renewable energy generation and storage technologies with non-fossil-fueled transportation. They can focus on environmentally sensitive business development, green job creation, and healthy social activities. Scientists describe this as sustainable development or the integration of a community's energy and infrastructure requirements, economic needs, and social activities for the protection and preservation of the environment. Business and new commerce is stimulated by this interaction, which in turn provides economic reasons for pursuing and creating sustainable communities.

Most modern cities have the potential to implement some, if not all, sustainable activities. With a little guidance, most communities can have locally-distributed renewable energy, clean water, recycled garbage and waste, and efficient community transportation systems that run on renewable energy sources for power. Global cities can lead the way in creating sustainable lifestyles that are free from the carbon-intensive, fossil-fuel-based, inefficient centralized energy generation of the past.

The Green Industrial Revolution's Key Components

Just as coal and steam engines were central to the development of the First Industrial Revolution, today's Green Industrial Revolution relies on core renewable energy components.

RENEWABLE ENERGY AND DISTRIBUTED ON-SITE POWER

Renewable energy generation is the foundation for a sustainable community, and the heart of the Green Industrial Revolution. Basically, renewable energy is a source of energy that is not carbon-based and will not run out. Renewable energy sources are described as distributed energies, because unlike the massive centralized fossil fuel power plants, they are spread out through many sources. For example, the solar installations on numerous rooftops in Germany or Arizona are on-site which is a decentralized system.

Such distributed energy resources are found in every inch of the world—the sun, the wind, wave and tidal action, the geothermal heat under the ground, and biomass like garbage, agricultural, and forest waste. Other renewable sources include bacteria, algae, and hydrogen when it comes from renewable electrolyzed sources.

Wind has been used as a power source for tens of thousands of years. Ancient civilizations used wind power for sailboats, and this original technology had a major impact on the first windmills, which used sail-like panels to catch the wind. Today, a large propeller is placed in the path of the wind. The force of the wind turns the propeller and a gear coupling interacts with a turbine, which generates electricity. The concept of wind generation may be ancient, but technological advances have transformed it. New generation wind turbines are extraordinarily sophisticated machines that use new materials like carbon fiber. They are strong, quiet, and cost-efficient.

Wind farms harness the energy of dozens, even hundreds, of wind turbines. Turbines can be installed on land or offshore. Small ones can be placed on rooftops, or in highway medians to capture airflow.

The major technology developments that enabled wind power commercialization have already been made, but there will be more refinements and improvements. Based on the way other technologies have developed, the eventual push to full commercialization and deployment of wind power will happen in a manner that is unimaginable today. There will be a major change in the demand for energy that will put several key companies or financial organizations in a position to regain their investments.

The use of wind, one of the most ancient power sources, is growing rapidly as the world moves into the Green Industrial Revolution. According to the World Wind Energy Association (WWEA, 2011), by June 2010, 196 GW (gigawatt) of electricity were being generated by wind power, which equated to about 2.5 percent of the world's energy production. Eighty countries are using wind power on a commercial basis. Several have achieved relatively high levels of wind power penetration by 2009: 20 percent of stationary electricity production in Denmark, 14 percent in Ireland and Portugal, 11 percent in Spain, and 8 percent in Germany.

Solar generation systems capture sunlight from the Earth's primary energy source. The sun radiates an enormous amount of power, about 170,000 TW (terawatts), and powers almost all natural processes that occur on the Earth's surface. There is no shortage or cost for energy from the sun's power. Harnessing and using sun energy can be done in both a centralized and de-centralized system. There are two technologies that directly convert electromagnetic energy from the sun into useful energy: solar PV and solar thermal.

PV systems convert light into electricity. Silicon cells capture sunlight, including ultraviolet radiation. The sunlight creates a chemical reaction and excites the electrons in a semiconductor, which generates a current of electricity. This PV reaction is at the core of solar panel systems.

A PV system includes mechanical and electrical connections, mountings, and a means of regulating or modifying the electrical output. Because the voltage of an individual solar cell is low, the cells are wired in series to create a laminate. The laminate is assembled into a protective weatherproof enclosure, thus making a PV module. Modules are then strung together into an array. Electricity generated by PV systems can be used directly as a standalone power source, stored, fed into a large electricity grid, or linked with many domestic electricity generators to feed into a small grid.

Silicon crystal and thin film are the two main categories of PV technologies. Silicon crystal is used more often because of its higher efficiency and greater abundance. However, the process of refining silicon is expensive. While thin-film technologies have a lower efficiency, they do have the potential to provide solar power at a lower cost per watt than silicon crystals. Now the third generation of PV design is developing that features low-cost, low-efficiency materials that may achieve significant scale.

A second process uses sunlight to heat liquid, which is then converted to electricity. On a large scale, thermal technology is concentrated in one location so that is it used for utility-scale power generation. These large systems use mirrors or lenses to focus solar energy on the liquid. The heated liquid then drives a turbine that generates electricity. These concentrated solar power (CSP) systems are of four basic types: trough, Liner Fresnel Reflector, tower, and dish. The most common is the trough system, which uses parabolic mirrors that concentrate solar heat on a fluid-filled receiver that runs the length of the trough.

The operation of a CSP solar plant requires large tracts of land and substantial volumes of water to provide cooling for the steam turbine. Many of the prime locations for these systems are remote, placing a burden on transmission lines and connection activities.

Although both PV and CSP are dependent on solar power input, CSP systems are easily fitted with thermal storage systems such as molten salt. Adding a storage component allows for operation at night or on cloudy days and turns solar energy into a more consistent power resource.

The US pioneered CSP technologies, and there are a number of large solar thermal installations in California, Nevada, and now Hawaii. In mid-2010, the

US produced more than half of all solar thermal power in the world, although Spain is rapidly building solar energy plants.

Solar, like wind, can be installed on homes and building complexes closer to the end user, instead of on distant farms. That is why, on-site renewable power generation is the key to becoming energy independent with solar and wind power as well as other renewable energy sources.

Use of solar energy is increasing rapidly. In 2000 there were only 170 MW (megawatt) of solar power generated globally. In 2010 the global market reached 20 GW of installed solar power capacity, according to Greentech Media. They anticipate that the global PV market will reach 25 GW by 2013, and come close to 100 GW by 2020. They also anticipate that a number of large solar firms will approach the 1 GW-capacity threshold in 2011.

PV systems can be integrated into a building that also links it to the infrastructures of surrounding buildings. This fast-growing segment includes incorporating PV solar panels in building elements such as roofs, window overhangs, or walls. This reduces the material costs of the building construction and the installation cost of the PV panels. Passive solar building design can also take advantage of solar energy, using windows and interior surfaces to regulate indoor air temperature. As the price of panels and generation drops, solar energy takes on a much bigger role in carbonless energy generation.

Biomass may be the oldest of all sources of renewable energy, dating back to the ancients and their discovery of the secrets of fire. It is biological material from living or recently living organisms such as plants that can be used to generate energy. This remarkable chemical process converts plant sugars like corn into gases like ethanol or methane. The gases are burned or used to generate electricity. The process is referred to as "digestive" and it's not unlike an animal's digestive system. Abundant and seemingly unusable plant debris—rye grass, wood chips, weeds, grape sludge, almond hulls, and the like—can then be used to generate energy. Algae can be grown in ponds and harvested and used for biomass fuel.

To create usable energy from biomass, materials like waste wood, tree branches, and other scraps are burned to heat water in a boiler. The steam is used to turn turbines or run generators to produce electricity. Biomass can also be tapped right at the landfill or waste treatment plant, by burning waste products.

Biomass can produce energy without the need for burning. Most garbage is organic, so when it decomposes it gives off methane gas, which is similar to natural gas. Pipelines can be put into the landfills to collect the methane gas, which is then used in power plants to make electricity.

Animal feed lots can process manure in a similar way using anaerobic digesters. The digesters can create biogas from the manure, which is then burned to produce power. For example, dairy farms can use methane digesters to produce biogas from manure. In turn, the biogas can be burned to produce energy or used like propane. Biogas can also be derived from poultry litter.

Although biomass is a renewable energy source, the combustion process creates pollution. Biomass resources also vary by area and depend on the conversion efficiency to power or heat. For these reasons, many countries see biomass as a transitional renewable energy source, for use as they look for new technologies to either convert the emissions or process waste differently. For example, Denmark creates much of their energy with biomass but they plan to start converting and limiting its use totally in the next 5–10 years.

On the positive side, biomass raw materials get their energy from the sun and regrow quickly. Through photosynthesis, plants use chlorophyll to convert CO_2 into carbohydrates. When the carbohydrates are burned, they release the energy captured from the sun. Energy crops can be grown on marginal lands and pastures or planted as double crops. While most scientists say that making ethanol from corn is not efficient, it has been produced in the midwest for years. Converting sugarcane to ethanol is considerably more efficient, and Brazil has adapted sugarcane to ethanol conversion as a major fuel source for transportation.

The Union of Concerned Scientists cites Minnesota's Koda Energy plant as an excellent example of generating energy from biomass. It is a combined heat and power (CHP) plant that uses biomass to generate renewable electricity as well as waste heat from the boiler (Tribe Koda Energy, 2014). In 2009 Koda began generating electricity from oat hulls, wood chips, prairie grasses, and barley malt dust. About 170,000 tons of these agricultural wastes are used a year.

Since the beginning of time, humans have captured the energy from biomass by burning it to make heat. In the First Industrial Revolution, biomass-fired heat produced steam power, and more recently this biomass-fired steam power has been used to generate electricity. Advances in recent years have shown that there are even more efficient and cleaner ways to use biomass.

Geothermal power is created from heat stored in the Earth. This heat originates from the formation of the planet, from radioactive decay of minerals, and from solar energy absorbed at the Earth's surface. It has been used for space heating and bathing since ancient Roman times, but is now better known for generating electricity. In 2007, geothermal plants worldwide had the capacity to generate about 10 GW, or 10 billion watts of power, and in practice generated enough power to meet 0.3 percent of the global electricity demand (GEO, 2014).

Most geothermal energy comes from heated water, or hydrothermal resources, that exist where magma comes close enough to the Earth's surface to transfer heat to groundwater reservoirs. This produces steam or high-pressure hot water. If the reservoir is close enough to the surface, a well can be drilled and the steam or hot water can be used to drive a turbine. The steam or hot water can also be used as a heat source. If the water temperature is moderate enough, it can be used directly to heat buildings, or for agriculture or industrial processes. Iceland has successfully done that so that 93% of its energy use for the entire nation comes from geothermal sources.

In the last few years, engineers have developed remarkable devices such as geothermal heat pumps, ground source heat pumps (GSHP), and geoexchangers that gather ground heat to provide heating for buildings in cold climates. Through a similar process they can use ground sources for cooling buildings in hot climates. More and more communities with concentrations of buildings, like colleges, government centers, and shopping malls are turning to geothermal systems.

Ocean power technologies vary, but the primary types are: **wave power** conversion devices, which bob up and down with passing swells; **tidal power** devices, which use strong tidal variations to produce power; **ocean current** devices, which look like wind turbines and are placed below the water surface to take advantage of the power of ocean currents; and **ocean thermal energy conversion devices**, which extract energy from the differences in temperature between the ocean's shallow and deep waters.

Tidal waves have power that can be harnessed to create usable energy. That is the concept behind the revolutionary SeaGen tidal power system, the world's first large-scale commercial tidal stream generator, installed in Strangford Narrows in Northern Ireland (OPT, 2014).

Tidal turbines that would have less impact on the environment are in development. Because water is denser than air, tidal turbines are smaller than wind turbines and can produce more electricity in a given area. In 2006, Verdant Power installed a pilot-scale tidal project in New York's East River. Verdant received the go ahead to expand the project to 1 MW in 2012 (Verdant, 2012).

Waves are produced by winds blowing across the surface of the ocean. Buoys, turbines, and other technologies can capture the power of the waves and convert it into clean, pollution-free energy. Pelamis Wave Power, a Scottish company, may have developed a breakthrough technology for wave energy. Named after a sea snake, the Pelamis absorbs the energy of the ocean waves and converts it into electricity. About the length of a jumbo jet, but thinner, this extraordinary machine is made up of five large brightly colored tube sections (Pelamis Wave Power, 2014).

The potential for wave energy from oceans is enormous. The estimated wave energy around the British Isles equals about three times the UK's electricity demand and could become a major factor in the UK's energy mix. Europe's western seaboard offers an enormous number of potential sites off the coast of Ireland, France, Spain, Portugal, and Norway. The Pacific coastlines of North and South America, southern Africa, Australia, and New Zealand are also highly energetic. In fact, most seacoast areas have the potential to generate wave energy at competitive prices.

Run-of-the-river systems generate electricity without the large water storage required of traditional hydroelectric dams. Run-of-the-river systems are ideal for streams or rivers with consistent water levels or minimum loss of water flow during the dry season. In most cases, power turbines are mounted along the river and as the water flows the turbines generate electricity. This is being done in Europe and Asia, where the flowing river water generates considerable amounts of energy without harming the surrounding land or changing the natural elements in the water. These systems do minimal destruction to pristine environments and could easily be adapted to large inland rivers (Run of River, 2014).

Bacterial, or microbial fuels use living, nonhazardous microbial bacteria to generate electricity. British Petroleum has made a $500 million investment in this futuristic process, which is now being developed by researchers at the University of California, Berkeley and the University of Illinois, Urbana.

Researchers envision small household power generators that look like aquariums but are filled with water and microscopic bacteria instead of fish. When the bacteria inside are fed, the power generator—referred to as a "biogenerator"—would produce electricity. Ironically the funding for this technology comes from the same company that caused the April 2010 oil spill in the Gulf of Mexico that killed 11 people, damaged the Gulf waters, and polluted the coastland while destroying fishing and tourist businesses.

Clean, never-ending energy is available throughout the planet; existing technologies just need to be applied in a systemic way. Humans have been using water and wind power for thousands of years, and these sources are abundant and the energy is easily gathered. The sun is the most energy-intensive object in our galaxy and its offers far more energy than humans will ever need. Hydrogen is another abundant energy source, as is tidal action. Turning waste—organic and inorganic—into energy isn't a complicated process and can be adapted to almost every community. The more common renewable sources and their technologies are wind, solar, geothermal, biomass, and ocean waves. Not so common renewable sources include hydrogen cells, magnetic levitation, algae, and bacterial or microbial.

However, California has become the key state starting hydrogen refueling stations (focused mainly on renewable sources such as wind and solar power or water to electrolye into hydrogen fuel) as the automobile manufacturers are targeting the state for the large leasing and sales of hydrogen fuel cell cars in areas in 2015 and then extensively in 2016. Germany already has such an extensive network of hydrogen refueling stations. And Norway has had a hydrogen highway for almost a decade now. Next are the large number of hydrogen fuel cell cars into these nations too.

ENERGY STORAGE

Most renewable energy sources, particularly wind and solar, are called "intermittent" because the sun is not always shining and the wind does not always blow. To make renewable energy sources work smoothly, devices that can store the energy and release it when needed are critical. These storage devices can take the natural form of large salt formations, or artificial ones like batteries, fuel cells, or flywheels. Innovation is exploding in energy storage, including the use of hybrid and plug-in autos. Cost-effective energy storage is the Holy Grail of the renewable energy dynamic.

Fuel cells are electrochemical cells that change a source fuel into an electrical current. They generate electricity through reactions between a fuel and an oxidant, triggered in the presence of an electrolyte. The reactants flow into the cell, and the reaction products flow out of it, while the electrolyte remains within it. Fuel cells are energy storage devices that can operate continuously as long as the necessary reactant and oxidant flows are maintained (Clark, Paulocci and Cooper, 2002; Cooper and Clark, 1996).

Fuel cells are different from conventional electrochemical cell batteries in that they consume reactant from an external source, which must be replaced (Clark, 2007; Clark, 2008; Clark and Rifkin, 2005; Clark and Rifkin, 2006). Many combinations of fuels and oxidants are possible. A hydrogen fuel cell uses hydrogen as its fuel and oxygen as its oxidant. Other fuels include hydrocarbons and alcohols, and chlorine and chlorine dioxide.

Also under development are new batteries that can provide cheap efficient electricity storage. Tesla Motors, the US electric auto manufacturer is building a $5 billion battery factory—projected to be the largest of its kind. Tesla sees the factory and their more efficient battery as the key to making electric cars more affordable and expanding the auto segment. Additionally, this "gigafactory" will produce stationary battery packs—about the size of a washing machine—that can be paired with rooftop solar panels to store power for individual houses. Already, SolarCity, a company that will use Tesla's improved batteries is packaging solar panels and batteries to power California homes and companies. Eventually, customers will be able to buy solar panels and battery storage units from local retail stores like Home Depot or Ikea (Bloomberg, 2014).

FLEXIBLE ENERGY SHARING

The old centralized, one-way power lines of the traditional utility system must change. The old grids are inefficient and dysfunctional. Smart grids are necessary to maximize distributed energy from many small sources. These Internet-like grids need to be scalable and distribute electricity flexibly, moving energy multiple ways among users. The idea is that even though you are not at home, your solar panels are generating power. While you are gone, your neighbor is editing video in his home office, while washing his clothes and brewing coffee, plus recharging his plug-in auto. All of which is using more electrons than his solar panels can produce. The smart grid can seamlessly divert your excess power to him, track it, and bill it.

INTEGRATED TRANSPORTATION

Mobility and transportation are critical functions that cannot be done without in our modern world. Yet, transportation contributes massive amounts of greenhouse gases that need to be eliminated. Autos, buses, and other forms of vehicular transportation have to switch from fossil fuels to green and environmentally sensitive energy. The international transportation industry has started this transition and it will only accelerate, especially if China moves forward with its non-fossil fuel auto regulations. Automakers are under pressure to increase gas mileage in their vehicles, and the results are remarkably innovative concepts and technologies, including hybrids, electric cars, and hydrogen-powered buses and vehicles.

A new program called the Cash-Back Car is being tested in the US and has great promise. On a small scale, this new program connects hybrids and plug-in autos to a local grid. The cars are charged when needed, and if not, the cars can push electricity back into the grid. The system is easily regulated by computer, which can keep tabs on the kWhs coming and going. The system can calculate how much electricity each car uses and puts back, making them ideal storage devices. The concept is simple, efficient, and has enormous potential. It can be scaled to be a major part of the energy storage dynamic. Plus it adds one more incentive to own an electric car.

These components are technologically accessible, and individually useful. However, the real value is in connecting them together in a seamless and environmentally clean infrastructure. Connected, they allow us to conceive of a new energy and economic model that is independent of fossil fuels.

Government Support and Involvement is Crucial

The huge carbon energy industries were launched with government support. Even today, these mega-corporations receive vast sums in subsidies from governments. Similar support needs to go into the sustainable technologies of the Green Industrial Revolution. The EU has consistently taken this position, including its efforts to create a hydrogen highway. Incentives that are now going to the carbon-generating industries—$4 billion annually in the US to the oil companies—must be reduced and applied to renewable energy generation. This tax shift has been very successful in other industries and can be designed so there is little or no additional tax burden on consumers (Clark and Demirag, 2005; *Fortune*, 2012).

To move the Green Industrial Revolution forward will require modification to these deregulation rules and new policies. Central power plants are still the norm and regulations are needed to oversee supplies, costs, and delivery of energy. German and Danish central power plants, for example, have significant government involvement through partial ownership or by appointed directors. The concept has begun in the US and it is critical in China where large renewable power systems are partly state-owned (Borden and Stonington, 2014).

Local energy generation is critical. While some fossil fuels, like coal, oil, and gas, are still cheap and used in central power plants, they are the major global atmospheric polluters. If a carbon tax or some other method that calculated the damage to the environment and public health were added, the costs would be higher than renewable power systems. That public policy and economic strategy is beginning in the Europe and China.

China and the US rank at the top of the emission polluters, and in both cases coal is the major problem. If the human and environmental impacts of coal were calculated into its true costs, then the real cost of coal energy generation for power would soar.

The Second Industrial Revolution pushed the operation of large fossil-based power plants in the early part of the twentieth century and then nuclear power plants in the century's last half. The plants had to be powerful to withstand the degradations over the vast distribution of a central-powered grid system. At each conversion from alternating current (AC) to direct current (DC), electricity loses some power, but for the fossil or nuclear-fueled plants there is so much power coming out at the beginning that it did not matter at the end. This system resulted in the loss of efficiency in transmission over power lines as well as the constant need for repairs and upgrades.

Not so in the case of the environmentally friendly renewable systems. For best results, community energy systems need nearby renewable power generation connected to "smart" distribution systems so electricity does not have to travel far and lose efficiencies. An alternative is to hook into a transmission line. This way the local grid is added to the existing distribution system and the transmission line can act as a battery for the renewable energy that needs storage. A system like this is similar to the Internet where there is no single area for control over data, or in this case power, rather it is spread out and localized.

The Next Economics: Civic Capitalism

In light of the October 2008 world financial meltdown, which even in 2014 continues with the monetary crisis in Europe, it seems silly to think that the supply-side, deregulated, free-market economics so passionately espoused by President Ronald Reagan and Prime Minister Margaret Thatcher in the 1980s will work for a twenty-first century world threatened by irreversible environmental damage.

The 2008 economic implosion from trillions of dollars in hedge funds, sub-prime mortgages, credit swaps, and related marginal derivatives nearly pushed the western world's financial structure into the abyss. It underlined what happens when governments ignore their responsibility to govern. Market economists and others had argued that there was no need for regulation. Government would act as "the invisible hand."

In the end, the worst financial disaster since the Great Depression was a testament to the venal side of free-market capitalism—greed, stupidity, carelessness, and total disregard for risk management. These are not behaviors that can be repeated if the planet is going to survive climate change and its impact on the Earth and its inhabitants.

The Green Industrial Revolution must develop an economy that fits its social and political structures, similar to the First and Second Industrial Revolutions. The first one replaced an agrarian, draft animal-powered economy with one powered by steam engines and combustion machine-driven manufacturing, an evolution that was accelerated by colonial expansion. The second created a fossil fuel-powered economy that extracted natural resources in an unregulated, consumer-fed, free-market capitalist society.

As the Green Industrial Revolution grows, the world will become much more interdependent. What happens in one part of the world, be it weather, pollution, politics, or economics, impacts other regions.

The Arab oil embargoes of the early 1970s pushed Europe and Asia toward social policies that eventually led to the beginnings of the Green Industrial Revolution. Energy independence, climate change, and environmental protection became serious political issues. Both these regions have been developing economic forms of what has become known as social or collective capitalism, an economic view that includes sustainable growth, health and educational issues, environmental concerns, and climate change mitigation, along with interest in diverse populations, gender equality, and democratic processes. The essence of civic capitalism is that there are some social and political problems so complex and overriding that free markets and deregulation cannot address them.

Social and environmental factors—sustainable communities, climate change mitigation, and environmental protection—are growing in importance and will soon demand far greater international cooperation and agreement. Rampant economic growth and individual accumulation of wealth is being replaced by social and environmental values that benefit the larger community. For example, the EU is pushing for limits on the salaries of corporate executives.

Without a national policy and investment, countries and their corresponding cities cannot address basic infrastructures. Without government consensus, there can be no action, no improvement, no resources, and certainly no response to environmental degradation. Energy and infrastructure are extraordinarily important national issues, just as important as defense or entitlement programs. To address these basic systems for the greater good, a nation needs to have plans, which are outlined and offered by the central government.

The Peoples Republic of China, not the US, is showing real global leadership in responding to climate change. More than anything, China demonstrates how important a role the government plays in overseeing, directing, and supporting the economics of technologies and creation of employment. China's economic system is the prototype of civic capitalism. Since the 1949 revolution, the Chinese have moved away from communism toward economic development through a series of Five-Year Plans, now being referred to as guidelines.

Europeans adjusted their economies to fit the requirements of the Green Industrial Revolution early on. Both the Scandinavians and the Germans realized that the move away from fossil fuels to renewable energy distribution would require more than neoclassical free-market economics could deliver. While the Danes and the other Scandinavians shifted national energy resources toward renewable energy power by national consensus, the Germans developed the innovative FiT process.

Germany's FiT was part of their 2000 Energy Renewable Sources Act, formally called the Act of Granting Priority to Renewable Energy Sources. This remarkable policy was designed to encourage the adoption of renewable energy sources and to help accelerate the move toward grid parity, making renewable energy for the same price as existing power from the grid (Morris, 2014).

Creating an economy that can move the world into the Green Industrial Revolution is an exceptionally complex process. Various governments and states are approaching the problem differently. The European FiT program and China's direct government subsidies have been the most successful. Some US states, such as California with its newly designed Renewable Auction Mechanism (RAM), have developed possible improvements over the European FiT. But the RAM is much more limited and available only in California.

The Green Industrial Revolution is about climate change mitigation, renewable energy, smart grids, health, education, and environmental sensitivity. But achieving the benefits—a wave of new technologies, business enterprises, and green jobs—will require substantial public support.

Global cities have a key role to play in moving the world faster into the Green Industrial Revolution, since renewable energy can be generated independently of large centralized utilities. Distributive renewable energy connected to smart grids can monitor power and increase efficiencies. The process is particularly well suited to cities and communities of all sizes and types.

Humanity's lust for fossil fuels may be our ruin. In the June 6, 2012 issue of *Nature*, Anthony Barnosky of the University of California, Berkeley, along with 21 co-authors, publically worried about the same thing. The planet may be on the verge of a "tipping point" they cautioned, which is a point of environmental decline that cannot be reversed (Climate Change, 2013).

The authors called for accelerated cooperation to reduce population growth and per capita resource use. Fossil fuels need to be replaced with sustainable sources. We need to develop more efficient food production and distribution systems, and more protection for land and ocean is needed. Barnosky writes, "Humans may be forcing an irreversible, planetary-scale tipping point that could severely impact fisheries, agriculture, clean water and much of what Earth needs to sustain its inhabitants."

These scientists are among those urging the world to join the Green Industrial Revolution before it's too late.

References

Adams, Lucas and Ken Funaki, 2009. Chapter 15 "Japanese Experience with Efforts at the Community Level towards a Sustainable Economy," Woodrow

W. Clark II, Editor and Author. *Sustainable Communities*. Springer Press, New York.

Asian Age, 2010. India Car Sales Jump 21 Percent. December 8, www.asianage.com/business/india-car-sales-jump-21-cent-504.

Bloomberg, 2014. Why Elon Musk's Batteries Scare the Hell Out of the Electric Company. December 5, http://www.bloomberg.com/news/print/2014–12–05/musk-battery-works-fill-utilities-with-fear-and-promise.html.

Borden, Eric and Joel Stonington, Chapter 15, "Germany's Energiewende," *Global Sustainable Communities Design Handbook: Green Design, Engineering, Health, Technologies, Education, Economics, Contracts, Policy, Law and Entrepreneurship*. Elsevier Press, New York.

BP report, 2011. China the Fuel for Growth, Issue 1, www.bp.com/sectiongenericarticle.do?categoryId=9037009&contentId=7068199.

China Oil Demand, 2013. http://news.yahoo.com/platts-report-chinas-oil-demand-1500502.

Clark, Woodrow W. II, 2000. Developing and Diffusing Clean Technologies: Experience and Practical Issues, OECD Conference, Seoul, Korea.

Clark, Woodrow W. II, 2007. "The Green Hydrogen Paradigm Shift," *Co-Generation and Distributed Generation Journal*, vol.22, n.2. pp. 6–38.

Clark, Woodrow W. II, 2008. "The Green Hydrogen Paradigm Shift: Energy Generation for Stations to Vehicles," *Utility Policy Journal*.

Clark, Woodrow W. II and Istemi Demirag, 2005. "Regulatory Economic Considerations of Corporate Governance," *International Journal of Banking, Special Issue on Corporate Governance*.

Clark, Woodrow W. II, Emilio Paulocci and John Cooper, 2002. "Commercial Development of Energy – Environmentally Sound Technologies for the Auto-industry: The Case of Fuel Cells," *Journal of Cleaner Production*, Special Issue.

Clark, Woodrow W. II and Jeremy Rifkin, et al., 2005. "Hydrogen Energy Stations: Along the Roadside to a Hydrogen Economy," *Utilities Policy*, January, n.13, pp. 41–50.

Clark, Woodrow W. II and Jeremy Rifkin et al., 2006. "A Green Hydrogen Economy," Special Issue on Hydrogen, *Energy Policy*, vol.34, n.34, pp. 2630–2639.

Climate Change, 2013. University of Oslo, http://davis.patch.com/articles/are-humans-bringing-earth-to-an-irreversible-tipping-point.

Climate Group, 2008. China's Clean Revolution. August, www.guardian.co.uk/environment/2008/aug/01/renewableenergy.climatechang.

Cooper, John F. and Woodrow W. Clark, II., 1996. "Zinc/Air Fuel Cell: An Alternative to Clean Fuels in Fleet Electric Vehicle Applications," *International Journal of Environmentally Conscious Design & Manufacturing*, vol. 5, n.3–4, pp. 49–54.

Febvre, Lucien and Henri-Jean Martin, 1976. *The Coming of the Book: The Impact of Printing 1450–1800*. New Left Books, London.

Fortune, 2012. April 30, p. 96.

Georgano, G.N., 1990. *Cars: Early and Vintage, 1886–1930.* Grange-Universal, London. p. 39.

Geothermal Energy Association (GEA), 2014. http://www.geo-energy.org/data/2014.

Gipe, Paul, 2014. Feed-in-Tariff Monthly Reports 2014, http://www.wind-works.org/FeedLaws/RenewableTariffs.qpw.

Hong, Lixuan, 2013. Developing an Analytical Approach Model for Offshore Wind in China, PhD Thesis.

Hubbert, Marion King, 1956. Nuclear Energy and the Fossil Fuels 'Drilling and Production Practice' (PDF). Spring meeting of the Southern District, Division of Production. American Petroleum Institute. San Antonio, Texas (Shell Development Company, June), pp. 22–27.

Jafry, Naved and Garson Silvers, 2014. Chapter 25 "Micro Cities: The Case of India," Woodrow W. Clark II, Author and Editor, *Global Sustainable Communities Design Handbook: Green Design, Engineering, Health, Technologies,*

Education, Economics, Contracts, Policy, Law and Entrepreneurship. Elsevier Press, New York.

Luft, Gal and Anne Korin, 2012. The American Interest, The Folly of Energy Independence, July-August, p. 33.

Lund, Henrik and Poul Alberg Østergaard, 2010. Chapter 14 "Climate Change Mitigation from a Bottom up Community Approach: A Case in Denmark," Woodrow W. Clark II, Author and Editor, *Sustainable Communities Design Handbook.* Elsevier Press, New York.

Morris, Craig, 2014. Chapter 7 "Energiewende—Germany's Community-driven since the 1970s," Woodrow W. Clark II, Author and Editor, *Global Sustainable Communities Design Handbook: Green Design, Engineering, Health, Technologies, Education, Economics, Contracts, Policy, Law and Entrepreneurship.* Elsevier Press, New York.

Ocean Power Technologies (OPT), 2014. info@oceanpowertech.com.

Pelamis Wave Power, 2014. http://www.pelamiswave.com.

Rifkin, Jeremy, 2004. *European Dream.* Penguin Putnam, New York.

Run of River, 2014. http://www.runofriverpower.com/.

Slater, Joanna, 2015. Germany Recharged: EU Powerhouse Goes All in on Alternative Energy. *Globe and Mail,* April 10, http://www.theglobeandmail.com/report-on-business/germany-recharged-eu-powerhouse-goes-all-in-on-alternative-energy/article23886255/.

The Economist, 2012. Special Report—The Melting North. June 16, p. 3.

Tribe Koda Energy, 2014. http://www.shakopeedakota.org/enviro/koda.html.

USEIA International Energy Outlook, 2011. 20554.135.7/forecasts/ieo/.

Verdant, 2012. http://verdantpower.com/what-initiative/.

World Wind Energy Association (WWEA), 2011.

Chapter 4
Smart and Green are Sustainable

Twenty-first century cities face unprecedented challenges. The ravages of climate change and global warming threaten—drought in some cases, flooding and rising ocean levels in others. Wealth inequality destabilizes the social fabric, leading to crime and homelessness. The data on health costs and rebuilding communities is overwhelming. And how is there a value put on the loss of life?

Growing numbers of migrants strain resources and pit traditional cultural values against new ones. Middle Eastern Jihadist violence and radical Islam have spilled over into the developed world, creating fear, political and social vengeance. Basic infrastructure issues like public transportation and water conservation are left unattended by governments with dreadful results. For example, California's infamous San Bruno natural gas pipeline explosion (eight people killed along with extensive land and economic damage) was caused by public utility neglect with the lack of regulator oversight.

For the first time in human history, a majority of the planet's population lives in cities. Which will make environmental crises that are linked to climate change that much more severe. Megacities like New York that are along the world's coasts will be impacted the most. Greening cities is essential to the mitigation of climate change, since buildings, cars, and other city elements are major sources of GHGs. Replacing fossil fuel energy generation with its corresponding GHG emissions for carbonless renewable energy is critical. Cities need to be healthier and pollution free and new approaches to development and construction must be incorporated into how we work, live, and play. Instead of being centers for wealth inequality that bred alienation, resentment, and strife, our cities most be turned into centers that promote human interaction, healthy exchanges of ideas, and participation in a shared culture.

In short, people need to develop and implement green cities, so that they are capable of slowing climate change and facing the other looming challenges of the twenty-first century. At the same time, cities need to be smart as they are urban centers that encourage sustainable economic development which promote a high quality of life. Unfortunately, too many governments are not able to lead this transition, which is why leadership by city governments is required. In other instances, cities have had to act long before international laws and treaties were passed. For example, Tokyo, Beijing, and Los Angeles, along with other cities, had to act on air quality issues long before national or state governments got involved. California, now under the Governor's leadership and due also to the state's continuing drought (in its fifth year) has committed and with new legislation just signed into law (September 2015) a goal to have 50 percent of its energy come from renewable sources by 2030. Some nations (Nordic countries, Germany, and The Netherlands) have also enacted similar plans and actions along with the financing to meet their goals.

Sustainable Cities are the Answer

These issues are far too important for the cities to leave only to national governments. For the survival of much of the world's population and its economic well-being, global cities must become smart, green, and sustainable. Cities must become more walkable, bike friendly, and livable (Clark, 2014). They need to focus on environmental as well as economic sustainability. The quality of urban space must improve. The architecture should be inventive with sensitive urban design and a dynamic atmosphere. Sustainable living and sustainable business development must be promoted, along with infrastructure needs of water, recycling, transportation, waste, and materials. Above all else, a green sustainable city needs to generate renewable energy and use energy storage with a smart integrated grid system to balance and share energy (Clark and Bradshaw, 2004; Clark, 2009; Clark, 2010.)

Sustainable communities started in Europe and Japan as a reaction to the Arab oil embargo of the mid-1970s (Clark and Cooke, 2011). These communities gained a toehold in Germany, then Sweden, Denmark, Norway, and The Netherlands. These countries had historically used wind power as a source of renewable energy, and so they quickly embraced sustainability. Already experts with transmission and grid connections, they created on-site energy systems for farmers, communities, and towns.

Norway, for example, was one of the largest oil-producing nations in the world with its offshore drilling, but realized that there was a limit to oil, so planned in the 1990s to convert its economy into other areas, including the creation of hydrogen from renewable energy sources. In many ways, in the US, the state of Alaska is doing the same thing as it sees the need to get out of the oil and gas business due to the negative environmental impacts.

Other European nations followed. Germany led the way in solving the problem of paying for these renewable energy systems with its feed-in-tariff (FiT), which made it the world's largest manufacturers and installers of solar panels in 2006–2009. Scotland and Britain have major wind farms and biomass generation plants. Pushed by the EU, Spain, Italy, and the other European countries have adopted policies, governmental programs, and economic plans to move sustainable communities and the Green Industrial Revolution forward, reaping environmental and economic benefits along the way.

With a long tradition of conservation and sustainability, Japan led the movement in Asia (Funaki and Adams, 2009). After their modernization blitz during the first half of the 20th century ended with defeat in the Second World War, the Japanese regained their historic sense of sustainability. Of course, much of this was also triggered by a glaring lack of natural energy resources. Unfortunately, and despite being the target for US atomic bombs in the Second World War, the Japanese started building nuclear power plants a few decades later. In the 1970s, many nuclear plants were built to provide power to the growing Japanese economy. The tragic result was Fukishima, which is a warning to all nations about nuclear power generation.

Today, the rest of Asia with Japan and South Korea's leadership has embraced sustainability. Granted, the region has horrendous pollution and environmental issues to overcome, but it is rapidly developing renewable energy technologies. China now leads the world in solar and wind technology production. It also has a Five-Year Plan that focuses on sustainability. The plan is intended to reduce China's GHGs emissions and carbon pollution from fossil fuels.

The common theme in all these nations, and a theme that is lacking in America, is the notion that sustainability starts at home, in the behaviors and values of families. Communities are usually described as a group of interacting people living in a common location. Psychologists describe a community as one that includes a sense of membership, influence, integration, and fulfillment of needs, as well as shared emotional connections. Generally, communities are organized around common values or beliefs. They share resources, organize around a political structure, agree on preferences, needs, and risks, and agree to tax themselves for the benefit of the whole.

A smart green city has these elements, plus the core values of conservation, a respect for natural resources, and an appreciation for the environment. The concept of "achieving more with less" is broadly endorsed. Sustainability is a community, or city-centric activity: the more focused and integrated the community, the more it has a chance of achieving sustainable development through environmental policies that reduce, recycle, and reuse. For power, add energy that comes from renewable resources. The pay off from sustainable development is a cleaner environment and a healthier lifestyle.

Besides these core values, sustainable communities as smart green cities combine common social activities with education, business development and job creation. This concept was first defined as *sustainable development* more than a quarter of a century ago. The Brundtland Commission in its "Our Common Future Report" addressed emerging concern about "the accelerating deterioration of the human environment and natural resources and the consequences of that deterioration for economic and social development" (Brundtland Commission, 1987).

Even in the 1980s, the UN General Assembly recognized that environmental problems were global in nature. Subsequently, it was in the common interest of all nations to establish policies for sustainable development. The Brundtland Commission defined sustainable development as meeting the "needs of the present without compromising the ability of future generations to meet their own needs" (Brundtland Commission, 1987). Today, the term describes how a community's economic concerns interact with its natural resources. Addressing large global problems locally, on a city level, can generate new creative ventures and opportunities, which then provide strong business reasons to pursue sustainable development.

Green smart cities must address the essential infrastructure elements of energy, transportation, water, waste, and telecommunications. The critical component is renewable energy power generation. Renewable energy provides power generation in harmony with the environment and economic development. Europe and Japan have developed numerous cities that are sustainable and secure through the use of their own renewable energy sources, augmented by storage devices and emerging technologies. Consider some national cases that have worked:

Denmark

As a nation, Denmark is very close to being a classic sustainable community role-model. With gasoline today (2015) costing $10 a gallon, Danes prefer to take public transportation. In the mid-1990s, Denmark established a CO_2 tax to promote energy efficiency, despite discovering offshore oil. However, instead of risking environmental issues with offshore drilling, the Danes installed offshore wind farms. Since 1981, Denmark's economy has grown 70 percent and energy consumption is almost flat (Lund and Clark, 2002).

Denmark's early focus on solar and wind power has paid off, as those sources now provide more than 16 percent of its energy. One-third of the world's terrestrial wind turbines now come from Denmark, and Danish companies Danisco and Novozumes are two of the world's most innovative manufacturers of enzymes for the conversion of biomass to fuel (Lund and Østergaard, 2010).

As an additional benefit, these industries have provided green jobs. In the 1970s, people from the northern and western regions (Northern Jutland) were flooding Denmark's capital city of Copenhagen, an island in the nation's east. The government took political policy action along with funding to reverse that massive movement to one city by establishing universities, businesses and economic development in Northern Jutland in the west. People moved back which attracted more people coming from other nations and cities to live in areas that were once being abandoned. The move into the Northern Jutland has paid off tremendously, attracting companies that are large, profitable, and sustainable (Clark and Jensen, 2002).

On a local level, a sustainable community must have three components (Lund and Østergaard, 2010):

- First, it must have a government-accepted strategic master plan for infrastructure that includes renewable energy, transportation, water, waste, and telecommunications and the technologies to implement and integrate these systems.

- Second, facility planning and financing must be addressed from a green perspective. The planning must include standards that can be measured and evaluated. There is an array of issues pertaining to the design, architecture, and siting of buildings that affect sustainability. The community needs to consider efficient conservation and generation of resources that apply to multiple-use design. For example, communities should be dense and walkable and integrate transportation choices powered by renewable sources, which reduce energy consumption as well as eliminate greenhouse gases, carbon emissions, and pollution.

• Third, a sustainable community is a vibrant, "experiential" applied model that should innovate, catalyze, and stimulate entrepreneurial activities, education, and creative learning, along with research, jobs, and new businesses.

As the sustainable movement has developed, cities have sought policies that direct facilities and infrastructures to be smart and green. Originally, there were several certification processes; however, Energy Star and the US Green Building Council's Leadership in Energy and Environmental Design (LEED) certifications are now becoming universal. There are regional LEED certification councils in most parts of Europe and Asia, and in some cases the standards are higher than the US (Clark and Eisenberg, 2008). Additionally, the Nordic countries and others in Europe have legal requirements, supported by government incentives and funding.

LEED certification is a standard for measuring a building's sustainability. It promotes best-in-class building strategies and practices, and pushes architects and builders toward designing green and environmentally sound buildings. LEED-certified buildings save money and resources and have a positive impact on the health of occupants, while promoting renewable, clean energy.

LEED certification includes a rigorous third-party commissioning, and offers proof that a building has achieved its environmental goals and is performing as designed. The certification process is a rating system that corresponds to five green design categories: sustainable sites, water efficiency, energy and atmosphere, materials and resources, and indoor environmental quality. Points are accrued in each category and result in four certification levels, Certified, Silver, Gold, and Platinum. LEED standards cover new commercial construction and major renovation projects, interiors projects and existing building operations. Standards are under development to cover commercial "core and shell" construction, new home construction, and neighborhood developments.

The US Green Building Council's website offers numerous tips for LEED certification as well as case studies of projects done throughout the world. Interestingly, the world's luxury hotel industry has started to compete against each other based on LEED certification levels and to market green and sustainable facilities. Even Jumeirah, the owners of the some of the world's most luxurious hotels promote the LEED certifications of their facilities (USGB, 2015).

On the other hand, Energy Star, or ENERGY STAR, is focused on the appliances and products that are used within a building. Established in 1992, ENERGY STAR is a labeling program that was started by the US Environmental Protection Agency (EPA). The program identifies and promotes energy-efficient products and buildings. The program clearly tells consumers which household products are energy efficient. Over the years, ENERGY STAR has become the standard for most US consumer products like televisions, refrigerators, and washing machines.

The ENERGY STAR program has boosted the adoption of energy-efficient products, practices, and services through valuable partnerships, objective measurement tools, and consumer education. The program has helped consumers and businesses save energy while at the same time it has reduced GHGs. It is important since energy use in homes, buildings, and industry account for two thirds of greenhouse gas emissions in the United States (ENERGY STAR).

The design and construction of buildings needs to shift toward on-site power through renewable energy production. Small, relatively self-contained communities within larger cities are more easily made sustainable. It is simpler on a local level to reduce the dependency on central grid energy.

Local on-site power is more efficient and can use the region's renewable energy resources. For example, Denmark's many sustainable communities are generating energy with wind and biomass to provide base load power (Lund and Clark, 2008). Denmark has a goal of 50 percent renewable energy generation by 2020. (Lund and Ostergaard, 2010). The country is well on its way to meeting and perhaps exceeding that national goal.

Europe's combined power and heat systems (CPH) were developed to meet local needs, reduce the use of fossil fuels, and help communities become energy independent and more self-sufficient. Some US communities are now developing similar systems focused on renewable energy and using cogeneration or CHP systems (Andersen and Lund, 2007).

Agile Systems

The traditional energy model generated power from a central plant dependent on fossil fuels, hydroelectric, or nuclear energy. Historically, governments wanted to centralize power for the public good with control, oversight, and regulatory measures. The power was transmitted or piped great distances over a rigid, one-way grid to the user. The old central grids required long transmission lines, pipelines, or ships to deliver the raw fossil fuel for processing. Then it needed to be transmitted and distributed to the end user. The standard approach was for municipalities to manage the capital costs for the central plant with its processing of raw materials, but for ratepayers to absorb the transmission costs.

As we transition to the Green Industrial Revolution, a hybrid or integrated model has developed. This new model is agile—that is flexible—because it can accommodate both green on-site power generation and grid-connected power (Clark and Bradshaw, 2004). Agile systems combine electricity from on-site renewable energy with electricity from traditional central grids hundreds of miles away, and manage them both to meet demand.

The agile system is efficient, smart, and rooted in renewable energy power generation. Although there is usually a central grid that depends heavily on fossil fuels to generate power, agile systems allow and even encourage on-site renewable energy sources, then disperse the electricity accordingly. These distributed energy systems can be formed and operated on the local level to serve targeted communities and consumers (Clark and Bradshaw, 2004).

Regional and city-level solutions are needed to address the challenges of global warming and climate change. Rather than having centralized power plants that use fossil fuels or nuclear power to generate energy and then transmit it over power lines, local on-site generation of power from renewable sources is better for the environment, far less expensive, and much healthier for the planet.

Energy needs are growing more complex as population increases, cities expand, and power demands climb. Air and water pollution are causing serious and costly health problems for young and old. Regulators are now implementing CO_2 regulations to stop pollution.

Meeting the challenges of supplying energy for increasing demand, while reducing carbon emissions, calls for more complex and creative solutions based on local and national plans that have funding to implement them. The change starts with requirements to increase energy efficiency, use renewable energy generation, and create infrastructures for water, waste, and transportation that are integrated. Together these changes will help the way people live, think, and plan for all kinds of activities from using electricity to getting to work everyday.

Despite its car-centric lifestyle, California is trying to be on the forefront of this transition. Much of the effort is being led by smaller cities like Santa Monica, Berkeley, Beverly Hills, and San Diego, which are using on-site energy from renewable sources (McEneaney, 2009). They are sustainable models for other cities that want to generate their own power from renewable sources. California has considerable amounts of geothermal power as well as ocean and wave power along with significant numbers of wind farms and solar installations. Hydrogen can be produced from renewable or green sources and then stored close to the needs and demands of communities.

Energy systems are evolving and agile energy systems have now emerged. In the future, the central grid will be used for redundancy and back-up purposes or act as a battery for energy storage when the sun is not shining and the wind is not blowing. These agile systems combine renewable energy, sensors, and wireless Internet connections and similar technologies that direct market mechanisms. This type of system is a new economic model that is part of making cities green and smart.

Sustainability Starts at Home

Researchers and political decision makers around the world are slowly recognizing that they need to do something about climate change and global warming. Sustainability is achievable. It can be done, and must be done, at the local level. Block by block, cities can change how they function.

Mobility is an essential characteristic to the modern lifestyle and it, along with animal protein, are the most sought after requirements of people emerging from poverty. This behavior and the desire to experience the American dream by owning an auto will not change easily. Ward's Auto reported that, in 2010, the global number of cars exceeded 1.015 billion, jumping from 980 million the year before, despite the global recession in October 2008. That means new environmental pressures on the climate in terms of fuel as well as carbon, greenhouse gases, and emissions. The results are seen in the rise of health problems around the world with some cities limiting single driver days along with alternative methods of transportation.

Therefore, it is critical to reduce, eliminate, and replace fossil fuel use for transportation and buildings. Pressured to increase gas mileage and reduce carbon emissions, the vehicle industry is making changes. Automakers are upgrading gasoline engines, using more efficient turbochargers with computer-assisted transmissions. Ford is substituting aluminum for steel to shave 500 pounds off their F-150 trucks creating profound gas mileage savings.

Diesel and natural gas are both fossil fuels with substantial emissions. They may be cleaner but they are not green and the costs are dramatically high for the environment and human health. As was revealed in the VW scandal, the company rigged software to give inaccurate and false emission information. More and more research shows that the emissions and pollution from fossil fuels is particularly harmful to the older adults and young children, costing uncountable amounts of money.

Research with this focus is being done by health agencies in California as well as the American Lung Association. Reports and standards are showing how cities rank throughout California and the nation on lung disease, with a new focus on emissions and greenhouse gases. To support these fossil fuels with tax breaks and changes in environmental rules will only postpone the eventual use of clean energy for vehicular transportation.

Some cities are considering banning autos all together. Hamburg, Germany's second-largest city, has laid out an initial concept that would eliminate cars by 2034. Named Grünes Netz, or "Green Network," it would expand public transportation and add more routes for pedestrians and bicyclists. It will be constructed over the next 15–20 years, and create car-free paths between all major parks, playgrounds, community gardens, and cemeteries in Hamburg. The resulting network will cover 40 percent of Germany's second-largest city, and it should enable commuters and tourists alike to navigate the once-car-dependent city entirely by bicycle and on foot.

Hamburg is an environmental pioneer in the mold of its regional neighbor Copenhagen. The city has multiple goals for its Green Network. The city acknowledges the need to change in the face of global warming; in the past 60 years Hamburg's median temperature has increased by 1.2 degrees Celsius to 9 degrees Celsius. Sea levels are rising and impacting the city's port. The level has risen by 20 centimeters, and they are expected to increase another

30 centimeters by 2100. As a large city, Hamburg is truly at risk and needs its Green Network to help limit the effects of floods.

Additionally, such a network will contribute to the overall health of the city and its inhabitants, helping residents move in a sustainable fashion. City spokesperson Angelika Fritsch said that the network, "will offer people opportunities to hike, swim, do water sports, enjoy picnics and restaurants, experience calm and watch nature and wildlife right in the city. That reduces the need to take the car for weekend outings outside the city."

Hamburg's Green Network is part of a growing trend, particularly within Europe, to create comprehensive cycle networks that encompass not only city centers and ring-roads, but that also connect the city with the suburbs. Copenhagen has undertaken perhaps the most ambitious of these plans with the construction of 26 bicycle "superhighways," that extend out from the city center as part of the city's goal to become carbon neutral by 2050 (Inhabitat, 2015).

Hamburg's Green Network is in the early stages. Ever since Fukushima, the focus in Germany has been on moving away from nuclear power, not on climate change adaptation. However, some 30 city staff members are developing the Green Network, aided by personnel in the city's seven districts. When politicians make the green web a priority, it will be an extensive network covering some 7,000 hectares (The Guardian, 2013).

London and Florence have adopted "green rings" that discourage autos and encourage pedestrians. Paris and other cities faced with congestion are examining similar bans and restrictions. Even New York City has made parts of Manhattan, including blocks near the theater district, into pedestrian zones. The idea of banning or reducing automobiles in city centers has become a hot topic among urban planners struggling to deal with issues like congestion and smog.

Banning autos or using hydrogen or electric cars is not enough to achieve sustainability. More is needed and, throughout the world, communities are developing plans for smart, sustainable futures. The use of fossil fuel energy sources is losing political and community support as advanced carbonless technologies are developed. For example, Britain, a country that for years maintained its prosperous lifestyle as a financial go-between for the Middle Eastern oil trade, recently hit a milestone of 1 GW of installed offshore wind turbine capacity with the completion of the Gunfleet Sands and Robin Rigg wind farms. Future plans call for the development of 25 GW from offshore wind farms, with more than 7,000 wind turbines. Scotland, the Nordic countries, and Germany have been taking similar actions in political and economic decisions based on their national plans, technologies, and business leadership.

In South America, Brazil is 95 percent energy independent through a combination of sugar cane ethanol and domestic oil supplies. To the west, Chile is developing renewable energy as a power source, after numerous public demonstrations against additional hydroelectric dams. Chile is one of the world's most beautiful countries, with wild, pristine regions interlaced with extraordinary free-flowing rivers. The Chilean public is adamant about keeping the rivers free from additional dams, and the government is responding by opening the door to renewable energy. In Mejillones in the Atacama Desert region of northern Chile, Algae Fuels S.A. consortium is using microalgae in second-generation biodiesel production. Wind and solar energy development is also headed to the region.

In other parts of the globe, China and Spain are developing sustainability through public policies that support renewable energy power generation, such as FiTs, which fix rates to provide rebates to consumers. Communities in Japan have been sustainable for many years, since Japan must either import all of its energy or generate it within the island nation. Increasingly, Japan is using renewable energy, and until 2008, it was the world leader in solar manufacturing companies. Italy has been active regionally, for different reasons, but primarily due to the national historical regionalization and its city-focused policies and programs. In the Baltic Sea region that was part of the Soviet Union, Lithuania has been active and begun a national focus on sustainability.

Creating Sustainable Communities

Creating sustainable communities is an extraordinarily complex task. It begins with addressing key infrastructure elements—energy, transportation, water, waste, and telecommunications—and extends through incorporating the belief systems, values, and behaviors of residents. Codes and standards are required to guide how buildings are designed, sited, and constructed. Certification programs like LEED provide guidelines, expertise, and political influence on how to construct and retrofit environmentally sensitive facilities that allow for the maximum use with fewer resources. Public policies establishing goals are needed to reduce GHG emissions and set thresholds and benchmarks for renewable energy power generation.

Emerging technologies are providing additional tools for achieving smart green sustainable cities. This is not only apparent in the development of new renewable energy technologies, but also in the discovery of innovative ways to conserve valuable resources, particularly water. There are devices just coming to market that will help minimize the water used in large Heating Ventilation and Air Conditioning (HVAC) systems. These retrofit systems are gaining credibility in water-constrained locations.

These systems conserve the amount of water required to run the equipment, as well as greatly reducing the outflows. A city like San Francisco not only has high water costs, but the sewer costs are equally high. One recently installed device on a large San Francisco hotel is projected to save $50,000 a year in sewer costs alone. This saving, combined with the reduction in the original water use, means that the cost of the device is recovered in just a few months. Ozone laundry conversions for commercial laundry systems provide similar benefits and a comparable short-term payback.

Three Smart Green Cities

Here are three examples of cities that are moving toward sustainability and the benefits it brings.

SINGAPORE

In far southeast Asia, Singapore is considered one of the world's greenest cities. A sovereign city–state that is officially known as the Republic of Singapore, it is an island country that lies off the southern tip of the Malay Peninsula and is 137 km (85 miles) north of the equator. The country is highly urbanized; however, the city is continually adding trees and parks, and now calls itself the Garden City.

The vision as a Garden City was put forward by former Prime Minister Lee Kuan Yew in 1968, just after the republic's independence. The idea is to integrate the environment with urban development and soften the effects of a concrete jungle. This garden project has the aim of creating a continuous ring of greenery, with the three different gardens wrapping around the Marina Bay area. Called Gardens by the Bay, the project stretches over 54 hectares, approximately the size of 72 soccer fields. It includes enormous trees that provide shade, shelter, and a steady source of rainwater as well as a cluster of green conservatories.

Singapore literally does not waste a single drop of water if it can be helped. Using modern desalination technologies, the island recycles and conserves almost all rainfall and water reserves including non-potable wastewater. The result is NeWater, a high-purity H_2O that can be used for industrial development and even drinking.

To support the growing number of electric autos and other motor vehicles, Singapore has created Greenlots. This is an island-wide network of power stations for electric vehicles to plug in and recharge which runs off the national power grid. Many of these Greenlots are solar-powered, drawing their power from the sun.

Besides passenger vehicles, taxis, and buses are energy-efficient hybrids, and Singapore-based ST Kinetics has launched the world's first commercially ready Hybrid Hydraulic Drive (HHD) enhanced port prime mover (PPM) which captures and reuses the energy normally lost from braking, using a hybrid system that can be easily adapted to other commercial machines such as tractors, heavy trucks, and excavators.

In 2012, the Singapore Green Plan was introduced. It is a government blueprint for environment sustainability that was put together by the Ministry of the Environment and Water Resources. The plan looks at six main areas: Clean Air and Climate Change, Water, Waste Management, Public Health, Conserving Nature, and International Environmental Relations. Almost all the green efforts for Singapore are guided by this master plan, including the Sustainable Development blueprint and the Green Transport Week.

Remarkably, Singaporeans are subsidized to do the right thing. Mitsubishi is discounting up to 50 i-MiEV electric cars for use in the $20 million three-year study to test the infrastructure needed to keep them running. The Japanese carmaker will sell the cars for about half their market cost to those participating in the study. Additionally, the National Park Board will give a 20 percent discount for venues at the HortPark in Alexandra Road. Couples who want the discount have to show that they have taken at least eight environmentally friendly measures for their wedding. These include using recycled paper for their wedding stationary, holding the ceremony at non air-conditioned venues, and using a hybrid car for their bridal car.

The Clean and Green Singapore campaign started two decades ago and it is now the longest in the island's history. Formerly known as "Clean and Green Week" for about 17 years, it went full steam into a year-long campaign and morphed into simply Clean and Green Singapore in 2007, with regular events, activities and community projects all over the country all the time.

A community-based platform, Green Singapore 2050 (GS2050) is for youngsters to express their concerns about environmental issues, and think of solutions to them. Why 2050? It's because these youths will be the ones to inherit and run the country in 2050, and hopefully solve the world's problems. GS2050 runs environmental surveys, forums for discussions and projects aimed at solving real issues.

The Duke–NUS Graduate Medical School is a collaboration between North Carolina's Duke University, the US government and Singapore. Besides its mission to be the "biomedical hub of Asia," it is one of the great examples of green design and environmentally conscious construction while still architecturally beautiful. The use of sustainable design elements such as the eight-storey glass atrium that provides vertical circulation to the whole building and ceramic tiles, which contain titanium dioxide (a material which keeps maintenance down and withstands tropical mold) earned the building Green Mark certification. The massive Resorts World Sentosa also won an award from the Building and Construction Authority for integrating sustainable building concepts into the master design of its development.

Green Kampong is an eco-community started by supermodel and MTV VJ turned eco-activist Nadya Hutagalung and a group of like-minded Earth angels, including former magazine publisher Holman Chin, capital investor Desmond Koh, and Green Drinks Singapore founder Olivia Choong.

Singaporeans are genuinely aware of the need to be Earth-friendly and save its resources. A recent survey by the National Environment Agency showed an overwhelming number—87.2 percent—of Singaporeans who are willing to adopt a clean and green lifestyle. A Kelly Services study revealed that over 90 percent of people working in Singapore said they are more likely to work for an organization that is ethically and socially responsible, while nine out of 10 teens in another survey are concerned about protecting the environment, with 96 percent agreeing that it's their responsibility to take care of Mother Earth (CNN, 2009).

The citizens of Singapore could teach the US about becoming green. The US has not been quick to join this movement, but several American city governments, such as San Francisco and Santa Monica in California, are moving in the green direction. LEED-designed buildings are being promoted, as well as local renewable energy generation including solar, wind, and ocean power, along with electric vehicles and hydrogen-fueled cars. Interestingly, in California, the schools and college systems have been strong supporters of LEED-designed buildings, and many new university facilities are being built to at least LEED silver.

FREDERIKSHAVN, DENMARK

Denmark set a national goal to be sustainable and to use 100 percent renewable energy by 2025. CHP systems are a core approach in local energy systems. In 2006, Denmark chose Frederikshavn, a relatively small town on the northeast coast of the Jutland peninsula, to demonstrate how it was going to achieve this goal. The city government along with local industry and the Aalborg University were included in the project (Lund and Ostergaard, 2010).

Frederikshavn, or in English, Fredrick's Harbor, with about 25,000 residents, is a busy transport hub. As an international ferry terminal, over 3 million people move through its port each year. The city has become Denmark's model city for sustainability. Dubbed the Energy Town Project, the city intends to be 100 percent energy independent by using renewable energy systems like wind and biomass by the end of year 2015. Today in 2014, the city is over 45 percent of its goal.

Frederikshavn held community meetings on sustainability to educate residents. Plans were developed that could be publically reviewed, and websites created that allowed residents to keep tabs on which programs were being developed and how much progress was being made. To encourage participation, they conducted campaigns to create awareness and encourage sustainable practices by the residents.

To achieve its goal, the city identified key components, which are now being planned and implemented. A new highly efficient waste incineration CHP plant with a capacity of burning 185 GWh (gigwatts per hour) per year was built. The project includes a biogas CHP plant of 15 MW. The rest of the heat production will be supplied from a biomass boiler burning straw.

Expansion of district heating grid

The Frederikshavn project also includes an expansion of the existing district heating grid. This will replace about 70 percent of the heat demand in industry and individual houses. The rest will be supplied from biomass boilers and the individual house heating will be converted to a mixture of solar thermal and electric heat pumps.

Transportation

For transportation, Frederikshavn is using vehicles converted into the use of biogas in combustion engines (biofuel cars), electric cars, and plug-in hybrid cars. To implement electric vehicles or hybrids or combine the use of batteries with fuel cells based on either methanol or hydrogen, the city is establishing refueling stations. Furthermore, motorbikes and vans and buses will be converted into biogas, hydrogen, or methanol.

Biogas plant and methanol production

Frederikshavn includes a biogas plant using 34 million tons of manure per year for the production of biogas to produce methanol for transportation and to replace natural gas for electricity and heat production. The plant itself is being converted into methanol, which will provide heat for district heating.

There are concerns with methanol due to its waste and impact on the environment. Eventually, methanol will be fully or partly produced by electrolysis from renewable energy sources. Moreover, efforts are underway to convert cars to hydrogen. In that case some of the biogas will be replaced by wind power.

Geothermal and heat pumps

The city is located on top of potential geothermal resources, which may be included. The resources can supply hot water with a temperature of about 40 C. However the temperature can be increased to district heating level by the use of an absorption heat pump, which can be supplied with steam from the waste incineration CHP plant.

The plan calls for additional compression heat pumps to use the exhaust gases from the CHP plants. The boilers will be supplemented by other sources like wastewater.

Wind power

Finally, Frederikshavn includes wind turbines to cover the rest of the electricity supply, for about 40 MW.

Bristol, United Kingdom

Bristol in southwest England was chosen by the European Commission as 2015's European Green Capital. Each year, the Commission recognizes a city for its environmental achievements, future commitments, and its ability to inspire others. A city with a population of 441,300, Bristol beat Brussels in Belgium, Glasgow in Scotland, and Ljubljana in Slovenia for the title.

Bristol has made a long-term commitment to improving the environment and has been working to reduce the city's contribution to climate change since 2000. It has developed a series of strategies and action plans to achieve this, such as the Bristol Climate Protection and Sustainable Energy Strategy and the Local Transport Plan to 2026, and active participation with citizens in the Quality of Life Survey.

The city has consistently reduced carbon emissions since 2005, despite a growing economy. It has a goal of becoming a European hub for low-carbon industry with a target of 17,000 new jobs in creative, digital, and low-carbon sectors by 2030. The city had 4.7 percent growth in the green economy in 2012. As well as being an efficient city with a growing green economy, Bristol is the UK's greenest city, with very good air quality. It has doubled the number of cyclists in recent years and is committed to doubling this number again by 2020.

To win the Green Capital award, Bristol's application had to address 12 separate areas: The areas are listed below and include highlights. For a detailed description of each area, see the entire document at: http://ec.europa. eu/environment/europeangreencapital/winning-cities/2015-bristol/bristol-application/index.html.

- **Local contribution to global climate change**—the city developed the Bristol Climate Protection and Sustainable Energy Strategy that set a target to reduce emissions by 80 percent by 2050 from a 1990 baseline. Bristol was one of the first UK municipalities to adopt such a strategy. Between 2004–2012, some of the activities to implement this goal were:
  - a dedicated energy management unit and a robust system accredited to the Eco-Management and Audit Scheme;
  - improving 185 non-domestic buildings;
  - automatic meter reading of energy meters providing accurate, real time data to improve energy management;

- street-lighting modernization. A four-year retrofit program has so far replaced 10,500 lamps and fitted all illuminated bollards with LED lamps;
- Eco-schools program. Working with community organizations to improve energy performance and climate awareness in schools;
- a school solar PV and energy-efficiency program, with 32 schools and an installed capacity of 568 kWp;
- developing a 6 MW wind energy project on BCC owned land at the industrial port area; construction work has commenced and will be the first UK Council to own wind turbines;
- developing 15 biomass boilers, mainly feed by wood waste from parks and street trees.

- **Local transport**—reducing the transport system use of fossil fuels with compressed natural gas (CNG)-powered energy-efficient buses:
  - zero-emissions hydrogen waterbus;
  - reduced the impact of cars in residential areas;
  - UK demonstration cycling city and 22 million pounds were invested in infrastructure and cycling promotion.

- **Green urban areas including sustainable land use**—six new city center open spaces have been created.
  - network of multifunctional, interconnected green spaces;
  - adopted new core strategy land use plan to enhance and protect green areas.

- **Nature and biodiversity**—Bristol is at the forefront of wildlife management for people; a journey driven by national events and pivotal action by citizen.
  - adopted Biodiversity Action Plan;
  - improved the quality of wildlife spaces from a citizen perspective, to work with and support disadvantaged groups and to focus our community outreach program in a network of 16 local nature reserves, equally accessible across the city.

- Quality of local ambient air.

- Quality of local ambient air—Part 2.

- Quality of local ambient air—Part 3:
  - Bristol has one of the most comprehensive air quality monitoring networks in the UK and publishes its data online;

- reducing air pollution from transport through a Joint Local Transit Plan (JLTP).
- **Quality of the acoustic environment**—actively manages noise pollution and population exposure:
  - pioneered the mapping of transport noise in UK cities;
  - quiet areas have been created within the city.
- **Waste production and management**—leads the UK on waste reduction and management:
  - clear strategy and targets to achieve significant reductions in waste to landfill;
  - large-scale promotional campaigns for waste services.
- **Water Consumption**—water supply is managed sustainably and efficiently:
  - water consumption is lowest it has been in 20 years, although population has increased by 10 percent;
  - water network is monitored for flow and pressure and purity;
  - 10,000 water efficiency kits have been provided to domestic water users.
- **Waste Water Treatment**—100 percent of the population connected to sewerage:
  - all sewage treatment compliant with the Urban Waste Water Treatment Directive;
  - the city's Urban Waste Water Treatment Plant is 100 percent self-sufficient in its electricity needs—equivalent to the most efficient sites in Europe—with all power coming from renewable sources generated on-site.
- **Eco-innovation and sustainable employment**—Bristol and the surrounding municipalities, universities, businesses, and communities are working together to achieve environmental and social sustainability. There is a particular emphasis on:
  - innovation;
  - green jobs and businesses;
  - inward investment;
  - developing supply chains;
  - knowledge transfer and skills;
  - showcasing eco-innovation projects that widen community engagement and build awareness of the smart eco-city.
- **Environmental management of the municipality**—adopted a plan to improve its environmental performance. This plan was to:
  - adopt a corporate environmental policy;
  - set and achieve corporate environmental management targets;

- implement the EU Eco Management and Auditing System (EMAS) for every council department and accredit the whole organization;
- use the environmental management system to create and deliver an environmental program to achieve continual environmental improvement.
- **Energy performance**—Bristol is the most energy efficient of the eight major English cities outside London:
  - uses 20 percent less energy per person than the average;
  - reduced energy use by 15 percent per capita between 2005 and 2010, compared to an average 12 percent for the other major English cities and 10 percent for the UK as a whole.

Bristol has committed a budget of €500m for transport improvements by 2015 and up to €300m for energy efficiency and renewable energy by 2020 (this includes a confirmed €100m investment in renewable energy).

Bristol has great potential to act as a role model for the UK, Europe, and the world. An agreement negotiated by the city with the foreign office to promote the award across Europe and the world through the British Embassies has the potential to raise the profile of the Award. Bristol's tag line "Laboratory for Change" is based on innovation, learning, and leadership. Social media and the innovation lab, via live lab conferences, will be used to make Bristol available to Europe, and vice versa, while also reducing or entirely removing any carbon footprint.

Bristol is an innovator in terms of the green economy, with a powerful communication strategy and the commitment and enthusiasm required to develop its role as a model for Europe.

Developing sustainable communities requires a plan or a set of concepts that will lead to that goal. Frederikshavn set the ball rolling when the local government established a set of principles to guide the city toward sustainability. In 2009 the United Nations Intergovernmental Panel on Climate Change (UN IPPC) met in Copenhagen, Denmark and reviewed some of the Frederikshavn programs that were stated in 2008. The plan consisted of statements on how cities can become more sustainable. They are designed to be read by decision makers, and provide a starting point on the journey toward sustainability.

Singapore, Frederikshavn, and Bristol are examples of what has been done successfully. Other cities can follow their models. These three cities provide a conceptual framework for moving today's sprawling, ever-growing cities toward sustainability. Turning energy, waste, water, transportation, and telecommunications into sustainable processes is critical. Besides the plans, smart green cities must develop the financial resources to implement the processes. These infrastructure elements are integrated; transportation and energy are connected because transportation systems should use renewable energy. The same is true for water pumping and surface transportation, particularly in places like California that require enormous amounts of energy to move large quantities of water across miles of surface area.

One good example that provides a global perspective is the C-40 program of megacities first created by the Clinton Foundation at the beginning of the 21st century. The program is now part of former New York City Mayor Michael R. Bloomberg's programs, which is independent from the city government. C-40 works both locally and collaboratively with other cities around the world to reduce both greenhouse gases and mitigate climate risks. Over 4,700 actions have been taken around the world based on global criteria that cities need to meet to be considered sustainable. These actions range from planning, conservation, and efficiency for energy, mass transportation systems to food supplies, waste, and recycling.

Hurricane Sandy, which devastated New York City and the surrounding coastal areas, is solid evidence of the needs for communities to become sustainable. The rebuilding of the entire region is estimated at about $100 billion. While this rebuilding will most likely be done in a sustainable plan and program, it needs to be monitored and evaluated for greenhouse gas reductions and pollution elimination.

Each sustainable community must retrofit the traditional central power plant into one using renewable energy generation and smart grid distribution. Further, the sustainable infrastructure systems must provide for recycling, waste control, water, and land use, as well as green building standards that require energy-efficient and compact housing. Today, green sustainable cities and communities are necessary to reduce environmental pollution and to provide a healthier world for tomorrow. The solutions to global warming and climate change exist now; we need to design, finance, and implement them.

References

Andersen, Anders N. and Henrik Lund, 2007. "New CHP (Combined Heat and Power) Partnerships Offering Balancing of Fluctuating Renewable Electricity Productions," *Journal of Cleaner Production* vol.15, pp. 288–293.

Brundtland Commission (1983) Report, 1987. Our Common Future. UN Commission General Assembly 828 Resolution #38/161 for Process of Preparation of the Environmental Perspective to the Year 829 2000 and Beyond. Oxford University Press, Oxford.

Clark, Woodrow W. II. Editor and Author, 2009. *Sustainable Communities.* Springer Press, New York.

Clark, Woodrow W. II. Editor and Author, 2010. *Sustainable Communities Design Handbook.* Elsevier Press, New York.

Clark, Woodrow W. II. Editor and Author, 2014. *Global Sustainable Communities Design Handbook: Green Design, Engineering, Health, Technologies, Education, Economics, Contracts, Policy, Law and Entrepreneurship.* Elsevier Press, New York.

Clark, Woodrow W. II and Ted Bradshaw, 2004. *Agile Energy Systems: Global Solutions to the California Energy Crisis.* Elsevier Press, New York.

Clark Woodrow W. II and Larry Eisenberg, 2008. "Agile Sustainable Communities: On-site Renewable Energy Generation," *Utility Policies Journal,* vol.16, n.4, pp. 262–274.

Clark, Woodrow W. II and J. Dan Jensen, 2002. "Capitalization of Environmental Technologies in Companies: Economic Schemes in a Business Perspective," *International Journal of Energy Technology and Policy,* vol.1, n.1/2.

CNN, 2009. http://travel.cnn.com/singapore/none/12-reasons-why-singapore-greenest-city-914640.

ENERGY STAR, 2015. http://www.energystar.gov/about.

Funaki, Ken and Lucas Adams, 2009. Chapter 15 "Japanese Experience with Efforts at the Community Level towards a Sustainable Economy," Woodrow W. Clark II, Editor and Author, *Sustainable Communities,* Springer Press, New York, pp. 243–262.

Inhabit, 2015. http://inhabitat.com/hamburg-announces-plans-to-become-a-car-free-city-within-20-years/print/.

Lund, Henrik and Woodrow W. Clark II, 2002. "Management of Fluctuations in Wind Power and CHP: Comparing Two Possible Danish Strategies," *Energy Policy,* vol.27, n.5, pp. 471–483.

Lund, H. and Woodrow W. Clark II, 2008. "Sustainable Energy and Transportation Systems Introduction and Overview," *Utilities Policies Journal*, vol.16, n.2, pp. 59–62.

Lund, Henrik and Poul Alberg Østergaard, 2010. Chapter 14 "Climate Change Mitigation from a Bottom up Community Approach: A Case in Denmark," Woodrow W. Clark II, Editor and Author, *Sustainable Communities Design Handbook*. Elsevier Press, New York.

McEneaney, Brenden, 2009. "Santa Monica Sustainable City Plan: Sustainability in Action," Woodrow W. Clark II, Editor and Author. *Sustainable Communities*. Springer Press, New York, pp. 77–94.

The Guardian, 2013. http://www.theguardian.com/sustainable-business/hamburg-answer-to-climate-change.

US Green Building Council (USGBC), 2015. http://www.usgbc.org/leed.

Chapter 5
Technologies That Make a City Smart and Green

Creating smart green cities requires new solutions to old and new problems. Changing from a carbon-intensive, polluted urban environment to one that is sustainable, healthier, and with low toxic emissions is doable—and there are many cities around the world that are doing just that. Even the costs are being reduced and met on the local community level.

Human needs remain constant in urban environments, particularly in large, global cities. People need the basic infrastructure components such as energy, water, waste, telecommunications, and transportation, to work well. In a smart green city, the components are linked and integrated. That way, components overlap, reducing costs for construction, operations, and maintenance.

People need to understand how the new green world works, and now also the smart world today. Above all, they need to know how these two connect to one another and future systems. The connection starts at home as many in Europe and Asia are discovering because home is where a city's infrastructure components all come together. Understanding how the new smart green world works on a personal level, leads directly to the larger community in which people live and work. Europeans are beginning to connect sustainability with what they do on a personal level and how they work, go to market, or seek entertainment. When it comes to conservation and efficient use of energy, as well as renewable power generation, storage, and telecommunications, the issues are the same for the wider community as within a person's home or business.

A complete examination of a city's infrastructures is beyond the scope of this book. However, there are emerging smart green technologies that city planners and leaders need to be aware of, and to understand, that can help a city integrate both being smart and green.

The new smart and green technologies are extraordinary. Just as renewable energy is required to generate carbonless electricity, so are storage devices required to optimize that energy for base load and to minimize costs. Similarly, flexible grid systems that move electricity around easily and efficiently are needed to distribute renewable energy seamlessly for local on-site power which is distributed to the communities within a city.

Other green technologies like "smart" windows that maximize daylight and external heat, while minimizing the electricity needed to maintain interior comfort, are just now commercially available. Countries such as Denmark and Germany have national policies, requirements, and financing for smart windows. Other technologies, like the amazing underground waste vacuum system have been around for decades, but are just now being installed in ecocities and sustainable neighborhoods like London's Wembley development.

So much is changing and happening to green a city's transportation infrastructure that Chapter 6 describes how the world's city dwellers can move about efficiently and healthfully without being dependent on a fossil-fueled vehicle.

Storage Technologies

The biggest criticism of large-scale renewable energy is that it is intermittent, which means the power from the sun and wind are not always available. The sun is not always shining and the wind is not always blowing. Therefore power is intermittent and not as available for base load energy as fossil fuels. Extensive research has been done for decades for a cheap way to store renewable energy when it is plentiful, so that it can be used when it is not. There is huge potential in storage technologies and each has benefits.

Generally, energy storage separates into two broad categories: those that store electricity for a central or on-site power grid, and those that store electricity for transportation. The Table 5.1 from the US Congressional Research Service is based upon data from the National Renewable Energy Laboratory (NREL) and gives an overview of the uses for energy storage technologies (Parfomak, 2013).

Storage technology can make electric grids more efficient, inexpensive, and reliable. Furthermore, it can manage power flows and support the integration of renewable energy generation. In particular, renewable energy needs to be

Table 5.1   Energy storage applications and technologies

	Electric Grid (Stationary)	Transportation (Vehicular)
High Power/Rapid Discharge	Batteries • Lead-Acid • Nickel • Lithium-ion Capacitors Flywheels Superconducting Magnetic Energy Storage (SMES)	Batteries • Nickel Capacitors Flywheels
Energy Management	Batteries • Advanced Lead-Acid • Flow • High Temperature Hydrogen Compressed Air Pumped Hydro Thermal • Concentrating Solar Power • End Use	Batteries • Lithium-Ion • Lithium-Metal • Metal Air Hydrogen

Source: P. Denholm, National Renewable Energy Laboratory, 2011.

Note: Electric power and transportation applications may elsewhere be referred to as "stationary" and "vehicular," respectively.

integrated with storage devices and shared with a smart grid. Since green energy such as wind and solar is the key to reducing GHGs emissions and mitigating a city's impact on climate change, then storage technologies are critical.

Grid storage devices can provide electricity for several hours or more. These devices can shift energy during periods of low demand or high renewable supply, to periods of high demand or low renewable supply. Many can also provide the same services as high power or rapid discharge devices.

Currently, the main technology in this group is *pumped hydro storage* (PHS). Basically, this stores potential energy by pumping water from a lower elevation reservoir to a higher elevation one. The pumping is done during low-cost off-peak demand periods. Then during periods of high electrical demand, the stored water is released through turbines to produce electric power. While it does not save or increase energy, this system increases overall revenue by selling more electricity during periods of peak demand, or when prices are the highest. Some communities are getting their energy from wind power so that the entire system is at very little cost and based upon integrated green energy systems.

Flywheels are an old technology that have roots in the Neolithic spindle and the ancient Greek potter's wheel. The potter's wheel features a heavy round stone, connected to a pedal that is pumped by the potter. The flywheel stores the fluctuating pedal movements as inertia, and creates a smooth, steady, turn of the wheel. Through the wonders of mechanical engineering, this old technology is being refitted as a modern-day energy-storing device. Flywheel energy storage (FES) works by accelerating a rotor, or flywheel, to a very high speed and maintaining the energy in the system as rotational energy. When energy is extracted from the system, the flywheel's rotational speed is reduced; adding energy to the system correspondingly increases the speed of the flywheel (LLNL, 2014a).

Most FES systems use electricity to accelerate and decelerate the flywheel, but devices that use mechanical energy are in development. Advanced FES systems have rotors made of high-strength carbon filaments. The filaments are suspended by magnetic bearings and spin at high speeds in a vacuum.

Over the past two decades, scientists have studied flywheels extensively and created ways to use them as power storage devices in vehicles and power plants. Flywheels can be used to produce high-power pulses in situations where drawing the power from the public network would produce unacceptable spikes. A small motor can accelerate the flywheel between pulses. Another advantage of flywheels is that it is possible to know the exact amount of energy stored by simply measuring the rotation speed (Clark and Isherwood, 2010).

Some start-up companies have now commercialized flywheels into systems that supply all the power needed for buildings and complexes. The key factors are that these flywheel systems are self-contained, cost-effective, and with a zero-environmental impact (Eco-Gen Flywheel Company, 2014).

Eco-Gen, a southern California company, markets the JouleBox, which uses a hybrid system of flywheels with solar, wind, and lithium-ion batteries. The flywheel is teamed with conventional renewable energy to meet the base load needs of customers. Currently the Eco-Gen systems are being sold all over the world for on-site power using power purchase agreements to finance them (Eco-Gen Energy Company, 2014).

FES can even help regulate the line voltage for electrified railways. This will improve the acceleration of unmodified electric trains, and increase the amount of energy recovered back to the line during regenerative braking, helping to keep costs down. Several large cities including London, New York, Lyon, and Tokyo, have pilot FES projects.

Thermal energy storage (TES) is often overlooked as an electricity storage technology, because it does not store or discharge electricity directly. However, in some applications, it will provide efficiencies that exceed other storage technologies. TES can store thermal energy from the sun, which is later converted into electricity. Naturally occurring molten-salt formations are the low-cost storage mediums.

Another application of TES is hot and cold storage in buildings. Cold storage used to reduce peak demand from air conditioning has been used on a relatively large scale. This is a commercially mature technology that provides system capacity at very high round-trip efficiency, with the capability of providing multiple grid services.

There are two types of batteries that have electric grid applications—liquid electrolyte batteries and high-temperature batteries. High-temperature sodium–sulfur batteries are the most mature and commercially available, though manufactured by a single Japanese company. There are over 270 MW in use worldwide. They also have the advantage of relying on low-cost and abundant materials, although manufacturing costs have limited larger-scale use.

Energy storage plays a critical part in transportation. Hybrid or all-electrical vehicles depend on batteries to store electricity and regulate power flow. According to a report by the Electric Drive Transportation Association (2014), the number of plug-in electric cars sold last year almost doubled from the previous year to 96,702. Many of these new sales are the result of Tesla Motors remarkable Model S sedan. Tesla uses a different lithium-ion battery pack design that is superior to most.

In 2014, Tesla announced that it would build a giant battery factory in the US to feed a steady stream of lithium-ion batteries for its electric cars and other electric applications (Tesla GigaFactory, 2014). Calling it a "Gigafactory," Tesla said that it would cost about $5 billion, and open in 2017 and employ about 6,500 people near Reno, Nevada. It would reach full capacity by 2020, enough to supply power for 500,000 cars a year (Tesla GigaFactory, 2014).

As the new Gigafactory move toward battery production, Tesla announced a potential revolutionary battery pack for home use. Called the PowerWall, the battery pack is a rechargeable lithium-ion battery that will connect to a solar array or other on-site renewable energy generator. According to Tesla, there are two different models using two different generic cell chemistries.

The daily cycle 7 kWh batteries uses nickel–manganese–cobalt chemistry and can be cycled 5,000 times. The other is a 10 kWh battery, using a nickel–cobalt–aluminum cathode and is for weekly or emergency use and has higher energy density but a lesser cycle life of 1,000–1,500 cycles.

The PowerWall includes a DC converter to sit between a home's existing solar panels, and the home's existing AC inverter. Prices start at $3,000 for a 7 kWh model beginning in the second quarter of 2015, and $3,500 for the 10 kWh. Analysts had expected the 10 kWh to cost up to $13,000 and predict the lower price will cause other storage producers to follow.

The device will be sold to companies like residential solar company, SolarCity. SolarCity is running a pilot project in 500 California houses, using 10 kWh battery packs. A bigger battery called PowerPack at 100 kWh is available for industrial consumers, reaching a price point of $250/kWh. The reaction to Tesla's new storage devices has been remarkable; the PowerWall is sold out through to the middle of 2016. Reservations within the first few weeks were over 50,000 units of the PowerWall and 25,000 units for the PowerPack at combined orders of $800 million. Tesla's new PowerWall and PowerPack may be true game changers for the renewable energy industry. The batteries will make on-site energy generation and use much more flexible and convenient. They have the potential to revolutionize energy storage and distribution.

In the lithium-ion battery industry, there are other high-temperature battery chemistries under various stages of research, development, and commercialization (Tesla GigaFactory, 2014). Flow batteries are in the early stages of development and commercialization, with a few US demonstration projects of vanadium and zinc–bromine technologies, with several other technologies under development.

Other types of storage have been around for two to three decades now. The zinc air fuel cell (ZAFC) technology was developed in the 1990s (Clark, Paulocci, and Cooper, 2002). The research and commercialization for this battery was never implemented. Later, the original project scientists linked up with international groups that saw value in the technology for transportation and as a replacement for batteries (*The Economist*, 2014a). ZAF Energy Systems in Montana is now commercializing the technology (Confidential Information

Agreement, 2012). The ZAFC battery will be viable by 2016 as a cost-effective and environmental-neutral battery for vehicles and buildings.

Vehicle to Grid (V2G) Power Storage in Electric Cars

In the US, the University of Delaware is hosting a pilot project that pays electric car owners to store energy for the grid. "Cash-Back Cars" involves electric cars that interact with the grid and receive monthly payments. Besides drawing electricity from the grid, the plugged-in cars send electricity stored in their batteries back into the grid as needed, acting like tiny power plants.

Because the grid needs short-, medium-, and longer-term storage to run smoothly, car batteries could meet the short-term need, in a process called frequency regulation. The pilot project actually provides better frequency regulation than traditional methods.

The US Federal Energy Regulatory Commission (FERC) is supporting the project and proposed a mechanism that will pay participating car owners on a national level. To work, electric cars need to be retrofitted with a bidirectional power system, so energy can flow both from and to the grid, and software to allow the car to communicate with the grid. Because most regional transmission systems have to work with multiple cars, it is expected that auto fleets will be the first to participate. The US Department of Defense, with its fleet of 200,000 autos, is considering early participation. Historically in the US, the Department of Defense has taken the initial first steps in energy-efficient and renewable power sources.

The concept may become international. Nuvve, a company with offices in San Diego and Copenhagen, has stepped in as an aggregator outside the US. The company plans to have the program running in Denmark, Hong Kong, and Taiwan by the end of 2015. Soon after, it plans to move into Germany, the Netherlands, Spain, and the UK. According to Nuvve, the market could be huge. The company says that by 2020 it's projected to be $12 billion worldwide, with $9.5 billion outside of the US.

A large drawback to mass-scale battery storage is how to scale them up in size and make them cheaper. Scientists from Harvard University announced in March 2014 a technological breakthrough that may make giant, cheap batteries a reality. The scientists have developed a new, more durable, and cheaper chemical mix for a flow battery.

Flow batteries use two liquids, each in contact with an electrode and separated by a membrane that is permeable to hydrogen ions. Jointly, they store the energy put into the battery when it is charged. They do this with chemical reactions that push ions through the membrane without the liquids coming into direct contact. Later, the liquids can release the stored energy by transferring hydrogen back through the membrane. Electrons are generated and flow through an outer circuit to light a lamp, or do other useful work.

Since the media that stores the energy is liquid they can be pumped into large containers, or even holding tanks. They could in principle harbor huge amounts of electricity. However, they are expensive, needing the salts of expensive metals like vanadium, with coatings from platinum or other rare catalytic metals.

The solutions, argue Huskinson et al. in *Nature* (2014: 195–198), is to use quinones molecules, mixed with sulfuric acid on one side of the membrane, and a mixture of bromine and hydrobromic acid on the other. The electrodes, they suggest, will be made out of carbon. The advantage is that this type of battery could be made out of organic molecules instead of rare metals.

While not in production yet, this type of battery has enormous potential. The cost of batteries using these organic molecules would be around $30 per kWh, compared to about $80 for conventional metal molecules, say the scientists. The critical issue will still be the locations for waste and reuse of the batteries.

Hydrogen—a Breakthrough Technology

Hydrogen and electricity-derived fuel cells have enormous potential when used with renewable energy from sources like water, wind, and sun. In a hydrogen fuel cell, electricity is created through reactions between a fuel and an oxidant, triggered in the presence of an electrolyte. Unlike a conventional battery, fuel cells consume reactant from an external source, which must be replaced but lasts considerably longer. They are also more likely to be environmentally sound, in terms of their manufacturing and disposal. The reactants flow into the cell, and the reaction products are separated and flow out of it, while the electrolyte remains.

An electrical current is produced that can be directed outside the cell to do work, such as powering an electric motor or illuminating a light bulb. Fuel cells can power an engine or an entire city. Because of the way electricity behaves, the current returns to the fuel cell, completing an electrical circuit. There are several kinds of fuel cells, and each operates a bit differently. But in general terms, hydrogen atoms enter a fuel cell at the anode, where a chemical reaction strips the atoms of their electrons. The hydrogen atoms are now "ionized," and carry a positive electrical charge. The negatively charged electrons provide the current through wires to do work (Clark, Paulocci, and Cooper, 2002).

Membrane electrode assembly is the core component of a fuel cell. Oxygen enters the fuel cell at the cathode, where it combines with electrons returning from the electrical circuit and hydrogen ions that have traveled through the electrolyte from the anode. Whether they combine at anode or cathode, hydrogen and oxygen combine to form water, which drains from the cell. As long as a fuel cell is supplied with hydrogen and oxygen, it will generate electricity. Even better, since fuel cells create electricity chemically rather than by combustion, they are not subject to the thermodynamic laws that limit a conventional power plant. This makes them more efficient in extracting energy from a fuel. Waste heat from some cells can also be harnessed, boosting system efficiency still further.

The basic workings of a fuel cell are not complicated, but building inexpensive, efficient, and reliable fuel cells has proved difficult. Scientists and inventors have designed many different types and sizes of fuel cells in the search for greater efficiency. The choices available to fuel cell developers are constrained by the choice of electrolyte. Today, the main electrolyte types are alkali, molten carbonate, phosphoric acid, proton exchange membrane (PEM), and solid oxide. The first three are liquid electrolytes; the last two are solids.

Each type of fuel cell has advantages and drawbacks when compared with the others, and none is yet cheap and efficient enough to widely replace traditional ways of generating power. The real goal in the fuel cell industry is to perfect a hydrogen-based fuel cell to take the place of the gasoline-based internal combustion engine. Hydrogen fuel cells use hydrogen as the fuel and oxygen as the oxidant. For more than three decades, the US Department of Energy (DOE) national research labs have been investigating how to use hydrogen fuel cells for transportation, industry, and homes.

Most hydrogen cars use fuel cells to generate electricity and electric motors to power the car. A few use internal combustion engines modified to accept hydrogen and burn it as fuel, and some use a hydrogen compound to generate hydrogen-on-demand to power the vehicle. Significant funding is being poured into hydrogen fuel cell research, as this is seen as the ultimate in green-car technology.

Hydrogen should be produced from renewable resources. Using biomass is one method, but the process emits some CO_2. Hydrogen can also be derived by using wind, hydroelectric, or solar power to electrolyze water. Today, electrolysis is still expensive, but companies in Canada and Norway predict rapidly declining costs. Other companies around the world are developing hydrogen systems for fixed energy generation facilities, such as power plants. Declining production costs through lower-cost electrolyzers and the use of low-cost, off-peak, renewable electricity could dramatically reduce the future cost of electrolytic hydrogen.

Elemental hydrogen has been widely discussed as a possible carrier of energy on an economic scale. Used in transportation, hydrogen would burn relatively cleanly, with some NO_2 emissions, but without carbon emissions. The infrastructure costs associated with full conversion to a hydrogen economy may be substantial. However, if refueling was done in the home or workplace using water or other renewable sources, electrolyzers could produce the hydrogen needed for fuel cells.

Today, industrial production of hydrogen is mainly from the steam reforming of natural gas and, less often, from more energy-intensive hydrogen production methods, such as the electrolysis of water. However, hydrogen from electrolysis and other renewable energy sources is gaining momentum. This process using renewables is in line with smart green cities. The external and lifecycle costs are rarely part of the costs for hydrogen to be used for refueling vehicles and power in buildings. Chapter 12 covers these and other costs in terms of how to finance smart green cities. Already this is occurring in Europe.

Fuel cell technologies, particularly hydrogen fuel cells, are an integral part of the Green Industrial Revolution (Clark and Cooke, 2014); they offer an exceptional alternative to oil and natural gas dependency, along with other fossil fuels and nuclear power. Scientists and manufacturers have some work to do before fuel cells become a practical alternative to current energy production methods, but with worldwide support and cooperation, a viable hydrogen fuel cell-based energy system may be a reality. However, hydrogen fuel cell cars are already part of an international movement and are now supported by refueling structures and stations in California, some northeastern states as well as the Nordic countries and Germany (Idtechex, 2016).

Asian nations like Japan and China are moving in that direction as well as seen with the introduction of the Toyota Mirai.

Smart, Green Grids

To reach a house, electricity must first flow across hundreds of miles of power lines and pass along a series of stations and substations. A technical marvel of the fossil fuel era, this electrical transmission network ties a central power plant through transmission lines to a local distribution grid, and then to an end user.

The conventional central power plants burn coal, oil, or natural gas, or are driven by hydroelectric power from dams on rivers that were hundreds of miles away. The power plants were housed in large concrete structures with massive silos and pipes surrounded by high wire fences and security guards.

Large electrical generators produce what is called three-phase alternating current (AC) power, as opposed to direct current (DC) power. Electricity leaves the generator and enters a transmission substation. Large transformers then boost the voltage for long-distance travel along transmission lines. The transmission lines are usually held aloft by huge steel structures and a typical transmission distance is 300 miles.

Electricity must then be distributed, or shared, with the end users. The electricity produced by these older systems is so powerful that it must be stepped-down, or reduced, along the distribution grid to provide the power connected to the household switch.

A key problem is that the amount of electricity used by the consumer is about 30–40 percent of that generated at the power plant. The transmission over hundreds of miles dramatically reduces the amount that a consumer gets to use. It also degrades the environment and is subject to disruption by storms or grid failures.

In the transition to a greener world, renewable energy must replace fossil fuel to generate electricity at the power plant, but it can also be used to create on-site power for buildings. This distributed power will mitigate global warming and preserve the environment. To get the most out of renewable energy there needs to be a transition from the old central power grid with its overlapping lines to a local on-site power grid and distribution network that is technologically smart. The need for a smart grid to distribute large amounts of electricity and meet the on-site needs is fundamental to developing the modern energy networks. The end result will be a combination of central and on-site power—this combination is called an "agile" (meaning flexible and integrated) energy system because it combines both energy power sources (Clark and Bradshaw, 2004).

The term "smart grid" started to appear at the end of the twentieth century during the dot-com era. Basically, it refers to using digital or information technology to control and enhance the electricity networks that form a power grid. Originally, these systems used landlines, such as telephone wires, but today the systems are primarily wireless.

A smart grid starts with a smart meter, usually installed at the end users' building or home. The smart meters enable customers to provide immediate feedback to utilities that are able to use the data to set pricing and smooth fluctuations in consumption. Depending on the size and type, other energy control and monitoring devices, software, networking, and communication systems are installed along the electricity distribution network. Combined, these elements form the grid's nervous system, which allows energy managers and end users to monitor and control consumption in real time. Smart grids use transmission or pipeline systems covering miles from a central power plant to the customer. Or conversely as an on-site system, it can work on a micro level within a building or small community.

The smart grid with its digital communications ability can interact with smart appliances that can turn themselves on and off as part of a sophisticated energy management system (EMS). The smart technology would allow the grid to support a fleet of electric cars as well as the buildings where they are parked and being recharged. The smart grid would vastly improve the efficiency of transmission power, and lower the cost of electricity.

A smart integrated system merges Internet and grid features with power sources, the data response, and a load center such as a residential home. A smart meter collects power usage data for the utilities and consumers, and it has Internet communication and the capability of using the digital cloud.

These technologies are being incorporated in numerous companies including Facebook, Google, Twitter, and Apple. One company has created a cell phone application that can measure and evaluate products for their environmental, health, and production costs when shopping (Earth Accounting, 2014). Real time data are fed back to a large distribution and transmission power grid that will enable efficient overall load management. Energy storage is extremely important as part of a smart grid because it allows for the load to be leveled, or optimized, between major power activities and a load center. For example, power generation could be from solar, or a charge for an electric car battery. Real time data are critical to predict and hedge power usage.

The smart grid is ideally suited to meet the challenging demands of sharing electricity generated from multiple renewable sources. With the cost of fossil fuels rising from depleting resources along with the need to mitigate GHGs emissions, customers will need green energy. The challenge for engineers and regulators will be how to construct a smart grid system from a century-old infrastructure, connect it to numerous renewable energy sources, and manage it all in real time for conservation and efficiency.

Solar PV and wind power may have significant power output, but they must be managed with load leveling suited to their output. Moreover, power may be wasted since the traditional power plants do not shut down when the consumer is asleep.

Europe's Parallel Lines

Europe, and particularly Germany, is facing a major problem with their grid structures. Germany's decision to close down its aging nuclear reactors leaves areas of the country with insufficient electricity supplies. Bringing power from elsewhere means rebuilding transmission lines, which is not popular. Given Russia's 2014 incursion into the Ukraine, which threatened the natural gas pipelines to Germany, the concern about power and where it comes from is critical.

Amprion and TransnetBW, two German electricity transmission firms, are experimenting with a system that will run two parallel lines together. One of the cables will carry AC current and the other will carry DC current. At the start, engineers feared that the AC/DC cables would interfere with each other, causing problems. Experiments being done in March 2014, suggest that none of the problems are major (*The Economist*, 2014b: 6). It seems that the only required changes will be upgraded insulators that control the voltage as it passes through the cables.

This discovery has far greater impact than the solution of a local problem. It opens up the potential to move a lot more electricity around as DC and increase the grid capacity, in what is called the ultranet. This should reduce the need to construct new lines across Europe and help bring expanding wind and solar-generated power to the cities. These connections would help balance supply and smooth the variability from renewable energy.

In European cities, as most global cities, grids are aging and in need of repair and subject to weather disruptions and accidents. Germany's experiment with a parallel cable system argues that there is a practical way to make the existing transmission lines more efficient. It will go a long way in helping accelerate the transition to electricity generated by renewable energy sources.

Transforming the energy market requires an advanced grid infrastructure with superior energy efficiency and green technology. A smart grid is becoming increasingly important with the growing use of solar, wind, and other renewable energy. A careful upgrade to the old power grid should begin with rebuilding the backbone with a new system.

Scientists and engineers are now focusing on the micro-grid as well as nano-technologies. Additionally, the enormous opportunities that would be created by the transformation have caught the attention of major investors and businesses. Replacing the world's old grids with new smart grids represents a huge business opportunity. Investors will realize that they can make a substantial social contribution while generating a good return on the investment.

China's Leading Smart Grid

China is the world's largest consumer of electricity and demand is expected to double over the next decade and triple by 2035. Coal generation accounts for most of China's electricity generation, but now the Chinese government is investing heavily in renewable energy technologies. Connecting China's new clean energy capacity into the national power grid requires upgrades and ultimately, a national smart grid (*Wall Street Journal*, 2011).

The Chinese 12th Five-Year Plan enacted in March 2011 includes the development of national renewable energy systems along with a smart grid as a key part of the nation's power system. The plan has support from the nation's large government stimulus package. Rapid development of smart grid systems in China will show significant social and economic benefits (Lo, 2011).

China's smart grid development is extraordinary, according to Bloomberg News Energy Finance (Bloomberg, 2014). China spent $4.3 billion in 2013 on smart grids, almost a third of the world's total. Conversely, North America's spending declined as much as 33 percent. The Chinese-style power grid is trying to achieve the integration of power, information, and business flow, with a strong and secure grid. For example, China has installed over 250 million smart meters, planned for smart charging stations and networks to serve electric vehicles (with thousands of charging piles completed), and built the world largest wind and solar energy generation and storage system.

China's Zhangbei power station is the world's largest hybrid green power station. Built as a demonstration project for China's ambitious smart grid system, the power plant was commissioned in December 2011, in Hebei province. With an initial investment of $500 million, the power station combines 140 MW of renewable wind and solar energy generation with 36 MWh (megawatts per hour) of energy storage and smart power transmission technologies.

The Zhangbei project was a great success. A battery storage system enhances the renewable power generation. The wind turbine production rate has been increased by 5–10 percent, and its whole renewable energy efficiency improved by 5–10 percent. During its first 100 days of safe and stable operation, the power station generated over 100 GWh. Overflow or excess energy that is generated is fed back into the utility grid after the storage has been filled. The Zhangbei project is an excellent example for the renewable energy solution.

Another high-profile demonstration project is the China Huaneng Group's micro-grid in the Future Science and Technology City, Beijing (Bloomberg, 2014). A smart micro-grid with 50 kW (kilowatts) of PV was set up in 2012. This project is being hailed as a model for constructing a scalable smart grid. It is the first smart micro-grid power system, and indicates that the company has begun to enter the field of distributed micro-grid power generation. Based on a micro-grid controller, the system integrates its PV power, with 300 VAh (Volts-Ampered per hour) of energy storage, grid power, and 30 kW load. Under normal circumstances, the load is completely powered by the PV modules.

When PV power decreases, the controller uses battery energy for base load demands. Under the extreme cases that the DC energy is too small to meet the base load, the controller can switch the electricity supply to grid power within 8 milliseconds, to ensure a stable power supply.

These large-scale smart grids are safe, reliable, and stable while accommodating production from renewable energy sources. China has a very uneven distribution of electricity production and demand, which requires that the nation pay more attention to smart transmission grids. So far, the Chinese smart green grid has handled the world's largest wind, solar, and energy storage integrated demonstration project.

China with its Five-Year Plans does something unique, which is not seen in other countries; it puts financing into the plans to make them work and become viable. For the current Five-Year Plan, smart grid construction investment amount will be over $300 billion and the total investment will reach $600 billion by 2020 (Lo, 2011).

Meanwhile, the national smart grid investment funds will be multiplied ten-fold. According to the China Huaneng Group's (2014) analysis for the central government, the national smart grid plan will focus on renewable energy systems. The range will be extensive and new industries will be added so that the market size is extremely attractive.

The attributes of a Chinese smart green grid are substantial, and include:

- strong, robust and flexible;

- clean and green: the smart grid makes the large-scale use of clean energy possible;

- transparent: the information of grid, power, and user is transparently shared, and grid is non-discriminatory;

- efficient: improve the transmission efficiency, reduce operating costs, and promote the efficient use of energy resources and electricity assets;

- good interface: compatible with various types of power and users, promote the generation companies and users to actively participate in the grid regulation.

China's successful integration of renewable energy into smart grid systems is a prime example of what can and should be done. Solar, wind, and other on-site distributed energy resources are becoming common and evermore important to our electricity hungry lifestyles. Smart green grid systems will optimize these resources and make the way we share and distribute electricity simple and efficient.

Greener Waste Collecting

The collection of waste and trash is a major problem for global cities. It is particularly acute in European or Asian cities with narrow or congested streets. Modern trash trucks are huge, they block traffic as they lumber along, making frequent stops and spewing out emissions. Making matters worse, most trash pick-up systems in large cities are highly politicized, or unionized, creating a very inefficient process.

Automated vacuum waste collection, which was developed in the early 1960s in Sweden, is starting to be adopted by cities wanting to be environmentally friendly and seeking a replacement for massive trash trucks, or rusty steel bins in the alley. Also known as pneumatic refuse collection, the system transports waste at high speed through underground pneumatic tubes. Porthole sensors indicate when the trash needs to be emptied and help to ensure that only one kind of waste material is travelling through the pipe at a time. The pipelines converge on a central processing facility that uses automated software to direct the waste to the proper container. The waste is compacted and trucked to its final location, such as a landfill or composting plant.

Developed by Sweden's Envac, the first installation was in 1961 at Sollefteå Hospital. The first vacuum system for household waste was installed in the new residential district of Ör-Hallonbergen, Sweden in 1965.

The system is now used in more than 30 countries, including in China at the Tianjin Eco-City. Other systems are working in southeast Asia, Korea, the Middle East, the US, south and north Europe. In the US, this type of system is installed in several places but Disney World and Roosevelt Island are the most well known.

Major cities in which the system is operating include Copenhagen, Barcelona, London, and Stockholm.

In 2008, the first UK system was installed in Wembley City in Brent, a northwest area of London. An older industrial area, the area is now one of the city's major regeneration, or redevelopment projects. The underground waste vacuum management system serves 4,200 mixed-use residential units, a designer outlet shopping center, a new Hilton Hotel, and retail, leisure, and entertainment venues. The area surrounds 85 acres around Wembley stadium that the developers are transforming into a sustainable region.

The system uses over 2,500 meters of pipe. A single waste collection station services the entire development; each collection cycle lasts only a few minutes making waste collection more efficient and cost-effective. More importantly, the process is driven by hot air instead of diesel-powered vehicles.

The system has generated international acclaim and received awards for its innovative approach to waste management. In 2013, the system connected to Brent Council's new Civic Centre, which is herald as the greenest building in London and the UK's first BREAAM outstanding-rated public building.

Evaluation of the system shows that it has increased Brent Council's recycling levels by 50 percent, or twice the London average, and reduced waste collection vehicle movements by 90 percent. It is estimated that, when the whole project is completed, the system will remove over 400 tons of carbon emissions annually and manage approximately 160 tons of waste on a weekly basis.

Jätkäsaari, a residential neighborhood in Helsinki, Finland, is using the system to serve housing cooperatives and apartment buildings. The system helps facilitate the separation and recycling of waste. Each building has a collection point with five waste bins or portholes, each for different types of waste and with the capacity to store several bags of waste. The underground tube network acts in a manner similar to a packet switched telecommunication network, transporting one kind of waste at a time. Once an input bin is filled it is transferred to the central collection site combined with the same class of waste.

Other cities in Finland, Tampere and Vuores, are installing the system. In Vuoures, the system's daily collection capacity for dry waste, bio waste, paper, and recyclable cardboard is a combined total of 13,000 kilos. Additionally, waste from computers, electronic and wireless systems need to be recycled and used. ReMedia (Milan, Italy), a founder in this area, has a vast network in the EU for remaking electronic and modern technologies back into useful and viable products.

The world's largest system is being built in the vicinity of Islam's holiest mosque in Mecca, Saudi Arabia. During the Ramadan and Hajj, 600,000 kilos, or 4,500 cubic meters, of waste is generated each day, which puts a heavy demand on the collection of waste and litter. In the new system, the waste is automatically collected from 74 waste feeding points spread out across the area and then transferred via a 20 km pipe network to a central collection point, keeping all the waste-collecting activities out of sight and below ground with the central collection point well away from the public areas.

Envac, with its underground-automated vacuum waste collection, has become an official partner in the EU-funded GrowSmarter project. The five-year project, which forms part of the EU's Horizon 2020 program, is to be coordinated by the City of Stockholm. The Horizon 2020 program is a major effort to make Europe more sustainable and environmentally "smarter."

Stockholm, Barcelona, and Cologne will act as "lighthouse cities" and be responsible for implementing 12 smart city solutions throughout the duration of the project, with the aim of reducing energy consumption and carbon emissions attributable to transport miles by 60 percent.

Envac is the only company involved that provides a waste-handling technology. It plans to introduce the system in Årsta, south of Stockholm's city center, hoping to create a best practice model of how to successfully integrate sustainable infrastructures. The system will introduce an optical sorting waste technology, and is expected to create 1,500 new jobs over the duration of the project's lifetime, which runs from 2015 to 2020.

Emerging Green Technologies

The Green Industrial Revolution is spawning truly remarkable technologies that are exponentially more stunning, numerous, and revolutionary as the inventions that emerged from the First and Second Industrial Revolutions. From Aalborg to Tokyo, and Beijing to Berkeley, amazing technologies—from tiny nanocrystals to 200 mph trains propelled by magnetic force—are being designed by scientists and engineers who are changing human history. A look at a few emerging green technologies will provide a sense of what can be implemented by cities.

Government-led initiatives are encouraging nations to research and develop innovative storage devices and to create systems that better integrate and share renewable energy. More pressure is being put on consumers to conserve and on manufacturers to create products that are more efficient. This helps drive the development of new technologies for lights, smart meters, and green grids to maximize energy use and efficiency. ENERGY STAR from the US DOE took the lead in measuring and setting standards to reduce the use of energy for appliances and other building items (US EIA, 2013). The US Green Building Council's LEED created domestic and international standards to measure buildings in the reduction of carbon pollution and greenhouse gases while promoting better energy management. In the initial stages, these programs focused on individual buildings, but are slowly expanding to communities.

A Revolution in Lighting Technologies and Peak Demand Response

The US, in common with most developed nations, uses about 15–18 percent of its total electrical consumption to light facilities (US EIA, 2013). This includes exterior parking and street lamps (Nularis, 2014). For most of the twentieth century, lighting came from incandescent bulbs and fluorescent tubes.

The lighting industry is quiet and low key, so new technological advances come into the marketplace without great fanfare. However, digital communications and Internet connectivity have stimulated a whole new generation of commercial lights that are energy efficient, dimmable, and most importantly, able to adjust to exterior daylight or high-peak load demands. Electrical and chemical engineers who are intent on providing the perfect lighting at all times are creating these transformative technologies. Optimal energy-efficient commercial lighting is a combination of building design and task-ambient lighting placement. The essence of this new generation of lighting is the Internet-connected dimmable ballast, working in combination with a high-output, low-wattage LED lamp.

LED bulbs are an extraordinary new generation of lighting. A 6-watt LED can provide the same amount of light as a standard 60-watt commercial overhead interior light. LED bulbs have a longer lifetime (measured in 8–10 years, instead of months), improved robustness, smaller size, faster switching, and greater durability and reliability. As a new technology, they are more expensive than traditional light bulbs, but the price is dropping quickly as new manufacturers come to market and cost-effective ways are developed to finance lighting projects (Nularis, 2015).

Efficiencies also come from building end user equipment that can respond to the ebb and flow of consumer and grid demand, rather than providing a constant stream of electricity that may not be needed during non–intensive use periods. For example, why use a constant pulse of electricity to light an office that is flooded with daylight in the morning hours, but shadowed in the afternoon? Ideally, the sun would be used for lighting in the morning, and electricity would be used in the afternoon.

This new generation of lighting responds to these changes by using smart sensors on the window glass. The sensors determine the light level and transmit the information through an Internet connection to dimmable ballast that then provides just enough electricity to power the lights at the optimal level for worker comfort and productivity.

Throughout the world, major cities as well as emerging nations are struggling for economic growth and growth means more electricity. Additional electricity is needed to power new businesses and an increasing number of electronic devices—iPads, smartphones, computers, televisions, and so on, but the grids and generation systems are at their maximum load. The only way to get quick relief is through conservation and an energy-efficiency program that reduces demand at a pace that is faster than the growth of new commerce.

For many reasons, utilities have difficulty responding to large swings in demand. For example, HVAC systems demand more power on hot summer afternoons. Demand also rises in the evening, when people return home after work.

The easiest way to prevent surges, or overload, is to keep everything in balance. So, when demand spikes, electricity is delivered, but not at such a high level. There comes a point when, to avoid major problems, electricity delivery has to be rationed, which means that some people have to get less. In this world, rationing doesn't work, so the world's utilities have been pushing what is called demand response, or "peak-load management," which offers the ability to reduce electricity use during extreme demand times.

Peak-load management tries to transfer some of the electricity use from high-demand periods to low-demand periods. Originally, peak-load strategies centered on offering utility rate discounts to customers willing to reduce their energy use during surge time periods, referred to as incidents. For example, a utility program might offer a large industrial customer a 5 percent rate discount if it reduces electricity use during days that are declared incident days. Incident days may happen 10–15 times a year in some areas. Once notified of an incident day, the customer would turn off lights or non-essential machinery, reduce the amount of air conditioning, or take other measures to meet the agreed-on reduction in electricity use. If the customer fails to meet the reduction, then a penalty is assessed.

Notification of an incident day was initially done by phone, then through an email to the customer. Now, with emerging technologies and smart devices, peak-load management is rapidly becoming more flexible and more effective. Utilities are offering deeper discounts to lure customers into letting the utilities connect directly to the customer's EMS. The EMS is connected via the Internet to the facility's dimmable ballasts for the lights, and the large central HVAC systems for air conditioning. In this way, the utility can automatically reduce a customer's systems to meet the agreed-upon level.

Eventually, as the new technologies come into the marketplace, simple equipment like thermostats, refrigerators, washing machines, and dryers will have Internet connectivity and smart operating systems. They can then be controlled remotely, and the utilities will notify the machines to reduce demand during peak-load periods. While most people would consider this intrusive, this type of mass-marketplace energy management will go a long way toward optimizing and balancing energy use throughout a smart grid system that integrates renewable energy generation with other technologies.

Technological advances in lighting may seem mundane compared to some of the other emerging technologies, but lighting impacts every office, home, and room in the modern world. It can even be life changing. In a mud-walled shack in a rural village in an undeveloped part of the world, solar-powered lighting can offer a child a chance to study his or her lessons and slip the bonds of poverty.

Cool Roofs Will Offset Carbon

One uncomplicated technology that has a huge potential impact on mitigating climate change and reducing carbon emissions is "cool" roofs. Basically, a cool roof is a roof coating or outside layer that is white or light in color, which will reflect the sun's rays. A black or dark roofing material absorbs the sun's heat, causing excess air conditioning in warm climates. Usually a cool roof is made from some sort of acrylic fluid or membrane material and is applied over a flat roof as new construction or a retrofit.

In hot or warm climates cool roofs can have an enormous effect on reducing building heat and, subsequently, building cooling. Not only does it reduce the heat of an individual building, but it also reduces the amount of heat that is carried in the wind. This is particularly important in cities where ambient heat from dark rooftops often cause urban heat island effect.

A 2010 study from researchers at Lawrence Berkley National Laboratory (LBNL, 2010) calculated that if 80 percent of the roofs in urban areas in the tropical and temperate climate zones were white or cool, it would offset 24 billion metric tons of CO_2 emissions. This is about the equivalent of removing the emissions of 300 million autos. Cool roof technology would reduce energy consumption in over 90 percent of India.

The study also pointed out that the urban heat island effect would be greatly reduced if highway or roadway pavement were changed from a dark to a reflective color. The combination of white, reflective roofs and pavements would have a dramatic impact on mitigating excessive heat in cities, since half the world's population now live in cities. By 2040, the number of people in cities is expected to reach 70 percent, adding urgency to reducing the urban heat island problem.

Nanotechnology – "Really" Small Things

Nanotechnology is the study of really small things—substances at the subatomic or molecular levels. Like additive manufacturing, it is another marvel of the new age with unlimited potential. To grasp the concept, think of the smallest distance that can be formed between the thumb and finger without actually touching. This is about a millimeter. Divide that space by a million, and that is a nanometer.

A variety of disciplines—biologists, chemists, physicists, and engineers—are converging on this new field and studying substances at the nanoscale. Astoundingly, at the nanoscale not all things behave normally. For example, a person cannot walk up to a wall and immediately teleport to the other side of it, but at the nanoscale an electron can—it's called electron tunneling. The nanoworld is one where quantum mechanics plays a major role. The rules of quantum mechanics are very different from classical physics, which means that the behavior of substances at the nanoscale can sometimes contradict common sense by behaving erratically.

For example, substances that are insulators, meaning they cannot carry an electric charge, might become semiconductors when reduced to the nanoscale.

Melting points can change due to an increase in surface area (How Stuff Works, 2014a).

Scientists working in this field are coming up with major advances in biomedicine; renewable energy, light modification, and carbon capture, among many, many other applications. In California, the scientists at LBNL's Molecular Foundry have created electrochromic glass, or "smart windows." When the glass is embedded with a thin coating of nanocrystals, it can permit visible sunlight into a room while deflecting its near-infrared heat, or conversely, block out visible light while allowing in heat. The change can be done with low-voltage current and a light switch (LBNL, 2014).

Another discovery, also from the Molecular Foundry, is a Metal Organic Framework that is designed to capture CO_2. Sort of like a high-tech sponge held together by metal joints, the system can be fitted inside a smokestack.

While most elements will pass through it, the system's little organic chambers capture and bind CO_2. This technology could result in a practical carbon capture system that would have major implications for the coal industry.

Nanotechnology has invented many new building products. For example a company called Nano-Architech makes advanced building materials like "nanocement," which is high-tech cement. Nanocement is far superior to normal stucco or concrete as a building skin. The product is lightweight, easy to work with, strong, and can be embedded with PV, LEDs, or sensors. Of particular importance to a world of increasing climate change, is that the product is largely disaster proof, offering superior building protection to extreme weather patterns.

A major breakthrough in LED technology was announced in spring 2014. Using nanotechnology, an international team working under grants from different nations has developed new thin, flexible LEDs. About three atoms thick, these are the thinnest-known LEDs that can be used as a light source. The LED is based off of two-dimensional, flexible semiconductors, making it possible to stack them or use them for applications not allowed by current technology.

Besides light applications, the technology can be used as interconnects to run nanoscale computer chips instead of standard devices that operate off the movement of electrons. This would reduce heat and be far more efficient, and allow for the development of highly integrated and energy-efficient devices in areas such as lighting, optical communication, and nanolasers (UW, 2014).

Regeneration Braking: From Trains to Cars to Trains and Back Again

When a vehicle uses its brakes to slow down, the reduction in speed creates kinetic energy. With conventional braking systems, excess kinetic energy is converted to heat by friction in the brake linings. As a result, the energy is wasted. Regenerative braking systems transform kinetic energy into another form of energy, which can be saved in a storage battery. This energy recovery mechanism is used on hybrid gas and electric automobiles to recoup most of the energy lost during braking. The stored energy is then used to power the motor whenever the car is in the electric mode. The most common form of regenerative braking is used in hybrid cars like the Toyota Prius, and involves using an electric motor as an electric generator (Toyota, 2014).

Regenerative braking has emerged as a viable technology for electric railways. For railways, the generated electricity is fed back into the onboard energy supply system, rather than stored in a battery or bank of capacitors, as is done with hybrid electric vehicles (Toyota, 2014). Energy may also be stored using pneumatics, hydraulics, or the kinetic energy of a rotating flywheel (LLNL, 2014).

Regenerative braking has been in limited use on railways for many decades. For example, the Baku-Tbilisi-Batumi railway (Transcaucasia railway or Georgian railway) started using regenerative braking in the early 1930s. This technology was especially effective on the steep and dangerous Surami Pass. In Scandinavia, the Kiruna to Narvik railway carries thousands of tons of iron ore from the mines in Kiruna in the north of Sweden down to the port of Narvik in Norway. These trains generate large amounts of electricity with their regenerative braking systems. For example, on the route from Riksgränsen on the national border of Sweden to the Port of Narvik, the trains use only a fifth of the power they regenerate. The regenerated energy is sufficient to power the empty trains back up to the national border. Any excess energy from the railway braking is pumped into the power grid and supplied to homes and businesses in the region, making the railway a net generator of electricity (Hellmund, 1917 and retrieved 2014).

Combined Heat and Power (CHP)

Engineers hate to let a good idea go to waste, or so it seems with CHP systems. In the 1880s, reciprocating steam engines powered the first electric generators.

Because these plants were inefficient, a large amount of waste steam was available for process use or building heat. Early developers provided electricity to customers and sent the waste heat through steam pipes for space heating. New York City's Manhattan still uses steam from decades-old cogeneration plants to heat over 100,000 buildings.

Modern engineers have brought this idea back and renamed it as Combined Heat and Power (CHP) systems. CHP produces heat as a byproduct of producing power, or electricity. With a fuel source that can be fossil fuel, like natural gas, or a renewable energy like hydrogen or biomass, a turbine is driven by an engine to produce power. As the turbine generates power, heat or thermal energy is also generated. This heat is captured and used to heat buildings (CEERE, 2014).

New technologies are allowing CHP to enter new markets, including small commercial buildings, food service operations, even for heating Olympic-size swimming pools. Cooling seems the opposite of heating with the hot thermal outputs from CHP plants. However, by using another marvel from mechanical engineers, an absorption cycle chiller, the hot thermal output of the CHP plant can be converted to a chilled water supply for use in the summer for space cooling.

CHP systems are most efficient in colder climates where heat can be used on-site or very close to it. Northern Europe is a large user of cogeneration, particularly Denmark where biowaste and biomass is used to power the systems. As a whole, the EU generates 11 percent of its electricity using cogeneration. Denmark, the Netherlands, and Finland have the world's most intensive cogeneration economies (Finish Energia, 2014).

Other European countries are also making great efforts to increase efficiency. Germany reported that over 50 percent of its total electricity demand could be provided through cogeneration, and plans to double electricity cogeneration to 25 percent of the country's electricity by 2020. The UK is also actively supporting CHP and encourages its growth with financial incentives, grant support, a greater regulatory framework, and government leadership and partnership.

According to the International Energy Association (IEA) 2008 modeling of cogeneration expansion for the G8 countries, the expansion of cogeneration in France, Germany, Italy and the UK alone would effectively double the existing primary fuel savings by 2030 (IEA, 2008).

Under the EU, a public–private partnership called the Fuel Cells and Hydrogen Joint Undertaking Seventh Framework Programme project was established. The partnership intends to do 1,000 residential fuel cell CHP installations by 2017 (EU HFC, 2014).

Heat Pumps and Seawater Heat Pumps

Simply, a heat pump is a mechanical device that uses a small amount of energy to move heat from one location to another. Typically, heat pumps are used to pull heat out of the ground to heat a home or office building, but they can be reversed to cool a building (How Stuff Works, 2014b).

Advances in heat pump technology have made these systems extremely efficient, and unlike a typical HVAC unit there is no need to install separate systems for heating and cooling. A geothermal heat pump or GSHP is a central heating and/or cooling system that transfers heat to or from the ground. In winter, it uses the Earth as a heat source and inversely uses it to cool in summer. The system uses the moderate temperatures in the ground to boost efficiency and reduce heating and cooling costs. Combining it with solar heating to form a geosolar system gives even greater efficiency. GSHPs are usually called "geothermal heat pumps" although the heat comes from the Sun, not the planet's center. GSHPs harvest heat absorbed at the Earth's surface from solar energy. Like CHP systems, heat pumps are popular in northern Europe. In Finland, a geothermal heat pump is now the most common heating system for new homes (How Stuff Works, 2014b).

One remarkable adaptation of the heat pump is the seawater source heat pump, like the ones being tried in Alaska and cities in China like Dalian and Rizhao (Kwan, 2009: 215–222). A seawater heat pump is a water-to-water system that harnesses the energy released by seawater temperature differences to provide buildings with air conditioning and heating, bringing huge potential energy savings and environmental benefits.

Electric compressors are used with a refrigerant, which is an evaporating and condensing fluid. Latent heat from raw seawater is "lifted" and transferred to building heat. The Alaskan system uses a dual high-efficiency rotor screw to help lift the heat from the cold temperatures. A stainless steel and titanium coated plate-and-frame heat exchanger is also required to prevent corrosion during the process of removing heat from the raw seawater flow in advance of the heat pump.

While this technology has been used in Europe, this innovative process of removing latent heat from seawater and using it to heat buildings is an emerging technology in Alaska (Alaska Energy Wiki, 2014).

Biofuel: A Transitional Energy Power

Although renewable energy is the goal, transitional energy sources are an interim step. Ironically, Henry Ford, since he was a farmer in Michigan, used biofuels from his farm crops to fuel his cars for several decades until 1923 when the oil and gas industries pushed him to use their fuel sources.

This approach to technologies from basic products and sources has been called "from the bottom-up" and seen to work well in Denmark where recycled products from waste have been used to create environmentally friendly energy supplies as well as the reuse of waste (Østergaard and Lund, 2010: 247)

Biofuels, then and today, are fuels made from living or recently living organisms (for example algae) that can be burned and used in ways similar to fossil fuels, but they are not carbon-based. Ethanol from corn or sugar cane is an example of a biofuel. Unfortunately, it takes about the same amount of fossil fuel energy to make corn-based ethanol, so there is no real benefit to its use as an alternative to gasoline. Ethanol from sugar cane is more efficient, and it is widely used in Brazil.

Two promising sources for biofuels are algae and a process called metabolic engineering. Though both must be burned to create energy, they are significantly cleaner than fossil fuels as substitutes for gasoline and diesel, and they can be sustainably produced. In one of history's most delightful ironies, metabolic engineering produces a clean fuel from switchgrass. This is the plant that the great herds of prairie bison fed on for centuries before America's Great Plains became Nebraska, Iowa, and Kansas, and were crisscrossed by the highways and cornfields used to support the fossil fuel industry.

Algae as a Biofuel Source

Algae are a group of simple organisms that are among the world's most ancient creatures. They have a fossil record that goes back 3 billion years to the Precambrian era. The US Algal Collection lists almost 300,000 specimens, ranging from one-cell organisms to large plants like the giant ocean kelp that grows to

150 feet in length. The glory of algae is that they are photosynthetic (able to use sunlight to convert CO_2 and produce oxygen), and "simple," because their tissues are not organized into the many distinct organs found in land plants.

Scientists and researchers are particularly excited about algae's rapid growth cycle—up to 30 times faster than corn—and the ease with which they can be turned into lipids (a green, goopy vegetable oil). This oil, much like any vegetable oil, can be burned and used as a substitute for carbon-based diesel oil or corn-based ethanol. In a strict sense, burning algae or other biofuels does not reduce atmospheric CO_2, because any CO_2 taken out of the atmosphere by the algae is returned when the biofuels are burned. However, it does reduce the introduction of new CO_2 by reducing the use of fossil hydrocarbon fuels.

Algal oils have many attractive features. They can be farmed on land that is not suitable for agriculture. They do not affect fresh water resources and can be produced using ocean and wastewater. They are biodegradable and relatively harmless to the environment if spilled.

At current production costs, oil made from algae is more expensive than other biofuel crops such as corn, but could theoretically yield between 10 and 100 times more energy per unit area. One biofuel company claims that algae can produce more oil in an area the size of a two-car garage than soybeans can produce in an area the size of a football field, because almost the entire algal organism can use sunlight to produce oil. The US DOE estimates that if algae fuel replaced all the petroleum fuel in the US, it would require just 15,000 square miles of farming area, which is only 0.42 percent of the nation's land mass. This is less than one-seventh the area that is currently used to grow corn in the US. The US Algal Biomass Organization claims that algae fuel can reach price parity with oil in 2018, if granted production tax credits (Feldman, 2010).

While much of the research on algae is focused on creating oils, either for food or as a transitional fuel for vehicles, one Canadian cement company has discovered a unique application. Ontario's St Mary's Cement plant is using algae from the nearby Thames River, which runs through Ontario, to absorb CO_2. The plant started a pilot project in 2010, using algae's photosynthesis to absorb the CO_2 produced during cement manufacturing. Martin Vroegh, the plant's environment manager, says the algae project is believed to be the first in the world to demonstrate the capture of CO_2 from a cement plant (Hamilton, 2010).

Through this process, the St Mary's plant is turning CO_2 into a commodity rather than treating it as a liability. The CO_2-consuming algae will be continually harvested, dried using waste heat from the plant, and then burned as a fuel inside the plant's cement kilns. Additionally, the goopy oil can be used as a biofuel for the company's truck fleet.

The company is preparing for a carbon-constrained future that will not treat cement makers and other energy-intensive industries kindly. "The amount of exposure to carbon pricing we face as an industry is very high," says Vroegh. "If we want to be around tomorrow we have to be sustainable. This project helps us achieve that." (Hamilton, 2010).

Algae can be used to make vegetable oil, biodiesel, ethanol, biogasoline, biomethanol, biobutanol, and other biofuels. Algae-based oil can be used for a variety of products, ranging from jet fuel to skin care and food supplements. The potential for large-scale production of biofuel made from algae holds great promise, because algae can produce more biomass per unit area in a year than any other raw material. The break-even point for algae-based biofuels should be within reach in about 10–15 years.

Green Industrial Revolution Fuel from Plants

Some of the most advanced scientific minds in biology, chemistry, and now metabolic engineering are working to develop useful microbes that will break down simple plants into starches and sugars, and eventually into clean fuel.

For over a century, scientists have made fuels and chemicals from the fatty acids in plant and animal oils. The hope is that a synthetic microbe can cost-effectively break down tough plant materials like wood chips and plant stalks and extract the simple sugars so they can easily be converted to fuel. In the US, the University of Illinois, Urbana, and the University of California, Berkeley, have a 10-year, $500 million grant program to develop algae and other biofuels.

While scientists are engineering fuel-producing microbes, farmers and agriculture experts are developing the inexpensive plants needed to produce biofuels.

Wood waste can also be a source of ethanol. Two US companies, Ineos Bio of Florida and KiOR Inc., are using gasified wood waste to create biofuels (Ineos, 2014). KiOR (2014) built the first commercial scale cellulosic fuel facility in Columbus, Mississippi and says it will make 1–2 million gallons of diesel fuel from its plant.

A major breakthrough for biofuels may have been made in February 2014 by chemists at the Davis campus of the University of California. While it is relatively easy to create diesel from biofuels, until now creating gasoline from farm and forestry waste has eluded researchers. Led by Mark Mascal, professor of chemistry, the researchers invented a new process for making a gasoline-like fuel from cellulosic material.

Gasoline requires branched hydrocarbons with a lot of volatility, and Mascal and his researchers used levulinic acid as a feedstock for the process. Almost any cellulosic material like straw, corn stalks, or municipal waste can produce Levulinic acid. While biodiesel fuel from plant-based oils are commercially available for modified diesel engines, a plant-based gasoline replacement would open up a much bigger market for renewable fuels. (UC Davis, 2014).

Waste to Energy

California's Sierra Energy is selling the US Army a breakthrough technology that turns waste—basically, any kind of trash—into clean energy. Called the FastOx Pathfinder, the technology uses a waste gasifier to heat trash to extreme temperatures without combustion. The output includes hydrogen and carbon monoxide, which together forms synthetic gas, or syngas. This syngas can be burned to generate electricity or made into ethanol or diesel fuel.

About the size of a shower stall, the FastOx is basically a small, portable blast furnace that uses a chemical reaction to heat waste. The company says the system can use organic or inorganic materials—such as banana peels, old iPods, and raw sewage. The concept comes from the old steel blast furnaces and, in fact, was patented by two retired engineers from Kaiser Steel, a long-closed US steel company.

Rugged, simple to use, and modular, the FastOx would be used by the Army to reduce its oil consumption. It can also be used to supply the front lines with fuel for its vehicles and generators (Sierra Energy Group, 2014).

Commercializing Emerging Technologies

Truly innovative technologies are not transformative solely by themselves. Today's mass market is far too vast and complex to support these remarkable technologies by traditional means. To be commercialized, these technologies need government support through a consistent and long-term incentive process from the research and development stage to public financing. Similarly, today's electricity companies were made possible because local governments supported the costs and the electricity could be made available at reasonable prices. Since the end of the Second World War, the industrialized nations have all used government research and development monies to support the commercialization of everything from diesel fuels to the Internet.

Government incentives, tax breaks, and even procurement are critical to the commercialization of new technologies. Governments can also assist in the introduction of new technologies through regulations and standards. When such government actions are geared to climate change issues, environment, health care, and other societal concerns, they are described as social capitalism similar to some Nordic countries and Chinese national policies (Clark and Li, 2012). Today, the advancements of technology to speed communications and to slow climate change are all linked to government regulations and oversight. Nations all over the world should consider their own unique ways to foster and support these emerging industries.

References

Alaska Energy Wiki, 2014. Seawater Heat Pump, http://energy-alaska.wikidot.com/seawater-heat-pump-demonstration-project.

Bloomberg, 2014. http://www.bloomberg.com/news/2014–02–18/china-spends-more-on-energy-efficiency-than-u-s-for-first-time.html.

Bloomberg, 2015. New Energy Finance, Business Council of Sustainable Energy, February.

Center for Energy Efficiency and Renewable Energy (CEERE), 2014. http://www.ceere.org/iac/iac_combined.html.

China Huaneng Group, 2014. http://www.chng.com.cn/eng/.

Clark, Woodrow W. II and Ted Bradshaw, 2004. *Agile Energy Systems: Global Solutions to the California Energy Crisis*. Elsevier Press, New York.

Clark, WW II and Cooke, Grant, 2014. *The Green Industrial Revolution: Energy, Engineering and Economics*. Elsevier, New York.

Clark, Woodrow W. II and William Isherwood, 2010. "Creating an Energy Base for Inner Mongolia, China: 'The Leapfrog into the Climate Neutral Future'," *Utilities Policy Journal*.

Clark, Woodrow W II, Li Xing, 2012. Social Capitalism: China's Economic Rise. Chapter 7 in *The Next Economics*. Springer, New York.

Clark, Woodrow W. II Emilio Paulocci, and John Cooper, 2000. "Commercial Development of Energy—Environmentally Sound Technologies for the Auto-industry: The Case of Fuel Cells," *Journal of Cleaner Production*.

Confidential Information Agreement with Dr Woodrow Clark, November 2, 2012.

Earth Accounting, 2014. www.EarthAccounting.com.

Eco-Gen Flywheel Company, 2014. eco-genenergy.com.

Electric Drive Transportation Association, 2014. http://www.electricdrive.org/index.php?ht=d/sp/i/2324/pid/2324.

EU Hydrogen Fuel Cells (EU HFC), 2014. http://www.h2fc-fair.com/hm13/images/ppt/10we/1420–1.pdf.

Feldman, Stacy, 2010. Algae Fuel Inches Toward Price Parity with Oil Reuters, November 22, http://www.reuters.com/article/2010/11/22/idUS10859941182 0101122?pageNumber.

Finish Energia, 2014. http://energia.fi/en.

Hamilton, Tyler, 2010. CO_2-Eating Algae Turns Cement Maker Green. *The Toronto Start*, March 18, http://www.thestar.com/business/2010/03/18/co2eating_algae_turns_cement_maker_green.html.

Hellmund, R.E., 1917. "Discussion on the 'Regenerative braking of electric vehicles' Pittsburg, PA." *Transactions of the American Institute of Electrical Engineers*, vol.36, p. 68.

How Stuff Works, 2014a. Nanotechnology, http://science.howstuffworks.com/nanotechnology1.htm.

How Stuff Works, 2014b. Heatpumps, http://home.howstuffworks.com/home-improvement/heating-and-cooling/heat-pump.htm.

Huskinson, Brian, Michael Marshak, Changwon Suh, Süleyman Er, Michael R. Gerhardt, Cooper J. Galvin, Xudong Chen, Alán Aspuru-Guzik, Roy G. Gordon, and Michael J. Aziz, 2014. "A Metal-free Organic-Inorganic Aqueous Flow Battery," *Nature* n.505, January, pp. 195–198.

Idtechex, 2016. http://www.idtechex.com/electric-vehicles-europe/conference.asp).

Ineos, 2014. http://www.ineos.com.

International Energy Association (IEA), 2008. https://www.iea.org/publications/freepublications/publication/chp_report.pdf

KiOR, 2014. http://www.kior.com.

Kwan, Calvin Lee, 2009. "Rizhao: China's Beacon for Sustainable Chinese Cities" *Sustainable Communities*. Springer Press, New York, pp. 215–222.

Lawrence Berkeley National Laboratory (LBNL), 2010. Global Model Confirms: Cool Roofs Can Offset Carbon Dioxide Emissions and Mitigate Global Warming. July 19, http://newscenter.lbl.gov/news-releases/2010/07/19/cool-roofs-offset-carbon-dioxide-emissions/.

Lawrence Berkeley National Laboratory (LNBL), 2014. http://foundry.lbl.gov.

Lawrence Livermore National Laboratory (LLNL), 2014a. Flywheels, www.llnl.gov.

Lawrence Livermore National Laboratory (LLNL), 2014b. www.llnl.gov/energy/regenerativebreaking.

Lo, Vincent, 2011. China's Role in Global Economic Development, Speech by Chairman of Shui On Land, given at Asian Society, Los Angeles, CA, April 25.

Nularis, 2014. LED Bulbs. www.nularis.com.

Østergaard, Poul Alberg and Henrik Lund, 2010. "Climate Change Mitigation from a Bottom-up Community Approach," Woodrow W. Clark II, Editor and Author, *Sustainable Communities Design Handbook*. Elsevier Press, New York, p. 247+.

Parfomak, Paul W., 2013. Energy Storage for Power Grids and Electric Transportation: A Technology Assessment. Congressional Research Service, http://www.fas.org/sgp/crs/misc/R42455.pdf.

Sierra Energy Group, 2014. http://www.sierraenergycorp.com.

Tesla GigaFactory, 2014. http://blogs.marketwatch.com/energy-ticker/2014/02/26/teslas-gigafactory-what-elon-musk-didnt-say/.

The Economist, 2014a. Going with the Flow, March 8, *The Economist Technology Quarterly*, p. 4.

The Economist, 2014b. Can Parallel Lines Meet? March 8, *The Economist Technology Quarterly*, p. 6.

Toyota, 2014. www.toyota.com/regenerativebreaking.

UC Davis, 2014. http://news.ucdavis.edu/search/news_detail.lasso?id=10823.

University of Washington (UW), 2014. LEDs, http://www.washington.edu/news/2014/03/10/scientists-build-thinnest-possible-leds-to-be-stronger-more-energy-efficient/.

US Energy Information Administration (US EIA), 2013. Residential Lighting Consumption, http://www.eia.gov/tools/faqs/faq.cfm?id=99&t=3.

Wall Street Journal, 2011. China's Energy Consumption Rises. T the Wall Street Journal.

Chapter 6

Sustainable Green Transport

Cities are the largest and most complex structures that humans make—and they should be made well. One of the key elements to a well-made city is how residents move around, accessing life's necessities. How flexible and effective this movement is reflects a city's livability and impacts residents' feelings of contentment, achievement, and connection to their community and other city dwellers.

For example, in New York and London, the rich and the poor, and everyone in between, rides the subway or Metro. They are the best ways to get around, and an accepted part of both cities ethos. Unlike NYC or London's streets, people on subways, or Metro, are classless and status is non-existent. There are no first-class or second-class seats; the rich are pressed against the poor. Businessmen in slim-fitting dark suits wearing Gucci loafers and holding fast to elegant leather brief cases stand next to workmen in rough canvas jackets and nob boats, with a satchel of hand tools.

The environment is democratic and equalitarian, and everyone is jostled and pushed together during commute hours. Despite what is shown on crime shows, the subway and the Metro are relatively crime free, and while people keep to themselves, civility and a bespoken humanity rules.

Traditional urban transport strives for mobility, especially for vehicles. But the real purpose of transport is access—to work, education, goods and services, friends and family—and there are techniques for cities to improve access while reducing environmental and social impacts, and managing traffic congestion. Cities that are improving the sustainability of their transport infrastructure networks are creating more vibrant and livable communities.

Transport systems account for about 20–25 percent of world energy consumption and CO_2 emissions (World Energy Council, 2007). Greenhouse gas emissions from transport are increasing at a faster rate than any other energy-using sector (UN IPCC, 2007, 2014). Road transport is also a major contributor to local air pollution and smog in the atmosphere that spreads around the world.

Other social costs of transportation include road crashes, air pollution, physical inactivity, vulnerability to fuel price increases, and time taken away from the family while commuting. These negative impacts usually fall harder on those social groups who are least likely to own and drive cars. Additionally, traffic congestion imposes economic costs by wasting people's time and by slowing the delivery of goods and services.

Greenhouse gas emissions from transportation can be reduced by increasing the production and use of green, highly efficient vehicles powered by sustainable fuels, along with better designed communities that include accessible and convenient alternatives to driving. For example, the US metropolitan areas of Washington, DC and San Francisco are served by mass transit systems that run on electricity not fossil fuel.

The US environmental group, the Sierra Club, is working on a national sustainable transport initiative. The group's initiative hopes to achieve three primary outcomes:

- *Clean and efficient vehicles*: A fleet-wide new vehicle fuel economy average of at least 60 mpg by 2025 through a combination of state and federal standards and a shift to vehicle electrification and hydrogen.

- *Lower-carbon fuels*: Reduce the carbon content of the fuels used for transportation by 15 percent below the 2005 level by 2030.

- *A twenty-first-century transportation system*: Reducing vehicle miles traveled per person by increasing public transit use, fostering compact communities with transportation choices (rail, bus, walking, biking), and by cutting the number of car trips taken.

The Sierra Club's initiative is extremely bold for the US, which typically lags behind Europe in developing national and even regional plans to mitigate climate change. However, there is a grass-roots effort developing in the US called the Citizens Climate Lobby. This group is advocating for a fee and dividend plan that would be levied on carbon generators. The Sierra Club's initiative is closely allied with the efforts of the Citizens Climate Lobby.

Sustainable Transport

The term *sustainable transport* comes from sustainable development, and is used to describe modes of transport that are consistent with wider concerns of sustainability. There are many definitions for sustainable transport, and of the related terms *sustainable transportation* and *sustainable mobility*. One such definition, from the European Union Council of Ministers of Transport, defines a sustainable transportation system as one that:

- Allows the basic access and development needs of individuals, companies, and society to be met safely and in a manner consistent with human and ecosystem health, and promotes equity within and between successive generations.

- Is affordable, operates fairly and efficiently, offers a choice of transport mode, and supports a competitive economy, as well as balanced regional development.

- Limits emissions and waste within the planet's ability to absorb them, uses renewable resources at or below their rates of generation, and uses non-renewable resources at or below the rates of development of renewable substitutes, while minimizing the impact on the use of land and the generation of noise.

Sustainability extends beyond operating efficiency and emissions. A lifecycle assessment involves production and post-use considerations. A cradle-to-cradle (C2C) design is more important than a focus on a single factor such as energy efficiency.

A sustainable transport system uses renewable energy and is sustainable in regards to social, environmental, and climate impacts. The components for evaluating sustainability include the vehicles used for road, water, or air transport; the source of energy; and the infrastructure used to accommodate and refuel the transport (such as roads, railways, airways, waterways, canals, and terminals). Another component for evaluation is pipelines for transporting liquid or gas materials. Transport operations and logistics as well as transit-oriented development are also involved. Transportation sustainability is a function of effectiveness and efficiency as well as environmental and climate impacts.

Sustainable transport systems can contribute positively to the environmental, social, and economic sustainability of their communities. Transport systems should provide social and economic connections so that people quickly take up the opportunities offered by increased mobility.

Moving large numbers of people around with zero carbon emissions and pollution is essential for a smart, green, and sustainable city. Cities have evolved differently, and their transportation needs are often dependent on their geography. However, basic forms of transportation such as walking, bicycling, autos, and public transportation are common to all cities. And with renewable energy and other technologies that do not pollute the environment, zero carbon emissions are doable and economical.

Walking Empowers Residents to Experience Their Environment

For many of its residents, particularly those that do not travel, the city is an entire world, and as such it should be livable and beautiful. Much of what makes a city livable is the ability and the encouragement to walk along its boulevards, pathways, and parks. Walking motivates residents to experience their environment and to interact with themselves as well as their larger community. It relieves tension and alienation. Additionally, there is a large body of research that shows that walking improves health and prolongs life.

In fact, the key to a vibrant, robust urban core, as a rich and satisfying urban existence, may come down to a city's walkability. Urban planners offer several insights into what makes a city walkable. Jeff Speck a renowned US urban planner and author of *Walkable City: How Downtown Can Save America One Step at a Time* (Speck, 2012) insists that to make a city walkable and livable, planners must start with the concept that streets should be designed for people.

Vibrant street life draws people into the city, and a successful public realm is one that people can inhabit comfortably on foot. Too often, Specks says, streets are designed by traffic engineers who ignore the real needs of pedestrians. For example, parallel parking, essential to protect people on the sidewalk, is often eliminated to speed the traffic. Every aspect of the streetscape, including lane widths, curbs, sidewalks, trees, and lighting can be designed to the needs of people, not of cars.

Creating a 24-hour city is another key to active street life. Neighborhoods should be diverse in use so that they are occupied around the clock. Eating, shopping, working, and socializing reinforce each other, so that together they flourish. Pedestrians must feel safe, comfortable, and entertained, and things should be kept in scale.

People are small, and the most walkable cities, like those in Europe, or Portland, Oregon in the US have small blocks, small streets, small buildings, and small increments of investment. Portland owes much of its success as a lively and walkable city to its tiny blocks that create an incredibly porous network of streets, each of which can be quite small as a result. Building height is another place for smallness, and only in the densest cities, where land does not sit empty as parking lots, are tall buildings justified.

Some cities owe their livability and walkability to luck or geography. London is one such city, being built on a rocky promontory that was split by a majestic river that required a huge crossing bridge to allow commerce, food, and natural resources to enter the city, and to keep enemies out. Paris, on the other hand, owes its great and everlasting beauty to ruthless politics.

After the French Revolution collapsed and the First Republic failed, Louis-Napoleon Bonaparte, the heir of Napoleon I, came to rule France. First he was elected as the President of the French Second Republic. Then after a coup d'état, he took the throne as Emperor of the Second French Empire. Determined to rule without challenge, Bonaparte crushed all opposition and set a plan in motion for a major reconstruction of Paris. In 1853, under the guise of bringing air and light into the medieval city center, he had Baron Georges Haussman replan the city. Bonaparte's intent was to remove the threat of rebellion from those who would take to the barricades clogging the city's narrow streets and bringing his government to its knees.

Haussman, a brilliant architect and engineer, set about his work with abandon, tearing out huge swaths of homes and apartments and creating wide boulevards that crossed Paris, making it impossible to restrict the Emperor's horsemen. As ruthless as he was, Haussman also had an architect's eye for beauty and he created grand squares, beautiful parks, and built the Palais Garnier for the Paris Opera. Modern Paris with its Avenue des Champs-Elysees and other majestic boulevards, its grand squares that link the arrondissements together and open its citizens to its beauty, was but an afterthought to the maintenance of political power.

Nonetheless, Paris, with its boulevards lined with cafes, small, friendly back streets, magnificent parks, and miles of walkways along the Seine River, is a city that beckons residents and tourists to walk and enjoy the vibrant street life. Paris made Frommer's, the travel guide publisher's top 10 of the World's Most Walkable Cities. In 2012, Frommer's listed Florence, Paris, Dubrovnik, New York, Vancouver, Munich, Edinburgh, Boston, Melbourne, and Sydney as the most walkable cities in the world.

Other cities great for walking include London, New York, Washington DC, and Venice. The most attractive cities for walking invariably have high-profile destinations, but they make a virtue of the journey, says Frommer's. Walking is a sufficient end in itself rather than just a means of getting to the next museum or gallery. Some cities have constant surprises or vistas as you walk round a corner, step up onto a bridge, or chance upon a square or park. London, for example, offers numerous bold architectural surprises.

Some cities have lots of intimate public spaces and walking is often made markedly more pleasant by minimizing the presence of cars. Florence has made the historic portion of the city that surrounds Palazzo Vecchio an auto-free zone. It is remarkably pleasant to stroll around the center of this extraordinary medieval city with its stunning outdoor sculptures and not have to sidestep traffic. It is also a wonder to inhale the rich odors of Italian cuisine without the stench of exhaust fumes.

Other cities, like Venice, have public spaces that buzz. Their streets burst with life and energy fed by a variety of shops and restaurants and a population that lives publicly. In some cities where the architecture might be unremarkable—like Hanoi—the vitality comes from the interplay of commerce and everyday lives played out on the streets.

Cities like Paris or Ireland's Dublin, combine both. These are cities where even if their prime high-profile attractions were closed, aimlessly walking the streets for hours on end would be a delightful and rewarding experience. Almost every city that attracts international tourists is walkable—they reveal themselves best on foot and most of what they have can be accessed easily. Visitors do not come because the cities are walkable, but some might stay away if they were not.

In the very best cities, though, walking the streets is like walking in a rainforest—it's a worthwhile end in itself (The Urbanist, 2012).

Bicycling

Bikes and bicycling are becoming more and more popular as a form of transportation. On many large US college campuses, like the University of California at Davis, there are more bikes than students. Northern European cities like Aalborg, Denmark and Amsterdam, Netherlands have long histories of residents using bicycles as their key mode of transportation. These cities are compact with defined centers and narrow streets making bicycling easy, convenient, and safe.

While some places like Hoge Veluwe national park in the Netherlands have bicycles for free use (called white bicycles since they are painted white), other larger cities have sophisticated bicycle-sharing systems. These systems make bicycles available to individuals on a very short-term basis. Bike-share schemes allow people to borrow a bike from point "A" and return it at point "B." Many bike-share systems offer subscriptions that make the first 30–45 minutes of use very inexpensive, encouraging their use as transportation. This allows each bike to serve several users per day. In most bike-share cities, casual riding over several hours or days is better served by bicycle rental than by bike-share. For many systems, smartphone mapping apps show nearby stations with available bikes and open docks. Some college and university campuses are adopting this bike-sharing scheme.

Bike-share began in Amsterdam in the mid-1960s, and various cities tried different systems over the years. Finally, in the mid-2000, thanks to the introduction of GPS and information technology, the bike schemes have blossomed. These new smart bikes are safe, reliable, and less prone to theft. They are spreading throughout the world, and now are operational in five continents, and include over 700 cities, operating about 806,200 bicycles at 37,500 stations (Shaheen et al., 2015).

The Wuhan and Hangzhou Public Bicycle bike-share systems in China are probably the world's largest with around 90,000 and 60,000 bicycles respectively. The countries with the most systems are Spain, Italy, and China. As of July 2013, the systems with the highest market penetration are operating in France, the Parisian Velib' with one bike per 97 inhabitants and Vélo'v in Lyon with one bike per 121 residents.

Generally there are two types of bicycle-sharing systems—community bike programs that are organized by local groups or non-profit organizations, and smart bike programs that are implemented by government agencies, sometimes in a public–private partnership. The central concept of these systems is to provide free or affordable access to bicycles for short-distance trips in an urban area as an alternative to motorized public transport or private vehicles, thereby reducing traffic congestion, noise, and air pollution. Bicycle-sharing systems have also been seen as a way to solve the "last mile" problem and connect users to public transit networks.

Bike-sharing systems that use "smart cards" or smart pay cell phones allow the bicycles to be returned to any station, which facilitates one-way rides to work, education, or shopping centers. Thus, one bike may take 10–15 rides a day with different users and can be ridden up to 10,000 km (6,200 miles) a year. Often the distance between bike stations is only 300–400 meters (1,000–1,300 ft) in inner city areas.

It was found—in cities like Paris and Copenhagen—that to have a major impact there had to be a high density of available bikes. Copenhagen has 2,500 bikes, which cannot be used outside the city center zone. Since Paris's Vélib' program operates with an increasing fee past the free first half-hour, users have a strong disincentive to take the bicycles out of the city center.

Outside of Europe and China, bike-sharing systems have developed in some US and Canadian cities, including Denver, San Francisco, and Montreal. In addition to bike-sharing programs, bicycling of all sorts has been on the upswing. Bike enthusiasts have successfully pushed for more and safer bike lanes and paths, and now are active elements of many cities commute traffic.

It is truly amazing to stand on the sidewalk by London Bridge at commute hour and witness the horde of bicyclists plunging into busy traffic, fearlessly jockeying for space between buses and autos. Many of these young daredevils are investment bankers who work in office buildings along the Queen's Walk. As they pour out of the offices, they quickly replace their banker's suit coats with bright yellow slickers, hook a clamp on their suit pant leg, and tie down a bike helmet under their chin. Then in one motion, they leap onto their expensive carbon-framed bikes and burst into traffic, inches away from huge buses, cursing cabbies, and whizzing autos.

As an alternative to pedaling, electrically powered or assisted bikes are becoming more popular. These e-bikes are often available along with pedal-powered rental bikes and generally recharged when they are parked at their station. E-bikes extend the range of the bikes and make cities with difficult topographies more accessible.

A London designer, Chiyu Chen, has conceived of an ingenious transit system that encourages the use of sustainable transportation by crediting people for renting and riding bicycles. His Hybrid2 system consists of a fleet of rentable bicycles that are capable of generating and storing kinetic energy, which is then used to power the city's hybrid electric buses. Simply rent a bike, charge it up with kinetic energy from pedal power, and then return it to a kiosk—the station feeds energy into the city's smart grid, and you receive a credit toward a bus pass.

Public Transportation

Not all cities are compact and accessible by bike or walking. In megacities, which have huge populations and extremely expensive real estate in the city centers, mass transit is critical. For most cities, big and small, creating mass public transit that is green is key to reducing carbon and other GHGs emissions.

While fossil-fueled buses and trains are common in developing nations, most of the world's cities recognize that non-fossil-fueled mass vehicles are part of their future transport mix.

BUSES

Pike Research, a US research firm focused on the transport sector, estimates that 64,000 new transit buses will be sold in 2015. Half of these, they predict, will be fueled by alternative energy sources, compared with 28 percent of new bus deliveries in 2010. The most significant growth will occur in North America and Asia, where more than 60 percent of all new buses will be powered with alternative fuels within five years. According to Pike, buses are the easiest option to making mass transit greener, because the power system can be changed without changing or upgrading the infrastructure (Green Car Congress, 2015).

The three common types of energy efficient, "green" buses being manufactured are:

Hybrid and electric

These buses combine a conventional internal combustion engine, usually fueled with diesel, with an electric propulsion system. The electric system is usually a "plug-in" type and the buses have large batteries to hold the charge. Some of these buses can run on a mix of diesel and biodiesel fuel, which further reduces greenhouse gas emissions and petroleum consumption.

A US company, Proterra, has developed a heavy-duty, fast-charge, and battery-powered electric bus. The company introduced its second-generation all-electric bus in 2014. Called the EcoRide, the 40-foot bus has a leading design and engineering that delivered a longer, lighter, and more fuel-efficient bus.

It weighs about 27,500 lbs, which is less than any other 40-foot transit bus on the market. The bus is built from lightweight, durable composite that uses fiberglass and balsa wood. It offers a great strength-to-weight ratio and its overall lower weight helps reduce wear and tear on streets. It has no tailpipe and runs virtually silent.

The drive-system uses an electric motor and regenerative braking—similar to a Toyota Prius—that captures 90 percent of the available energy and returns it to the energy storage system. The system increases the total distance that the bus can drive by 31–35 percent. It can travel 30–40 miles on a single charge, and may be 600 percent more fuel-efficient than a typical diesel or CNG bus. It produces 44 percent less carbon than a bus run on natural gas.

Proterra's buses use a rapid charge technology that provides transit operators the ability to have their buses run 24/7 without lengthy stops at transit bus barns. The 68-passenger machine relies on lithium titanate—a feature that allows the bus to fully recharge in less than 10 minutes. The buses can charge on-route, with an overhead connection system that links the bus to a high-capacity charger without driver involvement. The buses can be fully recharged in a few minutes during a layover stop while passengers are boarding. As one of the world's most efficient transit buses, it also leaves the smallest carbon footprint. Since it's an all-electric vehicle, there are zero tailpipe emissions.

Proterra is in competition with a Chinese company called Build Your Dreams, or BYD Motors, the world's other all-electric, or EV-bus manufacturer. BYD's electric buses can run for an impressive 30 hours and charge to full capacity in three to four hours. According to the Society of Automotive Engineers International, one of BYD's buses ran for a total of 1,481 miles in New York City.

In January 2015, BYD unveiled the world's first long-range, 100 percent battery electric road coach. This electric coach, named the BYD C9, is a two-axle, 40-foot coach, with the seating capacity to carry 47 people at highway speed for over 190 miles.

This is the first of three 100 percent battery electric coaches the company is launching. The other two, a 45-foot three-axle coach named the C10 and a 23-foot coach with executive and transport configurations named the C6 will arrive by the end of 2015.

Overall, Pike Research forecasts that the global market for all electric-drive buses—including hybrid, battery electric, and fuel cell buses—will grow steadily with a compound annual growth rate (CAGR) of 26.4 percent from 2012 to 2018. Pike finds that China's market will constitute the majority of global electric drive bus sales, while some of the more developed markets will see fluctuations in electric bus uptake (Green Car Congress, 2015).

Pike suggests that North America will experience a rebound, as the economy stabilizes along with public transit funding levels. Sales of electric drive buses in western Europe will experience steady growth (around a 20 percent CAGR), as the hybrid market begins to take off and there is continued interest in building the electric and fuel cell bus markets. The Latin American market will be driven largely by Brazil, but other countries will also spur adoption. For example, Uruguay recently indicated it would purchase 500 battery electric buses (Green Car Congress, 2015).

Electric trolley, or streetcar, bus systems are starting to make a comeback, particularly in Europe. Trolley buses are connected by overhead wires to the grid. The design of modern trolley bus operations overcomes the existing disadvantages of conventional buses. Germany has an efficient trolley industry that mixes braking energy recuperation and energy storage in modern super capacitors. Modern trollies are emission-free with a low-noise transit system. Gentle but powerful when starting and braking, the modern trolley bus is cost-effective and easy to integrate into an existing infrastructure. Such an electric bus system is ecological, customer-friendly, and suitable for cities. It has a high economic efficiency and it also expands the traffic-planning field toward an ecological future technology (Kühne, 2010).

Compressed Natural Gas (CNG)

Buses and other vehicles that run on gasoline or diesel, can be converted to run on CNG which is basically methane stored at high pressure and which, when burned or ignited, produces fewer undesirable gases than diesel or gasoline. It is also safer than other fuels in the event of a spill, because natural gas is lighter than air and disperses quickly when released. CNG may be found above oil deposits, or may be collected from landfills or wastewater treatment plants where it is known as biogas.

CNG is made by compressing natural gas that is stored and distributed in hard containers under pressure, usually in cylindrical or spherical shapes.

This compression creates added risks and costs, which are not usually calculated in a cost–benefit analysis. Drilling is one thing but then storage and transportation by pipelines, trains, and ships (as Liquid Natural Gas or LNG) are very dangerous and costly. CNG is used in traditional internal combustion engines that have been modified or in those manufactured for CNG use, either alone ("dedicated"), with a segregated gasoline system to extend range (dual fuel) or in conjunction with another fuel such as diesel (biofuel).

Natural gas buses are increasingly used in Iran and Pakistan, also in the Asia–Pacific region. India is starting to use them in Delhi, and other large cities like Ahmedabad and Mumbai. CNG is also starting to be used in tuk-tuks and pickup trucks, transit and school buses, and trains.

High costs, fuel storage tanks, and transfer difficulties are the major barriers to wider adoption of CNG as a fuel. It is also why municipal government and public transportation vehicles were the early adopters, as they can more quickly amortize the money invested in the new and usually cheaper fuel. The number of vehicles in the world using CNG has grown steadily and the cost of fuel storage tanks have been brought down to a more acceptable level.

However, the added issues with CNG (called externalities) have made the use of natural gas and its byproducts more and more costly. For example, numerous train accidents have occurred in the US and Canada where people have been killed and property damaged. The costs from these accidents have been in the millions of dollars. A natural gas accident near the San Francisco Airport several years ago resulted in the death of six people. The costs for the San Bruno gas pipeline explosion were in the billions of US dollars. Increased insurance, accident, and operation along with maintenance costs have also made natural gas more and more expensive.

Hydrogen buses

Most transit experts speculate that hydrogen will soon replace diesel and gasoline as the most common means of powering vehicles. How soon that happens is the major question, but that reality gets closer each day as concern for the environment increases. While the technical ability to convert to hydrogen is here, the number of hydrogen-refueling stations is limited. Though in Europe, and soon to be in California, hydrogen highways with refueling stations are being developed and installed. To enhance and support sustainability, these stations and the buses that use them should get hydrogen from renewable energy resources like water or electrolyzed from solar and wind power (Environment 360, 2011).

A hydrogen-powered bus uses a hydrogen fuel cell as its power source for electrically driven wheels, sometimes augmented in a hybrid fashion with batteries or a super capacitor. A hydrogen fuel cell vehicle emits only water and heat, without tailpipe pollutants and is considered a Zero Emission Vehicle. It also has a quick refueling process and has a high-energy density relative to battery technology, so it is not as limited in range.

There are several demonstration models of hydrogen-powered buses, with over 100 fuel cell buses in use. Most of these buses were produced by UTC Power, Toyota, Ballard, Hydrogenics, and Proton Motor. Ford has hydrogen-powered shuttle buses, mostly for airport transit. Fuel cell buses have a 30–140 percent higher fuel economy than diesel buses and natural gas buses. They have been used around the world including in Whistler, Canada; San Francisco, US; Hamburg, Germany; Shanghai, China; London, England; Sao Paulo, Brazil, as well as several other locations.

Germany also started the use of hydrogen fuel cell buses at the turn of the twenty-first century when Daimler commissioned 33 buses (three each to 10 cities in the EU). Brazil introduced a hydrogen fuel cell bus prototype in Sao Paulo. The bus was manufactured in Caxias do Sul and the hydrogen fuel will be produced in Sao Bernardo do Campo from water through electrolysis. The program, called *Ônibus Brasileiro a Hidrogênio* (Brazilian Hydrogen Autobus), includes three additional buses.

Hydrogen-powered fuel cell buses began operating in Beijing on an experimental basis in 2006. Three fuel cell buses, made by Daimler in Germany, were purchased with a grant from the UN Development Programme.

In recent years, many of China's major cities have experienced record smog levels. The pollution has been so intense in Beijing and Shanghai that airplanes have been unable to land due to poor visibility. China's smog is also responsible for hundreds of thousands of premature deaths each year and makes China the number one country that is polluting the atmosphere.

The Chinese government is urgently pursuing ways to improve air quality. It has made the development of hydrogen and fuel cell technology a high priority, and the industry is eager to grow. Ballard Power Systems, for instance, announced in September 2014 that it will provide the license and related equipment to assemble its next-generation FCvelocity HD7 bus fuel cell modules in China (Scientific American, 2013).

Probably, the most active market for hydrogen fuel cell buses is in Europe. Ballard Power Systems is partnering with the Belgian bus manufacturer Van Hool to launch 27 hydrogen buses. Hydrogen bus fleets have also been deployed in Norway, Italy, Scotland, the Netherlands, and elsewhere (Scientific American, 2013).

Tower Transit of London has been running zero-emission hydrogen fuel cell buses on route between Covent Garden and Tower Gateway since 2011. They now have eight buses in operation, which means it is the first time a whole route has been fully operated by hydrogen-powered buses in the UK (Transport for London, 2014).

London is part of CHIC, the Clean Hydrogen In European Cities Project, which is the essential next step leading to the full market commercialization of fuel cell hydrogen-powered buses. The project involves integrating 26 buses in daily public transport operations and bus routes in five locations across Europe—Aargau (Switzerland), Bolzano/Bozen (Italy), London (UK), Milan (Italy), and Oslo (Norway). The CHIC project is supported by the European Union Joint Undertaking for Fuel Cells and Hydrogen with funding of €26m, and has 25 partners across Europe, which includes industrial partners for vehicle supply and refueling infrastructure (Chic Project, 2013). (http://chic-project.eu/TFL case study).

In addition, the EU has launched a major program to accelerate the use of hydrogen-based energy and transport solutions across Europe. Called the Fuel Cells and Hydrogen 2 Joint Undertaking (FCH 2 JU) the program will bring together six public–private partnerships with a total investment of €1.33 billion. FCH 2 projects will improve performance and reduce cost as well as demonstrate on a large scale the readiness of the technology to enter the market, particularly for transport—cars, buses, and refueling infrastructure—and energy with hydrogen production and distribution, energy storage, and stationary power generation. One of the projects aims is to accelerate the deployment of fuel cells and hydrogen-based mobility in Europe by rolling out at least 100 new vehicles and 23 hydrogen-refueling stations (FCH 2 JU, 2014).

Although hydrogen-powered vehicles are expensive now, the cost of fuel cell buses has dropped dramatically. The costs will continue to drop as more hydrogen buses are deployed. As demand increases, hydrogen technology will become a more affordable and viable alternative.

TRAINS

There are a variety of urban rail systems in use throughout the world. Unlike freight train systems that run on diesel, most of these urban passenger systems are electric and have low GHG emissions.

- A *tram, streetcar or trolley* system is a rail-based transit system that runs mainly or completely along streets, with relatively low capacity and frequent stops. Passengers usually board at street- or curb-level, although low-floor trams may allow level boarding. The term "tram" is used in most parts of the world. In North America, these systems are referred to as "streetcar" or "trolley" systems; in Germany, such systems are called *Straßenbahn* which literally translates as "street train" or "street railway." Originally, horses drew trams—a horse-drawn tram service still exists in Victor Harbor, south Australia—then steam-powered trams were developed in the mid nineteenth century. Finally, in 1881, the world's first electric tram line opened in Lichterfelde, Germany. Most of the world's tram systems are electric-powered.

- A *light rail*, or *Stadtbah* in German is a rail-based transit system that has higher capacity and speed than a tram, but is not fully grade-separated like rapid transit. It emerged as an outgrowth of trams and streetcars. Light rail systems vary significantly in terms of speed and capacity. They range from slightly improved tram systems to systems that are essentially rapid transit with level crossings. Light rail vehicles are typically driven electrically with power being drawn from an overhead electric line via a trolley pole or a pantograph. Light rail systems are usually driven by an operator on board, and may have either high-platform loading or low-level boarding using steps.

- A *rapid transit*, underground, subway, tube, elevated, or metro system is a railway—usually in an urban area—with high passenger capacities and frequency of service, and full grade separation from other traffic. In most parts of the world these systems are called "metro," short for "metropolitan." The term "subway" is used in many American systems, such as New York's as well as in Glasgow and Toronto. In San Francisco, the system is called BART for Bay

Area Rapid Transit. In London, it's called the "Underground" and "Tube." Systems in Germany are called U-Bahn, which stands for *Untergrundbahn* (underground track). Many systems in east and southeast Asia such as Taipei and Singapore are called MRT, which stands for Mass Rapid Transit. Systems that are predominantly elevated may be referred to as "L" as in Chicago or "Skytrain," as in Bangkok and Vancouver. Other less common names include "T-bane" (in Scandinavia) and "MTR." London's Tube is probably the oldest. It opened in January 1863 between Paddington and Farringdon using gas-lit wooden carriages hauled by steam locomotives (Day and Reed, 2010) Like most of the world's rapid transit systems, London's uses electricity to power its annual load of 1.23 billion riders.

Other similar passenger train systems include the monorails or commuter rail systems of Europe and Asia. Funicular systems, which are cable-driven inclined railways, use the weight of descending cars to help pull the ascending cars up. Finally, cable car systems like the one in San Francisco use rail cars that are hauled by a continuously moving cable running at a constant speed. Individual cars stop and start by releasing and gripping this cable as required.

MAGLEV TRAINS FOR A CARBONLESS FUTURE

The Chinese economic marvel, which has pulled an undeveloped nation of 1.4 billion people into a world leader in a few short decades, has produced many extraordinary creations. None may be as impressive as their magnetic levitation trains. A high-speed train powered by magnets is a remarkable concept, a stunning application of mechanical engineering and physics. The Chinese took a cutting-edge German technology, based on a 1934 patent, and implemented the world's first commercial magnetic levitation train.

Maglev train systems use powerful electromagnets to float the trains over a guideway, instead of the old steel wheel and track system. Electromagnetic suspension suspends, guides, and propels the trains. A large number of magnets provide controlled tension for lift and propulsion along a track. Maglev trains do not need an engine and, therefore, produce no emissions. They are faster, quieter, and smoother than conventional systems. The power needed for levitation is usually not a large percentage of the overall consumption. In fact, most of the power is used to overcome air drag, which is a factor with any high-speed train.

The first system, the Shanghai Maglev Train, was built in 2004. The train connects the city subway network to the Pudong International Airport. This system transports people more than 19 miles in just over seven minutes.

The line has since been extended to Hangzhou, about 105 miles away. Speeds are over 260 mph, which allows the train to travel the distance in 27 minutes. The line is the first inter-city maglev rail line in commercial service in the world and also the fastest inter-city train. The Chinese have plans for similar maglev trains throughout the country. They reason that going from one city to another via a maglev train is far easier, more efficient, uses less fuel, and is better for the environment than any other form of transportation except the bicycle. A super-meglev train is now under development. Chinese researchers at the Applied Superconductivity Laboratory of Southwest Jiaotong University claim their fast transportation concept based on magnetic levitation technology could potentially be three times faster than an airplane. The researchers have been testing a concept train encapsulated in a vacuum tube, thus decreasing the speed limitations imposed by air resistance on regular maglev trains.

Should the project be successful, the prototype will set the standard for future evacuation tube transportation (ETT). Such trains may reach speeds as high as 3,000 km (1,800 miles) per hour (RT, 2014).

Though only a concept, a similar high-speed transit system is being proposed for a potential solar-powered ecocity in California. The system would provide transportation in and out of Quay Valley, a sustainable city proposed for the state's Central Valley. Passengers would ride in small capsules floating on a thin cushion of air inside sealed tubes. Rather than carrying engines, the capsules would be propelled by electromagnetic pulses through the pipes. The Quay Valley Hyperloop would stretch just five miles as a first phase. This would allow the designers to study other aspects of the system, such as the process of loading and unloading passengers, while providing a service to the new city's residents. The Hyperloop, or high-speed transit system, is being proposed by Elon Musk, the inventor and businessman behind the Tesla Motor Company (SF Gate, 2015).

Hybrids, Electric, and Hydrogen Vehicles

Cities throughout the world struggle with how to deal with autos. Many have eliminated auto traffic from city centers or other prominent areas. Regardless, autos cause an extraordinary amount of congestion and tons of polluting CO_2. Still residents insist on buying and driving cars, even in cities like London that have excellent public transportation and legends of cabs.

Fortunately, the world's auto industry is undergoing a dramatic shift toward more efficient and less polluting vehicles. The EU and other government regulators are insisting that the manufacturers increase gas mileage of their vehicles. Europe has the world's highest standards, requiring a carmaker's fleet to average 45 mpg (miles per gallon) in 2015, and attaining a proposed 61 mpg by 2020. Japan and China have similar requirements, and the US is requiring 35 mpg by 2016, and a proposed 56 mpg by 2026.

This trend toward more efficient vehicles is having a profound effect on automakers. For example, Ford has made a major change in its iconic F-150 pickup series. The 2014 full-size trucks replaced portions of heavy steel with aluminum, shaving off 500 pounds of mass. This yields an increase of as much as 5 mpg in mileage, and considering that the F-150 is the most popular vehicle sold in the US, this mileage increase represents huge gasoline savings. Other automakers have now developed drivetrain technologies like direct-injection engines, advanced transmissions, and drive gears.

China is also considering new policies along with funding that will address the horrendous smog and miserable air quality of major cities like Beijing. Speculation is spreading that some sort of restriction on carbon-fueled autos will be developed, forcing new car owners to electric or possibly hydrogen-propelled vehicles (Clark and Isherwood, 2010).

Electric, hybrid, and biofuel cars are not new. Germany's Lohner-Porsche Carriage originally developed hybrid electric cars in 1903. Henry Ford ran his cars originally on biofuels from his agricultural products. These early hybrids disappeared as gasoline-powered engines came to dominant the industry before the Great Depression. It was not until Toyota introduced the Prius in 1997 with its regenerative braking technology that hybrid vehicles began their extraordinary success story.

Toyota's hybrids, as do most other hybrids, have two engines—a gasoline and an electric motor. From start to about 15 mph (24 kilometers per hour or kph), the car runs on its electric motor before switching on the gasoline engine. The electric engine is used under low-power conditions like city driving, and the gas engine is used for higher-speed driving. A computer controls the process and the transition between engines is seamless. Regenerative braking systems transform kinetic energy into another form of energy, which can be saved in a storage battery. This energy recovery mechanism is used to recoup most of the energy lost during braking. The stored energy is then used to power the motor whenever the car is in the electric mode. The most common form of regenerative braking involves using an electric motor as an electric generator (Toyota, 2014).

While introduced first in Japan, Toyota took the bold step in launching Prius in 2001 into the California market with 2,000 vehicles. Since then, the cars underwent several upgrades making them bigger, faster and even more efficient. In 2012, Toyota introduced a plug-in Prius hybrid. A common sight as taxis in world capitals, the Prius with its 4.4-kWh lithium battery has proven to be remarkably durable and appealing.

Toyota now sells 27 different hybrid passenger car models and one plug-in hybrid model in more than 90 countries and regions. In October 2014, Toyota said that its total global hybrid sales surpassed 7 million-unit. By achieving global appeal, Toyota hybrids have significantly lowered the amount of gasoline consumed and emissions generated by driving. To date Toyota hybrid vehicles have resulted in about 49 million fewer tons of CO_2 emissions and saved 4.75 B gallons of gasoline that would have been emitted or used by gasoline-powered vehicles of similar size and driving performance (PR Newswire, 2014).

Ironically, the Prius's regenerative braking concept was developed in the US by the DOE through its research labs. The first auto to use it was the 1967 AMC Amitron. The American Motor Car Company developed an energy regeneration brake for this concept car. The AMC Amitron was a completely battery-powered urban car, with batteries that were recharged by regenerative braking, which increased the range of the automobile. However, AMC went out of business. So the Lawrence Livermore National Laboratory, which is part of the US DOE, refined regenerative braking further and offered the intellectual property rights to all three American car companies in the late 1990s. Each one turned it down (Clark and Bradshaw, 2004; Clark, 2009).

The Japanese bought the rights and then commercialized the technology. Almost a decade later, Ford and Chevrolet licensed it back from Toyota for their hybrid cars. Meanwhile regenerative braking is also used in the Vectrix electric maxi-scooter. The success of hybrids shows that the future is in technologies that are good for the environment.

United Parcel Service, or UPS, the huge worldwide logistic company, delivers about 16.3 million packages a day to over 220 countries. During 2012, it delivered a total of 4.1 billion packages. For decades, UPS has used diesel-powered large brown trucks. In fact, the company is often referred to as Big Brown because of the trucks and the distinctive rumble of their diesel engines.

Now UPS is actively slashing its carbon emissions, first by converting their fleet to alternative-fuel vehicles, and now by using zero-emissions, all-electric vehicles. The first 130 of the electric trucks went into service in California in 2013, and the company is marketing their green efforts, saying that they are committed to electric vehicles as a way to clean the air and reduce carbon emissions. The trucks have a range of 75-miles and use a regenerative braking system to augment the stored electricity in the battery.

Most major automakers are now offering hybrid versions of their cars, and hybrids are gaining steadily in popularity. Manufactures like Chevy and even Porsche are offering plug-ins that are gaining market share. However, Tesla Motors out of California's Silicon Valley has proven to be the true game-changer.

Named after Nikola Tesla, a late nineteenth-century electrical engineer and physicist, the car uses an AC motor directly descended from Tesla's original 1882 design. Barely 10 years old, Tesla Motors was founded by Elon Musk, a successful Silicon Valley high-tech entrepreneur. Musk set out to prove that an all-electric car could compete directly with the world's high-end luxury automobiles. In 2006, the company released the Tesla Roadster, which was the first highway-capable all-electric vehicle in serial production in the US. The car was the first BEV (all-electric) car to travel more than 200 miles per charge, and could do over 125 mph. Selling for over $110,000, it was featured as *Time* magazine's "Best Invention 2006—Transportation Invention."

While the Roadster sold in limited quantities, Tesla's next auto, the Model S has seen strong demand. Released in 2012, the Model S is a sleek four-door sedan that has become the "go-to" luxury car of Silicon Valley and northern California techies. They can be seen plugged into electric fuel stations at tech campuses like Google and Intel, or cruising through San Francisco. Parking structures and airports now have recharging stations but the demand is so high, electric car owners are all having trouble finding places to recharge their cars.

Beautifully designed with high performance and a range of over 260 miles, the Model S sells for around $80,000. In Europe, the Model S was Norway's top-selling car in September and December 2013. Also in 2013, the Model S was the top-selling luxury car in the US, outselling Mercedes-Benz, BMW, Lexus, Audi, and Porsche. Globally, the Model S sold over 25,000 units in 2013 and sales are even stronger in 2014.

Hydrogen Fuel Cell Vehicles

Hydrogen fuel cell vehicles have long been considered the ideal replacement for the gasoline internal combustion engine if refueled from electrolyzing of renewable energy sources. They are zero emission and run on compressed hydrogen to power the vehicle. A fuel cell can be used in combination with an electric motor to drive a vehicle—quietly, powerfully, and cleanly.

A hydrogen fuel cell electric vehicle is powered by a group of individual fuel cells, known as a fuel cell stack. Each fuel cell has an anode, a cathode, and a proton exchange membrane sandwiched in between. Hydrogen, from a tank onboard the vehicle, enters into the anode side of the fuel cell. Oxygen, pulled from the air, enters the cathode side. As the hydrogen molecule encounters the membrane, a catalyst forces it to split into electron and proton. The proton moves through the fuel cell stack and the electron follows an external circuit, delivering current to the electric motor and other vehicle components. At the cathode side, the proton and electron join again, and then combine with oxygen to form the vehicle's only tailpipe emission, water.

In Norway, a hydrogen highway using renewable electrolyzed water resources stretches 375 miles or 600 km from Oslo to Stavanger. It opened in 2009 with the first hydrogen station in Stavanger followed by one in Porsgrunn. A modified Toyota Prius can travel 200 kms using just 2 kilograms of hydrogen. While slightly more expensive than regular gas, the vehicles are odorless, noiseless, and free of CO_2 emissions. Japan, Sweden, Denmark, Germany, and California in the US have built hydrogen-refueling stations in major cities with plans for more. To provide vehicles for the hydrogen highways, car companies are quietly producing hydrogen fuel cell cars. Every automaker is planning on having hydrogen fuel cell cars in California after the state awards funds in 2015 for hydrogen-refueling stations in 2016. The cars, like other innovative vehicles (Prius, Tesla, and so on) coming into a market will be available first by leasing them and later for sale. The leasing has already started for some cars in mid-2015.

Other cities are also working to combine the demand for transportation with electric and hydrogen fuel cell cars, along with the need to have local recharging and refueling stations. In April 2014, the California Energy Commission awarded almost $50 million for these stations. Unfortunately only six stations (out of 28) will use solely renewable energy to electrolyze into hydrogen (CEC, 2014).

In spring of 2015, Hyundai Motor Co. released for leasing a hydrogen-powered version of its Tucson crossover in the southern California market. The Tucson seats five and has a 134 hp engine and a driving range of 265 miles. For 2015, the Hyundai zero-emissions fuel cell engine earned a spot on Wards 10 Best Engines list. It was described by Wards, as a "great engineering achievement and giant leap for zero-emission vehicles." (Wards Auto, 2015).

The car is available only in southern California where there are nine public hydrogen-fueling stations.

Toyota Motor Corp. and Honda Motor Co. have also announced that they will have hydrogen models available by 2016. All three automakers want to take advantage of California's coming hydrogen highway with its new refueling stations.

Uber and Zip Cars

The marketplace often has interesting solutions to a social problem. In the case of city dwellers needing convenient, inexpensive, but only occasionally, auto transportation, Uber and Zipcars have emerged.

Uber is a remarkable auto transportation network that started out as a taxi company in San Francisco in 2009. Focusing on San Francisco's young, technologically savvy residents, the company leveraged the advantages offered by the new smart cell phone world. It developed an application-based system to receive ride requests from customers' phones; then sends these trip requests to their drivers. Customers use the app to request rides and track their reserved vehicle's location.

Besides using cell phone apps to request an Uber ride, the company uses a credit card, non-cash system of payment. A user can log onto the Uber website, by computer or smart phone, and set up an account that includes a credit card for payment. A user's account is automatically charged at the end of a ride, and no money is exchanged between rider and driver. Since the drivers carry no cash, and the customers don't have to think about payment, this eliminates any confusion and anxieties about money. Another safety feature is that with a cell phone app, and constant vehicle and customer tracking, both customers and drivers have a sense of well-being and safety. In addition, Uber cabs are often half of what a traditional taxi charges, making the whole experience especially appealing to women and tourists.

The Uber service has expanded rapidly and in December 2014 it was available in 53 countries and more than 200 cities worldwide. In cities like London, Uber cars compete directly with the traditional "Black" cabs; however, since Uber drivers use GPS to navigate London's maze of streets, the drivers don't have to go through the extensive learning process that "Black" cab drivers do. Nor do they have to read and speak perfect English to find their way around.

This makes the job appealing for first-generation immigrants. Most Uber drivers in London were not born in the UK, and most drive a Prius, which has a reputation for durability, efficiency, and low-GHGs emissions.

Taxi services in many cities and nations are often controlled by regulators, or are heavily politicized, and Uber has drawn its share of protests from taxi drivers, taxi companies, and governments, who believe that it is an illegal taxicab operation that engages in unfair business practices and compromises passenger safety. However, the service is extremely convenient, user-friendly, and significantly less expensive than most traditional cab services.

Zipcars is another service that has evolved because it fits the lifestyles of the modern, technology savvy city residents. Basically, an urban car rental service, Zipcars makes use of smartphone applications and IT technology to track and rent its cars. In fact, a customer's cell phone can be used to lock and unlock the car. Instead of having a large lot full of cars available for day-to-day rentals like those at airports, Zipcars has two to three cars parked in convenient locations throughout a city. The cars can be rented for a day or by the hour, and dropped off at various locations—all of it tracked by computer. This makes the service extremely convenient for city dwellers that don't own a car, but need one for the occasional trip or project. Most of the cars are hybrids or low emission, efficient, and clean.

While Zipcars is a US-based company, it has expanded into Canada. A variety of other short-term car rental and car-sharing services have been inspired by Zipcars, including eHi in China, Zazcar in Brazil, and Zoom in India. Similar services are in Germany and other European countries.

Cities without Autos

While electric, hydrogen, Zipcars, and other low-emission autos are being developed by auto manufacturers, some cities are considering banning autos all together. As mentioned in Chapter 4, Hamburg, Germany's second-largest city, has laid out an initial concept that would eliminate cars by 2034. Named Grünes Netz, or "Green Network," it would expand public transportation and add more routes for pedestrians and bicyclists. It will be constructed over the next 15–20 years, and create car-free paths between all major parks, playgrounds, community gardens, and cemeteries in Hamburg. The resulting network will cover 40 percent of Germany's second-largest city, and it should enable commuters and tourists alike to navigate the once car-dependent city entirely by bicycle and on foot.

Hamburg is an environmental pioneer in the mold of its regional neighbor Copenhagen in Denmark. The city acknowledges the need to change in the face of global warming; in the past 60 years Hamburg's median temperature has increased by 1.2 degrees Celsius to 9 degrees Celsius. Sea levels are rising and impacting the city's port. The level has risen by 20 centimeters, and they are expected to increase another 30 centimeters by 2100. As a large city, Hamburg is truly at risk and needs its green network because it will help limit flooding.

Hamburg's Green Network is part of a growing trend, particularly within Europe, to create comprehensive cycle networks that encompass not only city centers and ring roads, but that also connect the city with the suburbs. Copenhagen has undertaken perhaps the most ambitious of these plans with the construction of 26 bicycle "superhighways," that extend out from the city center as part of the city's goal to become carbon-neutral by 2050 (*The Guardian*, 2013).

Modern city life is changing as we live it. Walking, biking, and watching nature is becoming a part of where we live. Mitigating climate change is critical to our planet's health and future, and it is generating a surprising mix of non-carbon futuristic and back-to-nature solutions for our global cities.

References

CEC, 2014.

Chic Project, 2013. http://chic-project.eu/TFL case study.

Clark II, Woodrow W. Editor /Author, 2009. *Sustainable Communities*. Springer Press, New York.

Clark II, Woodrow W. and Ted Bradshaw, 2004. Agile Energy Systems: Global Solutions to the California Energy Crisis. Elsevier Press, New York.

Clark, Woodrow W. II, Lead Co-Author and Co-Editor and William Isherwood, 2010. Special Issue on China: Environmental and Energy Sustainable Development. *Utilities Policy Journal*, Winter 2010.

Day, John R. and John Reed, 2010 [1963]. *The Story of London's Underground* (11th ed.). Capital Transport Publishing, London.

Environment 360, 2011. http://e360.yale.edu/digest/majority_of_new_buses_will_use_alternative_fuels_by_2015_report_says/2940/.

Fuel Cells and Hydrogen 2 Joint Undertaking (FCH 2 JU), 2014. http://www.fch-ju.eu/sites/default/files/Press%20Release%20FCH%202%20JU%20final.pdf.

Green Car Congress, 2015. http://www.greencarcongress.com/2012/08/pike-20120820.html.

http://www.tfl.gov.uk/corporate/projectsandschemes/8444.aspx

Kühne, Reinhart, 2010. Electric Buses – An Energy Efficient Urban Transportation Means. *Energy*, vol.35, n.12, pp. 4510–4513.

PR Newswire, 2014. http://www.prnewswire.com/news-releases/toyota-is-global-hybrid-leader-with-sales-of-7-million-279077081.html.

RT, 2014. http://rt.com/news/158116-china-super-maglev-train/.

Scientific American, 2013. http://www.scientificamerican.com/article/hydrogen-buses-struggle-with-expense/?print=true.

SF Gate, 2014. http://www.sfgate.com/news/article/Hyperloop-s-1st-home-may-be-Central-Valley-6102049.php.

Speck, Jeff, 2012. *Walkable City: How Downtown Can Save America One Step at a Time*. Farrar, Straus and Giroux, New York.

The Guardian, 2013. Hamburg's Answer to Climate Change, http://www.theguardian.com/sustainable-business/hamburg-answer-to-climate-change.

The Urbanist, 2012. http://blogs.crikey.com.au/theurbanist/2012/08/26/whatre-the-worlds-most-walkable-cities/.

Toyota, 2014.

Transport for London, 2014. http://www.tfl.gov.uk/corporate/projectsandschemes/8444.aspx.

United Nations Intergovernmental Panel on Climate Change (UN IPCC), Fourth Report 2007 and WGII AR5, Phase 1 Report Launch, April 2014.

Wards Auto, 2015. http://wardsauto.com/diesel-resource-center/2015-ward-s-10-best-engines-winners#slide-0-field_images-1175431.

Chapter 7

China—Revolutionary Green Transformation

The Peoples Republic of China's "miracle" or "Golden Era" as they call it, required tremendous amounts of new energy systems. Pulling hundreds of millions of people out of poverty took countless tons of coal and other fossil fuels. Because China had lots of coal and it is relatively easy to extract, it was used as the prime energy driver for the nation's rapid growth. According to an analysis by Climatescope, from 2008 to 2013, China's annual energy consumption rose 51 percent, with almost 70 percent of electricity coming from the burning of dirty coal. Largely because of all its coal use, China has become the world's biggest carbon polluter, surpassing the US (Climatescope, 2014).

In 2012, China burned almost as much coal as the rest of the world put together. The burning of that much coal to power China's development and the country's rapid industrialization has resulted in severe environmental pollution (Clark and Isherwood, 2007; 2010). The air quality in China's largest cities is bad, with much of the water and soil contaminated. The growing Chinese middle class is becoming concerned and speaking out, with the new Chinese government responding.

The environmental situation is dangerous both economically and politically, as the new Chinese leadership is taking decisive actions to pursue green low-carbon development. In fact, China is showing real global leadership in addressing climate change. In 2013, China's carbon intensity (a way of measuring carbon emissions per unit of GDP) fell almost 29 percent from 2005 levels, reported Vice Premier Zhang Gaoli at the UN summit in September 2014 when he also announced that China intends to reduce its carbon intensity by up to 45 percent by 2020 (Cho, 2014).

To reach this goal, in 2016 China may launch the world's largest carbon trading system, having tested various regional pilot ones. CO_2 emissions from coal plants, factories, and other big emitters will be capped, and permits must be purchased for emissions that exceed the cap. By 2020, China's carbon market is expected to be twice as large as the EU emissions trading system and worth up to $65 billion.

In 2014, China strengthened its Environmental Protection Law, making it easier to fine and detain polluters, take public-interest legal action against those who violate the law, and link the performance reviews of local officials to the environmental performance of their regions rather than just economic performance and growth.

China's Renewable Energy Law includes a FiT that is a fixed price above market for renewable energy sources. This will encourage grid operators to purchase all the renewable energy that is produced and made available in their regions. A renewable energy quota sets the amount of energy that provinces and cities must get from renewable sources. The government is also planning to spend $277 billion to deal with air pollution and $333 billion on water pollution (Cho, 2014).

China instituted strict policies to curb coal consumption at the provincial level. In 2014, for the first time, the nation's use of coal dropped, despite the economy continuing to grow at 7.4 percent (Greenpeace, 2014.) Output at 14 of the biggest coal producers is being cut, and beginning in 2015, the sale and import of highly polluting coal with high ash and sulfur content will be banned. Also, 50,000 small coal-fired plants are being shuttered, and no new coal plants will be built in large eastern cities like Beijing and Shanghai. In 2020, coal burning will be banned altogether in Beijing and replaced by renewable energy.

New technologies are being developed and commercialized to deal with carbon emissions, and China is collaborating with the US on carbon capture, utilization, and storage. The Earth Institute's Lenfest Center for Sustainable Energy is working with Zhejiang University on researching pre-combustion and post-combustion carbon capture and developing new technologies. Demonstration projects in China have already captured about 270,000 tons, using over 120,000 tons and storing 100,000 tons of CO_2 per year, according to the World Resources Institute.

China's energy consumption is expected to double by 2030, so to simultaneously cut fossil fuel use and keep the economy healthy, China must develop alternative energy sources (Clark and Isherwood, 2007; 2010). Global Renewal reported that China has become the world's largest investor in clean energy technology, spending $61.3 billion on renewables in 2013. China's goal is to generate 550 GW of electricity from renewables by 2017, almost 50 percent more than in 2013 (The Renewable Energy Policy Network for the 21st Century (REN21), nd).

In the post-Mao era, China moved aggressively in the 1990s into a market–capitalism system due to influences from western economists promoting the conventional neocapitalist model, but one where state institutions were owned in part by the Chinese government and shared in joint ventures with foreign companies. Companies wanting to do business in China had to keep their profits there for reinvestment as well as have at least 49 percent of the company owned by the Chinese government. Today's new Chinese government leadership is putting more controls on industrial growth, and more focus on mitigating climate change (Lo, 2011).

China is vast with an enormous landmass, and millions of people are migrating from the countryside to urban centers to share in the "Chinese Dream." In fact, this internal migration may be the most extensive in world history. The McKinsey Global Institute (2009) has estimated that China's urban population will expand from about 600 million in 2008 to 926 million in 2025 and more than one billion in 2030.

Making it even harder for urban centers, the migrants are commonly members of a floating population, which refers primarily to migrants in China without local household registration status through the Chinese Hukou system (Liang and Ma, 2004). In general, rural–urban migrant workers are excluded from local educational resources, city-wide social welfare programs, and many jobs because of their lack of Hukou status. This is a major problem for Chinese cities and one that is being addressed by the national government. The Chinese government has committed to eliminating institutional discrimination of migrant workers on the grounds of the Hukou system but the reform is complicated since it involves restructuring political and social systems, which will impact every aspect including employment, social security, and property rights.

Similar to most developing nations, the Chinese emerging middle class has adopted the automobile, which increases the smog and pollution that surrounds cities like Beijing. Once a nation where everyone commuted by bicycle, China now has 60 million cars on the road, with 12 to 18 million more new cars predicted annually. To solve it's demand problem, China state-controlled oil and gas companies have been buying massive amounts of oil and gas from around the world.

However, as China prepares for its 13th Five-Year Plan (from 2016–2020), there is speculation that the nation will allow only electric and hydrogen fuel vehicles to be sold. That would be monumental for China's own auto manufacturing, and it would force other nations to convert rapidly to non-fossil fuel transportation.

With strategic plans and large sums of government investment and support, China's environmental and climate difficulties are being addressed. Meanwhile a large-scale effort is underway in China to overtake other countries in the new Green Industrial Revolution. In 2008 the Climate Group, an international think tank, reported China's rapid gains in the race to become the leader in developing renewable energy technologies via its 12th Five-Year Plan. This plan that started in March 2011 committed the nation to spending the equivalent of over 3 trillion dollars in funding for renewable energy (Climate Group, 2008; Clark and Isherwood, 2010; Lui, 2012; Sun et al., 2013)

China's Wind Power

With the help of its central planning process and funding, China has leapfrogged other nations into the new green era. As part of China's social capitalism economic model the Chinese leadership merged their interest in making money with their concern for protecting their society and the environment.

China's huge energy needs will continue to grow as more and more of its citizens rise into a middle class, and the nation is making an ever-growing investment in renewable energy. In 2009 China led the US and the other G-20 nations in annual clean energy investments and finance, according to a 2010 study by the Pew Charitable Trusts. In May 2010, it was reported that China used 34 percent of its stimulus funds, about $590 billion for clean technology energy generation. It will have the capacity for more than 100 GW of renewable energy installed and operating by 2020. Much of this will come from wind (Pew Charitable Trust, 2010).

China created its own semi-state owned corporation, Hanergy, that advanced renewable energy in the country primarily through hydroelectric power systems and then other renewable energy sources like solar and wind (Li, 2014). Now Hanergy has expanded around the world through the technological and economic development of hydropower along with new technologies like thin film solar and storage systems (Li, 2014) that are integrated into China's Green Revolution (Clark et al., 2015). However, China's centralized renewable energy plans in its current Five-Year Plan needs to focus also on the local or decentralized use of renewable energy. These systems are "distributed," which is "on-site" power, since they use renewable energy resources that fit local community needs.

The Danish wind turbine manufacturer Vestas saw early on that China and Asia were large emerging markets. In the early 1990s, Vestas agreed to China's business model that had state-owned companies be majority owners in international partnerships. The result was that the wind industry and supporting businesses grew rapidly. Jobs were created and people were hired to install, repair, and maintain the equipment. Today, China is the world leader in wind energy production, manufacturing, and installation.

Wind power is China's most economically competitive new energy source. The nation's wind industry emerged in 2005, after a decade of joint ventures and collaborations with northern European companies. Favorable government policies were key to doubling the country's wind power capacity each year. According to the Chinese Renewable Energy Industries Association—CREIA—China has the world's largest installed wind turbine capacity.

In 2012 China had a total wind power capacity of 75 GW, an increase of 21 percent, from a year earlier. China is predicted to reach 250 GW of installed wind capacity by 2020, almost 3.3 times more than current capacity, and 42 times more than 2007 (Hong, 2013).

The wind industry is essential to achieving China's goals of secure and diversified energy production for its rapid and extensive growth in land development and transportation needs. The wind energy industry also contributes to economic growth, environmental, and pollution control. If the Chinese wind power industry installs 250 GW by 2020 it will reduce GHG emissions by 500 million tons. China will also limit air pollution by reducing coal consumption, and CREIA predicts that at the same time the country will generate more than 400 billion RMB in added value and create 500,000 jobs.

While engineering and new smart grid technologies are needed to integrate renewable energy into China's electricity grid, the country is intent on a massive increase in wind generation. China is rich in wind energy resources, with a long coastline and large western open plains. Wind energy resources are particularly abundant in the southeast coastal regions and the islands off the coast. In the northern part of the country as well as western inland regions, mass wind energy systems have been built—now the wind power must be transmitted to the coastal cities.

Offshore wind energy resources are plentiful, and in 2010 the first large offshore project was completed at Shanghai's Donghai Bridge. Thirty-four large 3 MW turbines, producing 100 MW, were installed. Analysts estimate that as much as 32,800 MW could be installed by 2020 (Hong, 2013).

Wind energy has enormous potential in China and could easily become a major part of the country's energy supply. Some scientists estimate that the total capacity for land-based and offshore wind energy could be as high as 2,500 GW.

China's wind turbine equipment manufacturing industry has developed rapidly. Substantial new business and job growth has resulted with the development of new green technologies. Domestic wind turbine manufacturers now account for about 70 percent of China's supply market and are beginning to export their products. The largest manufacturers are Sinovel, Goldwind, and Dongfang Electric. China now leads the world and accounts for roughly a third of the global total, both in installed wind turbine capacity and in equipment manufacturing capability (Sun et al., 2013).

The state-owned power supply companies have developed the largest wind farms. These companies are given direction and funding to steadily increase their proportion of renewable energy. CREIA reported that by the end of 2009, a total of 24 provinces and autonomous regions in China had their own wind farms, and more than nine provinces had a cumulative installed capacity of more than 1,000 MW, including four provinces exceeding 2,000 MW. The Inner Mongolia Autonomous Region (IMAR) was the lead region, with newly installed capacity of 5,545 MW and a cumulative installed capacity of 9,196 MW (Clark and Isherwood, 2010).

At the UN's 2009 Copenhagen Conference on climate change, China committed that by 2020 it would meet 15 percent of the nation's energy demand with non-fossil fuels. Achieving this goal will require a huge increase in green energy development, including a much greater concentration on wind power.

With its Five-Year Plans, Renewable Energy Law, and other policies, China has made a major commitment to wind energy and soon to solar. A major part of China's future efforts involves the creation of seven large-scale wind power bases. Each wind base has potential for at least 10 GW of installed capacity.

The Chinese National Energy Bureau is developing these bases. They plan a total installed capacity of 138 GW by 2020, but only if the supporting grid network is established. A significant problem is that many of these bases are located in remote areas with a weak transmission grid and a long distance from China's main electricity load centers. There are also concerns about how to integrate large quantities of variable wind power into a grid built for coal-burning power stations.

Pricing is another important element. China's support mechanism for wind power has evolved from a price based on return of capital to a FiT, with variations based on differences in wind energy resources.

Introduced to China in 2009, the FiT system divides the country into four categories of wind energy areas. This regional FiT policy seems to be a positive step in the development of wind power and is stimulating stronger economic growth, increasing manufacturing output, and adding jobs. Additionally, the Chinese see the need for trained workers for building, operating, and maintaining these new systems, so they have created engineering and science programs to train people to work in wind and other renewable technology industries.

China faces several challenges when it comes to integrating large-scale wind-generated energy into its local and regional grid networks and infrastructures. Wind farms in China are located mainly in areas far from load centers, and where the grid network has transmission issues and needs high maintenance. This causes a loss in efficiency, so the present design of the infrastructure grids places constraints on the development and use of wind power. This has become the biggest problem for the future development of wind power throughout the country. Nonetheless, the Global Wind Energy Council projects exceptional growth for China's wind power capacity. Wind power could account for 10 percent of total national electricity supply by 2020 and reach 16.7 percent in 2030. These figures do not take into account more local and regional wind farm systems as well as smaller systems that are integrated into buildings.

Wind energy, in contrast to fossil fuels, is plentiful, renewable, widely distributed, clean, and produces no GHG emissions during operation. While there is some criticism of wind farms because of their visual impact, any effects on the environment are generally among the least significant of any power source.

Large-scale wind farms are not the only solution. Today's new technology allows for the installation of wind turbines in small communities. Even smaller systems can be placed on rooftops to capture the natural flow of air over buildings.

Advances in turbine construction have increased efficiency to the point that wind energy is quickly becoming the most cost-effective source of electrical power.

China's Solar Valley City

Toward the end of 2010, China overtook Germany as well as Japan to become the world's largest manufacturer of solar panels. However, the Chinese solar industry is primarily an export industry with over 90 percent of PV sales for exports.

Solar industry leaders have lobbied for a more regionally and city-focused active set of government policies to subsidize the domestic use of solar power. Because there is so little domestic use, the potential for growth is strong. Policies intended to jumpstart domestic solar power demand are emerging in their next Five-Year Plan (LO, 2011).

To provide more domestic use of solar, the Chinese Ministry of Finance is pushing an on-site or local Solar-Powered Rooftops Plan. This plan will develop demonstration projects for building solar power systems in medium to large cities that are economically developed and want to be sustainable. The plan calls for rooftop units and PV curtain walls and supports the development of systems in villages and remote areas that are outside of the power grid. As part of this effort to improve domestic use of solar panels, the Ministry of Finance has earmarked a special fund to provide subsidies for PV systems that are at least 50 kW in size and have 16 percent efficiency. The subsidy will cover the cost of the equipment, or approximately 50 to 60 percent of the total cost of an installed system.

Industry analysts say that much needs to be done to develop a thriving solar industry in China. The country will need to reorient the industry to one that is balanced between domestic consumption and export. To achieve this balance, the Chinese will need to create a new domestic system that matches the industry's export capabilities (LI, 2015).

To showcase its commitment to solar energy, the nation built the Solar Valley City in Dezhou, Shandong Province in 2008. This ambitious project created a new sustainable, environmentally sound center for manufacturing, research and development, education, and tourism focusing on solar energy technologies. Solar Valley City is part of China's efforts to promote green energy technology and grow global market share.

More than 100 solar enterprises, including major solar thermal firms, are based in Solar Valley City. The solar industry in China employs about 800,000 people, and China's solar thermal industry and the accompanying industrial chain are examples for the rest of the world. A leading company, Himin, produces more than twice the annual sales of all solar thermal systems in the US and is quickly expanding into solar PV and other technologies.

Now hydrogen fuel cells—using water and renewable sources for electrolyzing into hydrogen—have been developed for major car companies and are being sold internationally. Eventually, hydrogen refueling will not be done by station; instead hydrogen will be produced at home for the refueling of all hydrogen fuel cell cars.

China's Leading Smart Grid

China is the world's largest consumer of electricity and its demand is expected to double over the next decade and triple by 2035. The Chinese government is investing heavily in renewable energy technologies and wants to dominate the clean energy technology market worldwide. To implement China's new clean energy capacity into the national power grid requires upgrades, local grids, and ultimately, a national smart grid (*Wall Street Journal*, 2011).

China's power industry began in 1882 with the birth of the Shanghai Electric Power Company, and the completion of the first-generation energy grid. By 1949, the nation's installed capacity reached a modest level of 1.85 GW. Then in the 1970s, construction of a second-generation grid began with the aim of creating a national power grid. The northwest Power Grid's 750 kV (kilovolt) transmission line was put into operation in 2005 and China's first 1,000 kV UHV transmission lines were built in 2009. As of July 2010, China's 220 kV or above transmission lines were over 375,000 km in length, the largest in the world.

The Chinese 12th Five-Year Plan, enacted in March 2011, includes the development of national renewable energy systems along with a smart grid as a key part of the nation's power system. The plan has support from the nation's large government stimulus package. Rapid development of smart grid systems in China will show significant social and economic benefits (LO, 2011).

China's smart grid development is extraordinary, according to Bloomberg News Energy Finance, for many reasons (Bloomberg, 2014). China, for example, spent $4.3 billion in 2013 on smart grids, which is almost a third of the world's total. Conversely, North America's spending declined as much as 33 percent. The Chinese-style power grid is trying to achieve the integration of power, information, and business flow, with a strong and secure grid. Therefore China has installed over 250 million smart meters, planned for smart charging stations and networks to serve electric vehicles (with thousands of charging piles completed), and built the world's largest wind and solar energy generation and storage systems.

China's Zhangbei power station is the world's largest hybrid green power station. Built as a demonstration project for China's ambitious smart grid system, the power plant was commissioned in December 2011, in Hebei province. With an initial investment of $500 million, the power station combines 140 MW of renewable wind and solar energy generation with 36 MWh of energy storage and smart power transmission technologies.

The Zhangbei project has been a great success. A battery storage system enhances the renewable power generation. The wind turbine production rate has been increased by 5–10 percent, and its whole renewable energy efficiency improved by 5–10 percent. During its first 100 days of safe and stable operation, the power station generated over 100 GWh. Overflow or excess energy that is generated is fed back into the utility grid after the storage has been filled. The Zhangbei project is an excellent example for the renewable energy solution for China and elsewhere.

Another high-profile demonstration project is the China Huaneng Group's micro-grid in the Future Science and Technology City, Beijing (Bloomberg, 2014). A smart micro-grid with 50 kW of PV was set up in 2012. This project is being hailed as a model for constructing a scalable smart grid. It is the first smart micro-grid power system, and indicates that the company has begun to enter the field of distributed micro-grid power generation. Based on a micro-grid controller, the system integrates its PV power, with 300 VAh of energy storage, grid power, and 30 kW load. Under normal circumstances, the load is completely powered by the PV modules.

When PV power decreases, the controller uses battery energy for base load demands. Under the extreme cases that the DC energy is too small to meet the base load, the controller can switch the electricity supply to grid power within 8 milliseconds, to ensure a stable power supply.

These large-scale smart grids are safe, reliable, and stable while accommodating production from renewable energy sources. China has a very uneven distribution of electricity production and demand, which requires that the nation pay more attention to smart transmission grids. So far, the Chinese smart green grid has handled the world's largest wind, solar, and energy storage integrated demonstration project.

The 12th Five-Year development plan for smart grids by the Chinese State Grid, has the following goals:

- Generation link: Grid to meet the demand of 60 GW wind generation and 5 GW PV generation by 2015 and 100 GW wind generation and 20 GW PV generation by 2020. The capability is over 400 GW.

- Transmission link: The next five-years' construction will connect large-scale energy bases and major load centers that will build "three vertical three horizontal" backbone for the Extra High Voltage (EHV) grid. This will provide a high-level transmission smart grid and transmission line availability factor of 99.6 percent and a "five vertical six horizontal" backbone EHV grid will be built by 2020.

- Transformer link functions at high voltages: 6,100 smart substations above 110(66) kV should be completed by 2015, which will account for about 38 percent of the total number of China's substations. 110(66) kV or above smart substations will account for about 65 percent of the total substations in 2020.

China with its Five-Year Plans does something unique, which is not seen in other countries; it puts financing into the plans to make them work and become viable. For example, the last two Five-Year Plans set the stage for the full-scale construction and improvement of China's smart grid. Now in accordance with the Chinese Five-Year plan for 2011 to 2015, the smart grid construction investment amount will be over $300 billion and the total investment will reach $600 billion by 2020 (LO, 2011).

Meanwhile, the national smart grid investment funds will be multiplied ten-fold. According to the China Huaneng Group's (2014) analysis for the central government, the national smart grid plan will focus on renewable energy systems. The range will be extensive and new industries will be added so that the market size is extremely attractive.

Moreover, smart grid construction provides a huge benefit. Specifically, by 2020, the benefits will be:

- The power generation benefits will be around $5.5 billion, saving the system effective capacity investment, and reducing power generation costs by 1–1.5cents/kWh.

- Grid link benefit will be about $3.2 billion; grid loss will be reduced by 7 billion kWh, and the maximum peak load decreased by 3.8 percent.

- User benefit will be about $5.1 billion, including new offerings of a variety of services, saving 44.5 billion kWh of electricity.

- The environmental benefits will be about $7 billion, conservation of land about 2,000 acres per year, emission reduction of SO_2 about 1 million tons, CO_2 emission reduction of approximately 250 million tons.

- Other social benefits will be about $9.2 billion, increasing employment opportunities of 145,000 per year, and significant electricity cost savings, and the promotion of balanced regional development.

China is committed to being the world's largest smart green grid user in the power industry. It is imperative to have a robust and low-cost smart grid that can accommodate clean renewable energy. In fact, China's total installation reached 1 TW by the end of year 2011 with an annual total electricity consumption of 4.7 trillion kWh. The grid-connected new energy power generation capacity reached 51.6 GW, of which: 45.1 GW of wind power, accounting for 4.27 percent of the total installed capacity; grid-connected solar PV capacity of 2.1 GW, accounting for 0.2 percent; and biomass installed power capacity of 4.4 GW, accounting for 0.4 percent; geothermal power generation capacity of 24 MW, ocean energy power generation capacity of 6 MW (China Huaneng Group, 2014).

The attributes of a Chinese smart green grid or third-generation grid are substantial, and include being:

- strong, robust, and flexible;

- clean and green: the smart grid makes the large-scale use of clean energy possible;

- transparent: the information of grid, power, and user is transparently shared, and grid is non-discriminatory;

- efficient: improve the transmission efficiency, reduce operating costs, and promote the efficient use of energy resources and electricity assets;

- good interface: compatible with various types of power and users, promote the generation companies and users to actively participate in the grid regulation.

China's successful integration of renewable energy into smart grid systems is a prime example of what can be done to replace aging infrastructure. Solar, wind, and other on-site distributed energy resources are becoming common and evermore important to world's electricity hungry lifestyles. Smart green grid systems will optimize these resources and make the way we share and distribute electricity simple and efficient.

The results are critical. China is now measuring and evaluating the results in which they have found some issues that need to be resolved. A critical one is the installation of wind and solar farms far from the energy consumers, which require massive transmission, monitoring, and smart grid connectivity. That issue needs to be solved. In part the resolution will be a focus on distributed or on-site power, which does not require massive transmission systems.

While the Green Industrial Revolution surprised America, it did not catch China napping. Starting in the 1990s, China was thinking ahead with its Five-Year Plans. Since the 1949 revolution, Chinese leaders have consciously set in motion Five-Year Plans and polices with strong economic backing in terms of funds, resources, and long-term relations. The latest is the 12th Five-Year Plan that began in March 2011. In the first decade of the twenty-first century, the Chinese leaders saw the need to use their latest Five-Year Plan to "leapfrog" the infrastructure and environmental mistakes made by western developed nations to gain social and economic advantages to mitigate climate change. The result is that China has become a global financial leader with its technological, economic, and commercial applications through state-owned and involved joint venture companies.

Now with the new Chinese national government in place through to 2023, there will be significant changes in the 13th Five-Year Plan because of China's strong concerns with urban growth and the subsequent demands for energy, water, waste, and transportation. Under the 13th Five-Year Plan market economics will be more controlled, regulated, and evaluated in terms of environmental and societal impacts throughout China.

Over the past two decades, China converted many of its government-built and operated infrastructure industries into state-controlled companies that included foreign investors and public shareholders. This joint venture business model is similar to the one used in Germany and the Nordic countries when they converted their infrastructure industries during the 1990s. As the world saw with the spectacularly successful 2008 Beijing Olympics, China has successfully leapt into the Green Industrial Revolution.

China used the 2008 Olympics to show that it had arrived as a world leader. While criticized for air pollution and violations of individual human rights, China set the stage and demonstrated its leadership for the twenty-first century with extraordinary displays, performances, and buildings using solar energy to generate power. The Chinese central government is fully aware of the nation's environmental and social issues and has taken aggressive steps to rectify them with its 13th Five-Year Plan.

In early 2011, China replaced Japan as the second-largest economy in the world based on GDP, behind the US. China has shown how focusing new green technologies can spur economic growth through industrial and manufacturing expansion and by building high-speed trains, magnetic levitation train systems, subways, housing, renewable energy systems, and on-site power for heating and cooling that are environmentally sound.

By the end of 2011, the US lost the "distinction" of being the world's worst air polluter. China is now number one. However, if the data were calculated on a per capita basis, the US would still rank first. Given its focus on sustainable energy sources, China will certainly reverse that trend and be well below the US and other western nations in a few years. China's next Five-Year Plan will begin to move the entire country into renewable energy, including electric and hybrid vehicles. The Chinese have the money and resources to make these goals not only achievable, but also sustainable. The new Chinese central government leadership will make such decisions as they move further into the 13th and 14th-Year Plans.

The shift to renewable energy requires a more educated workforce, upgraded labor skills, and businesses that can be certified as environmentally responsible for the short and long term. Along with environmentally sound technologies comes a new green workforce that must learn new technologies that range from nanotechnology to chemical engineering systems. China knows this, and understands that the shift to renewable energy will require extensive workforce retraining. Most of China's senior leaders have degrees in engineering or science, unlike other nations whose elected leaders tend to have backgrounds in western economics and law. China's dominance in the wind turbine and solar panel manufacturing sectors is a good example why having leaders with scientific and engineering knowledge can be beneficial to national leadership.

China intends to learn from the west's mistakes as it moves its energy infrastructures into the Green Industrial Revolution. The nation plans to do this through a centralized economic policy that is mainly shaped by the Communist Party of the National Government of China (CPC) through plenary sessions of the People's Republic of China Central Committee. The Committee plays the leading role in establishing the foundations and principles of Chinese policy by mapping strategies for economic development, setting growth targets, and launching reforms.

Long-term planning is a key characteristic of centralized social economies, as the overall plan normally contains detailed economic development guidelines for the various regions. There have been 12 such Five-Year Plans; the name of the 11th plan was changed to "guideline" to reflect China's transition from a Soviet-style communist economy to a social capitalism economy.

In October 2010 China announced the 12th Five-Year Plan with final approval and implementation plans for early 2011 and beyond when it ends in 2015. The guideline addresses rising inequality and sustainable development. It establishes priorities for more equitable wealth distribution, increased domestic consumption, and improved social infrastructure and social safety nets. The plan represents China's efforts to rebalance its economy, shifting emphasis from investment to consumption and from urban and coastal growth to rural and inland development. The plan also continues to advocate objectives set out in the

11th Five-Year Plan to enhance environmental protection, which called for a 10 percent reduction of the total discharge of major pollutants in five years.

The 12th Five-Year Plan focuses the nation on reducing its carbon footprint, and will address climate change and global warming. Not only will it be well financed, with the equivalent of $1 trillion US dollars, but it will set in motion the possibility that China will be able to surpass western nations in the technologies and industries that support and make up the Green Industrial Revolution. One key element is that the Chinese will change their central power plants into agile, sustainable, and distributed energy infrastructures with local on-site power systems that use renewable energy to power the facilities.

Emerging World Leader in Environmental Sustainability

There has been a dramatic transformation in Beijing and several other major cities in the world's most populous nation. In the 1990s Beijing was ranked third among world cities with the highest levels of air pollution. Today, air pollution has been reduced dramatically.

Sustainable development is now official government policy in China, and it has been implemented at a remarkable pace in some regions. The IMAR, north of Beijing, was one of the first (Clark and Isherwood, 2007; and 2010). At the same time, in the early part of the first decade of the twenty-first century, Shanghai built the first commercial high-speed magnetic levitation train line.

The Shanghai Maglev train connects the new Pudong International Airport to the city's rapidly growing subway system, making the 30 km trip in just seven minutes. The city wanted the train in operation since it was hosting the World Expo in the summer and fall of 2010. Furthermore, Shanghai, Beijing, Shenzen, Qingdao, and Chengdu are all building or planning new underground railway lines, and in some cases, light rail lines at ground level. High-speed rail now connects many Chinese cities, providing shorter travel times than can be achieved by airplane.

Meglev trains now connect Shanghai Pudong International Airport to Longyang Road Station at the record speed of 311 mph (November 12, 2003) in seven minutes and 30 seconds.

The transformation of Beijing, Qingdao, and Nanjing toward environmentally sensitive cities was driven in large part by China's goal of making their 2008 Olympics green. For example, PV panels and concentrated solar systems were constructed on many of the Olympic buildings. The determination to achieve sustainable development in other cities like Shanghai, which was not an Olympic city, can be explained similarly. For example, Shanghai did host the World Expo in 2010, which provided an opportunity to showcase its implementation of significant green technologies (such at the Meglev train) and the city's plans for the future.

Shanghai's urban planning and sustainable exhibition areas attract thousands of visitors and business people each day. Within the exhibit, the city says that it wants to become one of the world's leading commercial cities in the twenty-first century. To do this, Shanghai cleaned up its air and water and waste drainage systems. As new buildings, communities, and areas were added, the city installed subways and roads that allowed for bikes and walkways.

The Chinese recognize that sustainable development of an area or region is good for business and tourism, as well as its citizens. Numerous cities and regions are now labeled as sustainable and have established benchmarks and criteria for official certification. Hundreds of conventions and conferences are held in these cities, primarily to show visitors the positive environmental impacts, but also to create business opportunities.

To encourage sustainable development, the national government continues to strengthen environmental legislation and make huge investments in green technology and sustainable infrastructure improvements. The nation's environmental protection sector is projected to grow at a 15 percent annual rate. Cities are closing their most polluting factories and moving others to locations far from residential and commercial areas. China encourages industries to modernize, which has improved energy efficiency over the past decade. However, the growing demand for personal cars and new buildings and homes has increased national energy consumption.

A Green Technology Culture

In a pattern reminiscent of the post-Second World War rise of Asia's manufacturing sectors, China, Japan, and South Korea are leading the way in developing green energy technologies. As a result, these countries have been dubbed the "green technology tigers." The three nations have already passed the US in the production of renewable energy technologies. According to the Breakthrough Institute and the Information Technology and Innovation

Foundation 2009 report "Rising Tigers, Sleeping Giants," these nations will out-invest the US three-to-one in renewable energy technologies as confirmed by the latest studies in 2011. This will attract a significant share of private sector investments in green energy technology, perhaps trillions of dollars over the next decade. Asia's green technology tigers will, therefore, receive the benefits of new jobs and increased tax revenues at the expense of the US and Europe.

Government policies and investments are the keys to helping China, Japan, and South Korea gain a competitive advantage in the green energy sectors. These Asian nations are making a large direct public investment in green technologies. Government investments in research and development, green energy manufacturing capacity, the deployment of green energy technologies, and the establishment of enabling infrastructure will allow them to capture economies of scale, learning-by-doing, and innovation advantages.

Companies that can establish economies of scale and create learning-by-doing opportunities ahead of competitors can achieve lower production costs and manufacture higher-quality products. This will make it harder for new entrants to break into the market. Direct government investments will help Asia's green technology tigers form industry clusters, similar to California's Silicon Valley, where inventors, investors, manufacturers, suppliers, universities, and others can establish a dense network of relationships. Even in an era of increasingly globalized commerce, the structure of these regional economies can provide enduring competitive advantages.

In China, national, regional, and local governments are offering green energy companies generous subsidies—including free land, funding, low-cost financing, tax incentives, and money for research and development—to establish operations in their localities (Clark et al., 2015). It took just three years for the Chinese city of Baoding to transform from an automobile and textile town into the fastest-growing hub for wind and solar energy equipment makers in China. The city is home to "Electricity Valley," an industrial cluster modeled after Silicon Valley, that is composed of nearly 200 renewable energy companies that focus on wind power, solar PVs, solar thermal, biomass, and energy-efficiency technologies. Baoding is the center of green energy development in China, and operates as a platform that links China's green energy manufacturing industry with policy support, research institutions, and social systems.

In Jiangsu, a province on the eastern coast of China, local government officials have provided large subsidies for solar energy with a goal of reaching

260 MW of installed capacity. Jiangsu already houses many of China's major solar PV manufacturers, and the new policy is targeted to create substantial market demand and attract a cluster of polysilicon suppliers and solar technology manufacturers.

Another Chinese city, Tianjin, is now home to the Danish company Vestas, the largest wind energy equipment production company in the world. This base not only enhances the company's production capacity, but also increases the number of locally installed wind turbines and helps component suppliers develop expertise with the company's advanced wind power technology, while providing a learning laboratory for students and researchers.

Regionally-based programs provide cost and innovation advantages, including access to specialized labor, materials, and equipment at lower operating costs, as well as lower search costs, economies of scale, and price competition. A regional focus provides member organizations with preferred access to market, technical, and competitive information, while creating knowledge spillovers that can accelerate the pace of innovation. Relationships between companies are leveraged and integrated so they can help each other learn about evolving technologies as well as new market opportunities. Workforce mobility enhances the rate of innovation for the whole region, making it more sustainable. These regional areas provide an attractive business environment for particular industries; if one or two companies fail or move out of the area, others can quickly replace them.

Establishing industrial regions does not guarantee continued market dominance. In the case of the automotive industry, US firms lost market dominance after east Asian nations spent years implementing an industrial policy that sheltered their nascent auto industry from competition. At the same time, these nations invested billions in direct subsidies to support the industry's growth and technological progress. Above all, the Asian nations held a high regard and value for the environment and moved aggressively into hybrid, electrical, and hydrogen technologies that combined renewable energy and infrastructures like highways, rail, and air systems.

China's extraordinary emergence as a twenty-first century powerhouse is a tribute to the vision and practicality of its leaders. While too many western nations rested on their twentieth-century successes, China surged ahead, adopting the opportunities of the Green Industrial Revolution. By deftly using its system of planning and government-supported development, China leapfrogged the mistakes made by other nations that were bogged down in a carbon-intensive mindset (Clark and Isherwood, 2007; and 2010). Knowing that fossil fuels are a declining resource that is destroying a fragile global ecosystem, China has acknowledged the need to protect the environment through the expanded use of renewable energy and sustainable communities.

References

Bloomberg, 2014. New Energy Finance, Business Council of Sustainable Energy, February.

China Huaneng Group, 2014. http://www.chng.com.cn/eng/.

Cho, Renee, 2014. The Greening of China. University of Columbia, November, http://blogs.ei.columbia.edu/2014/11/08/the-greening-of-china/.

Clark II, Woodrow W. and Grant Cooke, 2014. The Green Industrial Revolution: Energy, Engineering and Economics. Elsevier Press.

Clark II, Woodrow W., Grant Cooke, Anjun Jerry JIN, and Ching-Fuh LIN, 2015. *China's Green Revolution*. Gower Press, Farnham and China Electric Power Press, Beijing.

Clark II, Woodrow W. and William Isherwood, 2007. Report on Inner Mongolia Autonomous Region. Asian Development Bank, December.

Clark II, Woodrow W. and William Isherwood, 2010. Report on Energy Strategies for the Inner Mongolia Autonomous Region. *Utilities Policy* vol.18, n.1, pp. 3–10.

Climate Group, 2008. China's Clean Revolution. August, www.guardian.co.uk/environment/2008/aug/01/renewableenergy.climatechang).

Climatescope, 2014. http://about.bnef.com/content/uploads/sites/4/2014/10/climatescope-exec-summary.pdf.

Greenpeace, 2014. October 11, http://energydesk.greenpeace.org/2014/10/22/chinas-coal-use-actually-falling-now-first-time-century/.

Hong, Lixuan, 2013. Developing an Analytical Approach Model for Offshore Wind in China, PhD Thesis, Aalborg University, Aalborg, Denmark.

LI, He Jun, 2014. *China's New Energy Revolution: How the World Super Power is Fostering Economic Development and Sustainable Growth through Thin Film Solar Technology.* McGraw Hill Education, New York.

Liang, Zai and Zhongdong Ma. 2004. China's Floating Population: New Evidence from the 2000 Census. *Population and Development Review*, Vol.30, n.3, pp. 467–488.

Liu, Wen, 2012. The Integration of Sustainable Transport in Future Renewable Energy Systems in China. PhD Thesis.

Lo, Vincent. 2011. China's 12th Five-Year Plan. Speech given by Chairman Shui, On Land and President of the Yangtze Council. Asian Society Meeting, Los Angeles, California, April.

McKinsey Global Institute, 2009. http://www.mckinsey.com/insights/urbanization/preparing_for_urban_billion_in_china.

Pew Charitable Trusts, 2010. Who's Winning the Clean Energy Race? Growth, Competition and Opportunity in the World's Largest Economies. G-20 Clean Energy Fact Book, http://www.pewtrusts.org/uploadedFiles/wwwpewtrustsorg/Reports/Global_warming/G-20%20Report.pdf.

REN21, nd. Global Renewal. http://www.ren21.net/portals/0/documents/resources/gsr/2014/gsr2014_full%20report_low%20res.pdf.

Sun, Xiaolei, Jianping Li, Yongfeng Wang and Woodrow W. Clark II, 2013. China's Sovereign Wealth Fund Investments in Overseas Energy: The Energy Security Perspective. *Energy Policy*, Vol.65, February, pp. 654–651.

Wall Street Journal, 2011. China's Energy Consumption Rises.

Chapter 8

The Next Economics for a Greener World

The impact of climate change on the economics of global cities is huge. While it is hard to calculate the cost per city—let alone individuals in terms of living and health—estimates are that climate change costs the world economy a potential 1.6 percent of annual output or about $1.2 trillion a year. This could double to 3.2 percent by 2030, if global temperatures continue to rise (DARA, 2012) as they have over the last few years (2012-2015) as NASA reports (October, 2015).

As the Earth's average temperature rises because of greenhouse gases, the effects on the planet, such as melting ice caps, extreme hot and cold weather, drought and rising sea levels, threaten populations and livelihoods. Costs are going to rise as regions and nations grow economically, needing more and more energy from other areas of the world. Even the biggest and most rapidly developing economies will not escape unscathed. The US and China could see a 2.1 percent reduction in their potential GDPs by 2030, while India could experience more than 5 percent loss of potential output. British economist Nicholas Stern, in a 2006 report on the economics of climate change, calculated that without any action, the overall costs and risks of climate change would be equivalent to a cut in per capita consumption of about 20 percent (Stern, 2006). In short, the prosperity and future of every nation is at risk.

Consequently, the effect on world cities is enormous, impacting the health and well-being of residents and worsening problems like wealth inequality, homelessness, and sprawl now and for future generations. The costs, particularly for coastal cities and islands, are even more extreme and immediate as the danger of flooding from rising sea levels increases.

The solution is to move to a carbonless and sustainable economy that is powered by on-site renewable energy and distributed by a smart power grid. However, the argument is made that fossil fuels are cheap and the convergence to renewable energy would be costly. However, it fails to consider the direct as well as the indirect, residual, and health costs known as externalities and lifecycle economics of using fossil fuels for energy generation. In many nations, including the US, the real cost of energy has never been reflected in the market because of the national and state governments land use policies and financial support for oil, gas, coal, and nuclear power. This has ranged from land grants and changes in environmental laws to actual subsidies, tax breaks, and financial grants that constituted the economic core of the Second Industrial Revolution that has now moved past a Third Industrial Revolution (Rifkin, 2011) into the Green Industrial Revolution (Clark and Cooke, 2014).

Consider the *Forbes* magazine article in April 2010 that, according to its 2009 Report to the Security Exchange Commission, Exxon Mobil Corporation (the largest grossing company in the world at the time) paid no US taxes, while reporting a record profit of $45.2 billion (*Forbes*, 2010). Exxon Mobil minimizes the taxes it pays by using 20 wholly owned subsidiaries in the Bahamas, Bermuda, and the Cayman Islands to legally shelter cash from its operations in Angola, Azerbaijan, and Abu Dhabi. Exxon Mobil did pay $17 billion in taxes to other countries, but paid nothing to the US (*Forbes*, 2010). While Exxon does not contribute anything to the US federal government, it spends millions on lobbying for the continuation of oil and gas subsidies, which are estimated at $4 billion for the industry. According to the Center for Responsive Politics, in 2009 alone, Exxon Mobil spent over $27 million on political lobbying (Kocieniewski, 2010).

In 2011, when gasoline prices spiked in the US and an angry public prodded Congress, Senate Democrats tried to repeal federal tax breaks and subsidies for five major oil companies. Following several days of hearings during which the Senate criticized "Big Oil" executives, the bill failed 52–48 when three Democrats from oil states voted against it. The bill would have stripped tax breaks from five major oil companies—Exxon Mobil, ConocoPhillips, BP America, Shell Oil, and Chevron. Ending their tax breaks would have saved the US taxpayer about $21 billion over 10 years, according to Congress's Joint Economic Committee (Kocieniewski, 2011).

In 2011, Dr Paul Epstein of the Center for Health and the Global Environment at Harvard Medical School tried to quantify the actual costs of coal in the US (Reuters, 2011). His comprehensive review of total economically quantifiable costs found that it costs the US economy annually some $345.3 billion, or close to an additional 17.8 cents per kWh. These externalities, which are other costs beyond supply and demand economics, are not borne by miners or utilities, but by the American taxpayer in multiple ways. Coal companies benefit from:

- *Tax breaks.* Just like the oil and gas companies, coal companies receive preferential treatment from the IRS. The Treasury Department estimates that eliminating just three tax preferences for coal would save $2.6 billion through 2022.

- *Public land loopholes.* According to the Energy Information Administration, 43.2 percent of the US coal comes from public lands. The coal industry benefits from various loopholes that make obtaining leases easier and cheaper.

- *Subsidized railroads.* Coal is the most important commodity transported on railroads. US railroads get loans and loan guarantees from the governmental agencies and have received numerous tax incentives for investments. This relationship is important when considering coal export, which have surged to all-time highs. A large portion of the exports going to Asia includes subsidies from the US taxpayer.

True Costs of Oil and Natural Gas

The externalities and actual costs of oil and natural gas are a subject that governments and the international oil and gas industry would rather not talk about. While the oil and gas industries are a powerful wealth builder, there are enormous long-term risks and impacts (Clark, 2012). Some costs are obvious. Oil spills and environmental disasters like the 1989 Exxon Valdez in Alaska and 2010 Deepwater Horizon oil spill in the Gulf of Mexico are never fully calculated when economists reckon the costs of fossil fuel-based energy generation. The actual costs of the destruction to the environment as well as the damage to the atmosphere are rarely recovered in full from the offending companies.

But the true costs of oil goes far beyond the obvious damage from spills, writes Richard Steiner, professor and conservation biologist in "The True Cost of Our Oil Addiction." (Steiner, 2014.) The additional or external costs, Steiner points out, are far less visible than oil spills. Little attention is spent on these considered costs that include ecological habitat degradation from exploration, production, and pipelines; health costs from breathing air polluted with fossil fuel emissions as well as the loss of lives from people killed in accidents and storms; urban sprawl and traffic congestion around all major cities of the world; and now the seemingly endless wars fought to secure oil supplies, like Iraq and Sudan, costing thousands of lives and trillions of dollars. Steiner notes that climate change from carbon emissions is incurring enormous present and future costs. Costs for storm damage, drought, wild fires, lost agricultural productivity, infrastructure damage, climate refugees, disease, forest decline, marine ecosystem collapse, species extinctions, and lost ecosystem services need to be considered.

Yet the world continues to use more oil, hitting a historic high of 91 million barrels a day in 2013. To date, the world has pumped and burned about 1 trillion barrels of oil (Steiner, 2014). Oil and natural gas-producing nations are heavily influenced by oil interests to limit regulation, lower taxation, and to favor production and demand for oil over development of low-carbon alternatives. The International Monetary Fund reports that worldwide governments provide annual subsidies of some $1.9 trillion, including $480 billion per year in direct subsidies to the oil industry. Such subsidies artificially depress prices and encourage overconsumption; detract from government spending on health care, education, and social services; and slow the adoption of alternative energy.

Milton Copulos, former president of the US National Defense Council Foundation, testified before the Senate Foreign Relations Committee in 2007 on the true cost of oil. He estimated that the true cost for a gallon of gas made from imported oil to the US consumer was $26 dollars. This amounts to about $15,400 per year for the average car in the US, or 70 percent of the median household income given 2.3 cars per household (Copulos, 2007).

These costs are ignored and taxpayers are paying for some through income taxes, but deferring most to future generations. With the use of cheap oil over the past century, human population has quadrupled and resource consumption has increased many times more. Without access to fossil fuels, humanity would almost certainly have evolved on a more sustainable path. But by not accounting for its true cost, oil has allowed us to dig ourselves deeper into an unsustainable hole. The environmental debt we are accruing is far larger and more consequential than our national financial debt, Steiner points out (Steiner, 2014).

The US government has estimated that the full social cost of carbon is about $50–$100 per ton of CO_2. Global emissions now exceed 39 billion tons per year, which amounts to $2–$4 trillion annually. Including these very real costs, sustainable alternatives become competitive. Much of the problem is that in the US and other developed industrialized countries, economics is sold to the public as based on the linear market of supply and demand, which it is not. The governments strongly fund and support these fossil fuel sources of energy.

Free-market Economics Has Failed

In light of the October 2008 world financial meltdown, it seems silly to think that the supply-side, deregulated, free-market economics, so passionately espoused by President Ronald Reagan and Prime Minister Margaret Thatcher in the 1980s, would work for a twenty-first century world threatened by irreversible environmental degradation (Clark and Fast, 2008). Even the bastion of supply-side economics, *The Economist*, ran a special issue in July 2009 showing a melting Bible on its font cover that discussed the failures of modern economic theory (*The Economist*, 2009).

In short, there is no linear economy based on neoclassical economics from Adam Smith: The debate in economics continues since it concerns the assumption that economics is a science. *The Economist* called it a "field of study" which now has become a debate within economics as to its being a science or not (Clark and Fast, 2008). Even the linear economics that exists in theory does not work today. What is needed is a new economic model (Clark, 2012) that today is being described as a "circular economy" (Circular Economy, 2014), which the EU has embraced as a possible international economic model but already has impacts in companies and even the US (Clark, 2015). Economics is not, and never was, a balance of supply and demand. Instead economics needs to be the financial mechanism that ties together different products due to their being monitored, reused, and recycled ranging from businesses in electronics to food products (Clark and Bonato, 2015).

The 2008 global economic implosion from trillions of dollars in credit swaps, hedge funds, sub-prime mortgages, and related marginal derivatives (which nearly pushed the world's financial structure into the abyss), underlined what happens when governments ignore their responsibility to govern. In the end, the Great Recession was the worst financial disaster since the 1930s, and a testament to the venal side of free-market capitalism—greed, stupidity, carelessness, and total disregard for risk management. New economic processes must be developed if the planet is going to survive climate change and its impact on the Earth and its inhabitants (Clark, 2012: 21–42).

To create a more sustainable planet and to maximize the benefits from the Green Industrial Revolution, the twenty-first century world must develop economies that fit its social and political structures. The First Industrial Revolution replaced an agrarian, draft animal-powered economy with one powered by steam engines and combustion machine-driven manufacturing, an evolution that was accelerated by colonial expansion. Then the Second Industrial Revolution created a fossil fuel-powered economy that extracted natural resources in an unregulated, free-market capitalist manner without regard to people, health, or environmental costs.

Globally, the economics of the Second Industrial Revolution resulted in a widely disproportionate amount of money in the hands of the industries involved with fossil fuels and related products, as well as the manufacturers who were able to prosper by using cheap energy. It was wealth built at a significant cost to the health of the general population, which had to live with polluted air and water, climate change, acid rain, and greenhouse gases that impacted health. The public, particularly in the US, has been forced historically to pay undeserved taxes to subsidize the oil, coal, and now the natural gas industry. All of which continue to be the wealthiest industries on Earth.

If the US developed a culture based on cheap fossil fuels, Europe and Asia offer a telling contrast (Clark and Cooke, 2011). In those regions of the world, consumers pay three to four times more than Americans pay for fossil fuels. This creates an economic barrier against overuse and provides an incentive to conserve fuel, seek other options, and use alternative energy to power buildings and transportation.

The world is becoming much more interdependent. What happens in one part of the world, be it weather, pollution, politics, or economics, impacts other regions. For example, the dramatic change in the Egyptian government in early 2010 has affected the rest of the Middle East and will result in global changes of oil and gas supplies. Further, the 2014 Russian incursion in Ukraine and the subsequent threats to reduce natural gas shipments to European and Asian nations were particularly unsettling. One lesson learned, however, has been for the EU and China to move more rapidly into renewable energy systems, which has caused the devaluation of the Russian currency in early 2015.

Social and environmental factors—sustainable communities, climate change mitigation, and environmental protection—are growing in importance and will soon demand far greater international cooperation and agreement.

Rampant economic growth and individual accumulation of wealth is being replaced by social and environmental values that benefit the larger community.

Countries, like the US, however, are severely hampered without a national energy policy. Without national consensus, nations struggle to address their basic infrastructures and there can be no action, no improvement, no resources, and certainly no response to environmental degradation. For example, the US's inability to develop a national energy policy that addresses climate change or renewable energy generation is often cited as a monumental failure of its free market and deregulation economic model. Energy and infrastructures, the argument goes, are extraordinarily important national issues. To address them for the greater good, nations like Germany, the Nordic countries, China, and Japan all have national plans, which are outlined and offered by the central government, to address these basic systems that interact with citizens and the environment.

The key is to have each of the major infrastructure components—energy, water, waste, telecommunications, and transportation—linked and integrated. That way, these components overlap and costs for construction, operations, and maintenance can be contained and reduced. If the basic infrastructure components can be constructed, operated, and maintained on the city level, and meet regional, state, and national goals such as carbon reduction, they take on a different perspective, format, and cost structure. While the US has no national energy policy, states such as California have created energy and environmental policies of their own. These days, America's leaders on energy policy are not in Washington, DC, but at the local and city levels.

Given the immense and increasing cost of global warming and extensive carbon emissions pollution, how are global cities going to pay for or much less recover from centuries of using the environment as a garbage can? Clearly, humanity cannot delay moving to a more sustainable existence, and this move must start with the global cities. The first and biggest step to sustainability is to replace carbon-based energy generation and its emissions with renewable energy, coupled with efficient storage and smart grid technologies that can maximize energy production and distribution.

While the US has not been able to develop funding mechanisms for sustainability, other parts of the world are coming to grips with the reality that they must if they want to preserve the planet's environment. The BRIC countries in particular are moving in this direction. Brazil and China are especially becoming both smart and green as exemplified by their policies, plans, and financing of non-fossil fuel vehicles (Harrop et al. 2014). Russia is showing some interest in moving in that direction, while India struggles with its growth and dependency upon fossil fuels and nuclear power.

China's Central Planning Model

The People's Republic of China (PRC) is showing global leadership as the world turns to a greener future (Clark et al., 2015). More than anything, China demonstrates how important a role the central government needs to play in planning, financing and then overseeing, directing, and supporting the economics of technologies and creation of employment. Nonetheless the actual implementation is at the regional and city levels where new communities and their infrastructures are being built. The market and capitalism have nothing to do with this remarkable sustainable growth. Instead it has more to do with the needs of the people to help improve their lives, work, and education as well as rest or retirement areas.

China's economic system is the prototype of civic capitalism (Clark and Li, 2012). Since the 1949 revolution, the Chinese have moved toward economic development through a series of Five-Year Plans. The central party plays the leading role in establishing the foundations and principles of Chinese policy by mapping strategies for economic development, setting growth targets, and launching reforms. Long-term planning and financing are the key characteristics of centralized social economies, as one overall plan normally contains detailed economic development guidelines for the various regions and communities. Each plan comes with considerable funding to implement the plans based on measureable results.

Now China's 13th Five-Year Plan addresses rising inequality and sustainable development. It establishes priorities for more equitable wealth distribution, increased domestic consumption, and improved social infrastructure and social safety nets. The plan represents China's efforts to rebalance its economy, shifting emphasis from investment toward consumption and from urban and coastal growth toward rural and inland development. The plan also continues to advocate objectives set out in the 11th Five-Year Plan to enhance environmental protection, which called for a 10 percent reduction in the total discharge of major pollutants in five years.

The current plan focuses the nation on reducing its carbon footprint, as well as addressing climate change and global warming. Not only is it well financed, with the equivalent of $1 trillion US dollars, but it also sets in motion the possibility that China will be able to surpass western nations in addressing environmental concerns, creating sustainable communities, and reaping the benefits of a new green economy. A case can be made that China has shifted to renewable energy as its key area for political stability, both within the country and for its international policies and programs (Clark and Li, 2012).

The significant change in China has been its economic growth, which required more secure supplies of fuel and energy. The question is, can China maintain economic growth in an environmentally sound and responsible manner according to its pledges and commitments? It is apparent that China has identified energy security as one of its vital national interests (Clark and Li, 2012). It has instituted plans and funds to provide for more energy from renewable sources, instead of relying on its own limited fossil fuels or importing fuel from other nations. Analysts predict that China will meet or exceed its 2020 renewable energy targets. China's rise today is in large part because of its rapid emergence as a major force in the energy geopolitics (Sun et al., 2013). With the new government leadership from Premier Li the rapid economic growth over the last three decades will slow down and focus on environmental and renewable energy strategies with economic and international support including a new collaboration with the US in November 2014.

The Feed-in-Tariff (FiT) Model

Europeans adjusted their economies early to move into the Green Industrial Revolution. The Nordic countries and the Germans realized that the move away from fossil fuels to renewable energy distribution would require more than the neoclassical free-market linear economics could deliver (Gipe, 2010–2014). While Denmark and other Nordic countries shifted to protect their environment through renewable energy power by national consensus, the Germans developed the innovative FiT financial process (Morris, 2014).

Germany's FiT was part of their 2000 Energy Renewable Sources Act, formally called the Act of Granting Priority to Renewable Energy Sources. This remarkable national policy, called Energiewende, was designed to create a total energy transformation by encouraging the adoption of renewable energy sources and to help accelerate the move toward grid parity, making renewable energy for the same price as existing power from the grid. Under a FiT, those generating eligible renewable energy, either homeowners or businesses, would be paid a premium price for the renewable electricity that they produced. Different tariff rates were set for different renewable energy technologies, based on the development costs for each resource. By creating variable cost-based pricing, the Germans were able to support the use of new energy technologies such as wind power, biomass, hydropower, geothermal power, and solar PV, as well as to support the development of new technologies.

The most significant result of the German FiT was that it stabilized the renewable energy market and reduced the financial risk for energy investment. By guaranteeing investors compensatory payments, the FiT program created a secure model for investment. The program covered up to 20 years per plant, with the exception of hydroelectricity installations, which required longer amortization periods. The law also offered a means for altering the compensation rates for future installations, if necessary. The executive summary of the original document says:

> This remuneration system does not mean the abandonment of market principles, but only creates the security needed for investment under present market conditions. There is adequate provision to safeguard the future existence of all the plants already in operation. The new act has abolished the regulation contained in the Electricity Feed Act, which limits the uptake at preferential rates of electricity from renewable energy sources to a maximum share of five percent of overall output.

> Instead, we have introduced a nation-wide cost-sharing arrangement. The act should put an end to any fears of excessive financial burdens. The contribution resulting from the new cost-sharing mechanism amounts to a mere 0.1 Pf per kWh. Even if, as we hope, there were powerful growth in renewable energy sources, this would still only rise to 0.2 Pf per kWh in a few years time. That, indeed, is a small price to pay for the development of this key sector (Federal Ministry for the Environment, 2000).

The designers of this policy had exceptional foresight and intuition. The result of the 2000 Energy Renewable Sources Act was the creation of Germany's renewable energy industry. The policy triggered the creation of wind turbine farms and launched the German solar miracle. Despite having an Alaskanlatitude climate, Germany was—for almost a decade—the number one world leader in solar power manufacturing and installation. Growth in solar and related businesses also meant jobs and expanded markets as well as reduction in greenhouse gas and carbon emissions. The German FiT sets in place a Green Industrial Revolution economic model which other nations can follow. By 2005, 10 percent of Germany's electricity came from renewable sources, when only five years earlier that portion was less than 1 percent. Germany estimated that the total level of subsidy was about 3 percent of household electricity costs. The FiT rates are lowered each year to encourage more efficient production of renewable energy. By 2008, the annual reductions were 1.5 percent for electricity from wind, 5 percent for electricity from PV, and 1 percent for electricity from biomass. In 2010 Germany met their goal of 12.5 percent of electricity consumption, thus avoiding the creation of more than 52 million tons of CO_2. They are on track to reach their goal of 20 percent renewable power generation by 2020 (Gipe, 2010–2014). By 2050, they hope to power almost entirely by renewable sources.

The German economic model is being adopted by other nations that are developing renewable energy sources. According to the Renewables Global Status Report: 2009 Update, FiT policies have been enacted in 63 jurisdictions around the world, including Australia, Austria, Belgium, Brazil, Canada, China, Cyprus, the Czech Republic, Denmark, Estonia, France, Germany, Greece, Hungary, Iran, Republic of Ireland, Israel, Italy, the Republic of Korea, Lithuania, Luxembourg, the Netherlands, Portugal, South Africa, Spain, Sweden, Switzerland, Thailand, and Turkey (Renewable Energy Policy Network for the 21st Century, 2009). Despite the lack of a national policy in the US, several states are considering some form of a FiT, and the concept seems to be gaining momentum in China, India, and Mongolia.

Recently, the European Commission and the International Energy Agency, among other groups, had completed various analyses of the FiT policy. Their conclusion was that well-adapted FiT policies are the most efficient and effective support systems for promoting renewable electricity.

The German FiT model continues to be highly successful, and certainly moves the country beyond conventional economic theory. The idea that ratepayers can get funds from higher rates to purchase renewable energy systems, which then generate power for their own buildings with the excess sold back to the central power company, is not part of the neoclassic economic model. This is because neoclassic economic theory does not consider infrastructure calculations (Borden and Stonington, 2014).

In 2012, Joke Schauvllege, Finland's Minister for Environment, Nature and Culture and President of the EU Environmental Council, supported the "circular economy" framework, which went beyond the linear economics of neoclassical economics. In 1976, Walter Stahel, architect and economist, and co-author Genevieve Reday published "The Potential for Substituting Manpower for Energy," a research report to the European Commission. Their vision was an economy in loops as the circular economy and they considered its impact on job creation, economic competitiveness, resource savings, and waste prevention. Stahel worked at developing a "closed loop" approach to production processes and created the Product Life Institute in Geneva more than 25 years ago with four goals:

1.   product-life extension;

2.   long-life goods;

3.   reconditioning activities; and

4.   waste prevention.

The circular was improved upon and applied to some businesses by William McDonough and other US architects and designers with the concept of C2C. The application was used with beverage products like Coca Cola and applied to farming as well as other products. But high-tech also has cases of circular economics that allows products, their parts, and even software to be reused in a variety of industries. For example, in the US, Dell (see below) and HP have been using the circular economy (although not calling it that) for over a decade (Clark, 2015).

When the circular economy framework is applied to major products in transportation, buildings, and the use of renewable energy sources, the significance becomes more dramatic. The McArthur Report noted how the Ford Model U concept car could have compostable body parts such as "polyester upholstery fabric, a 'technical nutrient' made from chemicals chosen for their human and environmental health qualities, and capable of perpetual recycling." The Ford Model U concept car would have a top that is made from a "potential 'biological nutrient,' a corn-based biopolymer from Cargill Dow that can be composted after use." Additionally, the Ford Model U concept car would use hydrogen for its "engine" which given technologies from Ford and all the other major carmakers would be a fuel cell, again a reusable product.

What is important in the circular economy is that it needs to go further, as the McArthur Report noted in a "New Report: Toward the Circular Economy, Volume 2" (Ellen McArthur Foundation, 2014: 10) with two goals for February 2015:

- report identifies global economic opportunity worth USD 700 billion for the consumer goods sector;

- new business alliance, Circular Economy 100, set to launch in February with blue-chip companies.

As of the summer of 2015, these goals have not been achieved. In the EU Commission, the circular economy has now come under "re-examination"—not to stop it from moving ahead but as a more cautionary and politically sensitive agenda. The future will be seen soon as the Ford Model U car and now others from every carmaker come into the EU and other nations, but especially California in the US where cars are a critical form of transportation. There the hydrogen fuel cell cars are coming in 2016 as Bloomberg (2015) research notes.

The key factor is that the circular economy applies to technologies and other goods, services and products. The next economics (Clark, 2012) is clearly this economic framework which helps define and implement the Green Industrial Revolution. Above all, circular economics must be scientific if it is to be successful and represent how economics is not linear but circular in that it composes a variety of resources as well as channels for the future use of waste materials. Consider the state of California in the US as a region that can explore and create smart green cities. The issue is always how are these communities paid for—and by whom?

The Nation State of California

Despite the basic intransigence of the US, California has moved forward toward a greener future. The state was the first to launch a major energy-efficiency effort after two decades of being the most conservation-oriented. The initial program has evolved into a multibillion-dollar effort that is now in its third cycle. As part of the state's commitment, California's goal is to generate 33 percent of its electricity from renewable sources by 2020. In 2010, to move this effort forward, California's Public Utility Commission approved a modified version of FiT called a Renewable Auction Mechanism (RAM). The program was much like the early version of the FiT from Germany in the early 1990s.

In short, it was too small and needed to be expanded. While not a classic FiT, the program is intended to drive small to mid-sized renewable energy development. It required investor-owned utilities to purchase electricity from solar and other renewable energy systems of 1.5 MW to 20 MW.

While it is too early to tell if the RAM program will be successful, the renewable energy industry—particularly the solar industry—is optimistic. Several industry leaders say that RAM improves the traditional FiT programs because it allows for market-based pricing, while still providing a long-term, stable power agreement for project developers. Other endorsers think that because it sets an outcome instead of fixing a price, it will help eliminate speculators and keep high-quality developers involved.

Paying to Mitigate Climate Change

Climate change is the greatest challenge of modern times, yet, addressing it offers the potential for tremendous economic growth. Mitigating climate change will unleash a wave of new economic development, generating jobs and revitalizing local, regional, and national economies. However, some nations may have the technologies to jumpstart a green energy economy; developing the mechanism to curb climate-changing emissions is another matter.

Climate change stems from a single fact, human beings treat the atmosphere as a free dumping ground. No one has to pay to pollute the shared air. The result has been increasing concentrations of climate-warming gases, a blanket of carbon that is keeping heat in the Earth's atmosphere.

To transition to a green economy, a price must be put on climate-changing emissions (Nijaki, 2012). Mechanisms have to be developed that make the polluters pay, while guaranteeing that emission reduction goals are met. Further, a workable system has to be built on three principles: efficiency, effectiveness, and fairness. Increasing taxes in areas or for issues that society targets have resulted in a more aware public and subsequent behavior changes. The best example is the tobacco smoking taxes in California that reduced smoking, kept second-hand smoke under control and labeled California as a smoke-free state. Now, around the world, other countries are following that same lead with taxes on tobacco products as well as prohibitions on smokers in public places.

In theory, it seems straightforward. However, in practice, and in the political world, it is extremely hard to develop international agreements, especially on economic issues. While several schemes are being discussed, the one being promoted the most by Wall Street is cap and trade. Proponents say that a fair cap-and-trade system must be comprehensive, operate upstream, and allow energy to be auctioned, limit the use of offsets, and have built-in protections for consumers.

So what does cap and trade mean? A "cap" is a set limit on the quantity of greenhouse gases a nation's economy can emit each year. Over time, the legal limit goes down—the cap gets tighter—until the country hits its targets and achieves a clean energy economy. The cap serves as a guarantee that a nation reaches its goal. Countries would use energy-efficiency standards for vehicles and appliances, smart-growth plans, building codes, transit investments, tax credits for renewable energy, public investment in energy research and development, and utility regulatory reforms to ensure that the goals are met.

"Trade" refers to a legal market system that allows companies to swap (buy and sell) the ability to emit greenhouse gases among themselves, thus creating a market for pollution permits or allowances. The point of a trading system is to place a price on pollution that is dispersed through the economy, motivating businesses and consumers to find ways to reduce greenhouse gases (Dole, 2012). By turning the permission to pollute into a commodity that can be bought and sold, everyone up and down the economic ladder gets new opportunities to make and save money. Trade leverages the flexible power of the marketplace—the mobilized ingenuity of millions of diverse, dispersed, innovative, self-interested people—to help meet climate goals.

Several cap-and-trade climate policy schemes have already been created; one was being partially deployed in Europe. California has started a cap-and-trade system with Toronto, Canada. Critics claim that the trading system has not changed behavior. The evidence that it has been successful is questionable. For example, in 2006 only 15 percent of the companies covered by the Emissions Trading Scheme (ETS) were taking the future cost of carbon into account. Point Carbon and other researchers found that a year later about 65 percent of companies in the trading system were making their future investment decisions based on having a carbon price, which is the system's goal (Price of Climate Change, 2012). These statistics and numbers are from Wall Street trading companies, all of whom who provide questionable "evidence" in numbers as well as scientific facts.

The problem is that this cap-and-trade economic model does not change anything—it allows companies to continue to produce carbon emissions, rather than stopping them. Companies that agree to eliminate their carbon emissions at some point in the future can continue to pollute, postponing their commitment for decades.

A better approach to reducing carbon and stop greenhouse gases are programs like those proposed by the Carbon Tax Center. This New York non-profit organization argues for a carbon tax. They regard a carbon tax as superior to a carbon cap-and-trade system, for five fundamental reasons:

1. Carbon taxes will lend predictability to energy prices, whereas cap-and-trade systems exacerbate the price volatility that historically has discouraged investments in less carbon-intensive electricity generation, carbon-reducing energy efficiency, and carbon-replacing renewable energy.

2. Carbon taxes can be implemented much sooner than complex cap-and-trade systems. Because of the urgency of the climate crisis, we do not have the luxury of waiting while the myriad details of a cap-and-trade system are resolved through lengthy negotiations.

3. Carbon taxes are transparent and easily understandable, making them more likely to elicit the necessary public support than an opaque and difficult to understand cap-and-trade system.

4. Carbon taxes can be implemented with far less opportunity for manipulation by special interests, while a cap-and-trade system's complexity opens it to exploitation by special interests and perverse incentives that can undermine public confidence and undercut its effectiveness.

5. Carbon tax revenues can be rebated to the public through dividends or tax-shifting, while the costs of cap-and-trade systems are likely to become a hidden tax as dollars flow to market participants, lawyers, and consultants (Carbon Tax, 2011).

Arguments and criticism abound over cap-and-trade systems, economics, and their efficacy. Critics point to the big American companies that are creating trading desks to facilitate "carbon credit" trading (Dole, 2012). The market could be worth trillions of dollars as emissions reduction becomes an international priority, and critics say that this much money will lead to corruption and cheating. Most of these arguments are being pushed aside as Europe and

California adopt cap-and-trade systems. Momentum is building for some way to put a price on pollution. Most likely, an internationally regulated carbon credit trading process will be implemented.

The question is how can climate change be stopped and who will pay for it? Most people argue that the voters and politicians need to decide; however, few governments are focused on environmental issues and societal concerns. The Green Industrial Revolution economics combines civic capitalism with standard economic mechanisms that use externalities. The new economics is neither the form of economics used in the carbon-intensive era, nor a totally government-controlled form of finance, regulations, and markets. In short, there is a need for a new economics, which includes externalities, lifecycle analyses, and effective monetary policies that will reduce carbon emissions and pollution and can be measured and controlled.

After the Climate Conference in September 2014 and the UN Intergovernmental Panel on Climate Change (IPCC) Conference in December 2014, the World Bank has taken economic action against climate change. They have been joined by 73 nations and over 1,000 companies with a few examples:

- China launched pilot emissions trading systems in seven cities and provinces in 2013 and 2014 and plans to create a national system in 2016. It has a goal to reduce emissions intensity by 40–45 percent compared with 2005 levels by 2020.

- Mexico has a national climate change law and a target to reduce greenhouse gas emissions 30 percent below a business-as-usual scenario by 2020. It started a carbon tax in 2014, has a voluntary carbon market, and is exploring innovative approaches to carbon pricing as a member of the Partnership for Market Readiness, a group of 31 countries helping to develop the carbon pricing systems of the future.

- Chile approved a carbon tax to start in 2018 that will target large thermal power plants and charge US$5 per metric ton of CO_2 emitted. The country has a target of cutting greenhouse gas emissions to 20 percent below 2007 levels by 2020.

- British Columbia created a revenue-neutral carbon tax that directs the C$30 per ton of CO_2-equivalent charged back to taxpayers through lowered personal and business income taxes and into targeted support for low-income individuals and families.

- South Korea launched its ETS in January 2015, covering 525 businesses from 23 sectors that account for about two-thirds of the country's national emissions. South Korea has a target to reduce emissions 30 percent below business as usual by 2020.

- The EU pioneered international carbon emissions trading in 2005. The system, currently the world's largest, covers more than 11,000 power stations and industrial plants, along with airlines, in the 28 EU countries plus three other countries. It has struggled with low prices and excess allowances and has been developing plans for reform.

- California and Quebec both launched emissions trading systems in 2013 and formally linked their systems in 2014, allowing the two systems to trade each other's carbon allowances. Linking markets expands the pool of participants and can broaden emission reduction opportunities and reduce volatility (World Bank, 2015).

Green Jobs: A Key Benefit

The Great Recession of 2008 is fading away amid signs of slow growth. Most of the world's financial structures have stabilized. Regionally, Asia appears the strongest, though China's growth slowed in 2010–2011, but has now picked back up. In 2015, China's GDP was lower as world demand for its goods and services has declined. Europe is trying to maintain a unified structure while balancing the wealth and stability of the more prosperous nations such as Germany and the Nordic countries, against the near bankrupt smaller nations such as Greece and Spain, and the potentially 25 new central and eastern EU member nations that are rapidly trying to catch up.

The Chinese at the turn of the twenty-first century, leapfrogged the rest of the world into green economics, technology, and job creation (Clark and Isherwood, 2007; 2010). In fact, China still leads the world with economic and career innovations. The leapfrog however was mostly focused on buildings and development of land areas, especially in its cities. The concerns for overbuilding, environment, and infrastructures were lagging behind. Analyzing China's phenomenal economic growth, it is clear how much of that growth can be attributed to the development of green industries, which has now been a key area under the new leadership in China's central government (Clark et al., 2015). Not only is China creating massive systems to generate renewable energy for its own use, but also it has quickly become the world leader in exporting these technologies. If anyone around the world wants to buy solar panels, or wind turbines, China is able to provide the best pricing and quality.

What the Chinese clearly understand, and other nations do not, is that once committed to the Green Industrial Revolution, a nation creates new economic development and business opportunities that lead directly to job generation, new career paths, and the revitalization of local economies in a sustainable way (Clark et al., 2015). This results in further research and development supporting the Green Industrial Revolution. Because of the extraordinary interconnectedness of a modern nation's economy, once local economies start to come back, they revitalize the service industries and corporations that support them—the markets, retail stores, and small businesses, as well as schools, city governments, and all the other public agencies dependent on tax revenues.

So what exactly is a "green" job? The label is much like the "knowledge-based" job label, a generic term that describes an industry or service rather than a specific type of activity. Raquel Pinderhughes, a professor of urban studies at San Francisco State University, defines green jobs as a generic term for people doing any kind of work, whether mental or manual, that in some way relates to improvements in environmental quality (Pinderhughes, 2006).

The UN Environment Programme's "2008 Green Jobs Report: Towards Decent Work in a Sustainable Low-Carbon World," added a subset called "green-collar" jobs. The UN tried for a more rigorous definition of green jobs, saying, "This includes jobs that help to protect ecosystems and biodiversity; reduce energy, materials, and water consumption through high efficiency strategies; de-carbonize the economy; and minimize or altogether avoid generation of all forms of waste and pollution" (UN EP, 2008). Subsequent reports provide data and details for green jobs.

It is difficult to put a number on how many jobs would be created if the US economy focused on climate change mitigation. Economists struggle when they analyze green job data and try to interpret the results. Robert Pollin, co-director of the Political Economy Research Institute at the University of Massachusetts, wrote a report in 2008 that calculated the US could generate 2 million new jobs over two years with a $100 billion investment in a green recovery (Pollin et al., 2008).

While economists can provide calculations that show on average how many jobs would be created, based on the number of dollars invested, they cannot measure the corollary impact or predict the number of related jobs that will be created. However, one precedent for green job creation is Germany's FiT. Germany attributes strong growth in the renewable energy sector to blunting the recession. According to Deputy Environment Minister, Astrid Klug, there were 250,000 jobs in Germany's renewable energies sector and an overall total of 1.8 million in environmental protection. The number of jobs in the renewable energy sector will triple by 2020, and hit 900,000 by 2030.

Another example is California's world-leading energy-efficiency program, which has put thousands of people back to work retrofitting commercial buildings. At the same time, the program is driving the lighting industry to develop extraordinary new products like cost-effective LED lights, dimmable ballasts, and smart networks that make peak-load management simple and effective. This new generation of lighting products is transforming the market and along the way creating a $1 billion industry for California. If LED and dimmable ballast changeovers were made a national priority, it would be a multibillion-dollar industry in the US alone.

Private Investment is Needed

Reducing carbon emissions and mitigating climate change will require a radical transformation. It will require a rapid increase in renewable energy; sharp falls in fossil fuel use, or massive deployment of carbon capture schemes, mitigation of industrial emissions, and eliminating deforestation.

Given the growing awareness of the costs associated with global warming, business-as-usual is not an option. The World Resources Institute estimates that to make this transition to the carbonless economy will require massive amounts of capital by the world's nations, about $300 billion annually by 2020, growing to $500 billion by 2030. This compares against the $100 billion annual funding committed by industrialized nations in the UN Framework Convention on Climate Change's (FCCC) Green Climate Fund (Climate Finance, 2012).

Yet, this is modest considering the alternative of doing nothing. "The longer we delay the higher will be the cost," said the UN IPCC chairman Rajendra Pachauri in April 2014 (UN IPCC, 2014). The cost is relatively modest now, he added, but only if the world acts quickly to reverse the buildup of heat-trapping gases in the atmosphere. His comments came as the IPCC released a report projecting that shifting the world's energy system from fossil fuels to zero-or low-carbon renewable sources would reduce consumption growth by a minimal 0.06 percentage points per year.

The UN IPCC said large changes in investment would be required. Fossil fuel investments in the power sector would drop by about $30 billion annually while investments in low-carbon sources would grow by $147 billion. Meanwhile, annual investments in energy efficiency in transport, building, and industry sectors would grow by $336 billion (UN IPCC, 2014).

Given the large amounts of money needed to address climate change, public funds will be a small portion. Unlocking private sector investment will be the key, Rachel Kyte, World Bank Vice-President for Sustainable Development, told the September 2012's UN General Assembly meeting. Private investors—equity firms, venture capitalists, pension funds, insurance companies, and sovereign wealth funds—currently control several trillions of dollars' worth of assets that can provide climate-smart infrastructure development. They must be more actively engaged, to identify the risks that they perceive in green investment and to develop new policy and financing mechanisms that make for attractive returns (Climate Finance, 2012).

In 2011, $257 billion was invested in renewable energy, according to the Global Trends in Renewable Energy Investment 2012 report. This UN Environment Program backed study has tracked the finance flowing into green energy since 2004. China attracted more money than any other country with $52.2 billion. Even though 2011 represented the largest investment in renewable energy, renewables still only represented about 6 percent of the world's energy requirements. So there's a huge upside potential for investment capital (Renewable Finance, 2012).

Google Invests Over $1 Billion in Green Tech

Google, Inc., perhaps the most successful and innovative technology company in the world, is a gigantic user of energy. The company has farms of computer servers spread throughout the world to power its search engine function and related information technology. In Q1 2014, the company said it spent $2.25 billion on data center and infrastructure spending, a major cost for the company. Google is also one of the world's most aggressive major companies when it comes to advancing a clean energy agenda, investing over $1 billion in renewable energy (Google Inc., 2012).

The company says that they are getting about 34 percent of their power with renewable energy, either directly from solar panels or indirectly by buying green power near their data centers. Google says that renewable energy projects must make good business sense, and have potential for long-term significant impact. In 2007, they installed the largest corporate solar panel installation of its kind—a 1.9 MW system that provides 30 percent of the peak load for its massive Mountain View headquarters.

While Google says that it is striving to power its operation completely with renewable energy, it is also investing heavily in large-scale projects (Jensen and Schoenberg, 2010). As of April 2014, they had put money into 15 solar and wind power generation projects, totaling over 2 GW of power. While some of the projects are in South Africa and Germany, most are in the US like the huge Ivanpah project in the southwest desert. The project is one of the largest solar thermal farms in the world, and uses 347,000 sun-facing mirrors to help produce 392 MW. Ivanpah's green energy powers more than 140,000 California homes.

Google says they are investing in green energy because doing so makes it more accessible. Rick Needham, Google's director of energy and sustainability, says that their efforts in procuring and investing in green energy all make business sense. "They make sense for us as a company to do," he said. "We rely on power for our business" (Google Inc., 2012).

Venture Business Research (VB/Research), a leading data provider, tracks the international financial activity in the green industry. They reported in the second quarter of 2010 that venture capital and private equity investment in clean technology and renewable energy exceeded $5 billion worldwide, despite a 30 percent decline in early stage venture capital activity. They also reported that a record number of merger and acquisition deals valued at over $14.5 billion were transacted during that period.

The bulk of the money being invested in green and clean technology is going to China, according to accounting firm Ernst and Young, which does a quarterly assessment of the most attractive countries for renewable energy investment. In their September 2010 report, they noted that China was now the world's biggest energy consumer, as well as the world's most attractive country for renewable energy investment. China has been encouraging investment in its clean energy companies as part of its goal of generating 15 percent of its electricity from renewable sources by 2020 (Energy Assets, 2012).

Ernst and Young also compared regulations, access to capital, land availability, planning barriers, subsidies, and access to the power grid. The report ranked investments in onshore and offshore wind, solar, biomass, and geothermal energy projects. After China, the next most attractive countries for renewable energy investment were the US, Germany, India, and Italy. Ernst and Young noted that government support in China gives it a huge advantage over other countries in pursuing clean energy projects. In the second half of 2009, China almost doubled consumer subsidies for generating renewable power, bringing the amount to $545 million. The fact that China has both Five-Year Plans and substantial financial support for the green technology sector gives it a huge advantage. Even more significantly, the Chinese require government participation or partial ownership of many of the new firms, in keeping with their tradition of government control of infrastructures.

There are huge amounts of money at stake, as the world moves toward a carbonless economy. The big losers will be the entrenched fossil fuel and centralized utility industries. Both industries have business plans dependent on increasing demand and neither is capable of adjusting to a declining demand environment. Without a doubt, some of the world's most powerful and wealthiest industries have much to lose. It is no wonder that the fossil fuel interests are going to such lengths to argue against climate change science and putting enormous pressure on governments and geopolitics to maintain their privileged status.

References

Bloomberg, 2015. The Future of Energy, Summit. Bloomberg New Energy Finance.

Borden, Eric and Joel Stonington, 2014. *"Germany's Energiewende,"* Global *Sustainable Communities Design Handbook: Green Design, Engineering, Health, Technologies, Education, Economics, Contracts, Policy, Law and Entrepreneurship*. Elsevier Press, New York.

Carbon Tax Center, 2011. http://www.carbontax.org/.

Circular Economy, 2014. *Towards the Circular Economy: Economic and Business Rationale for an Accelerated Transition*. Ellen Macarthur Foundation, Cowes, UK.

Clark, Woodrow W. II, 2012. Editor and Author, *The Next Economics*. Springer Press, New York.

Clark, Woodrow W. II, 2015. The Circular Economy in the Green Industrial Revolution Framework, Keynote Speech, ReMedia 10th Anniversary, Milan, Italy, 10 June 2015.

Clark, Woodrow W. II and Danilo Bonato, 2015. Circular Economy and Raw Material Strategy: A Critical Challenge for Europe and the Rest of the World. Huffington Post, (Italian and English) March 31,   http://www.huffingtonpost.it/woodrow-w-clark-ii/economia-circolare-approccio-strategico- materi-prima-sfida-europa-mondo_b_6975304.html?1427799160.

Clark, Woodrow W. II and Grant Cooke, 2011. *Global Energy Innovation: Why America Must Lead*. Preager Press, New York.

Clark, Woodrow W. II and Grant Cooke, 2014. *The Green Industrial Revolution*. Elsevier Press, New York.

Clark, Woodrow W. II, Grant Cooke, Aujun Jerry Jin and Ching-Fuh Lin, 2015. *China's Green Industrial Revolution* (in Mandarin). China Electric Power Press, Beijing.

Clark. Woodrow W. II and Michael Fast, 2008. *Qualitative Economics: Toward A Science of Economics*. Coxmoor Press, Chipping Norton, UK.

Clark, Woodrow W. II and William Isherwood, 2007. Energy Infrastructure for Inner Mongolia Autonomous Region: five nation comparative case studies, Asian Development Bank, Manila, PI and PRC National Government, Beijing, PRC.

Clark, Woodrow W. II and William Isherwood, 2010. "Inner Mongolia Must 'leapfrog' the Energy Mistakes of the Western Developed Nations", *Utilities Policy Journal*, vol.18, pp. 29–45.

Clark, Woodrow W. II and Xing Li, 2012. *Social Capitalism: China's Economic Rise. The Next Economics*, Springer Press, New York, pp. 143–164.

Climate Finance, 2012. www.insights.wri.org/news/2012/10/wri-launches-project-climate-finance-and-private-sector.

Copulos, Milton R., 2007. Testimony of Copulos, President, National Defense Council Foundation, before the Senate Foreign Relations Committee, March 30, 2006; IMF, 2008; EIA; CleanTech Group, 2007; US Census Bureau; Experian Automotive; Paper presented to Congressional staff members by NDCF President Milt Copulos, January 8, http://www.sapphireenergy.com/learn-more/59518-the-true-cost-of-oil-.

DARA, 2012. http://daraint.org/climate-vulnerability-monitor/climate-vulnerability-monitor-2012/.

Dole, Malcolm Jr., 2012. "Market Solutions for Climate Change," Woodrow W. Clark II, Editor and Author, *The Next Economics: Global Cases in Energy, Environment, and Climate Change*. Springer Press, New York, pp. 43–70.

Ellen McArthur Foundation, 2014. New Report: Toward the Circular Economy, http://www.ellenmacarthurfoundation.org/assets/downloads/publications/Towards-the-circular-economy-volume-3.pdf.

Federal Ministry for the Environment (GR ME), 2000. Nature Conservation and Nuclear Safety, Germany.

Forbes, 2010. http://www.forbes.com/2010/04/01/ge-exxon-walmart-business-washington-corporate-taxes.html.

Gipe, Paul, 2010–2014. Feed-in-Tariff Monthly Reports, http://www.wind-works.org/FeedLaws/RenewableTariffs.qpw.

Google Inc., 2012. http://www.cnbc.com/id/101417698.

Harrop, Peter, Franco Gonzalez and Raghu Das, 2014. Global Sale of Hybrid and Pure Electric Cars Will Rise to over $185 billion in 2024. IDEC Tech Report, http://www.idtechex.com/research/reports/future-technology-for-hybrid-and-pure-electric-cars-2015–2025–000393.

Jensen, Thomas and David Schoenberg, 2010. "Google's Clean Energy 2030 Plan: Why it Matters," Woodrow W. Clark II. Editor and Author, *Sustainable Communities*. Springer Press, New York, pp. 125–134.

Kocieniewski, David, 2010. As Oil Industry Fights a Tax, It Reaps Subsidies. July 3, http://www.nytimes.com/2010/07/04/business/04bptax.html.

Morris, Craig, 2014. Chapter #7, "Energiewende—Germany's Community-driven Since the 1970s," *Global Sustainable Communities Design Handbook: Green Design, Engineering, Health, Technologies, Education, Economics, Contracts, Policy, Law and Entrepreneurship*. Elsevier Press, New York.

NASA, October 2015: http://climate.nasa.gov/evidence/

Nijaki, Laurie Kaye, 2012. "The Green Economy as Sustainable Economic Development Strategy," Woodrow W. Clark II, Editor and Author, *The Next Economics: Global Cases in Energy, Environment, and Climate Change*. Springer Press, New York, pp. 251–286.

Pinderhughes, Raquel, 2006. Study of Green Jobs: Small Businesses, http://www.sfsu.edu/~news/2008/spring/15.html.

Pollin, Robert, Heidi Garrett-Peltier, James Heintz, and Helen Scharber, 2008. Green Recovery: A Program to Create Good Jobs and Start Building a Low-Carbon Economy, University of Massachusetts: Center for American Progress and Political Economy Research Institute, September.

Price of Climate Change, 2012. http://www.huffingtonpost.com/thomas-kerr/paying-price-climate-change_b_2206791.html.

Renewable Energy Policy Network for the 21st Century, 2009.

Renewable Finance, 2012. http://www.cnn.com/2012/06/12/world/renewables-finance-unep/.

Reuters, 2011. Coal's Hidden Costs Top $345 Billion in US Study. Boston, February 16, http://www.reuters.com/article/2011/02/16/usa-coal-study-idUSN1628366220110216.

Rifkin, Jeremy, 2011. *The Third Industrial Revolution: How Lateral Power is Transforming Energy, the Economy, and the World*. Palgrave MacMillan. New York.

Steiner, Richard, 2014. The True Cost of Our Oil Addiction. Huffington Post, January 15, http://www.huffingtonpost.com/richard-steiner/true-cost-of-our-oil-addiction_b_4591323.html.

Stern, Nicholas, 2006. What is the Economics of Climate Change? *World Economics*, vol.7, n 2.

Sun, Xiaolei, Jianping Li, Yongfeng Wang and Woodrow W. Clark, 2013. China's Sovereign Wealth Fund Investments in Overseas Energy: The Energy Security Perspective, *Energy Policy*, vol. 65, pp. 654–661.

The Economist, 2009. Collapse of Modern Economic Theory. Cover page and special section. July 16.

Energy Assets, 2012. http://www.ey.com/Publication/vwLUAssets/Renewable_energy_country_attractiveness_indices_-_Issue_27/$FILE/EY_RECAI_issue_27.pdf.

UN Environment Programme (UN EP), 2008. Green Jobs Report: Towards Decent Work in a Sustainable Low-Carbon World, http://www.unep.org/documents.multilingual/default.asp?documentid=545&articleid=5929&l=en.

UN Intergovernmental Panel on Climate Change (IPCC), 2014. Fourth Report 2007 and WGH AR5, Phase 1 Report Launch.

World Bank, 2015. Report, March 18, http://www.worldbank.org/en/news/feature/2015/03/18/5-ways-reduce-drivers-climate-change.

Chapter 9

Smart Ecocities—New Ideas For Urban Living

Since ancient times, human beings have worked to solve problems with urban resource scarcity, energy use, environmental sustainability, and quality of life. Though always crucial, these problems increase exponentially as the world's population grows. As the planet heads toward the mid twenty-first century with an estimated 10 billion inhabitants, humanity is bumping up against finite limits of available natural resources. The planet is experiencing severe climate change along with social destabilization, while entire ecosystems are being threatened. Since the vast majority of humanity—the predications are for over 80 percent— lives in, or will live in an urban environment, it is becoming clear that cities, towns and villages must be restructured for greater sustainability and a reduced carbon footprint.

During the late 1800s, a movement developed in Britain focused on reducing the misery of the growing worker class. As the great mercantile colossuses of the First Industrial Revolution rose, more and more workers were becoming trapped in the grinding poverty of unsanitary and overcrowded slums of industrial centers. Several ideas were put forward to reduce this dilemma, and the one most fully conceived came from Ebenezer Howard in *Garden Cities of To-morrow* (Howard, 18981902). Howard envisioned a garden city that would balance the social and economic benefits of cities with the healthful effects of living in the countryside. A cleaner environment, efficient city sanitation services, and sufficiently spacious housing were the main strategies Howard described to reduce the harmful health effects of the gigantic industrial Meccas.

Howard had a holistic view of a new type of city development. He thought that by integrating rural settlements and industrial urbanization through upfront planning, it eliminated the contradictions among social groups, and improved economic development and environmental quality. His ideas remain radical even today because they require the high-speed creation of completely new large-scale developments and new self-governing societies.

Howard thought of new towns and cities of about 30,000 residents. They would be built in series with a radial layout plan so that residents lived close to self-sufficient industries, community services, and agriculture. Thus the cities would not exceed their resources and their growth potential was limited by a "green belt" of non-developed areas on the outskirts. Remarkably for nineteenth-century England, Howard suggested that to prevent the accumulation of speculative investment capital and the social discord resulting from conflicts of interest between landlords and tenants, each city was to be collectively owned by its occupants.

Physically, the garden city was to be laid out in a wheel-and-spoke pattern of sectors that would expand over time as small towns and villages grew around a larger central city. Economic growth would rely on each occupant becoming an artisan entrepreneur, producing the highest-quality goods for primary use in the community, with potential for export sales. Perhaps most important to Howard's vision was a strong interest in equity to reduce class conflicts and create sustainable community economic growth. Although garden cities would be newly built on purchased property, they were to be publicly owned by occupant collectives, and, after the original capital investment was paid off, rents paid by businesses and residents were to be reinvested in municipal works rather than going to investors (Orlando, 2013).

No garden city was ever built completely true to Howard's concepts, but several attempts were made, including Letchworth and Welwyn in England. Reduced in scale and components, they did not completely measure up to the ideal. However, many of his ideas lived on with widespread support. These include his focus on human health as a reason to pursue high environmental quality, and restricting outward sprawl development with green belts. He also advocated the close proximity of local jobs for residents, and the means to enhance social equity among all citizens.

Several of Howard's ideas were brought back to life in the mid-1970s, when a group of city planners, activists, and theorists came together in Berkeley, California with the idea of reconstructing cities to be in balance with nature. Founded by Richard Register, the group became Urban Ecology, the first US group focused on elements of sustainability for communities. The term "ecocity" came from Register's 1987 book, *Ecocity Berkeley: Building Cities for a Healthy Future* (Register, 1987). The group planted trees along Berkeley's main streets, built solar greenhouses, and worked within the legal system to pass environmentally friendly policies and encourage public transportation.

Eventually, they defined the term "ecocity" as an ecologically healthy city (Ecocity Builders, 2015). An ecocity, they said, is built on the principles of living within the means of the environment. The ultimate goal is to eliminate carbon waste, to produce energy through renewable sources, and to integrate the environment into the city. Ecocities intend to stimulate economic growth, reduce poverty, and to be organized with higher population densities to achieve higher efficiency, and improve health.

The definition of ecocity, they continued, is conditional upon a healthy relationship of the city's parts and functions, similar to the relationship of organs in a living organism. City design, planning, building, and operations are integrated and in relation to the surrounding environment. Natural resources are used to reverse the negative impacts of climate change, species extinction, and the destruction of the biosphere.

According to Register, the ecocity model provides a practical vision for a sustainable and restorative human presence on this planet and suggests a path toward its achievement through the rebuilding of cities, towns and villages in balance with living systems (Ecocity Builders, 2015).

Over the years, the ecocity movement has grown to include representatives from all over the world. In 2002, the Fifth International Ecocity Conference was held in Shenzhen, China. Out of the conference came a greater definition of what the ecocity movement was about. It was called Guidelines for Ecocity Development, which is a whole systems approach integrating administration, ecologically efficient industry, people's needs and aspirations, harmonious culture, and landscapes where nature, agriculture, and the environment are functionally integrated.

Ecocity development requires:

1.   Ecological security—clean air, and safe, reliable water supplies, food, healthy housing and workplaces, municipal services, and protection against disasters for all people.

2.   Ecological sanitation—efficient, cost-effective eco-engineering for treating and recycling human waste, gray water, and all wastes.

3.   Ecological industrial metabolism—resource conservation and environmental protection through industrial transition,

emphasizing materials reuse, lifecycle production, renewable energy, efficient transportation, and meeting human needs.

4.   Ecological infrastructure integrity—arranging built structures, open spaces such as parks and plazas, connectors such as streets and bridges, and natural features such as waterways and ridgelines, to maximize accessibility of the city for all citizens while conserving energy and resources and alleviating such problems as automobile accidents, air pollution, hydrological deterioration, heat island effects, and global warming.

5.   Ecological awareness—help people understand their place in nature, cultural identity, responsibility for the environment, and help them change their consumption behavior and enhance their ability to contribute to maintaining high-quality urban ecosystems.

The ecocity concept has grown into a diverse, international, and fast evolving phenomenon especially since the turn into the twenty-first century with the rise of nations like China, Russia, Brazil, and India. Since 2005, there has been a proliferation of new initiatives, which suggests that the ecocity phenomenon has gained momentum and become part of mainstream policy-making.

While there are no set criteria or standards for an ecocity, several have been suggested, encompassing the economic, social, and environmental qualities an ecocity should satisfy. The ideal ecocity has been described as a city that has the following characteristics, many of which are similar to Howard's "garden city" ideas.

The basic overview for an ecocity:

1.   operates on a self-contained economy, with local resources;

2.   is carbon neutral and uses renewable energy generation;

3.   has a well-planned city layout and public transportation system that makes the priority methods of transportation as follows possible: walking first, then cycling, and then public transportation;

4.   conserves resources—maximizing efficiency of water and energy resources, constructing a waste management system that can recycle waste and reuse it, creating a zero-waste system;

5.   restores environmentally damaged urban areas;

6.   ensures decent and affordable housing for all socio-economic and ethnic groups and improves jobs opportunities for disadvantaged groups, such as women, minorities, and the disabled;

7.   supports local agriculture and produce;

8.   promotes voluntary simplicity in lifestyle choices, decreasing material consumption, and increasing awareness of environmental and sustainability issues.

In addition to these initial characteristics, the city design must be able to grow and evolve as the population grows and the needs of the population change. This is especially important when taking into consideration infrastructure designs, such as water systems, power lines, and so on. These must be built in such a way that they are easy to modernize, in contrast to placing them underground, which makes them highly inaccessible.

Over the years, the ecocity movement has identified several cities, which have adopted initiatives and policies consistent with the ecocity concept. Ecocities also have to be smart. There are a number of ways to define and explain what smart ecocities (or green) are but some examples will help.

This example shows how wind turbines can provide renewable energy close to shore for a port city and surrounding areas. The city is smart as the systems *are* integrated with electric cars and buses and buildings that use Wi-Fi and mobile systems.

Above all, a smart city has sensors and monitoring systems. Everything from waste and energy resources can be monitored and measured in real time, including the use of cameras and meters for traffic flow within and around the city. The result is every section of the city has interlinked systems such that also connect people with government services like police, fire, and first aid.

The management of a smart ecocity depends on real time grid measurements that are set as standards and then implemented, monitored, and evaluated daily. The results can be changes and improvements in how people travel, live, work, eat, and have fun. In the end will be new ways to travel including in the air instead of on the ground.

Consider some actual cases of smart green cities:

Curitiba, Brazil

Curitiba started to address sustainable urban development in 1966 with a master plan that outlined future integration between urban development, transportation, and public health. Curitiba's plan has been realized with stretches of urban development surrounded by green space and low-density residential areas. The city was designed for the mobility of people, not the mobility of cars. The city's bus system is highly developed, with high-capacity buses and dedicated lanes, and reaches about 90 percent of the population. This bus system is used by 45 percent of the population, which has caused private automobile use to drop to 22 percent. To prevent congestion, the central areas of the city have been closed to cars. These road closures have led to dynamic economic growth for local shops and the development of community space for pedestrian.

Public health and education gains have also been substantial. Curitiba maintains the lowest air pollution rates in Brazil and over 300,000 trees in the city helps reduce natural flooding. Curitiba has also dedicated resources to environmental education in primary school, which has translated into environmentally conscious citizens. Over 70 percent of city residents participate in recycling programs which fuels the city's progressive waste processing system.

In 2010, Curitiba received the Globe Sustainable City Award (Suzuki, 2010).

Auroville, India

Auroville, or City of Dawn, is an experimental township in Tami Nadu, India. It was founded in 1968 as a project of the Sri Aurobindo a group led by Mirra Alfassa, "The Mother." The group believed that "man is a transitional being" and that this township would contribute to the progress of humanity with the intention of realizing human unity, and is now home to about 2,000 individuals from over 45 nations around the world. Its focus is its vibrant community culture and its expertise in renewable energy systems, habitat restoration, ecology skills, mindfulness practices, and holistic education.

Freiburg, Germany

A city of about 220,000 people, Freiburg is located at the edge of the Black Forest, near the borders of France and Switzerland. An early home to the Germany's Green Movement, Freiburg's sustainable policies go back to the 1970s, triggered by a community protest against a nuclear power plant.

As a sustainable city, Freiburg has won various national and international environmental awards. It is committed to its target areas of energy, transportation, and to its three pillars for sustainable development: energy saving, new technology, and renewable energy sources. The city's success at protesting the nuclear power plant led to the creation of a campaign for sustainable energy solutions. A network of environmentalists, research organizations, and businesses was established, helping to push the sustainable city agenda forward.

Freiburg is now considered to be a solar capital. Along with high solar electricity rates, Freiburg hosts such innovations as the world's first football stadium with its own solar power plant and the world's first self-sustaining solar energy building. In terms of both ecology and economy, Freiburg has been extremely successful in the fields of research and marketing of renewable energy. The Freiburg science network and solar industry embraces many research institutions, like the Fraunhofer Institute for Solar Energy Systems ISE, Europe's largest solar research institute.

In addition to solar initiatives, Freiburg made improvements to the transportation systems. Heavily bombed during the Second World War, the city center was rebuilt following the old street plan and architectural style. As the roads were rebuilt, they were widened enough for a tram track, not more car lanes. In 1969 Freiburg devised its first integrated traffic management plan and cycle path network. The plan, which aims to improve mobility while reducing traffic and benefitting the environment, is updated every 10 years. It prioritizes traffic avoidance and gives preference to environment-friendly modes of transport such as walking, cycling, and public transit. Traffic avoidance is achieved in conjunction with urban planning that makes Freiburg a city of "short distances"—a compact city with strong neighborhood centers where people's needs are within walking distance. The city has over 500 km of bicycle paths and more than 5,000 bicycle parking spaces as well as car-free centers, 30 kph zones, a region wide bus service, and tram lines.

Freiburg has resolved to cut CO_2 emissions. In 1966, the city resolved to lower CO_2 by 25 percent by 2010. Although they did not reach their initial goal by 2010, they extended their goals. By 2030, they resolved to cut CO_2 emissions by 40 percent and be climate-neutral by 2050 (Gregory, 2011).

Freiburg also focused initiatives on waste management. Paper products are 80 percent recycled materials. Financial incentive programs, like discounts for collective waste disposal and people who compost, are used to increase waste avoidance. Since 2005, Freiburg's non-recyclable waste has been incinerated and the heat energy released is converted to supply electricity to almost 25,000 households in the city.

Freiburg is a green city with 43 percent of borough area in woodland. In 2001, the Freiburg Woodland Convention was adopted and, since 2009, the city officially supported the Freiburg Convention on the Protection of Ancient Woodland. For over 20 years Freiburg has worked to maintain their public parks with principles that work with nature: they no longer use pesticides, grass is mown less, and almost 50,000 trees line streets and parks.

Stockholm, Sweden

Stockholm is an environmentally focused city that is redeveloping sustainability through efficient urban planning and resource use. Stockholm has established six environmental goals, called Vision 2030, which act as the foundation of this initiative. These goals include development of efficient transportation, sustainable energy, land, and water use, waste treatment improvements, and safe building and product materials. Beyond Vision 2030, Stockholm is planning to be fossil fuel free by 2050.

Stockholm requires mandatory reuse of land before urban sprawl can continue. Run-down and abandoned industrial areas have been transformed into modern, efficient, and integrated residential and business communities. The Hammarby Sjostad district is the primary example, as this resurrected industrial area has become twice as energy efficient as the rest of the city after an environmentally focused redevelopment.

These gains are measured by the environmental load profile of the area, a lifecycle assessment tool developed by the City of Stockholm, the Royal Institute of Technology, and a consultancy firm. This unique measure allows for environmental performance analyses, on both the small and large scale, in terms of environmental costs and benefits. These comprehensive qualitatively defined measures have allowed Stockholm to quantify their environmental progress and could be applied as a decision-making tool in other cities or districts to aid their environmental efforts.

Stockholm has pursued green development and optimization of urban systems and achieved results. These efforts were recognized in 2010 by EU, which selected Stockholm the European Green Capital for "leading the way towards environmentally friendly urban living" (City of Stockholm, 2010).

Adelaide, Australia

Adelaide in South Australia is a city of 1.3 million people. In 2003, the city started an urban forest initiative to plant 3 million native trees and shrubs on 300 project sites across the metro area. The projects ranged from large habitat restoration to local biodiversity projects. Thousands of Adelaide citizens have participated in community planting days. Sites include parks, reserves, transport corridors, schools, watercourses, and coastline. Only trees native to the local area are planted to ensure genetic integrity. The project's aim is to beautify and cool the city and make it more livable; improve air and water quality and reduce Adelaide's greenhouse gas emissions by 600,000 tons of CO_2 a year. It is also about creating and conserving habitat for wildlife and preventing species loss.

Adelaide has an established plan with funding support to install technologies that allows it be both green and smart. The city launched an initiative to lead Australia in the take-up of solar power. In addition to Australia's first FiT to stimulate the purchase of solar panels for domestic roofs, the government committed millions of dollars to place arrays of solar panels on the roofs of public buildings such as the museum, art gallery, Parliament, Adelaide's airport, and 200 schools. Australia's biggest rooftop array is on the roof of Adelaide Showground's convention hall, which is now registered as its own on-site power station.

South Australia went from zero wind power in 2002 to wind power making up 26 percent of its electricity generation by October 2011. In five years to 2011 there was a 15 percent drop in GHG emissions, despite strong economic growth.

For Adelaide, the South Australian government also embraced a zero-waste recycling strategy, achieving a recycling rate of nearly 80 percent by 2011 with 4.3 million ton of materials diverted from landfill to recycling. On a per capita basis this was the best result in Australia, the equivalent of preventing more than a million tons of CO_2 entering the atmosphere. In the 1970s, container deposit legislation was introduced. Consumers are paid a 10-cent rebate on each bottle/can/container they return to recycling. In 2009 non-reusable plastic bags used in supermarket checkouts were banned, preventing 400 million plastic bags per year entering the litter stream. In 2010, Zero Waste SA was commended by a UN-Habitat Report entitled "Solid Waste Management in the World Cities" (Climate Group, 2012).

Cities throughout the world are moving toward a lighter carbon existence and adopting sustainability behaviors and ecocity values. While several examples have been given already, the following case studies will provide greater detail and a better understanding of how cities are becoming much smarter and much greener.

Remarkably, today the Danes swim in Copenhagen's harbor. Once the water in this busy port harbor was heavily polluted with sewage, algae, industrial waste, and oil spills from commercial harbor transport. Now it is crystal-clear and water quality is extremely high. Thousands of Danes and visitors enjoy some of the best natural swimming waters in Europe.

Copenhagen has outdoor swimming areas in the inner city. The city also has a number of beaches, including the long white sand of Amager Beach, which you can get to by bike or metro. North, there are the popular beaches of Bellevue Strand and Hellerup Strand, and the outdoor baths at Islands Brygge are also extremely popular in the summer and well known for their distinctive design.

For years, the discharge of wastewater from sewers and industrial companies had a major impact on the harbor's water quality. In 1995, overflow channels fed wastewater into Copenhagen harbor and the adjacent coastlines. Since then, the city has built rainwater reservoirs and reservoir conduits, which store wastewater until there is space again in the sewage system. This has resulted in the closing of 55 overflow channels. Today, wastewater is only discharged into the harbor during very heavy rainfall.

The city invested in the modernization of the sewage system and expanded the city's wastewater treatment plants, which remove nutrient salts and minimize discharge of heavy metals. This has revitalized the harbor and, in 2002, the first public bath opened in the area of Islands Brygge, making Copenhageners the only people in Europe able to bathe in their harbor without jeopardizing their health. Today, an online warning system monitors the harbor's water quality. If the quality is poor, the swimming facilities are immediately closed.

Copenhagen, a city of 541,989 residents, is one of the world's greenest and most environmentally friendly cities. Much of the impetus for this effort came when Denmark implemented its environmental law, which originated from much of the EU legislation. The nation's Ministry of the Environment is the main authority for environmental policy and drafting law, and includes three agencies:

- *The Environmental Protection Agency* (EPA) is the main environmental law. The EPA sets out the fundamental environmental protection objectives and the means to meet them. It is supplemented with guidelines and statutory orders drafted by the agency and issued by the Minister of the Environment. The agency also administers other laws including: Chemical Substances and Products Act, Soil Contamination Act, and the Environmental Liability Act.

- *The Danish Geodata Agency* ensures that geographical information about land and sea is collected, quality checked, and made accessible on the Internet. Information includes the location of roads, houses, lakes and streams, what the landscape looks like and where boundaries are located. This information is used with climate protection, the provision of mobile access to data, information services to citizens, and by the police and emergency services when carrying out their tasks.

- *The Danish Nature Agency* and its local entities ensure the overall protection of nature. It is also responsible for the Planning Act, the Act on Environmental Objectives, and several other acts regulating nature-related issues. Denmark has implemented the Industrial Emissions Directive (IED). Under the IED, all industrial production processes, agricultural production, and waste treatment activities are covered. About 800 enterprises and 1,200 animal husbandries are governed. The IED also allows the authorities to impose a requirement for the enterprises and animal husbandries to use the best available techniques. In addition, the IED can impose requirements on combustion plants, and investigate soil and groundwater pollution.

Copenhagen plans to become the world's first carbon neutral capital by 2025, and has a municipal strategic climate action plan with 50 initiatives. Each initiative meets the 2015 mid-term goal of a 20 percent CO_2 reduction. Other European cities are trying to achieve sustainable growth without underperforming on environmental and economic indicators. However, Copenhagen has developed highly successful sustainable solutions. Studies show that Copenhagen's growth in the green sector has increased by 55 percent over the course of five years.

Examples of sustainable city solutions include increased mobility through integrated transport and cycling solutions that has reduced congestion significantly and improved citizens' health. Cleaning the harbor has led to attractive urban areas with better quality of life, improved local business, created jobs, and generated revenue in the area. Landfill from waste has been reduced while heating 98 percent of the city through district heating.

These urban green solutions are already being implemented on a large scale and used by everyday people. These solutions have had significant effects on CO_2 emission and the city's livability.

One of the keys to Copenhagen's climate action plans and the city's subsequent success has been its approach to transportation, a critical infrastructure element. Every day 1.1 million km are bicycled in Copenhagen. It's not just the commute, Copenhageners cycle everywhere, from shopping trips and nights out to visits to friends. As a visitor to the city, it's easy to saddle up and cycle with the flow, thanks to the groundbreaking free city bikes, which have been offered since 1995.

The City is relatively small and attractions are concentrated in and around the center, making it easy to cycle around. People feel at ease, cycling around the city on the safe bike lanes, separated from the road traffic. About 40 percent of the city's residents cycle to and from work. Copenhagen also has a well-developed public transport system, which means less cars and more space to breath in the city center. A second ring of the underground metro system is being built and the city has buses, metro, and S-trains. The rings around cities exist in many other EU city areas. Copenhagen also has a central station for trains to other Danish cites as well as on a bridge to Sweden. The international airport services other Nordic nations as well as the EU and nations around the world. Infrastructures are key to smart green local cities as they connect them to other cities (Clark and Jenssen, 2001).

As one of the world's greenest cities, Copenhagen has numerous beautiful city parks such as the King's Garden in the grounds of Rosenborg Palace and

Frederiksberg Garden, and a short cycle ride north or south of the city will bring you out into nature. The atmospheric Deer Park at Klampenborg lies just north of the city and the way there is lined with beaches and stunning coastal views. To the south is the vast open expanse of Amager Common covered in walking and cycle routes.

The City also promotes organic food, and one in ten food purchases is organic, making it the leading organic city in the world. It has high targets for organic food production and consumption, and features a range of organic food in cafes, restaurants, and shops. Copenhagen has also been ranked as the world's leading city for clean technology, clean businesses and sustainable buildings (Visit Denmark, 2015).

Masdar City, United Arab Emirates

About 17 km southeast of Abu Dhabi, near the international airport, a remarkable futuristic city is slowly emerging from the barren desert. Designed by the British architectural firm Foster and Partners, Masdar City will be the latest of a small number of highly planned, specialized, research, and technology-intensive municipalities in the United Arab Emirates (UAE) that incorporate a living environment, similar to King Abdullah University of Science and Technology (KAUST) in Thuwal in Saudi Arabia or Tsukuba Science City in Japan.

Masdar City was proposed in 2006 and construction started in 2008, only to be delayed as funding was slowed by the 2008 global recession. However, progress is being made. Planners say that the first phase was be finished at the end of 2015, and overall completion for this $20 billion city is sometime between 2020 and 2025.

Built by Mubadala Development Company, with the majority of capital provided by the Abu Dhabi government, Masdar is an ambitious project planned to showcase sustainability and to "position Abu Dhabi as the hub of future energy," according to Sultan Ahmed Al Jaber, Masdar's CEO.

With a center core of 2 square miles, the city will house 50,000 residents and support 1,500 new green businesses, creating a center for commercial and manufacturing companies that support clean technology. The first of these tenants are the International Renewable Energy Agency and the Masdar Institute of Science and Technology, which moved into its campus in 2010.

Both of these early arrivals serve as magnets for industry. Project designers expect as many as 60,000 workers will commute to Masdar daily as employees of green companies. The city is an example of arcology, which is architecture that has design principles for densely populated habitats focused on minimizing ecological impact.

Planners say that the urban layout is an attempt to "combine classic Arab design with 21st century technology," allowing the city to serve as a "living lab for a greener, cleaner future and a bridge for Abu Dhabi as it prepares for a day when the oil runs out," which is projected to happen within a century. The goal is to build a development that is sustainable and energy efficient in the arid heat of the Middle East. The developers want to look at the science behind sustainable living, and what could be done in terms of spin-off technology.

Masdar is a mixed-use development designed to be friendly to pedestrians and cyclists. Buildings have terracotta walls decorated with arabesque patterns. From a distance, the city looks like a cube. The temperature in the streets is generally 15 to 20°C (59 to 68°F) cooler than the surrounding desert. The temperature difference is due to Masdar's unique construction. A 45-meter high wind tower modeled on traditional Arab designs sucks air from above and pushes a cooling breeze through Masdar's streets. The site is raised above the surrounding land to create a slight cooling effect. Buildings are clustered close together to create streets and walkways shielded from the sun.

The Foster's design team toured ancient Middle Eastern cities such as Cairo and Muscat to see how they kept cool. They found that ancient city planners coped with hot desert temperatures by creating cities with narrow, short streets that were usually no longer than 70 meters. The buildings at the end of the streets create just enough wind turbulence to push air upwards, creating a flushing effect that cools the street.

The initial design for Masdar banned automobiles. Travel would be by public mass transit and personal rapid transit systems, with existing road and railways connecting outside the city. The absence of motor vehicles coupled with Masdar's perimeter wall, which was designed to keep out the hot desert winds, allowed for narrow and shaded streets that helped funnel cooler breezes across the city. In October 2010 it was announced the personal rapid transit system would not expand beyond the pilot scheme because of the cost to segregate the system from pedestrian traffic. Under a revised design, Masdar will now use a mix of electric vehicles and other clean energy vehicles for mass transit inside the city. The majority of private vehicles will be restricted to parking lots along the city's perimeter. Abu Dhabi's existing light rail and metro line will connect Masdar City's center with the greater metropolitan area.

The Masdar Institute of Science and Technology is a graduate-level research university focused on alternative energy, environmental sustainability, and clean technology. The institute was Masdar City's first occupant. The design of the campus emphasizes flexibility, the use of traditional architectural elements, and modern materials to provide for natural lighting and cooling that minimize energy use.

By 2013, 336 students were enrolled at the Institute. Remarkable by Middle East standards, 35 percent were women and 42 percent were from the UAE. Eventually 800 students are expected to enroll. Admitted students from all countries are offered a full-tuition scholarships, monthly stipends, travel expenses, laptop computers, textbooks, and accommodations to facilitate their studies. Masdar students and faculty are engaged in over 300 joint projects with academia, private enterprise, and government agencies. Their research tends to focus on renewable energy, smart grids and smart buildings, energy policy and planning, water use, environmental engineering, and electronics.

The Masdar Institute has been behind the engineering plans of Masdar City and is at the center of research and development activities. The Institute's building, developed in cooperation with the Massachusetts Institute of Technology, uses 51 percent less electricity and 54 percent less potable water than traditional buildings in the UAE, and is fitted with a metering system that constantly observes power consumption.

The International Renewable Energy Agency, commonly known as IRENA, is headquartered in Masdar. The city was selected after a high-profile campaign by the UAE. In its bid, the UAE offered rent-free offices in Masdar City, 20 IRENA scholarships to the Masdar Institute of Science and Technology, and up to $350 million in loans for renewable energy projects in developing countries.

The giant construction company, Siemens, has built a regional headquarters in Masdar City. This building is the most energy efficient in all of Abu Dhabi. About 800 staff members work in this LEED Platinum building that makes use of sustainable and energy-efficient materials and building techniques. It was designed to use 45 percent less energy and 50 percent less water than typical office buildings. The 130,000 square-foot building is built around the idea of a "box within a box." The structure includes a highly insulated airtight inner façade that insulates from the sun and a lightweight aluminum shading system on the exterior. The plaza beneath the building is funnel-shaped. This shape works to suck prevailing winds underneath the building. Due to the Venturi effect, a breeze flows up to the roof of the building through atria in the building's structure, cooling public spaces without energy costs. These atria also allow daylight into the center of the building to reduce the need for artificial lighting, further reducing energy consumption. The buildings automation systems are all from Siemens.

The Incubator Building includes retail and office space to house start-ups, small-and-medium-sized enterprises, and regional offices for multinationals. The Incubator Building is designed to accommodate roughly 50 companies. Some of the most notable tenants include General Electric, Mitsubishi, Schneider Electric, and the Global Green Growth Institute. The Incubator Building also houses the General Electric Eco-imagination Center. The center offers training and exhibitions on energy and water efficiency.

The city is powered by a 22-hectare (54-acre) field of 87,777 solar panels with additional panels on-site. There are no light switches or water taps in the city; movement sensors control lighting and water to cut electricity and water consumption by 51 and 55 percent respectively. The original plan called for powering the entire city through on-site methods such as rooftop solar panels. However, because of the desert's blowing sand, it was more efficient to build a large solar field.

Blowing sand presents problems for solar panels, so Masdar has been working with companies to engineer surfaces with pores smaller than sand particles to stop them from sticking on the panels. Scientists at the Masdar Institute are also working on coatings that repel sand and bacteria for use on solar panels and in other applications. Besides PV, CSP plants are being explored.

In a desert, water management is absolutely critical. Approximately 80 percent of the water used is recycled and wastewater is reused as many times as possible, with this gray water being used for crop irrigation and other purposes. Exterior wood is used as accents for buildings, entrance gates and doors. The wood is palm wood, a sustainable hardwood-substitute developed by Pacific Green using plantation coconut palms that no longer bear fruit (PFSK, 2014).

Tianjin—China's Ecocity

China has more than 1.3 billion people and is growing more now that the one-child policy has ended. Urbanization is one of the most important factors in

China's extraordinary economic growth and rapid industrialization over the past three decades, providing essential labor and new consumers. However, while the cities grow with people moving from the western regions to the eastern seacoast areas they are not all young people. Older and retired people are staying in their urban homes and more new retirement centers are being formed. More than half the population now lives in cities, which at 690 million is more than double the entire US population. In 1980, less than 20 percent of the Chinese population lived in cities. By 2030, this number is predicted to rise to 75 percent (CS Monitor, 2010).

This rapid rise in urbanization brings serious challenges, including housing, infrastructure, water, food and jobs, as well as rising pollution and social inequality issues. The Chinese government is working on these by moving the big polluters out of the biggest cities inland into rural areas or other cities. The slum populations, called "urban villages" have dropped from 37 to 28 percent since 2000, and China is in the midst of a building frenzy (CS Monitor, 2010).

In the middle of what were saltpans, an industrial dumping ground, and a 2.6 square km large wastewater pond, the Chinese have built a green, smart, and sustainable city. Forty km from Tianjin city center and 150 km from Beijing, Tianjin Eco-City is the shipping and port for most of central and western China which is now emerging from what was a heavily polluted industrial waste area. The city is a cornerstone for the Tianjin Binhai New Area, part of the Bohai Bay region. This is one of the fastest-growing regions in China, which has been identified as the next growth engine in China, after the Pearl River delta and Yangtze River delta.

In a landmark example of cooperation, China and Singapore agreed in 2007 to jointly develop Sino-Singapore Tianjin Eco-City (SSTEC, 2013). The city's goal is to be, "A thriving city which is socially harmonious, environmentally-friendly and resource-efficient—a model for sustainable development." This vision is underpinned by the concepts of "Three Harmonies" and "Three Abilities" (SSTEC, 2013).

"Three Harmonies" refers to:

1.   People living in harmony with other people, that is, social harmony.

2.   People living in harmony with economic activities, that is, economic vibrancy.

3.   People living in harmony with the environment, that
        is, environmental sustainability.

"Three Abilities" refers to the Eco-City being:

1.   Practicable—the technologies adopted in the ecocity must be
        affordable and commercially viable.

2.   Replicable—the principles and models of the ecocity could be
        applied to other cities in China and even in other countries.

3.   Scalable—the principles and models could be adapted for another
        project or development of a different scale.

In deciding on the site, the Chinese government set two criteria for the location
of the ecocity. The city should be developed on non-arable land and it should be
located in an area facing water shortages. Four possible locations for the project
were identified—in Baotou (Inner Mongolia), Tangshan (Hebei province),
Tianjin municipality, and Urumqi (Xinjiang).

After a thorough study, the Tianjin site was selected due to the consideration
for development of the surrounding infrastructure, ease of accessibility, and
commercial viability. China's 12th and now 13th Five-Year Plans also started to
focus on western China for environmentally planned sustainable development.
One of their models is Denmark, which had faced similar problems of rapid
urban growth to Copenhagen from rural farmland areas.

With a completion date of 2020, Tianjin Eco-City is a remarkable and
fascinating project. It is the largest of its kind in the world, the first attempt
to build a smart green city from the ground up. With a total land area of 30
square km, about half the size of Manhattan, the city will house an eventual
population of 350,000 residents, in a low-carbon, green environment. By 2014,
the start-up area was completed and had about 12,000 residents. The rest of the
site will be transformed in phases.

The master plan was developed by teams of experts from Singapore and
China, and incorporates the best ideas from these two countries as well as other
international communities. The city will showcase new green technologies and
use benchmarks to ensure that development will be environmentally friendly,
resource-efficient and economically sustainable. The two governments have

established a high-level joint steering council to monitor and support the progress of the Tianjin Eco-City.

Planners say it will create a green community where nature is integrated into daily living and adopt affordable technologies and practices to create a strong foundation for sustainable development. To reduce its carbon footprint, the Tianjin Eco-City promotes public and non-motorized fossil fuel transportation. Hybrid cars and buses will form the bulk of the general transportation. Residential and commercial developments are planned to be located close to either the main city center or sub-center so that residents can live close to work and amenities so that they can walk and ride their bikes (Feng and Zhang, 2012).

Buildings in the Tianjin Eco-City are green and comply with the Green Building Evaluation Standards, which were set by Singapore and Chinese expert teams as unique benchmarks for eco-solutions that are integrated into buildings to enhance sustainability and commercial viability. The minimum green buildings standards include water-saving sanitary fittings, insulated walls and double-glazed windows, as well as a south-facing orientation to optimize passive heat. While standard in some countries, these elements are rare in China but recognized as the future needs in all its cities (BBC, 2012).

To enhance livability, parks and green spaces are planned around the city with reed beds to attract birdlife and help clean the water. Lanes and alleyways intersect the usual grid layout of big blocks, meaning neighborhoods and communities can develop. The area is walkable and cycleable, so that people do not feel socially excluded. Recreation facilities are planned within a short distance of anywhere in the city.

A green spine, called the "eco-valley" runs through the heart of the city with cycle routes and a tram. Cars are not banned, but residents are encouraged to use regular low-carbon transport or walk, rather than drive. The city is set to be a hub for green tech enterprise and creative industries. Over 1,000 companies have settled in, including an animation studio that is powered by its own energy station, incorporating solar PV walls as well as roof panels.

Water is one of the bigger challenges in this naturally arid area. Tap water is piped in and drinkable, which is a rarity in China, particularly in arid northern China. To supplement water supply, a desalination plant is planned. Water conservation is a major focus, as is water recycling for irrigation and toilet flushing. The lakes and water pipes are lined in clay or concrete to prevent saltwater incursion, and wastewater undergoes anaerobic bio-digestion. The methane emitted in the digestion process is used to produce energy. A collective system of waste management and recycling is integrated with waste disposal and incineration processes to regenerate energy as well as minimize the strain on landfills.

Tianjin has an advanced light rail transit system and varied eco-landscapes ranging from a sun-powered solarscape to a greenery-clad earthscape for its estimated 350,000 residents to enjoy. A vast, beautiful eco-valley, which serves as an ecological green spine, will run through the city linking major transit nodes, residential developments, and commercial centers. Natural habitats will be restored and rivers, water bodies, and wetlands will be cleaned up (SSTEC, 2013).

Chosen by both Singapore and Chinese governments to show that it is possible to clean up a polluted area and make it useful and livable, the site clean up took three years, and included the development of a new technology that removed the heavy metals from a central reservoir, which is being converted to a boating lake. GSHPs, which use the temperature difference in the ground to create energy, supplement solar panels and wind turbines.

Some buildings have sound- and motion-sensitive lights from the Dutch-owned Philips lighting company. The lights will default to off unless the switch hears or feels someone approach. Buildings have smart controls, which can automatically rise and lower window blinds to regulate light and temperature. Other innovations include a pneumatic municipal waste collection system, produced by the Swedish company Envac, which eliminates the need for refuse trucks, and General Motors will road-test the next-generation of its driverless EN-V (Electric Networked-Vehicle) cars.

Tianjin Eco-City planners say that being green is not a luxury, but an achievable necessity. The city will be a practical, replicable, scalable model for cities elsewhere in China and the world.

Progress in Other Nation States

Europe and Asia are moving the fastest into the Green Industrial Revolution and making great strides and monetary commitments in creating smart green cities that are environmental responsible as well as sustainable. The US, with a dysfunctional Congress, lack of census of a national energy policy, and a monumental conflict over fossil fuel production is lagging. There are, however, signs of an emerging green push, primarily from the nations two leading states, California and New York.

As with many social issues, California is the most advanced. The state is rapidly adopting energy efficiency and renewable energy. Climate change has hit the state hard with an agonizing four-year long drought and water conservation is becoming more important, even crucial, as the state's population continues to grow.

The City of Davis, California, just 10 miles west from Sacramento, the state's capital, is a town of about 65,000 residents wrapped around the University of California, Davis, which has 35,000 students. Together the university and city probably lead the US in sustainable concepts and practices. A campus office of environmental stewardship and sustainability leads the university as well as most of the town in developing policies and regulations that promote sustainability. Multiple university departments like agricultural intertwine concepts of sustainability, renewable energy, and energy-efficient design into the curriculum.

In 2011, the university opened West Village for student and faculty residents, set on 130 acres next to campus. Conceived as a new campus neighborhood, it was built by a partnership that included private builders and state agencies. At first the university saw it as "an environmentally responsible campus housing project." However, it evolved into the US's largest planned zero net energy (ZNE) community, with a goal to generate as much energy as it uses. It is also home to the university's Energy and Transportation Innovation Center.

University of California Davis, West Village—a Net Zero Energy Community

A number of public agencies including the US DOE, California Energy Commission and the California Public Utilities Commission helped with UC Davis's West Village. The project will be a roadmap around the technological, financial, and regulatory barriers that other communities face in striving to be ZNE.

Since the first shovel of dirt, West Village has steadily contributed to the practical knowledge of how to plan, construct, operate, and improve on a large-scale, sustainable, mixed-use neighborhood. The university says that already it is becoming a living laboratory for energy-efficiency and renewable energy research, providing not only valuable data but also a test bed for new technologies and business models related to ZNE.

Eventually, West Village will be home to 3,000 students and 500 campus staff and faculty families. When completed it will include 662 apartments and 343 single-family homes, plus commercial space, a recreation center, and village square. West Village will also have a community college center, and what is being called "University Hub" or "uHub."

Located in the commercial space surrounding the village square, the uHub is home to the campus' energy research centers. Promoting sustainable development, the uHub helps commercialize the universities' scientific innovations and patents. This innovation center is aimed at fostering collaboration among related research units, enhancing interaction with the private sector, and accelerating the transfer of university inventions to the marketplace. The uHub at West Village is now the physical home for these UC Davis research centers:

- Center for Water-Energy Efficiency

- China Center for Energy and Transportation

- Energy Efficiency Center

- Institute of Transportation Studies

- Plug-In Hybrid & Electric Vehicle Research Center

- Policy Institute for Energy, Environment and the Economy

- Program for International Energy Technologies

- Sustainable Transportation Energy Pathways Program

- Energy Institute

- Urban Land Use and Transportation Center

- Western Cooling Efficiency Center.

West Village apartments are built on aggressive energy-efficiency measures and use on-site renewable energy. The apartments feature two-bedrooms, walk-in closets, a full-size washing machine and dryer, stainless steel kitchen appliances, unlimited high-speed Internet service, and air conditioning.

PLANNING PRINCIPLES

During the planning stages, the planning team realized that West Village had to be accessible for UC Davis faculty, students, and staff, and that the ZNE goal had to be balanced against affordability. In response to these competing principles, the following principles were adopted:

- West Village would strive to use ZNE from the grid measured on an annual basis.

- ZNE needed to be achieved at no higher cost to the developer.

- ZNE needed to be achieved at no higher cost to the consumer.

- West Village would adopt deep energy-efficiency measures to reduce energy demand.

- ZNE would be achieved through multiple renewable resources developed on-site at a community scale.

- West Village would be used as a living laboratory for further energy-related topics.

As part of the planning process, they found that by adopting deep energy-efficiency measures, they could reduce West Village's energy consumption by 50 percent compared to the California Energy Efficiency Building Code. The energy-efficiency measures include solar-reflective roofing, radiant barrier roof sheathing, and extra insulation. Energy-efficient exterior lighting fixtures, indoor occupancy sensors, and day lighting techniques help the community use about 60 percent less energy than if standard lighting had been used. A web-based tool enables energy monitoring by unit. And a smartphone app lets residents turn off lamps and plugged-in electronics remotely.

The first phase is powered by a four-MWh solar array on building rooftops and on parking lot canopies. A bio-digester that converts campus table scraps, animal and plant waste into energy ties into the on-site power system.

The community is sustainable in ways beyond energy generation. It offers an extensive bike network and is served by natural gas-powered buses that will be replaced soon by all-electric and hydrogen-fueled transportation. Drought-friendly landscaping, water-saving toilets, recycled building materials, and paints low in volatile organic compounds (VOCs) are just some of the green features incorporated into the design.

West Village demonstrates a green revolution in California's residential construction, showing how construction practices can be sustainable. In a remarkable leap toward building Smart Green Cities, the state's public utilities commission has called for shifting all new residential construction to ZNE by 2020, and all new commercial construction by 2030.

OTHER FEATURES

A variety of other sustainable features include battery-buffered electric vehicle charging stations. This combines on-site solar energy, a high voltage lithium-ion battery pack with electric vehicle charging stations to store PV energy and charge vehicles, day or night, without adding loads to the grid. The system's primary source of energy is a PV tower located in the village square, but it is also grid-connected. This allows the system to be operated in a number of ways including controlling electric vehicle charging loads, reducing demand during peak hours and load shifting for vehicle charging and building loads. Soon hydrogen fuel cell cars and vehicles will be leased in the community with refueling stations, which electrolyze their hydrogen from renewable energy sources as well as wastewater.

To demonstrate advanced ZNE technologies, a 24-panel PV plus-thermal hybrid solar system has been installed at Solstice student housing. The system provides PV electricity to one apartment and supplies thermal energy to the building's central hot water system. The PV plus-thermal system was integrated with the central hot water system to interact with the high-efficiency air-to-water heat pump to investigate how to optimize both water heating systems for multi-family applications.

As a companion project, a single-family hybrid solar and demand-side management technologies have been installed at Aggie Village, an university faculty and staff community in downtown Davis. The technologies in the test home include a PV plus-thermal hybrid solar system, a lithium-ion second life battery, and a home EMS. The EMS monitors and controls plug loads, appliances, battery storage charging and discharging, and electric vehicle charging. Future plans include installing a ground source heat pump system for heating and cooling of the home. The goal of the project is to achieve ZNE in a retrofit environment and transfer learned lessons to future single-family homes in West Village and elsewhere.

Architectural Energy Corporation, in conjunction with PG&E and Sustainable Design + Behavior, is working closely with the West Village management team to create a monitoring and outreach program for the community. This program includes monitoring 140 apartment units to understand end-use loads and provide specific monthly intervention messages to those units, based on their observed consumption. The program has initiated a community-wide outreach program that provides messaging and information on energy consumption. This includes regular outreach activities, such as contests, that promote education and energy conservation within the community.

A unique, high-tech sustainable home, called the Honda Smart Home, was built to demonstrate an approach to meeting California's goal of requiring all new residential construction to be ZNE by 2020. Technologies featured in the home include: a solar power system, a smart-grid Honda Energy Management System, direct solar PV-to-vehicle charging, and high-efficiency HVAC (heating, ventilation and air conditioning) and lighting systems designed by UC Davis.

LESSONS LEARNED

West Village's planners defined ZNE as "zero net energy from the grid measured on an annual basis." More specifically, this means the community would produce enough energy on-site to offset its annual consumption. It is connected to the regional electrical grid and during peak hours it feeds electricity into the grid while at night it draws electricity from the grid.

A thorough energy consumption and evaluation of Phase 1 of West Village was completed in spring 2013. West Village was successful, achieving 87 percent of the initial ZNE goals years ahead of the fully completed community. However, several important issues arose in the evaluation that will help future phases.

Commissioning newly constructed systems is critical to achieving optimum performance. Commissioning is a process that ensures that new systems function at the levels that are intended. The central heat pump water heaters (HPWHs) were not properly commissioned and this contributed to more energy use them necessary.

The installed heat pump water heaters failed to perform according to specification, which caused the heating control system to automatically shift to less energy efficient, back-up resistance-type electrical heaters to meet the water heating demand of the residents. Unfortunately, the use of the backup water heating systems added substantial unanticipated power demand to the project. However, this problem was identified and resolved by proper commissioning.

From the commissioning process, West Village planners identified Lessons Learned:

- With new technologies and strategies, it is important to test and commission building systems to ensure that they are operating as designed.

- Provide alarms on the heat pump water heaters that can notify operations staff when a system goes down. The manufacturer is now installing alarms on heat pump water heater systems.

- Implement ongoing commissioning of the more complex building systems, such as the central heat pump water heaters and the mechanical systems at the recreation center.

The evaluation process also uncovered issues with the original energy modeling assumptions. The original assumptions were based on sources for standard multi-family projects. The planners found that there is a distinct difference between student housing and other multi-family projects. In a typical multi-family setting, there may be only one or two computers for the household, one gaming system, and other multi-user appliances. In contrast, a four-bedroom student housing apartment turns out to resemble four separate households, each with its own computer, smartphone, gaming system, television, and other separate appliances. West Village is developing educational programs to encourage students to conserve energy. Additional solar PV alternatives to offset overconsumption are being evaluated.

In the initial design modeling for the community, energy demand for the recreational swimming pools and common area lighting were not included. The modeling focused on the buildings that make up the student apartments. Strategies to reduce overall consumption and other ways to offset overconsumption due to incorrect modeling assumptions are being developed.

Individual apartment consumption for high energy-use apartments was up to three times higher than low energy-use apartments. This large difference suggests significant behavioral variability between occupants. High energy-use is primarily occupant related and most likely due to occupant-supplied plug loads. Since occupants do not directly pay for their utilities and do not have access to records of how much energy they consume, there is little awareness of their consumption habits or how their behavior affects energy use. An educational program to encourage students to conserve energy is being implemented.

The planners identified the following Lessons Learned:

- Develop and implement community engagement strategies to encourage energy conservation. Educate the community to the occupant's role in a ZNE building and better translate the ZNE vision. Strategies include incentives for apartments that deviate from the targets, contests, and awareness campaigns.

- Identify "high-use" apartments early in the school year and develop a strategy to discourage excessive (larger than estimated) energy consumption.

- Provide means for occupant feedback and control of consumption. Evaluate currently available products on the market to determine if there are cost-effective solutions to providing occupant feedback and control (UC Davis West Village Report 2012–2013).

References

BBC, 2012. China's eco-cities: Sustainable urban living in Tianjin, http://www.bbc.com/future/story/20120503-sustainable-cities-on-the-rise.

Christian Science Monitor (CS Monitor), 2010. http://www.csmonitor.com/World/Global-News/2010/0318/India-China-lead-in-lifting-people-out-of-urban-slums-UN-says.

City of Stockholm, 2010. http://international.stockholm.se/city-development/european-green-capital-2010/.

Clark, Woodrow W. II and J. Dan Jenssen, 2001. The Role of Government in Privatization: An Economic Model from Denmark. International Journal of Technology Management, Vol.21 N.5/6.

Climate Group, 2012. http://www.theclimategroup.org/what-we-do/news-and-blogs/hon-mike-rann-on-revitalizing-cities/.

Ecocity Builders, 2015. www.ecocitybuilders.org/why-ecocities/.

Feng, Yun and Mingzhuo Zhang, 2013. A Path to Future Urban Planning and Sustainable Development: A Case Study of Sino-Singapore Tianjin Eco-city. UCLA, Cross-disciplinary Scholars in Science and Technology Program.

Gregory, Regina, 2011. Freiburg, Green City. The EcoTipping Points Project, January, http://www.ecotippingpoints.org/our-stories/indepth/germany-freiburg-sustainability-transportation-energy-green-economy.html.

Howard, Ebenezer, 1902. *Garden Cities of To-morrow*. S. Sonnenschein & Co., Ltd., London.

Orlando, Ernest, 2013. An International Review of Eco-City Theory, Indicators, and Case Studies. Lawrence Berkeley National Laboratory, LBNL-6153E, https://china.lbl.gov/sites/all/files/lc_eco-cities.pdf.

PFSK, 2014. Futuristic Eco-City Masdar Keeps Rising, Right On (a New) Schedule http://www.psfk.com/2014/09/eco-friendly-city-masdar-rises-new-schedule.html.

Register, Richard, 1987. *Ecocity Berkeley: Building Cities for a Healthy Future*. North Atlantic Books, New York.

SSTEC, 2013. Eco-City Singapore, http://sstec.dashilan.cn/en/SinglePage.aspx?column_id=10304.

Suzuki, Hiroaki, Arish Dastur, Sebastian Moffatt, Nane Yabuki, and Hinako Maruyama, 2010. *Eco2 Cities: Ecological Cities as Economic Cities*. World Bank Publications, Washington, DC.

UC Davis West Village Energy Initiative Annual Report, 2012–2013. http://eec. ucdavis.edu/files/02–21–2014-wvei_annual_report_2012_131.pdf

Visit Denmark, 2015. http://www.visitdenmark.co.uk/en-gb/copenhagen/ transportation/green-and-laid-back-capital.

Chapter 10
Smart Green Cities

The Stone Age came to an end, not because we had a lack of stones, and
the oil age will come to an end not because we have a lack of oil.
Said Sheikh Ahmed-Zaki Yamani, the former Saudi oil minister and arguably the
world's foremost expert on the oil industry, in 2000. (Telegraph, 2014)

A decade and half later the world has come to the beginning of the end of oil age, and the domination of the world's geopolitics and economics by the fossil fuel interests for the past century. Correspondingly, the carbon coal and oil and then nuclear-powered centralized energy utility industry that was started by Thomas Edison in 1882 when he flipped the switch at the Pearl Street substation in Manhattan, has begun to decline.

Over the years, Big Oil and its related industries have wrecked havoc on our environmentally fragile planet and disrupted the way humans manage their lives. Today, the loss of a major section of the West Antarctic Ice Sheet and most of the North Pole from global warming caused by excessive carbon-generated heat appears unstoppable. The summers are hotter and longer, and diseases like dengue fever are spreading. Asthma is afflicting children around the world in record numbers. As the ocean levels rise, coastal cities and island nations become more and more threatened with flooding and severe storm damage.

It is not hard to conclude that if humans had not developed fossil fuels as a major source of energy, the planet would have industrialized slower, but been a much more sustainable environment for the future. Nor is it hard to conclude that human affairs would have turned out much differently if the oil industry had not gained so much political and economic power and come to dominate much of the world's activities.

Nowhere is the environmental decline from fossil fuels more pronounced, or its impacts more critical, than in the world's great cities. As more and more people transition from an agrarian to an urban lifestyle, the twenty-first century cities face increasing and unprecedented challenges. Climate change and global warming threaten with droughts in some cases, flooding and rising ocean levels in others, and declining air quality throughout the planet. Wealth inequality destabilizes the social fabric, leading to crime and homelessness. Sprawl, without planning or viable infrastructure, creates more pollution and destroys land better used for growing food.

To fight anthropogenic climate change, greenhouse gas emissions (GHG) have to be dramatically reduced. Cities and their leaders have a critical role to play, since, on a global scale, 70 percent of all greenhouse gas emissions are caused by cities. While they cover only 3 percent of the total land surface of the Earth, cities already hold more than 50 percent of the world's population, and the trend is increasing.

Emissions from big cities exceed those of some states. For example, the total annual CO_2 emissions of New York City (54 million tons) corresponds to those of Bangladesh. London's 40 million tons are almost equal to those of Ireland, and Berlin's CO_2 emissions (21.3m tons in 2010) equal those of Croatia, Jordan, or the Dominican Republic (Climate-Neutral Berlin 2050, 2015).

Cities need to reduce the emissions despoiling the planet's atmosphere. They must focus just as intently on the environment, as they do on creating jobs, wealth, and prosperity. Sustainable living and sustainable business development must be promoted, along with infrastructure needs of water, recycling, transportation, energy, telecommunications, waste removal, and reuse.

Cities and their leaders must come to understand that resources like energy and water are precious and must be limited and used wisely. New housing must be denser and constructed with the newest energy-efficient materials, smart windows, and energy-saving lighting. Water capture and reuse is critical in drier climates, and water pollution must be eliminated—if Copenhagen can make its harbor safe for swimming after centuries of pollution-laden shipping use, other cities can do the same. Above all else, a green sustainable city needs to replace carbon energy with renewable energy generation, store the energy on-site, and use a smart integrated grid system to balance and share energy.

The Green Industrial Revolution

Fortunately, circumstances and technologies are coming together to accelerate the change away from carbon-based energy generation. As pointed out in

Chapter 3, the Green Industrial Revolution (Clark and Cooke, 2014) is emerging in several parts of the world. Cities can now change and become greener and smarter, particularly as to the way energy is generated, supplied, used, and reused. The Green Industrial Revolution is a revolutionary global change from fossil fuels to renewable energy sources that has extraordinary potential and opportunities. It includes remarkable innovations in science, technologies, and energy. These advances are leading to sustainable, smart, and carbonless communities whose economies are powered by non-polluting technologies like solar, wind, and geothermal.

New advances in efficient batteries and hydrogen fuel cells will store energy for when it is needed most. Smart green grids will share electricity seamlessly. Water saving and purifying technologies are emerging to conserve precious resources, and startling new water technologies are being developed that squeeze potable water out of air. New scientific areas ranging from nanotechnology to social media are having a profound impact on business, human health, and the global economy.

This new era includes changes in technology, economics, businesses, manufacturing, jobs, and consumer lifestyles. The transition could be as complete as when the steam-driven First Industrial Revolution gave way to the fossil fuel-driven Second Industrial Revolution. In parts of Europe and Asia, this monumental shift is underway and spreading.

Toward a Greener and Smarter Future

The world is turning toward a greener future. New green and smart technologies are emerging rapidly from the laboratories, and global cities, especially the large megacities, can take advantage of many of these developments. In particular, and despite resistance from the fossil fuel interests, renewable energy generation is becoming cheaper, more efficient, and mainstream. Solar power is gaining so much momentum that PV competes directly in price now with oil, diesel, and natural gas in much of Asia (Evans-Pritchard, 2014). Even in the US, almost 30 percent of last year's added electricity capacity came from solar. According to the US Solar Energy Industries Association, more solar was installed in the US in the past 18 months than in the last 30 years.

Deutsche Bank, a leading German investment bank, reported in January 2014 that there were 19 regions around the world where unsubsidized PV solar power costs were competitive with other forms of generation. This equality of costs with fossil fuel and natural gas is creating a solar boom. Deutsche predicts that a huge 46 GW of solar PV will be installed in 2014, followed by an additional 56 GW in 2015 (Parkinson, 2014).

The bank notes that in the world's three largest economies—US, China, and Japan—solar power is booming. India, Australia, South Africa, Mexico, as well as regions in the Middle East, South America, and southeast Asia, are rapidly installing solar power. As seen below, China has now taken the lead in renewable energy (Mathews and Tan, 2014).

Almost daily, scientists in university and national research laboratories are making breakthroughs in developing non-carbon energy sources. Advancements in nanotechnology and smart grids are making electricity usage much more efficient.

Several nations, as well as California and other US states, are creating hydrogen highways. Norway, Sweden, and Germany have them in place. California will open its hydrogen highway in 2016. Hydrogen fuel cell cars are already being leased in Nordic countries, California, and Germany. China is considering a ban on fossil-fueled new cars, and major cities across the globe have limited the use of autos in downtown areas. Daimler, Honda, Chevrolet, and most major automobile manufacturers have hydrogen-powered fuel cell cars ready to go.

Tesla's Model S, a plug-in electric car, is outselling the high-end German autos in the US and Norway. Tesla's success comes from a superior lithium-ion battery pack that will soon come to market as a storage unit for on-site generated renewable energy. Superior batteries and hydrogen fuel cells will revolutionize the way renewable energy can be stored and shared across smart Internet-like grids.

Finally, there are key factors that will put to rest the fossil fuel industry and make the wise Sheikh Yamani's prediction come true.

The first is that the carbon emitters will be held accountable and made to pay for using the atmosphere as a garbage can. While still struggling to price the cost of pollution, most nations, as well as California, have come to realize that the heavy carbon emitters need to pay for the damage that they have done. A cap-and-trade process has risen from the bureaucracies as the first method to hold the emitters accountable. While imperfect and not nearly as effective as a straight carbon tax, this system is growing throughout the world.

In the US, California's program continues to grow and the carbon offsets are tradable in parts of Canada as well. Other US states and nations are watching California's program. However, there are better and more efficient ways to stop and control greenhouse gases such as direct taxes and the complete movement to the Green Industrial Revolution.

That the major carbon emitters must pay for their pollution is coming from the agreements made at the 2012 UN Conference on Climate Change in Doha, Qatar. At this conference world governments consolidated the gains of the last three years of international climate change negotiations and opened a gateway to greater ambition and action. Among the decisions was to concentrate on a universal climate agreement by 2015, which will come into effect in 2020. The 2015 United Nations Framework Convention on Climate Change (UN FCCC) conference was held in Paris, where world governments focused on much greater cooperation and agreement for carbon-reduction policies from the US, China, and other major emitters. Cities were a key target area of concern by all nations. Next will be the challenge to implement and evaluate what results.

The world is slowly accepting the reality that the mitigation of climate change is a massive problem. Millions of people are dying and the world's GDP will lose over a $1.2 trillion by 2030, if the world fails to tackle climate change now (Monitor Climate, 2012). Governments do not want to use their public funds for environmental clean up and climate change mitigation, so it will be the heavy emitters who will pay.

Grid Parity

Another factor hastening the change to renewables is grid parity which is a technical term meaning that the cost to a consumer for electricity from a renewable source (without subsidies) is about equal to the cost from a traditional source—be it fossil or nuclear fuel sources. The Germans used grid parity to price its FiT program, that launched Energiewende in the early 1990s.

Simply put a California utility's rate to a resident or small commercial consumer is about 20 (19.9) cents per kWh for electricity from traditional sources. If that same kWh came from a renewable source and cost the consumer an equal 20 cents, then the renewable source would be at "parity" or equal to the cost of the traditional source.

However, the cost of fossil fuel and nuclear energy is rising, driven by higher extracting costs, maintenance costs for natural gas pipelines, and increases in operating and waste costs at nuclear power plants. At the same time the costs for renewable energy—wind, solar PV, and biowaste fuels—are declining. The costs for wind generation have been and still are the lowest. However, the costs for solar are declining rapidly. Solar PV technology, which has been helped by the US military, is improving so fast that it has achieved a virtuous circle.

Energy Deflation

Sanford and Bernstein, the highly respected New York investment bank, released a report in spring 2014 that introduced the term "global energy deflation" where they argue that the fossil fuel-dominated energy markets will experience a major decline in costs over the next decade. However, the market is entering a new order that will erode the viability of oil, gas and the fossil fuel continuum over time (Greentechsolar, 2014).

According to Sanford and Bernstein, this global energy deflation will be created as the cost of PV (and other renewable energy sources) achieves grid and price parity with fossil fuels. They say that solar is now cheaper than oil and Asian LNG, and will get cheaper over time, while fossil fuel extraction costs will keep rising (Greentechsolar, 2014).

The report argues that the adoption of solar in developing markets will translate into less demand for kerosene and diesel oil. The adoption of oil in the Middle East means less oil demand and the adoption of solar in China and developing Asia means less Liquid Natural Gas (LNG) demand. Further, distributed solar in the US, Europe, and Australia will likely reduce demand for natural gas.

Bernstein reasons that while solar has a fractional share of the current market, within one decade, solar PV and related battery storage may have such a large market share that it becomes a trigger for energy price deflation, with huge consequences for the massive fossil fuel industry that is dependent on continued growth. The report concludes that it is inevitable that renewable technology and battery storage will turn into behemoths, and lead to energy price deflation.

The Citigroup in the US released a report titled "Age of Renewables is Beginning—A Levelized Cost of Energy" in March 2014. The report argues that there will be significant price decreases in solar and wind power, which will add to the renewable energy generation boom. The bank projects price declines based on Moore's Law, the same dynamic that drove the boom in information technology.

In brief, the bank is looking for cost reductions of as much as 11 percent per year in all phases of PV development and installation. They said that the cost of producing wind energy would also significantly decline. As the same time, the report says that natural gas prices will continue to go up and the cost of running coal and nuclear plants will slowly become prohibitive (Wile, 2104).

When the world's major financial institutions start to do serious research and quantify the declining costs of renewable energy versus the rising costs of fossil fuels, it becomes easier to understand the monumental green changes taking place.

Even the Saudis are betting on solar, investing more than $100 billion in 41 GW of capacity, enough to cover 30 percent of their power needs by 2030. Most of the other Gulf nations have similar plans.

Zero Marginal Cost

Another key development is "zero marginal cost." Marginal cost, to an economist or businessperson, is the cost of producing one more unit of a good or service after fixed costs have been paid. For example, let's take a shovel manufacturer. It costs the shovel company $10,000 to create the process and buy the equipment to make a shovel that sells for $10. So, after 1,000 or so are sold, the company has recovered its fixed or original costs. Thereafter, each shovel has a marginal of cost of $3, consisting mostly of supplies, labor, and distribution.

Companies have used technology to increase the productivity and reduce marginal costs and return profits. However, as Jeremy Rifkin points out, we have entered an era where technology has unleashed "extreme productivity," driving marginal costs on some items and services to near zero (Rifkin, 2014). File-sharing technology and subsequent zero marginal cost almost ruined the record business and rocked the movie business. Newspaper and magazine industries have been pushed to the wall and are being replaced by the blogosphere and YouTube. The book industry struggles with the e-book phenomenon.

A powerful smart green technology revolution is commercializing rapidly that will change all aspects of our lives, including how we will access renewable energy. The Internet is becoming sophisticated enough and soon it will seamlessly tie together how we share and interact with electricity. It will greatly increase productivity and drive marginal cost of producing and distributing electricity down, possibly to nothing beyond fixed costs.

This is almost the case with the early adopters of solar and wind energy. As they pay off these systems and their fixed costs are covered, additional units of energy are basically free. Eventually, city residents will be able to buy a home solar system at Ikea, Costco, or Home Depot, have it installed and recover costs in less than two years.

All three of these elements—carbon mitigation costs, grid parity, and zero marginal costs, (as well as others, like additive manufacturing and nanotechnology) are part of the Green Industrial Revolution. The new energy model is distributed, mobile, intelligent, and participatory and will rapidly replace the old energy model. As the nexus of declining prices for renewables and rising costs of extraction for fossil fuel is crossed—and we are there in several regions of the world—demand will rapidly shift and propel us into global energy deflation. It will change our cities and the way we live.

The era of sustainability and renewable energy has begun. The push for renewable energy and a carbonless lifestyle will become history's largest social and economic megatrend, with the potential of extraordinary benefits in the form of economic revival, innovation, emerging technologies, and significant job growth for those nations, and cities, capable of fast entry.

The Anthropocene Era

As mentioned in the introduction, geologists describe the current geological age as the Anthropocene period. Beginning with the first Industrial Revolution, it refers to the period during which human activity has been the dominant influence on climate and the environment. One of the key characteristics of this era is the mass migration from an agrarian society to an urban one. The Anthropocene is being populated by city dwellers, in contrast to the rural demography of the past millennia, and has profound implications for human society.

This vast migration to an urban environment is being fueled by many factors including jobs, social services, and safety against violent marauders, but it can be summed up by the human sense that a better way of life is available in a community, among like-thinking humans. As history teaches, this need to be connected and identify with a group is one of the most powerful forces in human history.

As this need manifests itself in the twenty-first century, with this burgeoning migration growing each day, architects and city planners are scrambling to envision the cities of the future. With only geographic restrictions, what will the "new" city look like? How can city planners halt sprawl and protect precious agricultural land, and still accommodate urban growth? How will cities be sustainable and robust on the future's carbonless economy? Finally, how can cities be designed so that people will flourish and be creative, and their overall lives enhanced?

These issues are besieging those working to design and create future cities. New cities are on several worldwide drawing boards, and their designers are searching for ways to avoid the mistakes of the past and adjust to the new realities. One such city on the drawing boards is Quay Valley, in the middle of California's Great Central Valley, half way between San Francisco and Los Angeles.

Quay Valley: A Smart Green Future City—California Style

Quay Valley, a proposed city of 75,000, has been in the planning stages for seven years with the designers working through the various environmental and financial issues. One key addition is a new academic division from California State University, Fresno, for a Sustainability Institute so that theory and practice can be combined and implemented all in one place.

Quay Valley is an ambitious project that will be constructed in California's mostly rural Great Central Valley. The Central, or San Joaquin Valley, is California's fastest-growing region in the state, with 10 million new residents expected over the next two decades. Since the Central Valley is the US's largest and most fertile agricultural area, the challenge for planners and developers will be to build towns and cities that lightly impact the surrounding agricultural economics and lifestyle.

The planners have coined a new phrase—the New Ruralism—for what they hope will be a model community for the Central Valley's expected growth. According to its planners, Quay Valley is grounded in the principles of smart growth, sustainability, green building, and environmental responsibility. The goal they say is to create a planned community that not only enhances the quality of life for people today, but also ensures that the needs of future generations can be met. It is a commonsense approach, they say, based on the understanding that sensibly meeting the San Joaquin Valley's expected population growth will require the careful planning and creation of entirely new towns, and that those towns must be self-sustaining, providing for the long-term viability of the community's natural resources and its social and economic systems.

The project is being watched carefully by state and local leaders, because California foresees continued population growth, particularly in the Central Valley. Despite the water drought in 2015, California's vast agricultural region is expected to house several million new residents in the next two decades. Managing this growth, creating sustainable cities that will not disrupt one of the world's most fertile valleys and destroy its corresponding rural culture is an extraordinarily delicate task. Quay Valley is at the end of the planning stage, and this book's authors are grateful that the planners have allowed such a liberal use of their preliminary design plan. (Note: Greater detail is provided in the appendixes.)

Berlin—To Become Climate-Neutral

Few world cities have approached the transition to a greener, smarter era as thoroughly as Berlin, the capital of Germany, and its largest city with 3.375 million residents. After several years of study and planning, Berlin released their feasibility study and plans for a "Climate-Neutral Berlin 2050." The report was published in late 2014 and the effort was led by the city's Senate Department for Urban Development and the Environment.

Berlin sees itself as a global model for the transition from a city dependent on fossil fuels and nuclear energy, to one developing a totally efficient-renewable economic strategy and economic model. This transformation process gives Berlin the opportunity to become a highly modern city with a power supply based on renewable energy sources. Berlin realizes that it cannot achieve the transition alone; it needs an improved grid system with more power lines and storage capacities. However, the city believes that it could be a leader of sustainable urban development.

Berlin is focused on becoming climate-neutral, but what does that mean?

The term comes from the United Nation's Climate Neutral Strategy and means that a city can be regarded as "climate-neutral" if its greenhouse gas emissions can keep global warming below the dangerous threshold of 2°C—assuming a world population of 9 billion people by 2050, each endowed with the same per capita emission rights of 2 metric tons of CO_2 equivalents based on a lifecycle (Greening the Blue, 2014).

Berlin is not new to working against climate change. The energy-related CO_2 emissions have been reduced from almost 30m ton in 1990 to 21.3m ton in 2010—a decline of 27 percent. The aim of becoming a climate-neutral city by 2050 presents an ambitious goal and also opens up long-term planning horizons. Environment and climate, including adapting to climate change, now play a crucial role. The city also is passing a new law promoting the implementation of the energy turnaround and climate protection ("Gesetz zur Umsetzung der Energiewende und zur Förderung des Klimaschutzes in Berlin"). This new law reflects the changing European and national energy and climate policy conditions as well as Berlin's particular circumstances and potentials.

Solar energy plays a key role in Berlin's future as it has for all of Germany over the last two decades. PV can be installed on the roofs and facades of buildings, the city distribution network can take on large amounts of solar electricity and the production costs are already significantly lower than electricity prices for private households and business enterprises are today. In both target scenarios, PVs are able to cover the yearly electricity demand of between 800,000 and 1.2 million two-person households. This rising electricity demand assumes that PV-generated electricity will be used more and more for transportation purposes—either for more private cars or more shared cars depending on the scenario. In any case, by 2050 Berlin's vehicle stock will produce significantly less emissions and make less noise.

The feasibility study shows that Berlin can become climate-neutral by 2050, meaning the city can reduce its CO_2 emissions by 85 percent relative to 1990. It can reach the goal with two different target scenarios, showing that climate neutrality can be achieved by more central structures and efficient technologies, as well as with a higher proportion of decentralized structures and sufficiency. Through the use of combined heat and power generation with solar energy, urban areas can generate enough energy for base load, but also to achieve surpluses, helping to reduce space requirements for energy production in other places.

Ultimately, the climate-neutral transformation of the Berlin energy system will stimulate growth of value-added activities and employment (Climate-Neutral Berlin 2050, 2015). (Note: Greater detail is provided in the case study in the appendixes.)

Smart Green Cities Are Here Now

For the first time in human history, a majority of the planet's population lives in an urban setting. This mass migration to the world's global cities puts added pressure on city leaders and urban resources. Environmental crises linked to climate change are much more severe and have much more impact. Creating smart green cities requires solutions to old and new problems. Changing from a dependency upon fossil fuels and their carbon-intensive, polluted urban environment to one that is sustainable, healthier, and with low toxic emissions is doable—and there are many cities around the world that are succeeding.

Human needs remain constant in urban environments, particularly in large, global cities. People need the basic infrastructure components such as energy, water, waste, telecommunications, and transportation to work well. In a smart green city, the components are linked and integrated. That way, components overlap, reducing costs for construction, operations, and maintenance.

Despite the extraordinary problems facing our cities, they need to change for the better. Cities need to be healthier and pollution free and new approaches to development and construction must be incorporated into how we work, live, and play. Instead of being centers for wealth inequality that breed alienation, resentment, and strife, our cities most be turned into centers that promote human interaction, healthy exchanges of ideas, and participation in shared values.

Overall, the quality of urban space must improve. Architecture should be more inventive with sensitive urban design and a dynamic atmosphere. Sustainable living and sustainable business development must be promoted. Cities must become more walkable, bike friendly, and livable. They need to focus on the environment as well as economic sustainability. They need to become smart and maximize the use of smart technologies to optimize the resources available for infrastructure upgrading.

In short, the world needs to develop and implement green cities which are capable of stopping climate change and addressing the other looming challenges of the twenty-first century.

References

Clark, Woodrow W. II and Grant Cooke, 2014. *The Green Industrial Revolution*. Elsevier Press, New York.

Climate-Neutral Berlin 2050—Results of a Feasibility Study, 2015. http://www.stadtentwicklung.berlin.de/umwelt/klimaschutz/studie_klimaneutrales_berlin/download/Machbarkeitsstudie_Berlin2050_EN.pdf.

Evans-Pritchard, Ambrose, 2014. Global Solar Dominance in Sight as Science Trumps Fossil Fuels. *The Telegraph*, April 9, http://www.telegraph.co.uk/finance/comment/ambroseevans_pritchard/10755598/Global-solar-dominance-in-sight-as-science-trumps-fossil-fuels.html.

Greening the Blue, 2014. http://www.greeningtheblue.org/resources/climate-neutrality.

Greentechsolar, 2014. Solar's Dramatic Price Plunge Could Trigger Energy Price Deflation. April 14, http://www.greentechmedia.com/articles/read/Solars-Dramatic-Price-Plunge-Could-Trigger-Energy-Price-Deflation.

Monitor Climate, 2012. http://daraint.org/climate-vulnerability-monitor/climate-vulnerability-monitor-2012/.

Parkinson, Giles, 2014. Renew Economy, Deutsche Bank Predicts Second Solar "Gold Rush." January 7, http://reneweconomy.com.au/2014/deutsche-bank-predicts-second-solar-gold-rush-40084.

Rifkin, Jeremy, 2014. Say Goodbye to Capitalism as We Know It. Marketwatch, May 15, http://www.marketwatch.com/story/say-goodbye-to-capitalism-as-we-know-it-2014–05–15.

Wile, Rob, 2014. Business Insider. CITI: 'The Age of Renewables is Beginning.' March 29, http://www.businessinsider.com/citi-the-age-of-renewables-is-beginning--2014–3.

Appendix A

Quay Valley: Future City California Style[1]

GRANT COOKE

A visionary form of supersonic transportation, called the Hyperloop is being planned for an ecocity in California. Located halfway between Los Angeles and San Francisco, Quay Valley is an ambitious project that will be constructed in California's mostly rural Great Central Valley. The Central, or San Joaquin Valley, is California's fastest-growing region in the state, with 10 million new residents expected over the next two decades. Since the Central Valley is the largest and most fertile agricultural area in the US, the challenge for planners and developers will be to build towns and cities do not surrounding agricultural economics and lifestyle.

The planners have created a new phrase: "New Ruralism" to which they hope will be a model sustainable community for the Central Valley's expected growth. According to its planners, Quay Valley is grounded in the principles of smart growth, sustainability, green building, and environmental responsibility. The goal they say is to create a planned community that not only enhances the quality of life for people today, but also ensures that the needs of future generations can be met. It is commonsense approach, they say, based on the understanding that sensibly meeting the San Joaquin Valley's expected population growth will require the careful planning and creation of entirely new towns, and that those towns must be self-sustaining, providing for the long-term viability of the community's natural resources, and its social and economic systems.

Quay Valley is named after its developer, an entrepreneur named Quay Hays, who says that his plan for the city of the future is the result of years of research and discussions with power companies, home builders, and other specialists.

---

1   This appendix is an overview of the Quay Valley Preliminary Design Plan. The author is
     grateful to GROW Holdings for its inclusion.

Proposed in 2007, Quay Valley has gone through a series of delays caused by the severe real estate depression and a nasty battle with an adjoining large farm over water rights. Now that the legal issues have been resolved, construction is set to begin in 2016. Originally planned for 150,000 residents, the city will now have about half that many residents, or roughly 75,000 (http://growholdings.com).

Located on 7,500 acres, Quay Valley is described by its developer GROW Holdings (Green Renewable Organic and Water), as a place for those interested in experiencing "the ideal community of the 21st century—sustainable, secure, spirited, and sound." The founding vision is "to build a model new town for the 21st century—a self-sustaining community that seamlessly melds the best qualities of the walkability and convenience of "New Urbanism" with the comfortable traditions of the San Joaquin Valley's small rural towns, while carefully preserving and enhancing the natural surroundings of the area. This foundation of an integrated stewardship process of conservation, protection, enhancement, and regeneration that balances the social, cultural, technical, economic, and environmental needs of the community will make Quay Valley one of the most modern, livable, and environmentally responsible communities in the world. At the same time, it will prove that the California Dream is alive and well in the Central Valley" (Quay Valley Preliminary Design Plan, 2015).

The project's Conceptual Land Use Plan describes a master planned community that embraces smart growth, including New Urbanism and New Ruralism, sustainability, green building, and green infrastructure principles. Other key concepts include:

- create a cohesive identity for the Project area;

- unify the Project area through implementation of a strong landscape and architectural design program;

- transform the Project into an aesthetic living environment;

- provide for a diverse range of housing opportunities responsive to local needs;

- provide for on-site retail/commercial/entertainment opportunities with "People Gathering Places" integrated;

- provide a convenient, safe, and aesthetic pedestrian circulation network;

- create the most efficient, cutting-edge "One Water" system possible that connects and utilizes all available water in the most sustainable manner;

- provide for advanced storm water management for the Project;

- incorporate a water quality treatment plant and storm water management and distribution system that can serve as an amenity to the community;

- provide for on-site state-of-the-art sewage, water treatment, water storage, and water reuse facilities;

- provide a comprehensive development approach that ensures adequate infrastructure is in place as each planning area comes online;

- "future proof" the infrastructure to provide a platform for future updates and help avoid obsolescence;

- create consolidated, connected open space systems that provide for conservation, mitigation, recreation, and enhancement of indigenous environmental systems;

- cluster development in order to minimize infrastructure impact and costs, and to maximize diversity of housing types;

- create a self-sufficient community where daily needs can be met;

- minimize the need for vehicle trips and vehicle miles travelled;

- provide for a fine-grained street network to avoid future traffic congestion within and outside of Quay Valley;

- provide the highest level of safety for residents and visitors alike;

- maximize opportunities for physical activity;

- emphasize a social network within the community.

There are five main land use components, including:

- A world-class sustainable community that will be home to over 75,000 permanent residents in 25,000 dwelling units, and will become a global showcase for sustainable energy, conservation, and pollution reduction for a higher quality of life.

- A high-energy, family-oriented entertainment destination featuring exciting and unique destination retail, themed resort hotels, museums, action sports complex, waterpark, gardens, convention hotel and facilities, cafes and restaurants, and other distinct attractions.

- Economic drivers to provide a significant job base and create employment self-sufficiency, including such uses as office and business park, innovation clusters, distribution hubs, industrial, retail hospitality, entertainment, service, tech, manufacturing, research park, educational institutions, and highway commercial.

- Sustainable permanent agriculture integrated into and overlapping with areas for wildlife and habitat management as well as areas for passive recreation.

- An embrace of the environment that will feature recreational waterways, wooded areas, walkways, and nature strolls, and will reintroduce habitat and species indigenous to the area.

Quay Valley landscaping will try to make the site a living part of the surroundings and to incorporate nature as part of daily life, enhancing Quay Valley's rural character while simultaneously preserving the resources and beauty of the area. Particularly, the water and energy sources have been designed using groundbreaking technologies to adhere to the principle of sustainable development—conserving and preserving natural resources to ensure that they can also be enjoyed by future generations.

The city will incorporate water sustainability into its design, and will be a model for water conservation and reuse, requiring significantly less water per capita than other towns. Additionally, PV solar power will be added to each energy-efficient home and business, complemented by large-scale solar generating stations to produce enough electricity for the project and provide surplus power back into the grid. As planned, homeowners will not have an electric bill, while enjoying the benefits of clean energy.

Extensive open spaces are planned to encourage a variety of naturalized wildlife habitats ranging from lakes and wetlands to woodlands that will support animals, birds, and fish. Walking paths will take residents along open spaces as part of their daily walk to school, work, or the local market. Lakes and waterways will connect neighborhoods, while also serving as storm water collectors and flood control facilities.

Smart technology and connectivity throughout the city will affect the way people live and how business is conducted. This connectivity infrastructure will grow with its citizens and the community at large. This network, both wired and wireless, will power commerce in new and innovative ways by enabling telecommuting and telemedicine, for example. An intended byproduct will be to reduce car trips and feed its population with the information it seeks when and where it is needed, providing a platform for evolving opportunities.

A 50-acre research ranch has been created to test various sustainable techniques. Experiments in the works include organic farming, renewable solar energy, water reclamation, and more. To get a better understanding of water quality, seepage, and other water issues, the planning team even built a three-acre lake and stocked it with various native species of fish with help from the California Department of Fish and Game.

To help this ecocity obtain its ultimate goal of sustainability, environmental friendly resources have gone toward organic farming. Miles of irrigation ditches have been built and thousands of acres of land have already been planted with organic wheat. The soil is regularly tested to ensure the time and effort put into the farming will continue to pay off. Orchards with nut trees, stone fruit, and citrus trees are planned, and buffalo and horses have been brought in to graze on the native grasses in the pastures.

A substantial educational effort will be made toward making sustainability part of the community's culture and mindset. Quay Valley hopes to teach its residents the benefits of green techniques for both the present and in the future. A large amount of planning is going into making the development sustainable. The planning commitments to sustainability objectives are:

- aim to produce more energy from renewable resources than we consume, with renewable energy as the mandatory primary energy source;

- provide for a "One Water" program consisting of a water treatment and recycling system that minimizes potable water requirements for municipal and industrial (M&I) uses through the use of non-potable water, such as reclaimed water, gray water, and rainwater harvesting and storage;

- create more biodiversity and habitat than existed when we started;

- significantly reduce the consumption and reliance on fossil fuels by the introduction of alternative fuel and green transportation choices;

- reduce building energy demands with passive and active alternative energy and solar uses, including PV or other solar thermal options, and efficient design and construction techniques;

- improve air quality by reducing auto dependence through a circulation plan that promotes walking, biking, and community electric shuttles or other alternative energy-saving transportation methods.

The Town Center is planned as a Main Street concept with about 55 acres in the core of the Quay Valley that will be readily accessible from all areas. As a subregional service area, it will house the local government facilities and Civic Center, as well as provide a variety of retail, service, cultural, recreational, and entertainment activities. Within the project itself, all roads and trails will eventually lead to the Town Center, where residents and visitors will be provided a variety of vibrant, colorful "people place" experiences. Both daytime and nighttime activities are ensured by the close proximity of residences to the Town Center, making it one of the most exciting components of the land use concept. It is envisioned as an eclectic, people-oriented gathering space that is used for living, work, play, dining, shopping, and entertainment.

Quay Valley is intended to be a mixed community that includes affordable housing. Housing will be available for families with low and moderate incomes to meet the county's affordable housing criteria. Other features include the development of a full service medical center and higher educational facilities provided by local colleges. A community activities services organization that promotes and organizes community activities is also planned.

The planners have also considered economic sustainability, expecting that over 30,000 jobs will be created. This strong employment base will make it possible for many Quay Valley residents to live, learn, work, shop, and play in their new hometown. Local colleges and universities as well as the county's economic development department are coordinating in "green collar" and other job training programs.

In addition, the community will be positioned to take advantage of telecommuters, who are the fastest-growing portion of the US workforce. The office parks and the community at large is smart, making use of high technology whenever possible. The project will feature state-of-the-art integrated fiber optic networks, high-speed Internet access, and reliable power supplies. Energy conservation and efficiency, the latest technology and telecommunication systems, and a desirable public environment will make Quay Valley an attractive business address for a wide variety of workers and companies, both regional and national.

Neighborhoods will be laid out to facilitate and encourage walking, bicycling, and mass transportation, decreasing the need for car trips and reducing air pollution and congestion. Charging stations will be provided for electric or hybrid vehicles, and fueling stations will allow for alternative fuel vehicles. The Hyperloop will provide fast, convenient transportation. Construction on the first stretch of the Hyperloop will coincide with the construction of the roads and city infrastructure. It is hoped the initial stage of the development will be finished by 2018, at which point the first residents will begin to move in, and Hyperloop will open for passengers.

Using a vacuum environment, the Hyperloop transports a 28-person capsule through a tube at speeds up to 760 mph. Hyperloop Transportation Technologies, the group of engineers building the system, will produce a $100 million first phase for Quay Valley. Eventually, the Hyperloop will be expanded between Los Angeles and San Francisco. The Quay Valley portion will be a five-mile test stretch, with reduced speeds. It will act primarily as a proof-of-concept for the technology, and its integration is intended to reduce the need for pollution-causing cars, buses, and trucks.

The planners say that the city is built on economical, environmental, and social sustainability, and part of this is reducing car dependency. The Hyperloop is the ideal clean community transit system for an ecocity.

Quay Valley is planning on several million visitors a year because of its convenient location and appeal as an "entertainment destination." It hopes to achieve this through 2 million square feet of retail outlets, three themed resort hotels, as well numerous attractions that include a surf park, basketball stadium, and an Olympic-class whitewater kayaking course.

The planners say that sustainability is a cross-generational community vision, not an objective that can simply be completed and forgotten. It must evolve and grow into a community mindset and culture. By creating, engineering, and embedding new sustainability practices into the core of the community, and by educating and sharing information about the benefits of sustainability practices, people will be better able to understand how these efforts impact their day-to-day lives.

Appendix B

Going Smart and Climate Neutral in Berlin: Insights from the German Capital

CORINNA ALTENBURG, FRITZ REUSSWIG, AND WIEBKE LASS[1]

European and National Context of Berlin

Berlin is not only the largest city in Germany with a population of 3.5 million but, as its capital, Berlin is also Germany's political, cultural, and economic center. Germany itself is one of the largest and most influential member states of the EU, which in turn sets standards and regulation relevant for all European member states, including local communities. Because of the strong influence of European and national legislation, we will shortly introduce some key aspects of green and smart policies on these levels.

When relating to green and climate policies, the EU climate goals for 2020 and more recently for 2030 are setting the framework for a number of more detailed regulations to be implemented by member states (see Appendix C, Potsdam case study). The EU original climate goals for 2020—the so-called 20–20–20 targets—aim to achieve a triple solution in terms of climate protection, energy efficiency, and renewable energies.[2] In preparation for the UN FCCC climate negotiations in Paris in December 2015, the EU has agreed on new goals for 2030. While green parties and environmental NGOs together with some green business lobbies criticized the updated goals as too weak and

---

1 Corinna Altenburg: corinnaa@pik-potsdam.de; Fritz Reusswig: fritz@pik-potsdam.de; Wiebke Lass: wiebke.lass@pik-potsdam.de.
2 Specifically, the EU targets a 20 percent reduction of greenhouse gases by 2020 (base year 1990), an increase of 20 percent share of renewables of primary energy and an overall reduction of primary energy by 20 percent. In preparation for the UN FCC climate negotiations in Paris 2015, these European goals were updated until 2030, aiming now for an increase of 27 percent share of renewables, 40 percent CO_2 reduction, and 27 percent increase in energy efficiency.

unambitious, European politicians defended the agreements, stating that other nations should take the targets as an example.

The new targets were negotiated between the 28 member states of the EU. Different interests and conditions of each member state needed to be considered to reach an agreement. For example, concessions were made to countries such as Poland, which heavily relies on coal. In the case of Germany, Chancellor Angela Merkel noted that as a nation, it will "not have a hard time [meeting the targets]" as it has already set more ambitious national targets. By 2020 Germany intends to reduce emissions by 40 percent (base year 1990), leading up to a reduction of 85 percent to 95 percent by 2050 with respective sub-targets for 2030 and 2040.

While there is a tendency in Germany to focus on national energy policies within its federal system, the relations between the EU and Germany are crucial for energy policy success. It is important to note that while Germany may be exemplary in some areas in the EU, such as the share of renewable energies, this is not the case for all issue areas. For instance, many other EU member states are doing better in implementing regulations for energy efficiency. Also, Germany has traditionally opposed stronger CO_2 limits for its car industries in the past.[3] Another example of the strong interdependencies between the EU-national (and also regional) level is one of the most successful policy instruments in Germany—FiT system.[4] The FiT is one of the reasons for the aggressive expansion of renewable energies in Germany (almost a 28 percent share of residential total gross electricity consumption in 2014, 11 percent share in total energy consumption including heat and transport).

A recent landmark in German energy policy, which also affects the federal states like Berlin, is the so-called German "Energiewende" (energy transition), agreed by the conservative–liberal government under chancellor Angela

---

3   However with the VW scandal in the early fall of 2015 over its incorrect data validating the diesel fuel reduced carbon emissions, German car companies and the Central government have instituted stronger vehicle oversight and restrictions. It is not clear whether the German car industry will continue to be a brakeman in the future, given its substantial—yet late— investments in the electric car. The German government has massively supported car manufacturers in this effort.

4   The first landmark at the federal level was the FiT law issued during the unification process in 1990. Green masterminds like Hermann Scheer, a social democratic supporter of renewable energies, and others from the Green party and the then young renewable energy industry developed the blueprint for the law. In 2000, the then red–green federal government under Chancellor Schroeder initiated a reform of the FiT system, leading to a massive roll-out of renewable energy in Germany. In 2014, the "great coalition" under chancellor Merkel issued another reform, adapting it to new conditions and goals under the German "Energiewende."

Merkel in 2011. Ironically, the same government a year before that had decided to suspend a decision of its red–green predecessor government to phase-out nuclear power by 2022. But then the nuclear accident of Fukushima happened in early 2011. Anti-nuclear protests had been shaking the former Federal Republic of Germany during the 1970s and 1980s, and the 1986 Chernobyl accident made this protest very popular. After Fukushima, the Merkel government immediately realized that one containment strategy of 1986—western/German nuclear power plants are much safer than Soviet ones, Chernobyl can never happen here—would no longer work given the high quality of Japanese technology. To prevent mass protests, Merkel and her government within one week jettisoned their own recent energy policy decisions and decided to phase-out nuclear power in Germany until 2022—just as the red–green predecessor government had decreed. Together with Germany's climate policy goals, to which Merkel had always felt committed, this phase-out decision led to a massive roll-out of renewable energy and energy-efficiency programs.

Considering its overall climate goals, however, it is still unclear if Germany can reach its 40 percent reduction target by 2020. Low world market prices for coal, in part triggered by the drop of US coal demand induced by increased use of shale gas, made coal more attractive for power plant investments. In addition to that, in some regions lignite is still an important domestic resource, and thus the phasing-out of coal has been developing slower than needed. The latest studies predict a reduction of only 33–34 percent instead of 40 percent. Therefore, in spring 2015 the ministry of economy and energy issued a plan to phase-out lignite-burning power plants older than 20 years. A lobby group from industry and labor unions protested against these plans. In addition, the government has issued an €80 million "Climate Action Plan" in December 2014, hopefully leading to a further reduction of 22 million tons, mainly through energy-efficiency measures.

The Berlin Context

Berlin's own history on green and smart actions has been diverse over the past 25 years marking the merger of East and West Germany and was often influenced by political changes. While the western part of Berlin has seen some energy and climate policy attempts even before reunification in 1990, mainly driven by civil society movements, science initiatives, and the Green party, similar attempts have been lacking in East Berlin until 1989. Environmental opposition groups played only a minor role in the GDR. Immediately after the reunification of the City in 1990, the Senate of Berlin officially launched an energy-saving law ("Energiespargesetz"). This was parallel to the administrative and economic process of integrating very heterogeneous economic and political systems and social cultures, and during a short period of a social–democratic/green coalition in Berlin. This law is still in effect today and will be followed up in 2015 by a so-called "Energiewendegesetz" (Energy Transition Law), which will function as new framework legislation for Berlin.

Until recently, Berlin was known, as a City, to be "poor, but sexy" —a famous remark by former Lord Mayor Klaus Wowereit in 2003. For many years, Berlin had to shoulder a hefty public deficit and a stagnant economy. While the public deficit is still huge (a total of €60 billion in 2013), promising developments are taking place as well. Berlin has a growing population and the economy is catching up. In 2014, the GDP growth was 2.2 percent compared to 1.4 percent for Germany. The recovering economy is also attracting new investment and new jobs. Berlin is especially attractive to many innovative start-ups in sectors such as bio-tech, energy, creative industries, media, IT, and life sciences. For the first time Berlin could even repay loans of €1.5 billion.

No light without shadow, however. From a climate policy perspective, a net annual growth of 25,000–30,000 people is a real challenge especially since the fall of 2015 when thousands of people escaping the middle-east and going to Germany. The top issue of the administration is to cope with the city's growth— in all dimensions. The average income in Berlin is still lower than in other large cities in Germany, but the pressure on the real estate market is growing. Eighty-six percent of all apartments in Berlin are rented, and the average Berlin rent is low, compared to places like Munich, Frankfurt, or Stuttgart. But rents go up, and there is a widespread fear of crowding-out lower income strata (Berlin is a focal point of Germany's gentrification debate). This is setting the scene for all attempts to make Berlin smarter and greener, for example by the energetic refurbishment of buildings, which usually leads to higher costs and rents. Despite its recent growth, Berlin is an old city, and a green and smart transition has to take place in a dominantly "adult" city. Compared to other cities in Europe, Berlin performs quite well. It ranks number 8 in the European Green City Index, and is the best City with a larger population (outperforming London or Paris for example) (EIT, 2012), and it is doing so despite the below-average per capita income of its citizens.

Where Berlin Stands Today: Toward a Smart and Green City

From 1990 to 2010, Berlin has managed to reduce its CO_2 emissions rather successfully by 27 percent (from 29.3 Mio. t to 21.3 Mio. t). But this de-carbonization success can only partially be attributed to a successful climate policy. A major part of this reduction can be attributed to the "renovation" of the eastern part of the city (the so-called "wall-fall profit"). Inefficient GDR buildings have been renovated, old industries either shut down or modernized, and the old car fleet substituted by more efficient—but also more powerful—new cars.

In 2011, parallel to the German "Energiewende," a new Senate emerged from the Berlin Parliament elections, formed by Social Democrats and Christian Democrats. Such a "great coalition" has been unusual for the City. However, the new Senate took the decision to develop Berlin into a climate neutral city until 2050. A couple of other developments, driven not only by the Senate, led to a remarkable dynamic of green and smart city development.

The Senate, right after its climate neutrality decision in 2011, established a new administrative unit, the special unit of climate protection and energy, with direct access to the undersecretary of state in the Senate Administration for Urban Development and Environment (SenStadtUm). One of the first steps of this unit was to specify what climate neutrality could mean for Berlin, and to find out how it could be achieved. To do so, they commissioned a feasibility study "Climate Neutral Berlin 2050," and a consortium of research institutes and planners led by the Potsdam Institute for Climate Impact Research (PIK) worked it out in 2013/2014. The feasibility study (Reusswig et al., 2014 a, b) is now a corner stone for the further process. It demonstrated that Berlin can achieve climate neutrality[5] by 2050 if consequent measures in all sectors of the City are taken and realized steadily.

The feasibility study worked with a lot of experts and stakeholders to develop its scenarios and measures. It developed two different scenarios for Berlin that equally achieve the goal, but on very different socio-technical pathways.

A more centralized and individualistic scenario (left) can be contrasted to a more decentralized and "communitarian" scenario (right). Individually owned cars for example do still play a large role in the first scenario, but of course all cars have to run on a renewable electric basis. In the "communitarian" case, we assume a significantly reduced number of privately owned cars, instead

---

5   Climate neutrality refers to the 2°C goal of the UN FCCC, trying to limit global warming in 2100 to that amount as compared to pre-industrial times. Combined with the assumption of a world population of 9 billion people in 2050 and equal emission rights per capita, this will leave for Berlin a tolerable emission space of about 4.4 million tons of CO_{2eq}, equaling a reduction of at least 85 percent as compared to 1990.

Berlin will have developed a substantial sharing economy with privately or commercially managed fleets.

Berlin's energy system will have become much smarter and greener in both scenarios, with a substantial increase in solar PV, together with a lower-temperature district heating system, heat pumps, and many decentralized CHP plants, fueled by a range of green alternatives, such as (renewable) power-to-heat (P2H) and power-to-gas (P2G). According to the feasibility study, all sectors will have to contribute, including the building sector and private households.

The feasibility study laid the intellectual ground for the process. But the institutional ground had still to be laid. For that reason, the Senate issued a new "Energiewende" Law, anchoring climate neutrality in the institutional landscape, and empowering the Senate to issue green and smart acts. The law has currently (summer 2015) taken the first institutional hurdles and will probably be passed by the Parliament in late 2015. It does refer to the follow-up activity of the feasibility study, the implementation study of the Berlin Energy and Climate Protection Program (BEK). This program is currently worked out by a consortium of research institutes and consultants, led by the Institute for Ecological Economic Research (IÖW), with PIK as a partner. Together with stakeholders, the project tries to specify next steps on the long way to climate neutrality, and to integrate stakeholders in the definition of near-term goals. These will later be formalized, for example in voluntary agreements between the Senate and the business sector, and they will be backed by the new law. In addition to a very cooperative process of goal definitions and measures design, the BEK process is accompanied by various formats of public involvement that include urban forums and online participation. Citizens have been invited to comment on measures, and to propose new ones. The final draft of the BEK will be handed to the Senate and the Parliament by end of 2015.

The Berlin City Parliament has also taken its own steps. Given the activities of the Senate, but also in the context of a vivid and controversial public debate on energy policy issues in Berlin, it has appointed a parliamentary committee "New Energy for Berlin" that will prepare the later decision process by exploring feasible ways for a green and reliable energy system for the city. The whole process is accompanied by a vivid public debate on the energy system, especially on the question of whether it should be managed by large private firms (as today), or if the Senate should bring it back into public ownership—of course at a high price. There are also green NGOs that want to buy the power grid in the regular licensing process.

Another development is very important for the climate neutrality goal, although it has not been driven by the environment department of the Senate: Smart City Berlin (Erbstößer, 2014). This initiative, advocated by the Senate Administration for Economy, is driven by economic considerations, trying to strengthen the competitiveness of Berlin by strengthening the role of IT in various economic clusters relevant for the city economy (for example, health or traffic). Despite being pushed by economic interests primarily, there are clear synergies with the green plans of Berlin, for example in the domains of energy efficiency or smart homes, and the environment administration has taken up the issue (Senate of Berlin, 2015). Already now Berlin is—together with Potsdam—one of the three national showcase areas for electro-mobility. So-called "BentoBox" bikes (electro cargo bikes) are used for the last mile of goods transportation. Smart metering and micro-smart grids are implemented. City-wide free Wi-Fi spots are implemented. In an EU-funded research project, 100 private households will be invited to voluntarily live by 1 ton CO_2 per year (instead of 11 as today), supported by green and smart business solutions (cf. http://www.climate-kic.org/projects/one-tonne-society/). PIK will support the households and monitor their performance via mobile phone apps. A prototype is already in use in Uppsala (Sweden) which, together with Bologna (Italy), is the partner city in this European project. Together with Paris and Bologna, Berlin applied for financial EU research fund support of €25 million for smart and green urban solutions. In case of a positive decision it will invest €7 million in green and smart pilot projects (Hoffmann, 2015).

One example of what the smart and green future might look like is already open to visitors: the so-called Energy Efficiency-Plus House, built in the city center by a consortium of famous German green architects, funded and monitored by the Federal Ministry for Education and Research (BMBF). Solar panels provide energy, including the electric car and bikes for the family that lives there, and all appliances communicate with the steering center.

There are many more examples in Berlin, driven by the Senate, but also by the business sector (Berlin has a vivid start-up scene) or by citizens, that show how the synergies between smart and green can lead to a new urban future. It remains to be seen whether the new BEK, which is currently under design, will be implemented fast enough to spur the intelligent de-carbonization of urban life that has slowed down a little recently.

Conclusions

Many cities in Europe have taken steps toward becoming green and smart cities. Some of them want to reach climate neutrality even earlier than Berlin. Copenhagen, for example, wants to be there by 2035. But what makes Berlin's efforts to become a climate neutral city especially valuable is the fact that the city is much bigger—3.5 million instead of 0.56 million—and thus more difficult to manage. Its huge building stock and the high share of low-income groups are also two big challenges.

Berlin is an example for a green and smart urban development strategy in which the elements of purposeful design and administrative agenda-setting play a much more important role than in, say, the case of Potsdam, its smaller neighboring city (see Appendix C, Potsdam case study in this volume). In addition, we find that not only is the environment administration involved, but also see synergistic activities from the economy administration, and investment programs of the business sector. In the case of Potsdam, a public utility company plays a key role in greening the city. In Berlin, where the Swedish company Vattenfall—a foreign private firm from a Berlin point of view, though a company owned by the Swedish state—owns large parts of heat and electricity provisioning, this actor to some degree has to be put in brackets, as it cannot be influenced directly. More indirect governance instruments, such as voluntary agreements for de-carbonization, are used. The conceptual preparation of a green and smart transition is very good in Berlin, and the anchoring in the wider public is better than in many other places. Other than Potsdam, for example, Berlin as a federal state has more legal and political means to put forward laws (the "Energiewende" law, for example) and to voice its interests in the national context. A big asset for Berlin is the large number of think tanks like universities or institutes in the city, many of which specialize in energy and smart city IT solutions. Associated with that, we find a high rate of related spin-offs in Berlin that nourish both the knowledge capital and the revenues needed to nourish a sustained green and smart transition. Other than Potsdam, Berlin has an explicit smart city strategy by the Senate and leading firms. While it has not officially been drafted to support the climate neutral goals of the City, the synergies and potential cooperation opportunities for the leading actors are obvious and have begun to be capitalized upon. Small pilot projects have already been implemented; a scaling-up is the next step.

And, last but not least, Berlin is well known for its creative scenery and its high quality of life, including a very broad and rich cultural scene and entertainment industry. Initiatives like Green Club Mobs, where people gather in music clubs to financially support more energy efficiency and renewable energy shifts, show that in Berlin two things can go together that often seem to be mutually exclusive: fun and greenness.

International city comparisons for green urban performance reveal that Berlin is performing quite well, especially when it comes to energy efficiency. All this has been achieved in a city that is—on average—poorer than say London, Paris, or Frankfurt. Berlin is sending an important signal to the world: you don't have to be rich to get green and smart—at least at a Europe-wide comparative level. Taken all together, Berlin is an encouraging case for smart and green urban transitions.

References

Caprotti, F., 2015. Building the Smart City: Moving beyond the Critique (Part 1): Ubiquitous Smart Cities, https://ugecviewpoints.wordpress.com/2015/03/24/building-the-smart-city-moving-beyond-the-critiques-part-1/.

Economist Intelligence Unit (EIT), 2012. European Green City Index: Assessing the Environmental Performance of 30 Major European Cities, http://www.siemens.com/entry/cc/de/greencityindex.htm.

Erbstößer, A.-C., 2014. *Smart City Berlin—Urbane Technologien für Metropolen: [Urban Technologies for Metropolises]*. Technologiestiftung Berlin, Berlin.

Hoffmann, K., 2015. Berlin will EU-Wettbewerb für Smart-Cities gewinnen. Berlin Wants to Win EU Competition for Smart Cities, http://www.tagesspiegel.de/wirtschaft/gemeinsam-mit-paris-und-bologna-berlin-will-eu-wettbewerb-fuer-smart-cities-gewinnen/11419344.html.

Reusswig, F., Hirschl, B., and Lass, W., 2014b. Climate-Neutral Berlin 2050. Results of a Feasibility Study. Berlin: Senate Administration for Urban Development and Environment, http://www.stadtentwicklung.berlin.de/umwelt/klimaschutz/studie_klimaneutrales_berlin/download/Machbarkeitsstudie_Berlin2050_EN.pdf.

Senate of Berlin, 2015. Smart City Strategie Berlin. Anlage. Berlin. Senate Administration for Urban Development and Environment, http://stadtentwicklung.berlin.de/planen/foren_initiativen/smart-city/download/Referenzprojekte_SCB.pdf

Appendix C

Green, Growing, and Smart: The Case of Potsdam, A Mid-size City in Germany

CORINNA ALTENBURG AND FRITZ REUSSWIG[1]

Overview

The activities of the city of Potsdam (population: 164,000) in Germany are quite different from those of newly built ecocities in states of transition. The mid-size city, bordering Germany's capital Berlin, is an example of a typical European city. Even though, medium-sized cities do not receive a lot of international attention, these cities (with a population of 100,000–500,000) host the majority of the urban population in Europe—more than 40 percent of Europeans live in these cities. This also holds globally: small and medium-sized cities form the majority of all urban communities, although megacities tend to receive most media attention and usually dominate the news (Van Staden and Musco, 2010).

Regarding smart and green activities, mid-sized cities face several obstacles in terms of limited economies of scale as well as restricted financial and institutional capacities. On the other hand, they offer interesting niche-potentials for smaller-scale innovations. Many green (and some smart) initiatives and programs have been implemented over time or are currently underway in Potsdam. Some were initiated through the support of state and federal or even European programs; others have been pushed by the city administration itself; and others again are bottom-up projects. This case study explains some of the opportunities and hurdles faced by an established European mid-sized city when going smart and green.

---

1   Corinna Altenburg contact email at: corinnaa@pik-potsdam.de and Fritz Reusswig contact email at: fritz@pik-potsdam.de.

The rest of the appendix is organized as follows: We first give some background information on the city and the national context that is needed to understand the specific pathway of smartness and greenness in Potsdam. We then give a short overview of important initiatives and projects that characterize Potsdam's green and smart profile. We end by focusing on the factors that drive the development of this profile—and that are hurdles to its stronger unfolding.

The Context

Potsdam can be seen as the small and beautiful little sister of Germany's capital Berlin, which is its direct eastward neighbor. Both cities share a common history of a Prussian kingdom that ended after centuries in 1945, when the four winners of the Second World War met in Potsdam to decide the fate of Germany.

Although Potsdam is more than 1,000 years old, the formative phase of the city structure can be traced back to the years 1750–1850, when a row of Prussian kings engaged gifted architects and landscape planners to design a new kind of royal residence and related urban living, both inspired by French, Italian, and English prototypes—and at the same time fueled by the idea of a more civic and aesthetic commonwealth. This led to a unique cultural landscape of castles, civic quarters, gardens, parks, and lakeside environments that had the power to survive two world wars and two totalitarian regimes in the twentieth century—today in large parts a UNESCO cultural heritage site.

Located in Eastern Germany, Potsdam after the Second World War has been a battle and experimentation ground for socialist urban planning during German Democratic Republic (GDR) times. The communist party deliberately fought the historical tradition of Potsdam as a stronghold of Prussian feudalism and militarism—deliberately neglecting large parts and aspects of that heritage. Highly symbolic architectural monuments have literally been blasted, such as the inner city castle and the Garrison church.

After the fall of the Berlin Wall—which was in its southwestern parts there was a "Potsdam wall" as well—the city invested a lot of energy and money into the restoration of many of these "vanished" monuments. The inner city castle for example, damaged in the Second World War, was wiped out by a party decree in 1960, but reconstructed in its historical shape in 2013 and today hosts the Parliament of the federal state of Brandenburg—Potsdam is its capital. This process of redesigning Potsdam after 1990 has been a constant process of conflict on different views on tradition, architecture, urban planning, and social development—to this very day.

As important as it is—the historically grown and partly reconstructed Potsdam is not the whole story. There is also a much less beautiful Potsdam, located mostly in the south of the city, hosting a majority of lower and middle-income citizens in former GDR multi-storage buildings. Many of them vote for left parties (if they vote) and feel excluded from the local mass media debates on how to reconstruct the inner city. And there is a "new north" of Potsdam: on the one hand garden-city types of new single housing quarters close to the center, and on the other hand rural settlements that have been newly incorporated to the municipality in 2003.

While many other municipalities in the state of Brandenburg—as in many other eastern German states—shrink, Potsdam has experienced population growth since about the year 2000. About 1,000–2,000 additional people migrate to Potsdam annually. This might seem a small number if we compare it to megacities in the global south. It is, however, a significantly high number for a German medium-sized city. Today, Potsdam is both proud of and worried about its own growth. Part of it is a side-effect of Berlin's growth, as the very good (public) transport connections between Potsdam and Berlin make it easy to work in the busy German capital and to live in its beautiful little sister Potsdam. But another part of it is the fact that Potsdam's quality of life is very high—even compared to western German standards—due to its location at river Havel and the lakes it forms.

Potsdam's economy is characterized by a lack of industry—not unusual for mid-sized German cities. The service sector is dominant, made up of mainly small and medium enterprises. Being the state capital and a regional center, Potsdam also hosts many administrative facilities. Besides being a cultural center in Brandenburg, Potsdam is also known for its leading global science institutes and universities, and has developed a promising location for green industries. Compared to its large neighbor Berlin, Potsdam's population is rather homogenous, with a share of foreigners of only 4.8 percent in 2013 (Berlin: 15.4 percent). This is now changing, mainly due to the influx of refugees from the Middle East and Africa. Potsdam is also a city of students with the second-largest share of university students (15 percent of total population; Berlin: 6 percent) among federal state capitals in Germany.

Potsdam's Climate Policy: Historical Background and National Context

Potsdam's climate policy—including mitigation and adaptation efforts—can be traced back to the early 1990s. It was a consequence of the German unification process, driven mainly first by a reformed political administration, and secondly by a local environmental civil society movement. The latter had two roots: on the one hand, "green" people and ideas from the west entered the scenery after 1990. But on the other hand, there is also a local history of an environmental and civil liberties movement, dating back to the 1980s under the GDR regime. One of their activists, Matthias Platzeck, even became lord mayor of Potsdam in 1998, before he moved on to become the prime minister of the state of Brandenburg in 2002.

In the case of Potsdam, international climate policy city networks had a catalytic effect in bringing forward local climate policies. Soon after 1990, the city of Potsdam joined the European Climate Alliance, a network of cities in Europe dedicated to reducing greenhouse gas emissions and to helping protect rainforests in South America. Potsdam adopted the reduction goals of the Alliance and a lot of Potsdam's early actions can be regarded as at least partially influenced by the network learning effect of being an Alliance member. [2]

However, very soon the city faced its own structural realities—and problems—and took its own decisions. One of the most important ones was the city's decision to end the long historic phase of lignite burning in its energy provisioning. The city is the majority owner of its energy provider EWP ("Energie und Wasser Potsdam") and in this role decided the phasing-out of the lignite era in 1995. Instead, a natural gas-fired combined heat-and-power plant was built, providing both electricity and heat for the district heating system, serving large parts of the city. The importance of this break with a path dependency has to be measured against the fact that the state of Brandenburg is a major lignite producer in Germany, and the coal-fired power plants in the south of Brandenburg that generate a large part of the state's GHG emissions export electricity to the rest of Germany. Of course there are also many jobs that hinge on the lignite industry. The decision of Potsdam to end lignite burning

---

2   The Climate Alliance (in German: "Klima-Bündnis") is one of the oldest European city networks founded in 1990 as an alliance between western cities and indigenous people. Member cities of the Climate Alliance commit themselves to reduce emissions every five years by 10 percent until 2050 when a baseline of 2.5 ton per capita should be achieved. At present, the Climate Alliance has about 1,700 members (about 1,200 cities, the rest are associated member (for example, Energy Non-Government Organizations or eNGOs)). The majority of members come from Austria, Germany, and Italy (April 2015—www.klimabuendnis.org).

in 1995 was thus perceived as a particularly "unfriendly act" of the state capital against the state interests—and the many protests of miners in Potsdam made that very clear. Nevertheless the decision was taken, and it has led to a significant drop in Potsdam's GHG emissions.

A next major step in Potsdam's climate policy has been the development of a comprehensive climate protection concept that covers all sectors of the city and is based on their actual emissions and their emission reduction potential. This study was completed in 2010, and the next section will report on it in more detail.

The last phase in Potsdam's climate policy history is characterized by two developments: the implementation of the 2010 concept, including the issue of monitoring and readjustment on the one hand, and the elaboration of a climate change adaptation concept on the other. To prepare the second issue, the city has commissioned a local adaptation strategy to a consortium of PIK and partners, completed in spring 2015. The implementation of this latest policy area is still in the making.

The latest phase of Potsdam's local climate policy has to be seen in a national and European context. For the German context, the so-called "Energiewende" is certainly a crucial factor. The immediate occasion for this major shift in the national energy regime was the Fukushima nuclear power plant accident in early 2011, which led the German government—then formed by a conservative-liberal coalition—to opt for a phase-out of nuclear power until 2022. Not without irony, the same government had, a couple of months earlier, decided to revise a phase-out decision of its red–green predecessor government. But given the historical experience of social irritation and protest against nuclear power in Germany, not least fueled by accidents like the Chernobyl disaster in 1986, the government was well advised to revise its own policy in 2011.

What has since been propagated as "Energiewende" can, however, be traced back to a longer history of energy efficiency and renewable energy policies of German governments, dating back to the 1970s and 1980s. Major policy tools, such as the national feed-in tariff (FiT) system, had been developed in the 1990s in a coalition of researchers, climate activists, administrative, and policy actors. The German "Energiewende" of 2011 can thus be seen as a continuation of pre-existing programs and tools, "radicalized" by ambitious climate policy goals and the bundling of various sector-specific policies under one coherent strategy. The long-term goal of becoming a climate-neutral society by 2050 especially reveals that this national project has major and more radical implications for the German economy and society. This is the reason why—despite a general consensus on these goals—the exact technical and organizational realization of this "Energiewende" is heavily debated in Germany and the combination of ambitious climate protection goals with a nuclear phase-out leads to very ambitious renewable energy targets. The questions of costs and local energy conflicts are the relevant topics in this context.

The policy goals and instruments of the German "Energiewende" since 2011 do have influence on the climate policy of German federal states ("Laender") and local bodies. Many German "Laender" have coordinated their climate policies in the light of national goals. And many cities have developed their own long-term strategies, trying to ensure coherence with national goals. The federal government has spurred this process by funding the elaboration of local climate policy concepts.

Green Urban Plans and Climate Projects

The target of the study commissioned by the city in 2010 was to develop a strategy for a reduction of the city's GHG emissions by 20 percent until 2020—measured against the 2005 level. It has already been mentioned that the city's emissions dropped significantly after the substitution of lignite by natural gas in its CHP plant erected in 1995. Given the additional fact that a lot of building refurbishments had already taken place in the 1990–2005 period, the 20 percent reduction goal can be assessed to be ambitious—especially if we take the city growth that Potsdam has experienced in recent years into account. As no further "wall-fall profits" can be gained, Potsdam needs to tap new potentials to become greener and smarter. Table AC1.1 gives an overview of current emissions patterns and goals on different hierarchical levels.

To develop concrete measures to achieve this goal, the city commissioned an "integrated climate protection concept" in 2010, funded by the already mentioned federal program for cities. A consortium of research institutes and planning offices worked on it during one year, led by the Potsdam Institute for Climate Impact Research (PIK, 2010). Based on a sector-wise wide assessment of urban GHG emissions and (mostly) qualitative cost–benefit assessments of almost 100 individual measures, the study developed a strategy for a cost-efficient and equitable GHG reduction for all sectors. The main field of actions in this concept included:

- energy provisioning;

- buildings;

Table AC1.1 CO_2 emissions and reduction goals in Europe, Germany, Brandenburg and Potsdam

Political Levels (Population in 2013)	Status Quo CO_2 Emissions—Total and Per Capita	Main Green and Climate Policies and Goals
Regional Level European Union (28 Member States) (Pop: 506m)	4,500 Mt CO_2 equivalents 9,0 t CO_2 equivalents per capita 7,4 t CO_2 per capita (2012)*,a	European Climate Package (20–20–20 goals) e.g. 20% GHG reduction by 2020 (base year 1990) New goals by 2030: e.g. 30% GHG reduction
National Level Germany (Pop: 80.7m)	953 Mt CO_2 equivalents (2013) 11.5 t CO_2 equivalents per capita 9.4 t CO_2 per capita[b]	Integrated Energy and Climate Package (2007) - 40% CO_2 reduction by 2020 (base year 1990);—long-term—80–95% CO_2 reduction by 2050 (base year 1990)
Federal State Level State of Brandenburg (Pop: 2.4m)	59 Mt CO_2 (2013) (24.4 Mt CO_2—including electricity exports (~ 12 ton CO_2 pc are exported)[c]	- 40% CO_2 reduction by 2020 (base year 1990) Brandenburg Energy Strategy 2030 -72% reduction (=25m CO_2 ton) by 2030 (~10t per capita)
Municipal Level City of Potsdam (Pop: 164,000)	1 Mt CO_2 (2012)* (6.33 ton CO_2 per capita)[d]	Potsdam Climate Decision in 2007 - 20% CO_2 reduction by 2020 (base year 2005) = 5.5t per capita

Note: [a] EEA 2014; [b] UBA 2014; [c] LUGV 2014; [d] City of Potsdam 2014; methodology not fully compatible with the other statistical levels due to a widely territory-based accounting approach.
* Due to statistical procedures some data is only available for 2012.

- solar roof potential;

- transport;

- urban planning and development;

- private households and communication.

The proposed measures were then evaluated with regard to their potential to reduce GHG, but also in terms of co-benefits, cost-benefits, and potential benefits for climate adaptation.

In 2011, the City Assembly, (the local Parliament), adopted the strategy as an orienting policy framework—not as a master plan with binding reduction goals. While from a science point of view this rather weak form of political adoption might be criticized, from a political standpoint the vote of the Assembly can be understood. From the 66 measures that have been finally adopted, almost every single one has the potential for a vivid political debate, often along the classical political cleavage lines in the Assembly. There is an inherent conflict potential in many measures, such as increased refurbishment rates or restrictions to car traffic.

Nevertheless, even endowed with a rather weak political mandate, the city has since then managed to implement a couple of measures that had been proposed by the concept. The latest trend projections of the city foresee that the 2020 goal of a 20 percent reduction in Potsdam is achievable (City of Potsdam, 2014). So far there has been a reduction of 91,000 tons of CO_2, which is about 8 percent, between 2005 and 2012.[3] The achieved reductions between 2003 and 2012 stem from a number of factors, such as:

- reduction of heating demand due to thermal refurbishment of buildings and increasing share of newly built dwellings, which—by German federal law—have to be more energy efficient;

- substitution of remaining individual coal-fired heating systems by gas, district heating, or geothermal energy;

- energetic use of sewage water residuals;

- more energy-efficient household appliances;

- more efficient-energy supply by the municipal energy utility EWP;

- increased share of solar power in private homes and some municipal buildings;

- increased share of bicycles and public transport.

---

3   The calculation model has been recently changed based on the emission tool by the network Climate Alliance. For instance, in the latest report the national electricity mix was used instead of the local one (which in fact is lower because of the efficient CHP plant). While this does not change the relative changes made, this procedure was criticized by members of the city council and is supposed to be changed in the next report.

As mentioned, the local energy provider EWP is a public utility with the city as the major owner. It was thus rather easy for the city to use EWP as a major tool in its climate policy. EWP has in 2013 adopted an "energy strategy 2020" that adopted the GHG reduction goals of the 2010 concept. Among other things, an originally planned third block of the natural gas-fired CHP plant was dismissed. Instead, the company invested in renewable energy projects (mainly solar and wind), and in 2015 erected a big heat reservoir, Storing the hot water that is cogenerated during electricity production in the summertime and shifting it to the winter phase, when the district heating systems needs more heat. In addition, this new reservoir is also endowed with an immersion heater that can transform wind and solar-generated electricity that the German grid cannot transport at times and would otherwise have to be exported— preventing the renewable facilities from being closed down for that "excess" period.[4] EWP has also adopted another measure proposed in the 2010 concept by issuing a public fund for its clients by which they could invest private money—for a defined return rate—into the renewable energy projects they conduct. The city of Potsdam has also taken first steps to specify a measure proposed in 2010: the linking of the salaries and bonuses of the CEOs of major public corporations to the degree to which they have achieved the sector-specific climate goals. A flagship project is the restructuring of the last multi-store quarter from GDR times, Drewitz (home of more than 7,000 people), into a climate-neutral "garden city" with more green and less car traffic space. The project received national awards and is an example of the close cooperation between the city, the largest public utility housing enterprise (ProPotsdam), and the local energy provider (EWP).

To monitor the progress of these and other proposed measures, the Climate Protection Unit of the city of Potsdam, has created a network of "climate partners" from science, the business sector, and local NGOs—or more precisely it has linked itself with existing networks. On the website of this network (www.klimapartner-potsdam.de) is an overview of individual actions, together with a short description and an assessment of compliance in percentage. The specific actions cover a wide range of topics, including more efficient and renewable energy supply and demand, urban planning including support of bicycle lanes and public transport, information and advising campaigns on energy efficiency, but also some actions on adaptation planning.

---

4   Due to the rapid growth of the share of renewables in German electricity generation (about 26 percent in 2014, goal for 2020: at least 35 percent, goal for 2050: at least 80 percent), the German grid has reached some limits and needs expansion and restructuring. This leads to situations in which "excess power" from renewables has to be turned off—or can be converted into hydrogen via electrolysis (power-to-gas) or to heat (power-to-heat).

For climate adaptation the city has recently commissioned a follow-up study in 2014, which will analyze current and future climate trends, such as rising temperatures and extreme weather events, in more detail. The final report was published in summer 2015, and the climate administration expects the City Assembly to adopt it as an orientating framework by the end of that year—just as in the case of the climate protection concept in 2011.

Even though the city of Potsdam seems so far on track with its reduction goals, and will on top of that complement it by an adaptation strategy, some remaining barriers and future tasks can also be identified:

- There are more specific goals for 2020, and according to recent reports the city is on track to meet them. However, 2020 will only be a step on the way to climate neutrality. This is the perspective provided by the German "Energiewende," and the neighboring city of Berlin has recently explicitly adopted this goal in an urban strategy. Although the 2010 concept offers some perspectives, no stringent strategy with concrete measures has yet been adopted.

- The rollout of solar PV systems on city rooftops has great potential for a greener city. The speed of this roll-out is still not satisfying, in part due to some slowing effects of a recent reform of the national FiT system, reducing the return rates for solar PV due to reduced production costs. This incentive problem also limits the use of a solar potential rooftop map, generated from the PIK-led concept consortium and available online.

- Once the incentive structure at the federal level has been changed again, this tool might become more effective.

- An accelerated energetic refurbishment of the city's building stock is needed, but so far no city-specific measures are available to realize this goal. National programs are available (for example, from the federal bank KfW), but Potsdam finds it difficult, given the still limited financial operation space of the city, to spur this process with "domestic" programs.

- Intervening in the traffic system, especially in the use of private cars in the city, is a politically hot topic. Fortunately, European and national legislation in the area of air quality improvement supports the climate goals in the traffic sector. However, even the rather strong and institutionalized policy area of air quality turns out to be a battleground for competing interests.

- In the area of urban planning and regulation of construction, the city is rather hesitating in setting energy standards that go beyond EU and national standards that have continuously improved in recent years. Given the considerable urban growth rate in the city, the amount of new buildings cannot be neglected.

An opportunity to overcome some of these barriers has been created recently. In early 2015, the lord mayor of Potsdam, mandated by the City Assembly, has initiated a visioning process ("Leitbildprozess"), by which the citizens are invited to express their views and visions for Potsdam's longer-term future. What should the city look like, in what direction and how shall it develop, what features should be strengthened, which ones weakened? In on- and off-line consultation processes citizens can post their preferences, which shall subsequently become an orientating framework for the work of the city administration and the City Assembly. Maybe Potsdam will become even "greener" by that "smart move."

Green City = Smart City?

Whether a city is smart or not depends of course of the definition of that term. In a conventional sense, smart cities need to capitalize on IT solutions to develop a smart economy, smart governance structures and procedures, smart people, a smart environment, smart mobility and smart living (Giffinger et al., 2007). In this volume, we would like to call cities smart if they make use of IT and human capital solutions to become greener. Measured against leading benchmarks in the *conventional* sense, Potsdam would probably rank only "medium."[5] While there are some activities at the administration level to push forward IT use in many domains, a coherent (conventional) smart city *strategy* for Potsdam does not exist—other than, say, in the case of Berlin.

However, Potsdam might qualify as a smart and green city as proposed by the definition used in this volume—for several reasons:

---

5   The study of Giffinger et al. (2007) develops indicators for all the dimensions of a conventional smart city and then ranks cities based on these indictors. Potsdam was not included.

- The city's energy system is becoming more *complex* and at the same time more *integrated*. More complex, as more renewable energy components are integrated and centralized large-scale systems (such as the district heating system) are merged with more decentralized system elements. The new hot water storage system, working both with fossil and renewable energy and shifting peak heat capacities seasonally into high-demand periods, is a good example of a smart solution, even if we neglect the IT components that are needed to manage it.

- At the EU and the federal level the roll-out for *smart metering* of energy use is currently prepared. The business sector will come first, the household sector will follow. Under current conditions, the high costs of these meters make them not attractive economically for private households with an annual electricity consumption of less than 6,000 kWh. In the future, however, smart meters will be key for virtual utilities and the integration of renewable energy systems as well as e-mobility solutions. Details of the applications of smart meters will depend on ongoing federal negotiations (BMWi, 2015). Potsdam has started to experiment with smart metering and—given its rather high share of well-off private households—might qualify for a national pilot study area in the near future.

- *Smart networks* are a core element of smart cities. In the case of Potsdam, energy and climate policy issues have led to the establishment of engaged and informed civil society actor networks. Representatives of environmental NGOs, energy experts, small and medium enterprises in the area, and engaged scientists have formed the "Energy Forum Potsdam" (http://www.energie-forum-potsdam.de/). The forum critically assesses the city's activities, and offers an arena for public debates. The city administration has established its own "official" network "climate partner" that links with the forum and taps into its knowledge and social capital.

- In the past couple of years, *participatory elements* have been introduced into the city government procedure. For example, there is an annual citizen budget campaign that collects the action priorities of the inhabitants. While the results of this public (including online) consulting are not binding for the City Assembly, endowed with the legal rights to pass the annual budgets, this "citizen budget" has had the power to exert some informal pressure on local decision makers. Another example is the already mentioned visioning process for Potsdam as a whole. First results show by the way that climate policy goals are put forward by the citizens themselves. Both examples can be interpreted as steps toward smart governance, in which the IT and online aspects are important, but the political implications are even more relevant for the process of becoming a smart green city.

A recent study on driving factors in Potsdam has found that implementation of proposed green measures was more likely to be successful when political promoters and legislative support existed. It also identified the crucial role of co-benefits: when promoters could link implementation of measures with their own agenda (for example, economic promotion, high publicity) implementation was also more likely (Twerdy, 2014). If this finding is seen together with the slight change of governance structures indicated above, the prospects for Potsdam to become smart and green are not bad.

The "beautiful" Potsdam, which is the historical center of the city today with its castles and parks, has been by and large a product of top-down decisions taken by kings and their consultants and planners. The smart green city that we can envision today as a possible future will—despite a non-negligible role of scientific consultants—by and large be a result of administrative action, democratic consensus, and citizen participation.

Conclusion focused on the near future

Potsdam stands for the large number of small- to medium-sized cities that fly under the radar of global megacities when it comes to debates about the future of urbanism, large touristic flows, and general public attention toward global prospects of the urban age. However, this city type hosts the majority of city dwellers worldwide, and its smaller size offers very interesting potential for becoming smarter and greener in the future.

This has to do with the city size: large enough to ensure that all classical features of the urban life (density, anonymous social relations, scale effects; cf. Bettencourt et al., 2007) are given, but small enough that the complexity of situations and decisions can be kept in manageable limits.

Potsdam is a growing city in the east of Germany that is characterized by a high quality of life, in part due to its historical heritage, but also by the vicinity of its big neighbor Berlin and a prospering service economy. Potsdam today has to face the challenges of urban growth (at least by German standards) in a shrinking state of which it is the capital.

There are many other German medium-sized cities that have managed to historically develop characteristic green features, such as Muenster with its huge share of bicycles in the transportation mix, or Freiburg with its solar architecture. These cities in the western part of Germany were able to create their green path dependencies as early as the 1970s or 1980s. Potsdam—as all other East German cities—could only do so since 1990. As we have seen, the flip side of this late-comer position was a rapid adoption of local climate policies, not least through the network effect of being a member in the European Climate Alliance. The lesson to be learned for other cities in the world that equally lack a long-standing tradition of green movements and/or green politics is that active membership in city networks can facilitate policy diffusion processes.

We have also seen that those network effects may form a necessary condition for becoming green and smart, but by no means a sufficient one. Not only do cities need a critical mass of engaged people both in the public administration and in civil society—if possible backed to some degree by the support of the political leadership, but certainly not hampered by it—they also need actors that are willing and able to invest in large infrastructure projects that break carbon-intensive pathways, or at least open up the option space for low-carbon solutions. The example of Potsdam's decision to move away from the local resource lignite shows that this can be realized even under unfavorable political conditions. It also shows that climate protection arguments alone in these cases lack the salience to convince political decision makers and investors. They need solid cost–benefit assessments, together with convincing narratives that they can tell the public and their shareholders.

Potsdam is also an example of the importance of smart actor networks and issue coalitions that bridge the gap between politics, the urban economy, and scientific expertise. We would like to generalize here: cities that host universities, research institutions, and/or think tanks can—if these intellectual capital holders are committed to invest their capital into solutions for a green and smart urban economy—move faster and, last but not least, be more sustainable toward that future. Besides the simple but important contribution they can make due to their expertise, their contribution lends credibility to green and smart projects.

The case of Potsdam reveals the fact that public administrations—or to be more precise: some "green" branches of these administrations that more often than not are confronted with many hurdles themselves—can realize their plans much better if the city has access or even decision power in terms of the urban economy, the public infrastructure, and the services that public utilities provide to businesses and private households.

A final conclusion we would like to draw has to do with visions and governance processes. More recently Potsdam has moved from the top-down mode of urban government to a more participatory approach of urban governance. In part, this participatory move is motivated by the combination of growing tasks and stagnating resources in dealing with them. But it is also a sign of a wider transformation process of public policies in general. Socio-technical innovations such as the Internet or social media have clearly pushed this transformation, which is by no means without risks, if we consider the fact that traditional forms of political representation—as limited as they might seem—have rather clear-cut standards of legitimation and transparency the new forms still have to develop. This makes it even more important that public bodies that are shifting to this new mode create new forms of public visioning and accountability. If—and we still do not know for sure—the citizens of Potsdam put forward smart and green issues in the city's current visioning process, another major step toward the public anchoring of a low-carbon urban future has been made.

References

Bettencourt, L.M.A. et al., 2007. "Growth, Innovation, Scaling, and the Pace of Life in Cities." *Proceedings of National Academy of Science*, vol.104, n.17, pp. 7301–7306.

BMWi (Bundesministerium für Wirtschaft und Energie)—Federal Ministry for Economy and Energy, 2015. Das Stromnetz wird intelligent BMWi veröffentlicht Eckpunkte für den künftigen Einsatz intelligenter Messsysteme und Zähler ("Smart Meter"). [Electricity Grid Becomes Smart—MoE Publishes Plan for Future Application of Smart Meters], February, 17, http://www.bmwi-energiewende.de/EWD/Redaktion/Newsletter/2015/3/Meldung/topthema-stromnetz-wird-intelligent.html.

City of Potsdam (LHP Potsdam), 2014. Klimaschutzberichte Potsdam 2010 und 2012. [Climate Protection Reports Potsdam 2010 and 2012]. Potsdam (15/SVV/0060).

European Environmental Agency (EEA), 2014. Annual European Community Greenhouse Gas Inventory 1990–2012 and Inventory Report 2014. EEA

Technical Report, Luxembourg, http://www.eea.europa.eu/publications/european-union-greenhouse-gas-inventory-2014, zuletzt geprüft am 09.05.2015.

Giffinger, R. et al., 2007. Smart Cities—Ranking of European medium-sized cities. Hg. v. Centre of Reigonal Science. Vienna University of Technology, Vienna, http://smart-cities.eu/download/city_ranking_final.pdf.

Landesamt für Umwelt, Gesundheit und Verbraucherschutz (LUGV) [State Agency for the Environment, Health and Consumer Protection], 2014. Klimagasinventur 2013 für das Land Brandenburg—Darstellung der Entwicklung der wichtigsten Treibhausgase und Analyse zur Minderung der energiebedingten CO_2—Emmssionen [Greenhousegas Inventory 2013 for Brandenburg—Trends and Analysis of Important Greenhouse Gases and Reduction Potential]. http://www.lugv.brandenburg.de/cms/media.php/lbm1.a.3310.de/klimagas_2013.pdf, zuletzt geprüft am 10.05.2015.

Potsdam Institute for Climate Impact Research (PIK), 2010. Integrated Climate Protection Concept Potsdam, https://www.potsdam.de/sites/default/files/documents/IntegriertesKlimaschutzkonzept2010.pdf.

Twerdy, F., 2014. Kommunaler Klimaschutz in Potsdam—Erfolgsfaktoren für die Umsetzung des Integrierten Klimaschutzkonzepts. [Municipal Climate Protection in Potsdam—Driving factors for Implementing the Integrated Climate Protection Concept]. Master Thesis, University of Potsdam, Potsdam.

Van Staden, M. and Musco, F. et al (Eds), 2010. *Local Governments and Climate Change. Sustainable Energy Planning and Implementation in Small and Medium Sized Communities*. Springer Science+Business Media B.V, Dordrecht.

Appendix D

Vilnius—A Smart Green City

NATALIJA LEPKOVA[1] AND DALIA BARDAUSKIENE[2]

Smart City Theoretical Approach

The Universities of Technology of Vienna and Delft, and the University of Ljubljana developed a definition of smart city that seems to have guided the first change of perspective: six axes along which the level of smartness of 70 medium-sized European cities could be evaluated. Not just data and information, but also mobility, environmental quality, governance, economy, social life, and sustainability which is liveability were all considered, bringing the concept of smart city within the orbit of the neoclassical economic theory on regional and urban development. This represented the first attempt to measure the level of smartness of a city, and pointed out the potential drivers to modify it to government and institutions (Mattoni et al., 2015).

The Analytic Network Process approach aims to identify the prevalent prototypes of smart cities from the four policy visions derived from the "Urban Europe" Joint Programming Initiative Urban Europe (JPI): Connected City (smart logistic and sustainable mobility), Entrepreneurial City (economic vitality), Liveable City (ecological sustainability), and the Pioneer City (social participation and social capital) (Mattoni et al., 2015).

A *smart city* (also smarter city) uses digital technologies to enhance performance and well-being, to reduce costs and resource consumption, and to engage more effectively and actively with its citizens. Key "smart" sectors

1 Associate Professor, Doctor of Technological Sciences at the Department of Construction Economics and Property Management, Civil Engineering Faculty, Vilnius Gediminas Technical University (Vilnius, Lithuania), Member of Lithuanian Association of Engineers. Contact: email: Natalija.Lepkova@vgtu.lt, natalijal2000@yahoo.com, Natalija.Lepkova@gmail.com.
2 Architect, Urbanist, past senior planner of City of Vilnius, Associate Professor, PhD of Humanities and Arts at Vilnius Gediminas Technical University (Vilnius, Lithuania). The member of International ISOCARP organization, Lithuanian architects association, President of Academy of Sustainable development. Contact: email: dalia.bard@gmail.com.

include transport, energy, health care, water, and waste and is therefore "green" due to its concerns for the environment. A smart city should be able to respond faster to city and global challenges than one with a simple "transactional" relationship with its citizens (Smart City, 2014).

Intelligent (smart) cities create more effective urban systems capable of addressing contemporary challenges and urban problems. They create more innovative and competitive cities, based on knowledge clusters, people-led innovation, and global networking; offering higher capacity of monitoring and management of environmental issues, improved city transportation, and more secure urban spaces (Smart City, 2014).

Vilnius—Capital of Lithuania

Vilnius is the capital of Lithuania, and its largest city, with a population of 529,022 as of 2014 (*Statistical Yearbook of Lithuania*, 2014). Vilnius is located in the southeast part of Lithuania and is the second biggest city of the Baltic states. The GDP of Vilnius was over 10 billion euros in 2014. Vilnius is classified as a Gamma global city according to Globalization and World Cities (GaWC) studies, and is known for its Old Town of beautiful architecture, declared a UNESCO World Heritage Site in 1994. Vilnius has some of the highest Internet speeds in the world, with an average download speed of 36.37 MB/s and upload speed of 28.51 MB/s (Wikipedia, 2015a). The current area of Vilnius is 402 square km (155 square miles). Buildings occupy 29.1 percent of the city; green spaces occupy 68.8 percent; and waters occupy 2.1 percent. Vilnius is the major economic center of Lithuania and one of the largest financial centers of the Baltic states (Wikipedia, 2015b). Vilnius is among the European cities with highest level of education.

Contemporary Vilnius is one of the fastest-growing cities in east and central Europe on the Baltic Sea, which is also the hub for political, economic, social, and environmental changes in Lithuania and the region as a whole.

Vilnius as a Smart Green City

After the Lithuania joined the EU in 2004, the government of Vilnius municipality made a decision to pursue smart solutions for the management of city's challenges and to engagement of inhabitants in the decision-making process.

The political decision is under implementation—the city boasts the fastest Internet connection in the world, a high quality of life, and the cleanest water and freshest air of any European city (The New Economy, 2014). The latest study by Eurostat shows 93 percent of inhabitants are satisfied with their life in Vilnius (European Commission, 2014).

Almost half of Vilnius is covered by green areas, that is, parks, public gardens, natural reserves, and others. Additionally, Vilnius is host to numerous lakes, where residents and visitors bathe and have barbecues in the summer. Thirty lakes and 16 rivers cover 2.1 percent of Vilnius's area, with some of them having sand beaches (Wikipedia, 2015b).

According to the "Quality of Life in European Cities" report, the percentage of inhabitants' satisfaction with the quality of the air in Vilnius city is 59 percent (European Commission, 2014).

Satisfaction with regard to green spaces is generally high in Vilnius—75 percent in 2012. Compared with 2009, the largest improvements in EU capitals in 2012 were noted also in Vilnius—75 percent (an increase of 14 percent from 2009) (European Commission, 2014).

SMART MANAGEMENT

The city's smart and forward-thinking management has been recognized by analysts and the media, and the rise in foreign direct investment and its effectiveness has also been reported (The New Economy, 2014).

The New York Times named Vilnius one of the world's 10 best-managed cities, alongside Berlin, Barcelona, Cape Town, Copenhagen, Montreal, Santiago, and Shanghai. Cities were evaluated not only on their quality of life but also on how wisely and well they are managed (*The New York Times*, 2011).

The Smart Vilnius concept is an effective city management tool; it creates urban systems capable of making democratic decisions addressing contemporary challenges and urban problems. The official website of Vilnius was developed to give greater information on the city's agenda.

The city government of Vilnius introduced e-participation platforms, which have involved citizens in the decision-making processes of the city. The official website of Vilnius was developed to give greater information on the city agenda. The site also allows citizens to express their opinions and make suggestions by interacting with the city council members, participating in polls, preparing e-petitions and even voting on the topics that are on the council's agenda. The online platform also makes it easy to access one of more than 100 online services for businesses and residents provided by the city—from licensing to permits and official documents (The New Economy, 2014).

GREEN PROGRAMS: LIGHTING THE CITY

Over the next two years, the city of Vilnius will be modernizing its street lighting. High-efficiency modern LED lighting fixtures will reduce energy consumption in the city by more than 70 percent. The technology will save over 2 million euros annually and will be implemented through a public–private partnership with Gemmo of Italy documents (The New Economy, 2014).

IMPROVING INFRASTRUCTURE

For the past decade, the city of Vilnius has been taking an integrated transport management approach and seeking the most suitable IT solutions to improve its public transportation. A number of projects have improved the mobility of both citizens and city guests.

The traffic monitoring and regulation system was deployed some years ago, while all the traffic lights in the city have been renewed and connected into a single traffic-monitoring center. It has had a tremendous impact on the traffic situation in the city: even though the number of cars increased by more than 40 percent during the past decade, the average journey time is shorter.

The public transportation system has also gone through positive changes. The city of Vilnius has introduced a single card for public transportation, together with dozens of new vehicles and fast-track buses to make journeys more comfortable and faster. What is more, a bike-sharing system has been launched to extend the possibilities of moving within the city. It has become one of the most popular means of transportation around the city center.

The city has recently launched a new mobile applications package, "Smart Vilnius" (m.Parking, m.Ticket, and m.Taxi). This mobile ticketing app allows commuters to buy tickets on their phones, plan a journey, and see live timetables. The mobile parking app—which has become extremely popular since its launch—has a start–stop function that allows users to pay only for the exact time they are parked, and removes the hassle of finding the correct change for the parking meter.

Improvements are also being made to the city's route planner app. It is being redesigned and will shortly include all kinds of transportation, from buses to city bikes, as well as the city's car-sharing system. It will also serve as a smart tool for planning journeys by car: it will inform drivers about traffic jams and suggest routes to avoid them.

In the city of Vilnius a bicycle hire system has been developed. There are 40 bike stations in the city. The stations are distributed in close proximity to each other in Vilnius city, so the user is never far away from being able to rent or return a bike. Open seven days a week, 24 hours a day, Cyclocity Vilnius is a self-service bike rental system open to everyone from 14 years of age. With 40 stations and around 300 bikes, it enables the user to travel through the city center, commute between home and work, and get out and about to enjoy the city of Vilnius at leisure. All stations are equipped to accept the Cyclocity Vilnius card, the Vilnius public transport card, and three-day ticket users. Once purchased, the user can use the three-day ticket in a similar way to the Cyclocity Vilnius or Vilnius public transport card in order to rent or return a bike from any station in the network. The first 30 minutes of use is free on every bike. After this first half-hour, a service charge applies (Cyclocity Vilnius, 2015).

By introducing the bicycle hire system, the city of Vilnius became more green and less polluted. The city's car-sharing system was developed in Vilnius. It provides the opportunity to use a car in the city at any time. There are several car renting and returning points in the city. The service is paid, and no contracts are required (Citybee Vilnius, 2015).

This approach to smart mobility was recognized by IBM, which awarded Vilnius a Smarter Cities Challenge grant. This money will help the city improve its transportation systems further, merging them and deploy different management and prediction tools (The New Economy, 2014).

RECENT INNOVATIVE PROJECTS IN THE CITY OF VILNIUS

- e-democracy tools;

- interactive map of the city;

- interactive energy classification map;

- mobile city applications;

- urban problems registry;

- e-services;

- centralized registration to preschool;

- online schools' sport halls renting system;

- social approach to public procurements;

- e-ideas room;

- safe city.

The city management of Vilnius needs a lot of information. The information flow is coming from different resources and needs to be integrated and used for different city management issues, as city planning and monitoring, transport, different registers, area pollution control, and so on. A web-based system (www.vilnius.lt/emiestas) provides this functionality and enables residents to participate in the decision making and implementation process, saving time, generating the economy, and so on.

E-democracy

E-democracy is web-based system which provides the opportunity for residents to access city council documentation, watch online streaming of council sessions, check voting results, submit proposals and ideas, participate in surveys, state opinion about legislation, create petitions, and so on. This service is only provided to registered users. Users can register via banking systems or using e-signature. All email messages from residents are registered via e-vice mayor direction and redirected to the appropriate municipality worker.

Interactive map of Vilnius city

The map has 25 layers (www.vilnius.lt/map):

- road load, traffic jams;

- schools;

- permits for construction;

- designed buildings;

- energy efficiency of buildings;

- urban problem registry;

- 3D model of the areas;

- outdoor cafés;

- bike lanes;

- and so on.

Interactive energy classification map

This map provides information on energy consumption of buildings in the town. The user of the system can select a particular building and receive information about its annual energy consumption along with other information.

Mobile City applications

There are three applications in operation

- **m. Parking**. The idea is to make parking in the city as easy as possible. This application is available for smartphones only. When a person arrives in an area, the application shows the payment zone (there are four zones in Vilnius with different rates and payment hours). When a zone is selected the user can enter the car number and click to make a parking booking.[3] This system means drivers do not have to carry cash for parking. Every 12 minutes the user received a text message with payment information.

- **m. Ticket**. This is a public transport ticket on a mobile phone. The user can buy, store, and use tickets on their smartphone. Using this application, the user can purchase the desired amount of any type of ticket.[4]

---

3   http://m-transportas.lt/lt/m-transport/m.Parking/.
4   http://m-transportas.lt/lt/m-transport/m.Ticket/.

- **m. Taxi.** This application allows the user to book a taxi. The customer can see the route and the rate per km. It also possible to read comments about the driver.[5]

URBAN PROBLEMS REGISTRY

Using this application it is possible to register a problem in the town online. Depending on the problem type, it will be registered and solved by the responsible subdivision of Vilnius municipality. For example, citizens of Vilnius could ask for a problem with a pavement to be fixed in a particular area of the city.[6]

E-SERVICES

Until 2014 there were 89 web-based e-services provided for residents and businesses: licenses, archive certificates, different type of permissions, applications for youth projects, permission for protected green pruning, and so on.[7]

ONLINE SCHOOLS' SPORT HALL RENTING SYSTEM

The procedures for residents to rent schools sports halls for leisure have been approved and from January 2013 an online system has been available on the Vilnius city website. Users are able to check whether the sports hall is available and pay via an e-banking system. It is helping to achieve transparency, increase school budgets, and encourage public participation in sport.[8]

E- IDEAS ROOM

The e-ideas room is a place in the administration building where Vilnius' residents can come and submit their own ideas or suggestions for municipality competence areas on how to improve management and reduce bureaucracy. An example of an idea is free Internet in the city for the citizens.

---

5   http://m-transportas.lt/lt/m-transport/m.Taxi.
6   www.vilnius.lt/problemos.
7   http://www.vilnius.lt/lit/E_paslaugos/691.
8   http://www.vilnius.lt/index.php?3652144830.

SAFE CITY

One of the applications is the centralized traffic control system. Vilnius's centralized traffic control system consists of the following subsystems:[9]

- traffic control center;

- traffic lights controllers;

- traffic lights;

- vehicle sensors (detectors);

- driver information system scoreboards;

- traffic video surveillance system;

- information system (web);

- speed measurement system.

The user of the system can see the interactive map of traffic in Vilnius.

Conclusion

Being a smart city makes life more convenient for both inhabitants and guests of the city. Being smart also provides green solutions for the city. Smart applications such as cyclocity and city's car-sharing systems reduce the pollution of the city and make life more comfortable and green. Smart and electronic applications allow the user to complete a lot of forms online, meaning that they don't have to spend time in special offices to solve particular problems. A lot of information is accessible online. Energy use monitoring systems can lead to effective solutions.

References

Citybee Vilnius, 2015. http://www.citybee.lt/en/, accessed April 27, 2015.

---

9   http://www.sviesoforai.lt/.

Cyclocity Vilnius, 2015. How Does it Work? http://en.cyclocity.lt/How-does-it-work, accessed April 27, 2015.

European Commission, 2013. Quality of Life in European Cities. Flash Eurobarometer 366 Report, p. 140, http://ec.europa.eu/public_opinion/flash/fl_366_en.pdf, accessed April 27. 2015.

European Commission, 2014. Quality of Life in European Cities. Flash Eurobarometer 366. Country Report Lithuania, p. 14, http://ec.europa.eu/public_opinion/flash/fl_366_nat_lt_en.pdf, accessed February 18, 2015.

Mattoni, B., Gugliermetti, F., and Bisegna, F., 2015. "A Multilevel Method to Assess and Design the Renovation and Integration of Smart Cities." *Sustainable Cities and Society*, vol.15, pp. 105–119.

Smart City, 2014. Wikipedia. http://en.wikipedia.org/wiki/Smart_city, accessed February 18. 2015.

Statistical Yearbook of Lithuania, 2014. Cities and Towns. Statistics Lithuania, Vilnius, p. 686.

The New Economy, 2014. Vilnius Becomes One of Europe's Smartest Cities. Business, July 21, http://www.theneweconomy.com/business/vilnius-becomes-one-of-europes-smartest-cities, accessed February 18, 2015.

The New York Times, 2011. Hip Cities That Think About How They Work, IHT Special Report: Smart Cities, http://www.nytimes.com/2011/11/18/business/global/hip-cities-that-think-about-how-they-work.html?pagewanted=all&_r=1&, accessed February 18, 2015.

Wikipedia, 2015a. Vilnius. http://en.wikipedia.org/wiki/Vilnius, accessed February 18, 2015.

Wikipedia, 2015b. Vilnius. Parks, Squares and Cemeteries. http://en.wikipedia.org/wiki/Vilnius#Parks.2C_squares.2C_and_cemeteries, accessed April 27, 2015.

Appendix E

Asia–Pacific Region: From Resource-hungry Cities to Smart Green Cities—Lessons from China and a Green Urban Development Agenda for the Asia–Pacific Region

STEFFEN LEHMANN, CURTIN UNIVERSITY, PERTH[1]

Introduction

Resource efficiency and greenhouse gas (GHG) emissions pose fundamental challenges for cities. Traditional urban planning methods and practices based on functionality and land use patterns are limited and unable to cope with fast-changing economic cycles and the requirements of rapid urbanization. To optimize resource use and renew planning methods, it is necessary to better understand and integrate the flows and inter-linkages between behavior on the one hand, and consumption of water, waste, food, energy, and transport on the other. Smart green cities are cities that are not necessarily more dependent on technology (for example, require more energy supply), but cities that have introduced urban systems and infrastructure that has made them more resilient and efficient.

---

1   Dr Steffen Lehmann is Head of the School of Built Environment at Curtin University in Perth, Western Australia. Prior to this, he was Chair and Professor of Sustainable Design and Director of the China-Australia Centre for Sustainable Urban Development at the University of South Australia in Adelaide; as well as Executive Director of the Zero Waste Centre for Sustainable Design and Behaviour. In 2008 he was appointed a UNESCO Chair in Sustainable Urban Development for Asia and the Pacific, a position he held for a number of years; since 2011 he has continued to work with UNESCO ex-officio, for instance as advisor for the UNESCO International Platform for Learning Cities. His latest books include: *Low Carbon Cities* (Routledge, 2015) and *Motivating Change* (Routledge, 2013). Email: steffen.lehmann@curtin.edu.au.

In this transformation process, not only technological innovation, but also economic, political, and social innovations will be essential. Some of the best opportunities for sustainable development are in small- to medium-sized cities, because these are transforming fast but can still be influenced. In this appendix case, I shall argue that the holistic concept of smart green urbanism offers systematic solutions to tackle the growth and complexities of cities and transform them into more sustainable urban settlements that maximize their use of resources while reducing emissions, pollution, and waste. While it is impossible to stop rapid urbanization, we can and must lessen its negative impacts. Policy-makers in the Asia and Pacific region, and worldwide, need to identify new approaches and development models to guide future urban growth. They need to look at the risk of "cities as usual" to civilization and the complexities of making the low-carbon paradigm shift.

The most intensive urbanization process in the Asia and the Pacific region is currently unfolding in China, which makes this country an interesting case study in regard to urban policy for ecocities. The dramatic scale and pace of urban growth and change in China has become a defining feature of the twenty-first century, with profound implications for people everywhere (Lehmann, 2015).

Urbanization in China is predicted to continue from 55 percent in 2015 to over 70 percent in 2030, with urban mega-regions developing, as currently around 20 million people are moving into cities annually. Chinese cities are, therefore, expected to swell by another 350 to 400 million residents in the next 25 years. Growth rates are highest in peri-urban areas, leading to further loss of productive agricultural land and biodiversity (UNEP, 2013).

Rapid urbanization throughout the Asia and Pacific region is likely to continue for at least another two decades. Therefore, its cities urgently need a new urban development agenda; one that implements the principles of green urbanism and transforms these cities into sustainable ecocities.

Forward-looking, future-focused cities are never at rest, but plan actively ahead. Approaching the key challenges of urbanization through the framework of green urbanism as a holistic strategy for tackling the challenges and curbing emissions from burning fossil fuels is not an option: it is the sole sustainable way forward.

Urbanization in the Asia and Pacific Region

The global urban population is expected to rise from 3.6 billion in 2010 to 6.3 billion by 2050. Cities in the People's Republic of China and India will be responsible for most of this urban population explosion. The projected growth of cities and towns in the Asia and Pacific region over the next two decades means that there is a need for urban planning principles that will create socially just, environmentally sustainable and economically prosperous cities (ESCAP, Lehmann and Thornton, 2014).

Electricity demand in Asian and Pacific countries is growing at around 4 percent annually. Over 90 percent of this electricity is generated from fossil fuels. This is especially important because, if we are to avoid the collapse of contemporary civilization predicted by researchers due to our obsession with economic growth and excessive use of finite resources (Ahmed, 2014; Beddington, 2009), our main hope of doing so lies with changing our urban systems. However, there are numerous perceptions of the notion of the "sustainable city" or "ecocity," which makes it difficult to compare and analyze existing proposals. In this discussion, the terms "ecocity" and "sustainable city" are used interchangeably.

The Principles of Green Urbanism: A Holistic Framework for Urban Development

There is plenty of scientific evidence that global warming will disrupt food and water supplies and cause irreversible damage to ecosystems. We can expect hotter cities, more heatwaves and urban flooding; rising sea levels; food and water shortages; and loss of biodiversity (plants and animals), which will cause drastic changes to natural systems and make cities more vulnerable.

The anticipated growth of cities and towns over the next two decades means that there is a need for urban planning principles that will create socially just, environmentally sustainable, and economically prosperous cities in the Asia–Pacific region. This can only happen if our economies and societies move away from high-consumption, fossil fuel-dependent, and wasteful "business as usual" urbanization models and investigate new concepts and approaches that generate wealth, jobs, and development without damaging the environment and ecosystems (Berners-Lee and Clark, 2013).

In most cities worldwide, where urban development over the past 50 years has been road-based, low-carbon urban cores are surrounded by suburbs emitting high levels of CO_2; a reason why we should limit suburban sprawl and increase population densities inside cities (ESCAP, 2011; UNEP, 2013). The concept of smart green urbanism shows that it is possible to do so. In the area of urban planning, green urbanism is a set of 15 holistic, interconnected principles that provide a way to plan for prosperous and sustainable ecocities that change in harmony with their environment (Lehmann, 2005; 2010). Introducing a practical post-fossil fuel urban agenda and shifting urban planning paradigms to green urbanism is urgent and essential.

There are four guidelines for creating sustainable ecocities (ESCAP, Lehmann and Thornton, 2014: 44–45):

1. Ecocities are holistic, so their planning and management must be cross-sectoral, integrated across urban services and infrastructure, and created through collaborative frameworks.

2. Ecocities grow from and rely on public awareness, so all residents, including city officials, need education about why sustainable urban development is essential and economically beneficial.

3. Ecocities require evidence-based research and sharing of knowledge and skills.

4. Ecocities (like any development) need stable sources of money, political will and long-term commitment.

With these guidelines in mind, Table AE1.1 sets out the 15 principles of green urbanism and some possible ways they could be implemented and measured.

Toward Resource-efficient Cities

Cities are getting bigger, busier, and denser. It's important for the Asia and Pacific region to develop new precincts of optimum urban density, avoiding outdated urbanization models that will create a range of problems. In the last 30 years, the availability of cheap fossil fuels has enabled rapid urbanization in the region, often with an urban form that followed sprawl models developed in the USA and Europe during the previous century and under radically different circumstances that allowed for private car-dependent suburbs and increasing

Table AE1.1   The 15 principles of green urbanism

The 15 principles of green urbanism	Sample recommendations and measures
Principle 1: Climate and context All urban development must be in harmony with the specific characteristics of each location.	Plan for development that works with the urban climate and bio-regional context. Improving the urban comfort conditions and air exchange rate at pedestrian level, through maintaining ventilation corridors and control of wind velocity through adequate massing.
Principle 2: Renewable energy for zero CO_2 emissions The city should be a self-sufficient on-site energy producer, using decentralized, district-based energy systems.	De-carbonize the energy supply; increase solar power to 10 percent of the energy mix by 2020; install smart grids and make solar hot water mandatory; generate at least 50 percent* energy on-site using precinct-scale renewable sources.
Principle 3: Zero-waste city The zero-waste city is a circular, closed-loop ecosystem that stops materials from going to landfill or incineration.	Implement "zero-waste city" ideas and plans; increase resource recovery rate towards 100 percent and stop land filling.
Principle 4: Water Ensure water security through and sensitive urban water management.	Use solar-powered desalination and recycle wastewater; keep fresh water consumption below 125 litres p. person p. day.*
Principle 5: Landscaping, gardens, green roofs, and biodiversity Maximize urban biodiversity through landscape strategies for productive open spaces.	Continue and increase tree planting programs. Constructing wetlands to purify and recycle grey water will also improve landscaping and biodiversity.
Principle 6: Transport and public space Anticipate future uses of public space so that it is more vital than simply a place of transit.	Invest over 6 percent of GDP in public transport,* expand tramlines and introduce free hybrid buses. Improve streets by giving greater priority to pedestrians and cyclists.
Principle 7: Local materials Use regional materials in construction and apply pre-fabricated modular systems.	Use engineered timber construction systems and make recyclability and re-use of construction elements compulsory.
Principle 8: Density and retrofitting Retrofit districts, encourage urban infill.	Continue street upgrading and introduction of bike lanes. Make public space more useful with natural elements designed for active living.
Principle 9: Green buildings and districts Apply deep green building design strategies for all new buildings using passive design principles.	Re-introduce passive design principles and demand higher ratings. Promote energy-saving building designs and full home insulation. Offer better housing choices and more diversity in urban infill.
Principle 10: Liveability, healthy communities, and mixed-use Emphasize affordable housing, mixed-use programs, and a healthy community; urban design being appropriate for children and an ageing population.	Include min. 25 percent affordable housing in every development* and use modular prefabricated construction systems. Reduce taxation of inner-city housing. Increase retrofitting and adaptive re-uses.

Table AE1.1   The 15 principles of green urbanism (*concluded*)

The 15 principles of green urbanism	Sample recommendations and measures
Principle 11: Local food Create a local food supply, with high food security and urban agriculture.	Introduce urban farming in at least 20 percent of the public parks.* Maintain urban hinterland for food production.
Principle 12: Cultural heritage A safe and healthy city, which is secure and just.	Consult and involve communities to ensure genuine commitment.
Principle 13: Governance and leadership Apply best practice for urban governance and sustainable procurement methods.	Create public–private partnerships to facilitate change, involve community groups and NGOs.
Principle 14: Education, research and knowledge-sharing Provide education and training for all in sustainable urban development.	Invest min. 3 percent of GDP in research and innovation.* Facilitate sustainable behaviors and provide incentives for long-term behavior change by positively influencing values to reduced consumption.
Principle 15: Special strategies for cities in developing countries To harmonize the impacts of rapid urbanization and globalization.	Cities require adjusted strategies appropriate for the developing world, e.g. mass housing typologies.

Note: *All suggested figures are benchmarks derived from current best practices.
Source: Lehmann, 2010.

urban footprints. Urban sprawl makes cities more car-dependent, less efficient, less resilient, and therefore less competitive. More compact and mixed-use urban development makes much more sense because it facilitates integrated and efficient low-carbon public transport (for example, light railway or metro); it enables low-carbon or carbon-free mobility, such as cycling and walking; and it promotes car sharing or car-pooling, all of which can dramatically reduce urban GHG emissions (John et al., 2013). Light rail in particular is now considered as a solution to a range of urban problems and there are numerous examples of cities in Australia that are now in the process of reintroducing light railway (from Sydney, the Gold Coast, and Newcastle to Parramatta, Bendigo, Canberra, Ciarns, and Hobart).

Light rail-based urban development brings reduced traffic, creates more walkable and lively places to live and work, and most of all attracts developers and financiers to enable denser, mixed-use development.

Middle suburbia offers good opportunities to accommodate population growth. Densification through urban infill can bring smaller environmental footprints and greater potential for services-rich, walkable areas to live in while avoiding the far less efficient sprawling urban fringe around a high-density urban core. There is now ample evidence that low-density suburbs account for more GHG emissions per household than compact urban areas where residents tend to live in smaller homes, use more public transit, and create much lower carbon footprints.

The most important factors that influence consumption (household income, vehicle ownership, and home size) all tend to be greater in suburbs. Transportation, typically responsible for 30 to 40 percent of overall household emissions in industrialized cities, is the most important factor in the emission differences between suburbs and core cities. Suburban transport emissions from cars can be as much as 2.5 times higher than urban ones. Residences 20 to 60 km from workplaces produce the highest emissions.

The focus of sustainable urban development has recently started to shift from individual buildings to the larger neighborhood and precinct scale, which will facilitate the integration of a new generation of green infrastructure and decentralized technologies. The higher densities common to the Asia and Pacific's cities allow for the implementation of decentralized and more efficient urban systems and infrastructure (for example, cogeneration, energy, and waste infrastructure, stormwater storage and re-use, cycling pathways) and facilitate a more compact, walkable urban form that influences any precinct's resource consumption patterns. Smart sustainable infrastructure for the twenty-first century must operate at the precinct scale: it includes smart grids, interconnected solar roof tops, bicycling path networks, light rail, wastewater recycling, local resource recovery stations, and community gardens—all as decentralized parts of an urban system that operates at the scale of the community or neighborhood.

Lessons from China's Experience and Redirection

The most intensive urbanization process in the Asia and Pacific region is unfolding in China which, combined with the fact that it is the world's most populous country, makes this nation an interesting case study. China now has 140 cities with over 1 million inhabitants and it is projected that 1 billion Chinese (70 percent of the population) will be urban by 2030 when China is projected to have 200 cities exceeding 1 million inhabitants. By 2050, China plans to complete its urban modernization process in which the development of mega-urban regions (urban clusters) in coastal areas plays an important role. It is expected that new urban populations will aggregate in eight to 10 coastal polycentric mega-metropolitan regions, each exceeding 40 million inhabitants and with residential densities of up to 8,000 people per square km (McKinsey & Company, 2009).

The dramatic scale and pace of urban growth in China has become a defining feature of the twenty-first century because of its profound global implications. The emerging Chinese middle classes will have consumption aspirations whose impacts will be felt around the world. Worldwide, cement and steel prices have risen because of Chinese demand. Therefore, if we can identify practical and successful solutions for China's urban sustainability, these will be of global benefit, especially if replicable.

China's urban transformation requires strategic interventions, innovative policies, and actions implemented at the local level, because cities will be the key actors in achieving sustainable development. It is particularly important for China to assess the impact of urban development policy on air and water quality, because these have emerged as major problems. Today, air pollution is driving all related environmental efforts in China, including sustainable urban planning, energy efficiency, renewable energy, and low-carbon development.

China's Pathway to Smart Sustainable Urban Development?

Urbanization has been one of the major facilitators in China's phenomenal economic growth. A key driver was rapid expansion of energy-intensive industries (Urry, 2013; Li, 2014). As a result, energy consumption increasing six-fold over 30 years, and coal accounted for around 70 percent of China's total energy mix. Perhaps not surprisingly, China now accounts for over a quarter of all global GHG emissions (EPA, 2014) and has major air pollution problems. In 2010, over 1.2 million premature deaths were attributable to outdoor particulate pollution (HEI, 2013). In some Chinese cities, air pollution has been 30 times the recommended upper limit. In January 2013 China experienced severe pollution levels in an area of 1.43 million square km and reached dangerous levels in 71 of 74 examined cities, negatively affecting health and productivity.

While China's 12th Five-Year Plan (2011–2015) includes important emission reduction targets, severe air pollution, rapidly rising consumption levels and rising emissions remain serious challenges. Air pollution is now the strongest driver to curb China's highly energy-intensive urbanization, which leaves little space for any growth in coal consumption. Although China has already increased its use of natural gas, its gas resources are quite limited and unevenly distributed. With Chinese cities expected to swell by another 350 to 400 million residents in the next 25 years, a post-fossil fuel urbanization agenda will be essential (China National Statistical Bureau/LBNL, 2012).

China's strategy of urban transformation entered a new period around 2013, in an attempt to leave behind single-minded growth targets and rapid expansion, high consumption and emissions. China's government has recognized the environmental and social problems caused "disorderly and inefficient urban developments, an imbalanced urban-rural and regional development and the unharmonious social development" (Wei, 2013).

Creating livable and green cities is now an important part of China's modernization goals. But rapid urbanization can easily overwhelm municipalities, landscapes, and communities, and not only in environmental terms. The social challenges in times of rapid change are also immense, including affordability of housing and provision of age-friendly neighborhoods. Government and the private sector deliver housing and set the standards for subsequent developments by private developers. Strong development guidelines are essential as these dictate how cities will grow and develop their future character.

In the last two decades, China's urban boom has become synonymous with traumatic individual experiences, with poor farmers leaving the countryside in the hope of finding better job opportunities and dreams of an air-conditioned flat, private car, and supermarkets full of goods; but ending up instead as a new urban underclass. There is now an increasing awareness of socio-economic inequality and the need to base the economy on innovation and knowledge rather than simply on cheap labor and environmental exploitation. Now that the need to protect agricultural land (food supply) is also being acknowledged, urbanization models have started to move away from western sprawl concepts toward growth boundaries.

Chinese Policies and Recent Reforms

China is increasingly interested in altering its unsustainable development and introducing better standards and environmental values in their urbanization programs. The government has initiated pilot programs to explore sustainable urbanization in varied types of cities. The 2015 priorities include pursuing land reform, reforming urban planning and design, managing environmental pressures, and improving local governance. The Ministry of Housing and

Urban-Rural Development (MoHURD) has launched ecocity pilots, while the National Development and Reform Commission (NDRC) is leading efforts in low-carbon provincial and city pilots. Dozens of provinces and cities have been enrolled in such schemes, receiving political and technical support from the central government, research institutions, as well as international foundations and development agencies.

A younger generation of urban dwellers is now demanding higher living standards; better quality of life; and the type of environmental protection they have seen when visiting Seoul, Singapore, Sydney, or Tokyo. They are demanding a cleaner environment and social well-being, not just growth (World Bank, 2012: 36). But whether the Asia and Pacific region is innovative enough to meet its challenges of rapid urbanization, air pollution, and renewable energy remains a major question. Governments and municipalities throughout the region will also need to develop better participatory models to involve their communities and citizens, and implement incentives to encourage people to move to public transport and take better care of the ecosystem, which risks destruction if the consumption patterns of the last three decades perpetuate.

Cases of Ecocities in China

By adopting new approaches to urbanization, China can assure more balanced investment, address a major source of debt, and clean up the country's environment. Today, "master plans" are increasingly seen as inadequate, because these are too inflexible to deal with the speed of change and rapid developing cities; instead, more flexible and adaptable frameworks that can accommodate change are needed (Roseland, 1997; Satterthwaite, 1999). However, there are promising major developments about rethinking cities and planning instruments, and exploring urban solutions based on walkability, cycling, and public transport. Self-contained, compact ecocity projects are underway in China (for instance, ecocity projects in Chengdu, Wanzhuang, and Qingdao; and an eco-park project in Ningbo), which could become prototypes for other cities and countries.

There are generally two types of ecocity initiatives in China: new-built ecocity projects (for example, Sino-Singapore Tianjin Eco-city and Qingdao Eco-park); and eco-remodelling or retrofitting of existing cities (for example, Wanzhuang and Huainan). Because of the scale of the task, ecocity efforts are at risk of being just a drop in the ocean of China's rapidly looming environmental crisis and a lot more needs to be done than a few show-pony ecocities.

While China is working hard to create its sustainable future and to enhance the well-being of its urban citizens, actually implementing the various ecocity projects and overcoming barriers has proven sometimes difficult. For instance, Tianjin Eco-city, currently under construction and thought to be the most advanced of China's ecocities, is widely seen as too conventional in its plan and energy supply and lacking genuine green ambition, not living up to its early expectations (Girardet, 2010; ICLEI, 2012).

Tianjin Eco-city is an initiative by the Chinese and Singaporean governments for a new-built flagship urban development. They have identified 26 key performance indicators, mainly around resource efficiency, in this innovative demonstration project. The Sino-German Qingdao Eco-park initiative in Qingdao has recently adopted Tianjin's framework (Xie, 2012). Both developments are expected to accommodate a large number of residents upon final completion in 20 years: 350,000 in Tianjin and 60,000 in Qingdao; the common sustainability framework is based on four dimensions: economy, society, environment, and resources.

Other visionary ecocity projects across China have seen little progress when facing the harsh reality of investment decisions and lack of policy continuity. The pioneering green city project Dongtan (close to Shanghai), for instance, stalled in 2008 after political leadership changes. Other projects have only been realized as ordinary real estate developments and greenfield developments, or even as gated communities for high-income households, in conflict with true ecocity principles. Chinese "green-washing" advertisements for conventional developments have cast the ecocity concept in the wrong light, which is disappointing, given the importance of China's role in leading the way for other countries to pursue sustainable development (Lehmann, 2013a).

But there are also good signs: Ningbo City is planning an eco-park in an industrial zone in the Zhenhai District, with a large constructed wetland which will purify polluted water and reduce the amount of run-off; a wastewater treatment plant releases treated water into the wetland, where the plants, along with microbes and soil, will absorb the organic waste and heavy metal in the run-off. The factories will reuse the water from the park. Zhenhai District has already significantly invested in five forest areas to separate the industrial from the residential zone with a 200-meter-wide forest belt with a total area of 10 sq. km and 1.5 million trees.

Chinese cities will continue to be the engine of the country's growth story, but they must continue their transformation toward real long-term sustainability and better social integration (Lehmann, 2013b). The upside is that China now has more researchers than any other country exploring better urban futures. With this shift to a knowledge-based economy and the global center of gravity shifting to Asia and the Pacific, it is timely to learn from sustainability efforts and experiments in China.

Policy Approaches for Smart Green Ecocities

Cities have an important role in showing what is possible, not only in terms of reducing emissions, but also in terms of creating low-carbon prosperity. The capacity to formulate strategic urban policies, the unique decision-making capabilities of municipalities and the operational scale at the community level all ensure that cities are well placed to innovate in sustainable urban development and to make well-informed integrated decisions. While cities are key actors in sustainable development, they also require supportive partnerships and adequate funding to fulfill the high expectations for a post-fossil fuel urban development agenda that implements the principles of green urbanism.

Asian and Pacific cities need new vision, to turn them into eco-positive powerhouses of dynamic innovation and to lead development in green urbanism. That requires partnerships among municipalities as well as learning valuable lessons from cities in China that have been able to accommodate urbanization on a scale that is, no doubt, difficult to grasp. The aim is to better understand the drivers and barriers to (and consequences of) effective climate governance in Asian and Pacific cities. There is growing agreement that urbanization has to be shifted onto more sustainable pathways to address pollution control and climate change challenges at the same time; the principles of smart green urbanism provide a conceptual model and map for that pathway.

Understandingly, the sheer complexities of resource transformations to support green urbanism will be immense, posing a huge challenge to break away from unsustainable pathways.

Action is a matter of urgency, collectively and individually, to bring the benefits of sustainable urban development to all Asian and Pacific cities. Behavior change has been recognized as a key factor in the transition toward low-carbon cities and the acceptance of new low-carbon technologies; it will be important to integrate this understanding in the formulation of new urban policies. Pro-environmental behavior requires a change in values and mindsets (Lehmann, 2015).

Urbanization is a force that has changed our ways of thinking and acting, ways of using space, lifestyles, social and economic relations, and consumption patterns. If we want to avoid the imminent collapse of our technologically-based civilization we need to revise and rethink the city and our urban futures in keeping with the principles of green urbanism. This new urban agenda can encourage innovation, harness the transformational power of cities, and achieve sustainable development.

Clearly, innovation is the key to better urbanization models: utilizing urban data and new technologies—but not only technological, also economic, political, and social innovations are essential so that people can participate in creating the healthy and sustainable future that all of us want. Integrated models of participatory planning approaches are a promising way forward. We know that being more resource-efficient and less carbon-intensive in production and more equitable in distribution are the only viable ways forward for our citizens, our cities, and our planet. The question is: do we have the will to act upon it?

References

Ahmed, Nafeez, 2014. NASA-funded Study: Industrial Civilisation Headed for "Irreversible Collapse"?, *The Guardian*, http://www.theguardian.com/environment/earth-insight/2014/mar/14/nasa-civilisation-irreversible-collapse-study-scientists, accessed March 20, 2014.

Beddington, John, 2009. Food, Energy, Water and the Climate: A Perfect Storm of Global Events?, UK Government Office for Science, London, http://www.bis.gov.uk/assets/goscience/docs/p/perfect-storm-paper.pdf, accessed March 20, 2014.

Berners-Lee, Mike and Duncan Clark, 2013. *The Burning Question*. Profile Books, London.

China National Statistical Bureau/Lawrence Berkeley National Lab (LBNL), 2012. China.

Energy Statistical Year Book 2012, report by the China Energy Group, Berkeley/Beijing, http://china.lbl.gov/sites/all/files/key-china-energy-statistics-2012-june-2012.pdf, accessed February 15, 2014.

Environmental Protection Agency (EPA), 2014. Global Greenhouse Gas Emissions Data, published annually by the EPA USA, Washington, DC, http://www.epa.gov/climatechange/ghgemissions/global.html, accessed May 5, 2014.

Girardet, Herbert, 2010. *Regenerative Cities*. World Future Council and HCU, Hamburg.

Health Effect Institute (HEI), 2013. *Outdoor Air Pollution among Top Global Health Risks in 2010: Risks Especially High in China and Other Developing Countries of Asia*. HEI, Beijing.

International Council for Local Environmental Initiatives (ICLEI), 2012. *Local Governments for Sustainability Report: Building an Eco City, Building a Sustainable City*. ICLEI, Bonn.

John, Mabel, Stefan Lehmann, and Alpana Sivam, 2013. "The Sustainable Design and Renewal of Water's Edge Public Spaces in the Asia–Pacific Region: Sydney, Hong Kong and Singapore." *Journal of Sustainable Development*, vol.6, n.8, pp. 26–52.

Lehmann, Stefan, 2005. "Towards a Sustainable City Centre: Integrating Ecologically Sustainable Development Principles into Urban Renewal." *Journal of Green Building*, vol.1, n.3, pp. 83–104.

Lehmann, Stefan, 2010. *The Principles of Green Urbanism: Transforming the City for Sustainability*. Earthscan, London.

Lehmann, Stefan, 2013a. Working with China on Urban Challenges, Eco-Business, Singapore, www.eco-business.com/opinion/working-with-china-on-urban-challenges/, accessed March 15, 2013.

Lehmann, Stefan, 2013b. "Low-to-no Carbon City: Lessons from Western Urban Projects for the Rapid Transformation of Shanghai." *Habitat International*, Special Issue: Low Carbon City, 37, pp. 61–69.

Lehmann, Stefan, 2015. *Low Carbon Cities. Transforming Urban Systems*. Routledge, London.

Li, Yun, 2014. Real Land Reform Requires More Than Words. *China Daily*, April 3, Beijing, p. 17, http://usa.chinadaily.com.cn/business/2014–04/03/content_17404151.htm, accessed April 10, 2014.

McKinsey & Company, 2009. *Preparing for China's Urban Billion*. McKinsey & Co., Beijing.

Roseland, Mark (Ed.), 1997. *Eco-City Dimensions: Healthy Communities, Healthy Planet*. New Society Publishers, Gabriola Island, BC.

Satterthwaite, David, (Ed.) 1999. *Reader in Sustainable Cities*. Earthscan, London.

United Nations Economic and Social Commission for Asia and the Pacific (UN ESCAP), 2011. *Are We Building Competitive and Liveable Cities? Guidelines for Developing Eco-efficient and Socially Inclusive Infrastructure*. UN ESCAP, Bangkok.

United Nations Economic and Social Commission for Asia and the Pacific (UN ESCAP), Lehmann, Stefan and K. Thornton, 2014. Planning Principles for Sustainable and Green Cities in the Asia-Pacific Region: A New Platform for Engagement, Report, Bangkok.

United Nations Environment Programme (UNEP), 2013. City-level Decoupling: Urban Resource Flows and Governance of Infrastructure Transitions. Geneva, UNEP, www.unep.org/resourcepanel, accessed November 15, 2013.

Urry, John, 2013. *Societies beyond Oil*. Zed Books, London.

Wei, Houkai, 2013. "China's Urban Transformation Strategy in New Period." *Chinese Journal of Urban and Environmental Studies*, vol.1, n.1.

World Bank, 2012. *Sustainable Low-Carbon City Development in China*. World Bank, Washington, DC.

Xie, Tonny H., 2012. "Tianjin Eco-City in China" in Simon Joss, Editor. *International Eco-Cities Initiative: Tomorrow's City Today. Eco-City Indicators, Standards & Frameworks* (Bellagio Conference Report), University of Westminster, London, p. 16.

Appendix F

Smart Cities in Small Island Nations: Paving the Way to Smart Green Mauritius

VISHWAMITRA OREE, ABDEL KHOODARUTH KHOODARUTH,
MOHAMMAD KHALIL ELAHEE, AND WOODROW W. CLARK II[1]

Overview

Mauritius is a small island nation of just 1,865 square km with a population of about 1.3 million located in the southwest of the Indian Ocean near East Africa. The last three decades has seen sustained and significant economic progress in the island. During this time, the country has successfully achieved the transition from a mono-crop economy, largely dependent on the sugar industry, to a thriving multi-sector and diversified economy resting on tourism, agro-industry, textile, financial services as well as information and communication technologies (ICT).

Against this backdrop, the GDP per capita has more than tripled during last three decades reaching around USD 10,000 in 2013 (Statistics Mauritius, Ministry of Finance and Economic Development, 2014a). According to economic statistics from the World Bank, Mauritius ranked first among countries in the Sub-Saharan Africa region in terms of GDP per capita (The World Bank Group, n.d.). Given their status as hubs for economic progress and employment, cities have experienced rapid growth. In line with their counterparts worldwide, Mauritius is facing unprecedented challenges mostly related to the relentlessly growing pace of urbanization. These challenges include population rise, traffic

---

1   Vishwamita Oree contact at: v.oree@uom.ac.mu, Abdel Khoodaruth contact at: a.khoodaruth@uom.ac.mu, M. Khalil Elahee contact at: elahee@uom.ac.mu and Woodrow W. Clark II contact at: www.clarkstrategicpartners.net.

congestion, pollution, social exclusion, growing energy and water needs, waste management, and security.

The sheer scale of these issues has motivated the government to consider new urban development paradigms that will encompass social, economic, and environmental sustainability. Pursuant to this goal, the government proposed to develop eight smart cities in its national budget 2015–2016. The smart cities will be spread across the island. Some 3,000 hectares of land and an estimated investment of USD 4 billion will be required to spur this new wave of development (Ministry of Finance and Economic Development, n.d.).

Introduction

Although this initiative underlines the efforts of the government to set the course for an overall urban transformation, it has not yet generated the expected enthusiasm among the population, mainly due to two reasons. Firstly, it comes on the heels of two resort development schemes introduced in the country and essentially aimed at rich foreigners. The Integrated Resort Scheme (IRS) and the Real Estate Scheme (RES) were designed to facilitate the acquisition of luxury residential properties in scenic locations by non-citizens. The underlying motivations for these projects were to boost economic growth through foreign currency inflow, support ancillary industries including construction and entrepreneurship, as well as job creation.

Besides, these policy and land-driven programs were expected to foster social inclusion through significant investment in social activities and infrastructure in neighboring regions. However, most of them turned out to be rich ghettos amidst much modest surroundings. Local communities in the vicinity of the luxurious gated communities felt alienated from the development. Secondly, the concept of smart city has been a buzzword increasingly used by policy-makers and researchers in recent years. It is often heralded as the panacea for all urban troubles and ranks high on the strategy agendas of many governments in both developed and emerging economies. Yet, there is no consensus on the definition and elements of a smart city (Dameri and Cocchia, 2013).

Moreover, there exists no framework to collect and share good practices from successful experiences that would have helped to chart a roadmap for the implementation of smart cities. Nevertheless, the design considerations of smart cities are largely dependent on some country-specific factors that go beyond its socio-economic indicators. These factors can capture a whole range of institutional, political, cultural, and climatic variables that have a bearing in assessing the needs and the approaches to the development of a smart city policy (Neirotti et al., 2014).

The Government of Mauritius has already taken a step in the right direction by constraining the planned smart cities to integrate four country-specific attributes (Board of Investment, 2015). At the outset, they should be driven by a priority theme for the country. For instance, the country is currently focusing on logistics and distribution, airport/port-related activities, ocean-based and knowledge-based economy. Then, the smart cities should exhibit a large-scale integrated development project that is environment-friendly, self-sufficient in terms of energy and water resources and enabled by state-of-the-art connectivity and modern sustainable transportation. They should also promote the live, work, and play concept. Finally, they should integrate a dedicated area for the dissemination of arts and culture where talent can be cultivated and nurtured (Board of Investment, 2015).

The ensuing sections will elaborate on the cornerstones of smart cities in Mauritius to ensure a holistic approach by embracing environmental, social, and economic sustainability measures. They also explore strategies that may help to steer the country through the urban transformation by adopting a proactive approach that anticipates future change and exploits new opportunities.

Priorities of Mauritian Smart Green Cities

According to the last census conducted in 2011, the population density of Mauritius had increased from 578 to 604 persons/ square km during the period 2000 to 2011, ranking it as the sixth most densely populated country in the world (Central Statistics Office, Republic of Mauritius, 2011). Forty percent of the total population lived in the five towns of the island, representing only 8 percent of the land. These figures amount to a population density of 3000 persons/square km in urban regions, about eight times denser than that in rural areas (Central Statistics Office, Republic of Mauritius, 2011). The obvious lack of proper planning of towns has led to citizens becoming increasingly frustrated with the environment they live in. The move toward smart cities will address several of the inherent environmental issues that would have been bolstered by a sustained population rise. In particular, energy and water consumption, pollution, traffic jams, and waste management remain the primary concerns in view of their high cost implications for both citizens and public administration.

ENERGY

Energy is a pervading issue as it influences other issues that will be tackled by smart cities, such as economy, pollution, and housing. The total primary energy requirement of Mauritius has been increasing consistently at an average annual rate of 2 percent during the last decade and nearly 85 percent of it was met from imported fossil fuels in 2013 (Statistics Mauritius, Ministry of Finance and Economic Development, 2014b). The remaining share was obtained from local renewable sources, mostly bagasse and hydro. The financial implications of such an over-reliance on fossil fuels is alarming, evidenced by the fact that petroleum products and coal accounted for around 21 percent of the total imports bill of the country in 2013 (Statistics Mauritius, Ministry of Finance and Economic Development, 2014a).

Mauritius has adopted several stringent measures in its long-term energy strategy to quash this unsustainable trend. Thus, the country has pledged to achieve 35 percent self-sufficiency in its electricity supply by 2025 through use of renewable energy sources and to improve energy efficiency in all sectors of the economy (Republic of Mauritius, Ministry of Renewable Energy and Public Utilities, 2009). The planned energy mix to reach the 35 percent target in 2025 is detailed in Table AF1.1. Energy will be central in the proposed smart cities given that it is required to power all fundamental urban functions. Traditionally, renewable sources of energy and enhanced energy efficiency have constituted the pillars of the energy conundrum for smart city projects.

The promising potentials of solar, both thermal and PV, and wind energy in the tropical island bode well with the aspirations of a substantial renewable share in the electricity mix. Meanwhile, innovations that merge ICT with the field of energy will lead to a new array of services that will facilitate monitoring and control of energy consumption. Thus, energy-efficiency mechanisms coupled with demand-side management programs may considerably curtail the continuous need to expand power generation capacity. In this context, the advent of micro-grids, with energy storage capacity embedded, will better leverage smaller renewable generation resources to create a shared demand profile and improve the power system performance and resilience.

MOBILITY

Transportation is the major final energy consumer in Mauritius, accounting for 50.4 percent of the total final energy consumption of the country (Statistics Mauritius, Ministry of Finance and Economic Development, 2014b). The number of vehicles

Table AF1.1 Targeted energy mix for the period 2015–2025

Fuel Source 2010		Percentage of Total Electricity Generation			
		2015	2020	2025	
Renewable	Bagasse	16%	13%	14%	17%
	Hydro	4%	3%	3%	2%
	Waste to energy	0	5%	4%	4%
	Wind	0	2%	6%	8%
	Solar Photovoltaic	0	1%	1%	2%
	Geothermal	0	0	0	2%
	Sub-total	20%	24%	28%	35%
Non-Renewable	Fuel Oil	37%	31%	28%	25%
	Coal	43%	45%	44%	40%
	Sub-total	80%	76%	72%	65%
TOTAL		100%	100%	100%	100%

Source: Republic of Mauritius, Ministry of Renewable Energy and Public Utilities, 2009

on the roads more than doubled during the last decade, from 291,605 in 2004 to reach 454,226 in 2013 (Statistics Mauritius, Ministry of Finance and Economic Development, 2014a). A study revealed that traffic congestions cost an estimated USD 33 million annually due to extra fuel consumption (Mauritius Employers Federation, 2007). The road network of the island is the fourteenth most congested in the world with 107 vehicles per km of road (Mecometer)(Mecometer). A largely inefficient public transportation system further encourages massive use of private cars and contributes to the degradation of the situation.

More than 100,000 vehicles enter the capital city of Port Louis every day. Port Louis not only represents the economic hub of the country but also accommodates most governmental departments. As such, the provision of urban mobility will be a key element in Mauritian smart city design. Already, one of the proposed smart cities will house government institutions. Several familiar measures are also envisaged to foster urban mobility: an efficient and sustainable public transportation service, electric and hydrogen fuel cell vehicles, car sharing, adequate parking facilities, and efficient road infrastructure with dedicated bike tracks. The charging systems for electric vehicles can in turn supplement the storage and regulation services of the energy system through the V2G technology, illustrating of the cross-cutting potential of these smart measures.

In addition to these conventional approaches, digital technology solutions can be integrated to plan transportation schedules and routes based on demand. For example, smartphones can be used to monitor traffic, detect congested areas, and determine alternative routes for a sounder use of existing transport infrastructure. Feedback of road users on social networks can be combined with traffic information from authorities to equip people with better and more reliable traffic status.

WATER MANAGEMENT

Water management is currently a highly intractable challenge for the Mauritian government with far-reaching socio-economic implications. Although the island receives a large amount of rainfall on an annual basis, water scarcity occurs due to several reasons. The limited water capture capability stands at 90.7 million m^3 which supplies the domestic sector together with other water-hungry services and industries like tourism, agriculture, textiles, and hydroelectricity. It is also highly likely that a large fraction of treated water leaks from the obsolete distribution system. Furthermore, only an estimated 10 percent of annual precipitation feeds the ground water recharge (Statistics Mauritius, Ministry of Finance and Economic Development, 2014a).

Finally, at a relatively cheap average price of USD 0.33 per m^3 of water, there is no compelling incentive to save water. Hence, efficient water resources management must form an integral part of the emerging vision for smart urban development in Mauritius. The move toward a sustainable water management model must be addressed as a package of long-term strategies that will aim at maximizing rain water capture, eliminate leakage in the distribution system, reduce operational costs, and improve customer control.

The inclusion of green water systems in building codes to promote rooftop rainwater harvesting, enhance groundwater recharge, and foster water-efficient landscapes constitutes a first step toward ensuring self-sufficiency. Moreover, the integration of ICT through smart water meters and sensor technology in the water production and distribution stages will be effective in identifying leaks and devise optimal pricing mechanisms to spur water conservation.

WASTE MANAGEMENT

Urban waste management is another tough challenge for many countries around the world and Mauritius is no exception. With urbanization accelerating at pace and the tourism sector ever-growing, solid waste is rapidly developing into a major and persistent issue. Until the early 1990s, waste was collected in cities under the responsibility of the five municipalities and was subsequently unloaded in open air dumping sites where it was often set on fire. The numerous environmental and health hazards associated with this practice led the authorities to review solid waste management. In 1997, the only landfill of the island became operational. Situated in the southern part of the island, the landfill was engineered for an initial surface area of 20 hectares and an expected lifetime of 19 years at a daily waste generation rate of 300 tons (Mohee et al., 2010). In 2006, the government announced that the landfill would continue to receive waste from the whole island for the next 20 to 30 years and extended the landfill area to 32 hectares. In the meantime, inhabitants from surrounding villages had to be relocated due to reports of water pollution from leachates and bad smell.

The extent of the problem can be gauged by considering the fact that the amount of waste landfilled has increased from 180,788 tons in 1999 to 429,935 tons in 2013 (Statistics Mauritius, Ministry of Finance and Economic Development, 2014a). Figure 5 presents the evolution of the amount of waste landfilled during the last 10 years. It must also be highlighted that no waste sorting is done before dumping and that landfills represent a major source of greenhouse (CHG) emissions, mainly CO_2 and methane, into the atmosphere. Accordingly, a new solid waste management paradigm that considerably reduces the amount of garbage sent to the landfill should be in the thick of the issues that Mauritian smart cities aim to address.

A plethora of relatively low-cost actions could easily help in bringing forward this agenda: waste sorting, promoting reuse and recycling of waste streams, encouraging green alternatives to plastic bags and packaging, composting and bio-energy. Mauritius has acquired some valuable operational experience in the implementation of some of these strategies. Following the successful initiation of composting on a household scale, it was extended to industrial scale with a full-fledged composting facility that processes about 180,000 tons of municipal solid waste annually. Only a small proportion of the total solid waste generated is recycled: 9 percent of paper, 3 percent of plastics and 31 percent of textiles (Mohee et al., 2010).

The private company responsible for the management of wastes at the landfill has started a Landfill Gas to Energy plant of 2 MW capacity in 2011. The capacity is expected to increase to 3 MW so as to generate nearly 22 GWh of electricity annually (Sotravic Ltd, n.d.). Government has also imposed an environmental levy on the purchase of plastic bags since 2006 in an attempt to curb its use. In yet another clear statement of intent from the government to tackle the waste problem, the sale of plastic bags will be banned in the country as from 2016.

INTEGRATION OF TECHNOLOGIES

Mauritius has undertaken to pursue a switch toward a low-carbon economy under the Kyoto Protocol. All the above-mentioned strategies pertaining to sustainable energy, mobility, water, and waste processes will a go long way toward reducing GHG emissions through the judicious management of natural resources. While a small carbon footprint is a crucial component of a smart city, the deployment of new technologies and innovation upgrades the quality of its core components to enhance its functionality and competitiveness.

Indeed, progress in the quality of life of citizens has been closely associated with the evolution of ICT. Consequently, the local government must ensure that digital technology networks are available throughout the smart cities to support the provision of effective public and private services to citizens. The 2014 World Economic Forum Networked Readiness Index ranked Mauritius first among African nations in terms of leveraging ICT for economic and social development and 48th in the world (World Economic Forum, 2014).

Nevertheless, efforts should be made to increase the penetration of Internet in families by enabling cheaper access. City administrators need to use ICT strategically to implement e-government for more efficient and personalized services to citizens. Furthermore, e-governance and e-democracy should be promoted to enable interaction of citizens with government and public participation in policy formulation respectively. It is equally important for smart cities to provide a favorable framework for businesses to thrive. Increasing the penetration of digital technology in businesses, promoting entrepreneurship, facilitating business development, and creating support infrastructure for business activities through science parks, incubators, and technology parks are some effective measures that can create and boost businesses (Clark, 2003).

Such stimulating environments where favorable economic conditions combine with state-of-the-art technologies are conducive to diversified employment opportunities. The whole framework must be backed by a holistic education system that tailors academic knowledge to the needs of the city. In addition, education system should consider the specific interests of individuals while fostering social, artistic and creative skills in them.

SOCIETAL DIMENSIONS

Often, the conceptualization of smart cities emphasizes so much on the application of technology that it runs the risk of ignoring the human and social dimensions. Neglecting the social aspect would defeat the very purpose of cities to improve the quality of life of people. Thus, any smart green city project should place its citizens at the center of the model. The influx of technology and innovation in urban processes will irrevocably modify the environment and experiences of citizens. Instead of alienating citizens by exacerbating digital, economic, and social divides, technology in smart cities should empower them. In order to achieve a smooth urban transformational change that garners widespread acceptance, it is imperative that technology adapts to the needs of the citizen and not the other way round.

Social inclusion should therefore be a decisive parameter in Mauritian smart cities so as not to repeat the mistakes of the real estate development schemes that are viewed as enclaves of economic privilege. In other words, "social capitalism," (Clark and LI, 2004) whereby economic gain is not just for a profit but also for the good of local and national communities, is a key strategy to undertake. To this end, all urban processes must consider the needs of all layers of the population through a high level of social security. Mauritius is already faring well in this field. In fact, it is the highest-ranked nation in the Sub Saharan Africa region on the Human Development Index (Economic Policy Research Institute, 2011). The government successfully promotes on a local level social equality and poverty reduction through numerous programs such as universal pension and free public transport for people above 60 years, free healthcare, free education, pension schemes for orphans, widows and handicapped, affordable housing schemes, and many supporting facilities for families living in poverty. The authorities can build up on the existing systems and improve access to as well as planning and management of the various services through the use of new technologies at the local level in what are called, on-site or distributed systems (Clark et al., 2004).

The multicultural nature of Mauritius underscores the importance of social justice as a vital tenet of the proposed smart cities. It will help to shape a community based on mutual respect for the different cultures and equal opportunities for everyone irrespective of background, creed, gender, age, and physical condition. All these social aspects taken together will ultimately contribute to a harmonious progress toward a caring society.

Challenges and Concerns

The Mauritian smart cities initiative, moreover, suffers from a three-fold challenge in terms of social aspects. Firstly, it is expected to rely significantly on involvement of foreigners and returning Mauritian diaspora (if they do return). It is not clear how locals will integrate into this endeavor, particularly people with low competencies and those who currently live in the neighboring areas. To date cohabitation has not been encouraged or even tried, with 28,300 manual foreign workers, mostly from Bangladesh, China, and Madagascar, living in Mauritius and with around 5,000 highly qualified or rich expats from Europe, India, South Africa, and elsewhere settling in the IRS and RES mainly (Board of Investment, n.d.).

The social tissue of the multifaceted Mauritian population remains fragile and risks should not be taken without due consideration to the willingness of the population to open up to "foreigners." To the very least, their attitudes should be investigated. Sensitization and dialog should not be neglected. Hospitality toward tourists is a different story and should not be misinterpreted as an open invitation to settle in the country.

Secondly, the smart cities proposal is to be privately funded in most cases. The institutional and regulatory framework for such projects cannot be identical to the existing one which was designed for another context, namely industrialization in the late twentieth century and then modernization of the economy at the beginning of this century. Equity and the so-called democratization of the economy have served more than slogans than anything else over that era. It is not yet clear how the benefits of smart cities will trickle down to the most vulnerable groups, particularly with the assumption that most of the investment in smart cities will be private sector-driven, probably foreign.

The third social challenge is no less awesome. Only a few months ago, the previous government was advocating a concept of Maurice Ile Durable (Mauritius Sustainable Island), building an "island-city" or an "ocean-state" which contrasts singularly with the current idea of micro "cities." Culturally a major paradigm change is needed, at all levels from the decision makers to the lay-people. A shared vision must be built. Will old villages and towns lose their historical cachet and be transformed into electronic jungles?

The happiness, well-being, and prosperity of the population is often evoked in Mauritius in terms of a return to simple living with the preservation of historical moral, religious, and traditional values. The destruction of the environment is much regretted and there is no indication that smart cities will restore the pristine beauty of Mauritius, even less the peaceful lifestyle of good old days. Reconciling with and rediscovering our past is undeniably a necessity if smart cities are to find a place in the hearts of the people.

Conclusions looking at the near turn future

Given the current state of urbanization in Mauritius that places severe stress on the city infrastructure, the government's ambitious plan to come up with a series of smart cities augurs an era of urban development characterized by environmental, social, and economic sustainability. Rather than copying successful western smart city models, which are not necessarily applicable to the local context, the authorities should focus on an approach that addresses the pressing issues specific to their urban regions. In a nutshell, the core guiding principles for this endeavor should be the application of innovative ICT to improve the overall performance and efficiency of infrastructure and processes, particularly the electricity grid, the water distribution system, transportation, public services, and waste management. Above all, a human-centred strategy must underpin all these efforts to promote safer and better standards of living for all citizens.

Sustainability criteria should be included in evidence-based decision making. The population should be involved through a participative democratic process right from the beginning. Politicians have to engage key stakeholders and not leave a few interest groups with the power to decide for others. Economic growth in terms of GDP should not be the only parameter of success. Good governance on the basis of clear ethical principles is needed. Everything should be done to avoid radical policy changes as a result of political instability. In other words, smart cities will not become a reality unless there is a departure from the ongoing business-as-usual approach.

References

Board of Investment, n.d. *Facts & figures*, http://www.investmauritius.com/work-live/facts.aspx, retrieved May 25, 2015.

Board of Investment, 2015. Mauritius National Budget 2015–16: Mauritius at the Crossroad. Republic of Mauritius.

Central Electricity Board, 2014. Integrated Electricity Plan 2013–2022: Demand Forecast for Mauritius, from http://ceb.intnet.mu/CorporateInfo/IEP2013/ Chapter4_Demand%20Forecast%20for%20Mauritius.pdf, accessed May 10, 2015.

Central Statistics Office, Republic of Mauritius, 2011. Population Census of Mauritius.

Clark, Woodrow W. II, 2003. "Science Parks (1): The Theory and Science Parks (2): The Practice." *International Journal of Technology Transfer and Commercialization*, vol.2, n.2, pp. 179–206.

Clark, Woodrow W. II, and Xing LI. 2004. "Social Capitalism: Transfer of Technology for Developing Nations." *International Journal of Technology Transfer and Commercialization*, vol.3, n.1, Inderscience, London.

Clark, Woodrow with William Isherwood, J. Ray Smith, Salvador Aceves, and Gene Berry, *"Distributed Generation: remote power systems with advanced storage technologies"*, Energy Policy, Elsevier Press, Fall 2004 (32) 14: 1573-1589.

Dameri, R.P., and Cocchia, A., 2013. Smart City and Digital City: Twenty Years of Terminology. *Proceeding of ITAIS Conference,* Milan.

Economic Policy Research Institute, 2011. Country Profile – Mauritius (EPRI), 17 from http://www.epri.org.za/wp-content/uploads/2011/03/32-Mauritius.pdf, accessed May 2015.

Mauritius Employers Federation, 2007. The Business Costs of Traffic Congestion, MEFeedback, n.3, October.

Mecometer, n.d. Vehicles per km of Road – by Country, http://mecometer.com/ topic/vehicles-per-km-of-road/, accessed May 16, 2015.

Medine Property, n.d. Medine Education Village, http://medineproperty.com/ downloads/project1364322417.pdf, accessed May 18, 2015.

Ministry of Finance and Economic Development, n.d. Budget Speed 2015–2016, (Republic of Mauritius), from http://budget.mof.govmu.org/budget2015/ BudgetSpeech.pdf, accessed May 5, 2015.

Mohee, R., Karagiannidis, A., Themelis, N., and Kontogianni, S., 2010. The Mounting Problems with Managing Waste in Rapidly Developing Islands: The Mauritius Case. *Proceedings of Third Symposium on Energy from Biomass and Waste*, Edulink, Venice.

Neirotti, P., De Marco, A., Cagliano, A. C., Mangano, G., and Scorrano, F., 2014. "Current Trends in Smart City Initiatives: Some Stylised Facts." *Cities*, vol.38, pp. 25–36.

Republic of Mauritius, Ministry of Renewable Energy and Public Utilities, 2009. Long-Term Energy Strategy 2009–2025, October.

Sotravic Ltd, n.d. Power Generation (Gas to Energy), http://www.sotravic.net/news/11-sefa-supports-sotravic-ltd-innovative-project.html, accessed May 15, 2015.

Statistics Mauritius, M.o., 2014. Labour force, Employment and Unemployment – Fourth Quarter 2014. Port Louis: Republic of Mauritius.

Statistics Mauritius, Ministry of Finance and Economic Development, 2014a. Digest of Energy and Water Statistics – 2013. Republic of Mauritius.

Statistics Mauritius, Ministry of Finance and Economic Development, 2014b. *Digest of Environment* Statistics – 2013. Republic of Mauritius.

Statistics Mauritius, Ministry of Finance and Economic Development, 2014c. Digest of Road Transport and Road Accident Statistics – 2013. Republic of Mauritius.

Statistics Mauritius, Ministry of Finance and Economic Development, 2014d. National Accounts of Mauritius – 2013. Repiblic of Mauritius.

The World Bank Group, n.d. World DataBank, http://databank.worldbank.org/data/views/reports/tableview.aspx, accessed May 5, 2015.

World Economic Forum, 2014. The Global Information Technology Report 2014, WEF and INSEAD.

Appendix G

Smart Green Micro Cities of South Asia

NAVED JAFRY AND GARSON SILVERS[1]

Introduction

The Indian subcontinent (otherwise known as South Asia) has always been a land of contrasts and we can get a glimpse of that by observing the gaps between the region's diversity and the synergy of a cohesive force that binds. From billionaires to beggars, skyscrapers and slums, bullet trains to bullock carts, and intellectuals to illiterates, South Asia has always been a place for organized chaos and greatness. This is the very land where great conquerors such as Alexander, Asoka, the Mughals, and the British Empire have come and settled. With its ancient history and place where the world's first university was established, South Asia boasts nearly 2,000 dialects and languages, multi-millennial history, countless gods and religious beliefs, fanatic nuclear armed dictatorships, and the building of the largest democracy.

Home to nearly 16 active and protracted conflicts, millions of internally displaced refugees and immigrants, this part of the world accommodates well over one-fifth of our planets population, making it the most densely populated geographical region. Since the region truly becomes ground zero for any ideas and ideologies, it first should prove its effectiveness in the subcontinents minds and markets, starting with smart green cities.

---

1   Naved Jafry (Chairman @ Zeons). Email contact at: Nj@zeons.org and Garson Silvers (CEO @ Zeons) Email contact at: Garson@zeons.org. Website for both authors is: www.zeons.org

Reasons to Deploy Smart Green Sustainable Micro Cities

Since the South Asian civilization is home to some of the world's most pressing challenges, one does not need to look far to find compelling reasons why Smart Green Sustainable Micro Cities should be deployed here. As South Asia's population continues to grow, more citizens will move to cities. Experts predict that about 25–30 people will migrate every minute to major cities from rural areas in search of a better livelihood and better lifestyles. It is estimated that by the year 2050, the combined number of people living in South Asian cities alone will touch 1.2 billion. To accommodate this massive urbanization, South Asia needs to find smarter ways to manage complexities, reduce expenses, increase efficiency, and improve the quality of life. To accommodate this growth, a McKinsey report suggests, India will need 20 to 30 new cities in the next decade alone. The state's solution has been to push for 24 new "smart cities" along high-speed regional transport networks. Economists argue that South Asian countries desperately need new cities: its urban population is expected to rise from 28 percent in 2001 to almost 36 percent in 2026.

A smart green sustainable city (SSGC) is an urban region that is highly advanced in terms of overall infrastructure, sustainable real estate, communications, and market viability. It is a city where information technology is the principal infrastructure and the basis for providing essential services to residents. There are many technological platforms involved, including but not limited to automated sensor networks and data centers. Though this may sound futuristic, it is now likely to become a reality as the "smart green cities" movement unfolds in India.

In a SSGC, economic development and activity is sustainable and rationally incremental by virtue of being based on success-oriented market drivers such as supply and demand. They benefit everybody, including citizens, businesses, the government, and the environment.

The Origins

The concept of smart green cities originated at the time when the entire world was facing one of the worst economic crises. In 2008, IBM began work on a "smarter cities" concept as part of its Smarter Planet initiative. By the beginning of 2009, the concept had captivated the imagination of various nations across the globe.

Countries like South Korea, UAE, and China began to invest heavily into their research and formation. Today, a number of excellent precedents exist that India can emulate, such as those in Vienna, Aarhus, Amsterdam, Cairo, Lyon, Málaga, Malta, the Songdo International Business District near Seoul, Verona, and others.

In India

India has planned 100 new smart cities. The "smart cities" effort, in 100 cities will develop modern satellite towns around existing cities. Another 500 cities will get infrastructure development where the government has allocated USD 2.4 billion for housing for all by 2022 and USD 1 billion for the smart cities project in its 2015–2016 budget. But according to TechSci Research, the entire projects could require more than $2 trillion.

The cities with ongoing or proposed smart cities include Kochi in Kerala, Ahmedabad in Gujarat, Aurangabad in Maharashtra, Manesar in Delhi NCR, Khushkera in Rajasthan, Krishnapatnam in Andhra Pradesh, Ponneri in Tamil Nadu, and Tumkur in Karnataka. Many of these cities will include special investment regions or special economic zones with modified regulations and tax structures to make it attractive for foreign investment. This is essential because much of the funding for these projects will have to come from private developers and from abroad.

Growth Engines

Today, it is evident that other than the six existing metros—Chennai, New Delhi, Kolkata, Mumbai, Hyderabad, and Bengaluru—new economic centers of growth are emerging. It is equally evident that we need to shift focus to these smaller cities, to plan carefully before growth overruns them. "We will have a better chance to integrate the city within its regional context, both in terms of space and economy," says Professor Shah. Smaller cities also allow for greater public interface and participation, the cornerstones of sustainable urbanization.

Indeed, Tier-II and Tier-III cities, once untapped assets, are now a part of the country's growth plan. Their progress will widen the market, help modernize rural India, and contribute to the overall development of the country. As it stands, several promising cities could qualify for the next set of major metropolitan cities. But what will it take to develop these cities optimally? Shah responds, "All cities need to identify through broad-based consensus their inherent and acquired economic strengths and develop plans to leverage their competitive advantages." He highlights the enviable advantage these cities have: "They can learn from the rest of the country and the world about successful good practices and models and replicate them." These practices include creation of an integrated and geospatially accurate development plan and the flexibility of land use.

Many of these cities do not have master plans—but this may actually be a boon as they can now prepare their plans on the basis of improved standards, more advanced knowledge about how cities work, and greater public participation. India aims to create urban spaces where green, high-tech initiatives bring more efficient management of resources, including water and energy, and better services to citizens. Public transport using clean energy, solar-powered streetlights, and green buildings are important low-carbon concepts for these cities.

The Challenges

The concept is not without challenges, especially in India. For instance, the success of such a city depends on residents, entrepreneurs, and visitors becoming actively involved in energy saving and implementation of new technologies. There are many ways to make residential, commercial, and public spaces sustainable by ways of technology, but a high percentage of the total energy use is still in the hands of end users and their behavior. Also, there is the time factor as such cities can potentially take anything between 20 and 30 years to build.

Another challenge is that the SSGC remains loosely defined in India and around the world, but many say the adoption of technology is a crucial element. Ambitious initiatives to build smarter cities include the use of data and digital infrastructure to manage energy and water usage to the creation of intelligent transport networks, according to a Brookings report earlier this year. India however should focus on fixing the lack of basic amenities and infrastructure such as housing, water supply, sanitation, and electricity in existing urban regions. A large part of these initiatives should just get the existing cities working in a more efficient ways.

Suggestions

Private companies may experience challenges working with the central, state, and local governments. To overcome this hurdle the government must create a stable policy framework for private investment, said an April report by Accenture Strategy and the World Economic Forum. A key component of this is for the government to develop a strong investor value proposition on a project-by-project basis. The government should not expect investors to accept a lower return simply because a project has significant social benefit.

Economical Reasoning

Smart Green Sustainable Micro Cities are a special reform zone, but on a larger scale with inhabitants sourced both locally and regionally. The reforms of Smart Green Sustainable Micro Cities involve considering the needs of the new settlement, as well as supporting a set of rules that allow a modern market to thrive. Through the power of their operating contracts, Smart Green Sustainable Micro Cities could make corporations and citizens accountable to their environment and their communities. Smart Green Sustainable Micro Cities ensure that there is better accountability through the production, supply, and marketing chain, while maintaining acceptable standards for security of life and property in the new city.

Lessons from Ancient Wisdom

Not all solutions to the SSGC developments have to come from the technology of the future, but much can be learned from the rich architectural and design history of the South Asian culture. One such growing trend among local architects is vernacular architecture. Falak Arora, a young architect from Mumbai, believes architects in new developments should strive to keep their focus on sourcing local materials. This not only helps in displacing huge carbon footprints but also creates local jobs. She has extensively studied vernacular architecture and is keen to apply the theory introduced by Adital Ela from Israel where she talks about "The Bridge Methodology" which is based on reviving objects, creating mediators, discovering abundances and design shares. Some of the application of the theory is best manifested in windy-lights, the self-sufficient outdoor lights that use clean energy.

Vernacular architecture is one of the most efficient approaches to produce sustainable architecture. Apart from reducing carbon emissions, because of the use of locally available materials, it also reflects the culture and traditions of the native place. Vernacular architecture is a little-known and less-explored field that is concerned with architecture, building traditions that are cost-efficient, ecologically sensible, and culturally relevant.

In South Asia several architects and organizations such as Housing and Urban Development Corporation Limited (HUDCO) deal in vernacular architecture. Due to its diverse and rich cultural heritage, the Indian subcontinent produces diversity in architecture from region to region.

The Laurie Baker Centre

Laurie Baker, a British-born Indian architect, initiated cost-effective and energy-efficient architecture using vernacular materials in India. He sought to incorporate simple designs with local materials and achieved fame with his sustainable architecture as well as in organic architecture. Baker used the methods and practices of vernacular architecture to deal with local problems. His buildings tend to emphasize profile-masonry construction, instilling privacy with brick jali walls, which invites a natural air flow, reducing the footprint. Also these jalis create patterns of light and shadow.

Baker is known as the "brick master of Kerala" for offering housing solutions to the roofless millions. In 1990 The Laurie Baker Centre was set up, which was jointly promoted by the Housing and Urban Development Corporation (HUDCO) and the Delhi Urban Shelter Improvement Borad (DUSIB). The cost-effective and eco-friendly technologies such as rat-trap bond, filler slabs, arches, and domes were adopted in addition to normal constructions. After Baker's death, his friends, students, and admirers created The Laurie Baker Centre for Habitat Studies to propagate his philosophy of concept of sustainable development through research, extension, training, documentation, and networking. Its main objective is to conduct and encourage research and development including action research, technology, and policy study relating to habitat studies within a larger perspective of green economy.

The Auroville Earth Institute

The Auroville Earth Institute was founded by HUDCO, Government of India in 1989 to promote earthen architecture in India and transfer their knowledge to 35 other countries. The work of the Earth Institute has attempted to revive traditional skills and to link ancestral and vernacular traditions of raw earth construction with modern technology of stabilized earth.

In the field, earth as a raw material plays a major role, but other appropriate technologies such as Ferro cement, biological waste water treatment, solar lighting, wind, and solar pumping are also extensively used.

The Centre for Vernacular Architecture (CVA) is a cooperative of building craft persons by R.L. Kumar, established in the late 1980s. The Centre works on the footprints of practioners like Laurie Baker and Hassan Fathy. The architectural practice promotes the use of locally available materials, traditional building techniques, culturally and climatically relevant designs. CVA has been designing and executing various vernacular architectural projects in South India and other parts of the country.

Chitra Vishwanath Architects

Chitra Vishwanath Architects is a firm based in Bangalore, India, focusing on ecology and architecture. The practice started in 1991 and, along the way, various architects joined and contributed projects throughout India and Africa. The philosophy followed is to employ local resources in an optimized way and to plan considering the natural elements, passively and actively, and to render the social impact of construction positive, improving lifestyle quality of both the doers and the users. As part of the range of resources used "mud" is a major component since it is well suited for local conditions, is relatively labor intensive, and locally available.

How to Fund Smart Green Sustainable Micro Cities in the Region

There are loan guarantees to help finance green sustainable projects in almost every state around the region along with grants by philanthropic trusts, funding through investment banks, hedge funds, socially conscious venture capital firms, and mortgage companies which also have loans with reduced rates for green sustainable homes. There are mandates at the local, state, and national level to stimulate investment policies within the region to fund and promote the use of sustainable industries. The immediate goals of these policies have always been to create new jobs and save existing ones, spur economic activity, invest in long-term growth, and foster unprecedented levels of accountability and transparency in government spending.

One can find many strategies which the state deploys to promote the renewable industries, including policies such as extending financial incentives, interconnection standards, net metering, output–based regulations, portfolio standards, and public benefits funds to name a few.

> *Public benefits funds* for renewable energy are a pool of resources used by states to invest in clean energy supply projects. Funds are typically created by levying a small charge on customers' electricity rates (that is, a system benefits charge).

> *Output–based* environmental regulations establish emissions limits per unit of productive energy output of a process (that is, electricity, thermal energy, or shaft power), with the goal of encouraging fuel conversion efficiency and renewable energy as air pollution control measures.

> *Interconnection standards* are processes and technical requirements that delineate how electric utilities in a state will treat renewable energy sources that need to connect to the electric grid. The establishment of standard procedures can reduce uncertainty and delays that renewable energy systems can encounter when obtaining electric grid connection in states that have not established interconnection standards.

> *Net metering* enables residential or commercial customers who generate their own renewable electricity (for example, solar PV panels) to receive compensation for the electricity they generate. Net metering rules require electric utilities in a state to ensure that customers' electric meters accurately track how much electricity is used on-site or returned to the electric grid. When electricity generated on-site is not used, it is returned to the grid; when on-site generation is not sufficient to meet the customer's needs, the

customer uses electricity from the grid. This system is perfect for micro cities as they can collectively generate additional renewable power to supply nearby communities.

Feed-In Tariffs (FiTs) encourage the development of renewable energy by obligating electric utilities to pay pre-established above-market rates for renewable power fed onto the grid. These tariffs, which may vary depending on the type of resource used, provide renewable generators with a set stream of income from their projects. With a transparent and fair accounting system this policy would be an ideal system to solve the problem of load shedding in the region.

Another avenue of funding green developments is to the Property Assessed Clean Energy (PACE) program. It is a financing option that attaches the obligation to repay the cost of renewable energy installations or energy-efficiency retrofits to a residential property rather than an individual borrower. This mechanism encourages property owners to invest in clean energy improvements even if the payback period is longer than the owner intends to keep the property. Similarly, in environmental finance districts a local government issues bonds to fund projects with a public purpose, and property owners that benefit from the improvement then repay the bond through assessments on their property taxes. We recommend that states and cities in the region create these programs to facilitate the use of sustainable technologies.

Overall we argue that a well thought out and executed plan for funding any sustainable project is the first key to success. Financial incentives such as grants, loans, rebates, and tax credits are provided in some states to encourage renewable energy development. The database of these state incentives for renewables and efficiency are available with their local town planning. Charity begins at home, a dollar saved is a dollar earned. We, collectively and as individuals. can finance this green revolution by transforming many of our daily habits and culture to one of reduce, refuse, recycle, and reuse. To sum it up best is to point to the recent special report by *Time* magazine dated July 7, 2014 and July 14, 2014 entitled that the smarter home gives hope that we are making choices in the way we live. The subtitle states, "The dwelling of the future will make you safer, richer and healthier and they already exist." In the special report it gives multiple examples of progress being made with technology and socially conscious individuals making a sustainable difference to improve the human condition. In short we truly think that as individuals we have the power and ability as consumers and investors and we can always vote with our dollars or feet to see the world transform to a sustainable place and financing is the place to start.

Discussion

In this land of so much diversity, we feel that there are common grounds of culture, art, music, tradition, and spirituality that many might call elements of soft power. Hence the great challenge for the region's leaders today may just be to look at the conflicts on economy, politics, and law and recognize that those challenges can be resolved through first implementing the SSGC and in turn creating relevant infrastructure, jobs, and a predictable source of security/judicial system for generations to come.

Throughout this case study we have demonstrated that SSGC/micro cities can aid in the growth of a country. But it is crucial that appropriate laws are enacted and enforced in order to transform our cultures from one of waste to that of sustainability. Micro cities are not just a mere idea; they can save lives and better the economy. Through the approaches listed above, a fresh, efficient lifestyle can ensure sustainability. When cities are governed by a good set of rules, people feel that they are safe from crime, disease, and bad sanitation, and where people have a chance to make a living. The concept of a micro city is gradually gaining acceptance on the Indian subcontinent. If all goes well, India should have at least 30 private cities across the country by the end of this decade. This number could increase, depending on the manner in which India's policy-makers allow this concept to germinate.

The concept of SSGC/micro cities is a promising and symbolic movement of our time. It is a new lifestyle with a transformed vision of the future, consisting of fitting laws and regulations, a healthy environment and population, and the financial means to sustain its existence. It is where the present and future well-being of humanity as well as the environment is a promising one. This revolutionary idea has the potential to impact communities around the world in profound ways. If the region is committed to a behavioral change, it will not be long until South Asians live in cities where residents experience high levels of satisfaction.

Index

net metering, usage 330–1
net zero energy community
(University of California Davis,
West Village) 225–31
New Ruralism 244
Newton, Isaac 42
New Urbanism 250
New York City: coast, impact 69;
growth 21–2
Nigeria, slum population 31
noise, generation/impact 131

occupant feedback 231
ocean current devices 56
ocean power technologies, types 56
ocean thermal energy conversion
devices 56
oil, true costs 179–81
One Water system 251
Onibus Brasileiro a Hidrogeno 141
output-based environmental
regulations 330

Pachauri, Rajendra 196
Paris, rebuilding/reconstruction 8,
133; World's Most Walkable
Cities 134
participatory elements, usage
(Potsdam) 278–9
Partnership for Market Readiness 193
peak-load management, electricity
transfer 113–14
People Gathering Places 250
per capita CO_2 emissions 17–18
Pew Charitable Trusts study 158
photovoltaic (PV) momentum 237
photovoltaic (PV) power: decrease
107; usage 245
photovoltaic (PV) systems:
integration 54; usage 52–4
photovoltaic (PV) tower, location 228

pig farming, impact 16–17
Pike Research 137, 139
plants, fuel source 122–3
Platzeck, Matthias 270
polar vortex 26
Pollin, Robert 195
port prime mover (PPM)
enhancement, Hybrid
Hydraulic Drive (impact) 82
post-use considerations 131
potential biological nutrient, usage
188
Potsdam, Germany (green smart
city) 267; barriers/tasks 276–7;
bicycles/public transport,
increase 274; buildings:
approach 272; refurbishment
276; carbon dioxide emissions/
reduction goals 273; climate
policy, historical background/
national context 270–2;
climate projects 272–7; coal-
fired heating systems,
substitution 274; construction,
regulation 277; context 268–9;
energy: provisioning 272;
smart metering 278; supply,
efficiency 274; system,
complexity/integration
(increase) 278; energy strategy
2020 275; field of actions 272–3;
future 279–81; GHG emissions
271; goals 276; green city,
smart city (equivalence) 277–9;
green urban plans 272–7;
heating demand, reduction
274; incentive structure, change
276; participatory elements,
usage 278–9; private homes/
municipal buildings, solar
power (increase) 274; private